About the Editors

Mary Lambkin is a Lecturer in Marketing and Director of the Master of Business Administration Programme at the Graduate School of Business, University College Dublin. She has published articles on marketing management and strategy topics in several international journals including the *Journal of Marketing*, the *Strategic Management Journal* and the *International Journal for Research in Marketing*. She is also the author of *The Irish Consumer Market: A Guidebook for Marketing Managers* (1993). She was Chairman of the Marketing Society of Ireland from 1993 to 1994.

Tony Meenaghan is a Lecturer in Marketing at the Graduate School of Business, University College Dublin. His main research interest is in marketing communications, in particular, commercial sponsorship, and he has published widely on these topics in such journals as the *European Journal of Marketing*, the *International Journal of Advertising*, the *Journal of Advertising Research* and the *Irish Marketing Review*. He has also worked with the International Advertising Association (IAA) and the World Federation of Advertisers (WFA) in preparing position papers on sponsorship, and he is the author of *Commercial Sponsorship*, published in 1983 by MCB University Press.

Irish Studies in Management

Editors:

W.K. Roche
Graduate School of Business
University College Dublin

David Givens
Oak Tree Press

Irish Studies in Management is a new series of texts and research-based monographs covering management and business studies. Published by Oak Tree Press in association with the Graduate School of Business at University College Dublin, the series aims to publish significant contributions to the study of management and business in Ireland, especially where they address issues of major relevance to Irish management in the context of international developments, particularly within the European Union. Mindful that most texts and studies in current use in Irish business education take little direct account of Irish or European conditions, the series seeks to make available to the specialist and general reader works of high quality which comprehend issues and concerns arising from the practice of management and business in Ireland. The series aims to cover subjects ranging from accountancy to marketing, industrial relations/human resource management, international business, business ethics and economics. Studies of public policy and public affairs of relevance to business and economic life will also be published in the series.

Perspectives on Marketing Management in Ireland

Edited by
Mary Lambkin and
Tony Meenaghan

Oak Tree Press
Dublin

in association with
Graduate School of Business
University College Dublin

Oak Tree Press
4 Arran Quay, Dublin 7

Cover Design: Robin Hegarty

ISBN 1-872853-58-7 paperback
ISBN 1-872853-66-8 hardback

A catalogue record of this book is available from the British Library.

© 1994 Individual contributors and:
"Long-term Trends in the Irish Economy" by Kieran A. Kennedy and "Developments in Irish Trade During the 1980s" by Dermot McAlesse and Michael Gallagher: © 1991 and 1993 *Irish Banking Review.*
"Irish Market Demographics" and "Consumer Spending, Saving and Credit" by Mary Lambkin: © 1993 Marketing Society, Dublin.
"Attitude Cycles in Customer Orientation" by Tony Meenaghan, "Sales Force Management in Ireland" by Seán de Burca and Mary Lambkin, "Quantitative Research" by Tom Harper and "Qualitative Research: Where it's At, Where it's Going" by Phelim O'Leary: © 1993 *Irish Marketing Review,* volume 6.
"Timing of Market Entry" by Mary Lambkin: © 1990 *Irish Marketing Review,* volume 4.
"Quality Improvements in a Services Marketing Context" by David Carson and Audrey Gilmore: © *Journal of Services Marketing.*
"Customer Service and Information Technology" by Christine T. Domegan and Bill Donaldson: © *Journal of Information Technology* and Association of Information Technology.
"Marketing Planning in Small Enterprises: A Model and Some Empirical Evidence" by David Carson and Stanley Cromie: © 1990 *Journal of Consumer Marketing.*
"Corporate Identity: A Strategic Marketing Issue" by Kathryn Stewart: © *International Journal of Bank Marketing.*
"The Role of Sponsorship in the Marketing Communications Mix" by Tony Meenaghan: © *International Journal of Advertising.*
"Meeting Source Selection Criteria: Direct Versus Distribution Channels" by David Shipley, Colin Egan and Scott Edgett: © 1991 *Industrial Marketing Management.*
"Manufacturer–Middlemen Relationships: A Case of Balancing the See-Saw" by Sean Ennis: © 1991 *Proceedings of the 1991 Annual MEG Conference,* Vol. 1.
"An Analysis of Competition in the New Europe" by John Fahy: © *European Journal of Marketing.*
"Successful SME Strategies for International Markets" by Frank Bradley and Seán Ó Réagáin: © 1992 *EMAC.*
"The Exporting Activities of Small Firms in Northern Ireland" by William Clarke: © *IBAR.*

All rights reserved. No part of this publication may be reproduced or transmitted in any form or by any means, including photocopying and recording, without written permission of the publisher and the individual contributors. Such written permission must also be obtained before any part of this publication is stored in a retrieval system of any nature. Requests for permission should be directed to
Oak Tree Press, 4 Arran Quay, Dublin 7, Ireland.

Printed in Ireland by Betaprint Ltd.

Contents

List of Contributors	ix
Acknowledgements	xi
Introduction	
Mary Lambkin and Tony Meenaghan	xiii

PART I
THE IRISH MARKETING ENVIRONMENT

1. Long-term Trends in the Irish Economy
   Kieran A. Kennedy — 3
2. Developments in Irish Trade During the 1980s
   Dermot McAleese and Michael Gallagher — 14

PART II
THE IRISH CONSUMER MARKET

3. Irish Market Demographics
   Mary Lambkin — 33
4. Consumer Spending, Saving and Credit
   Mary Lambkin — 45

PART III
CUSTOMER FOCUS

5. Fundamentals of Good Marketing Practice
   James J. Ward — 61
6. Attitude Cycles in Customer Orientation
   Tony Meenaghan — 71
7. Quality Improvements in a Services Marketing Context
   Audrey Gilmore and David Carson — 81
8. Customer Service and Information Technology
   Christine T. Domegan and Bill Donaldson — 100

PART IV
STRATEGIC MARKETING IN IRISH COMPANIES

9. Competitive Advantage: The Vital Edge
   John A. Murray — 123
10. Going for Growth:
    Strategies of High Growth Small Businesses
    Colm O'Gorman and John A. Murray — 134
11. Marketing Planning in Small Enterprises:
    A Model and Some Empirical Evidence
    David Carson and Stanley Cromie — 146

PART V
PRODUCT AND BRAND MANAGEMENT

12. International Brand Strategy:
    Its Relevance for Irish Marketing
    *Mary Lambkin, Tony Meenaghan
    and Marie O'Dwyer* — 167
13. Quality Standards and ISO 9000:
    Do the Results Meet the Expectations?
    Brian Fynes and Sean Ennis — 186
14. Timing Market Entry
    Mary Lambkin — 203

PART VI
MARKETING COMMUNICATIONS

15. The Changing Face of Marketing Communications
    Tony Meenaghan and Caolan Mannion — 221
16. Corporate Identity: A Strategic Marketing Issue
    Kathryn Stewart — 241
17. The Role of Sponsorship in the
    Marketing Communications Mix
    Tony Meenaghan — 257

PART VII
PRICING AND SELLING

18. Pricing Practices in Irish Companies
    Donal Keating — 275
19. Sales Force Management in Ireland
    Seán de Burca and Mary Lambkin — 295

Contents

PART VIII
DISTRIBUTION SYSTEMS AND PROCESSES

20. Meeting Source Selection Criteria:
    Direct versus Distribution Channels
      David Shipley, Colin Egan and Scott Edgett   321
21. Value-adding Partnerships as Alternatives
    to Vertical Integration
      Emily Boyle   336
22. Manufacturer–Middlemen Relationships:
    A Case of Balancing the See-Saw
      Sean Ennis   349

PART IX
MARKETING RESEARCH

23. Quantitative Research
      Tom Harper   369
24. Qualitative Research: Where it's At, Where it's Going
      Phelim O'Leary   380

PART X
INTERNATIONAL MARKETING

25. An Analysis of Competition in the New Europe
      John Fahy   393
26. Successful SME Strategies for International Markets
      Frank Bradley and Seán Ó Réagáin   409
27. The Exporting Activities of Small Firms
    in Northern Ireland
      William Clarke   435

Index   455

List of Contributors

Emily Boyle is a Lecturer in Marketing at the University of Ulster at Jordanstown.

Frank Bradley is R&A Bailey Professor of International Marketing, University College Dublin.

David Carson is Professor of Marketing Management at the University of Ulster at Jordanstown.

William Clarke is Head of Department, Department of Banking and Commerce at the University of Ulster at Coleraine.

Stanley Cromie is a Senior Lecturer in Organisation Studies at the University of Ulster at Jordanstown.

Seán de Burca is a Lecturer in Marketing at University College Dublin.

Christine Domegan is a Lecturer in Marketing at University College Galway.

Bill Donaldson is a Lecturer in Marketing at University of Strathclyde, Glasgow, Scotland.

Scott Edgett is a Lecturer in Marketing at Brock University, St Catherine's, Canada.

Colin Egan is a Lecturer in Marketing at the University of Bradford, Management Centre, Bradford, UK.

Sean Ennis is a Lecturer in Marketing at the University of Strathclyde, Glasgow, Scotland.

John Fahy is a Lecturer in Strategic Management and Marketing at Trinity College, Dublin.

Brian Fynes is a Lecturer in Business Administration at University College Dublin.

Michael Gallagher is a Research Assistant at Trinity College, Dublin.

Audrey Gilmore is a Lecturer in Marketing at the University of Ulster at Jordanstown

Tom Harper is Managing Director, Media Audits, Ireland.

Donal Keating is a Lecturer in Accounting and Finance at Dublin Business School, Dublin City University.

Kieran Kennedy is Director of the Economic and Social Research Institute.

Mary Lambkin is a Lecturer in Marketing at University College Dublin.

Caolan Mannion is a Research Assistant in the Department of Marketing, University College Dublin.

Dermot McAleese is Whatley Professor of Political Economy at Trinity College, Dublin.

Tony Meenaghan is a Lecturer in Marketing at University College Dublin.

John A. Murray is Professor of Business Studies at Trinity College, Dublin.

Marie Louise O' Dwyer is a Research Assistant in the Department of Marketing, University College Dublin.

Colm O'Gorman is a Lecturer in Business Administration at University College Dublin.

Phelim O'Leary is a Director of Behaviour and Attitudes, Dublin.

Sean Ó Réagáin is a Business Development Officer at the Industrial Development Authority, Dublin.

David Shipley is Associate Professor of Marketing at Trinity College, Dublin.

Kathyrn Stewart is a Lecturer in Marketing at the University of Ulster at Coleraine.

James J. Ward is Professor of Marketing at University College Galway.

Acknowledgements

A collection of readings such as this is a collaborative effort which requires the goodwill and co-operation of many people and organisations, and this particular book is no exception. We have been most gratified by the interest and co-operation extended to us by all those approached and we would like to acknowledge this assistance.

Firstly, we must thank all of the authors for allowing us to publish their work. We have derived much benefit and enjoyment from our search of the literature and we are most grateful for that opportunity. We have come away from this exercise with a sense that the academic side of marketing is alive and vigorous right throughout the country and that there is a considerable volume of good research being undertaken which will add to that which has already been published.

We would also like to thank the editors of the journals who kindly allowed us to reproduce their material. In particular, we would note the *European Journal of Marketing*, *Industrial Marketing Management*, the *International Journal of Advertising*, the *International Journal of Bank Marketing*, the *Irish Accountancy Association Conference*, the *Irish Banking Review*, the *Irish Journal of Business and Administrative Research* (IBAR), the *Irish Marketing Review*, the *Journal of Information Technology*, the *Journal of Marketing Management* and the *Journal of Services Marketing*.

We owe a particular debt of gratitude to Professor Bill Roche, Research Director of the Graduate School of Business at UCD for stimulating this project in the first place, for financial support, and for his continuing interest and encouragement.

A considerable amount of work in collecting, collating and preparing the material for this book was carried out by Marie O'Dwyer and we would like to thank her most sincerely. We are also most grateful to Fionnuala McCarthy of the Centre for Research for acting as an intermediary between all of the people involved.

We wish in particular to thank David Givens and his colleagues of Oak Tree Press for the professionalism and patience exhibited at all stages of this project from conception through to ultimate publication.

Finally, we must acknowledge that the choice and arrangement of material in this book is our own and we accept responsibility for any errors and omissions. We hope that the end result is a worthy addition to the marketing literature in Ireland and we look forward to reviewing and updating it as time progresses.

Mary Lambkin
Tony Meenaghan
September 1994

Introduction

The statement that marketing is important for Irish firms is a truism that is universally accepted and seldom questioned. Every report on Irish industry and commerce since the 1950s has repeated the call for greater emphasis on and additional investment in marketing, to match the investment in production facilities and production efficiency which has tended to receive a higher priority. Greater levels of marketing skill are particularly necessary for indigenous Irish firms which do not generally have the benefit of multinational parent firms or internationally recognised brand names.

The acceptance of the need for more and better marketing at a broad policy level has resulted in the development of a substantial infrastructure of state support through organisations such as the Irish Trade Board and those representing individual industry sectors such as Bord Bainne, Bord Fáilte, Bord Iascaigh Mhara, the CBF, the Irish Financial Services Centre and others. The universities and other third level educational institutions have also responded by offering a wide range of education programmes on marketing management and allied subjects which are consistently over-subscribed.

This practical support has undoubtedly contributed to the growth of the Irish economy and to the healthy trade balance enjoyed in recent years. It has further ensured a significant improvement in the standard of marketing practice and an increased sensitivity among modern-day Irish firms to the need for investment in marketing and the recruitment of skilled practitioners to expend this investment effectively.

One of the more welcome outcomes of this increased emphasis on marketing has been an increasing interest in research on marketing amongst managers, educators and students. Such research is a vital prerequisite to the continued development of high-quality education and practice. It serves to raise the collective understanding with regard to state-of-the-art ideas and best practice leading to regular progress and increasing sophistication in the application of marketing principles.

It is an unfortunate reality that while the quality and quantity of research in marketing have improved significantly, much of this research is presented in lengthy reports and dissertations which are available in university and college libraries but which are not published in a form that is accessible to marketing practitioners. This is a loss of which academics are keenly aware; however, an increasing number of publication opportunities are now available to assist the dissemination of this body of research work. One such publication is the *Journal of Business and Administrative Research* (IBAR) co-edited by University College Dublin, University of Ulster and the University of Limerick. The *Irish Marketing Review*, published since 1986 by Aidan O'Driscoll of the College of Marketing and Design, has a mission "to bridge the gap between theory and practice" and therefore represents a most important publication outlet in this field. Irish academics, North and South, have also contributed articles to many other publications at home and abroad, and their work has also appeared in conference proceedings and professional reports of various types.

By now, there is a significant body of published work available, addressing many different topics and spread across a wide range of publications. While individually these articles represent significant achievements, much of their benefit is lost because they are often not known to potentially relevant audiences, and because they are not placed in context by association with related material.

The objective of this book was to extract further value from these individual contributions by bringing together a representative collection of the best writing in this field. The intention was to compile a book of readings on marketing management topics of contemporary interest with particular relevance to Ireland, both North and South. The focus was to be broad and international, reflecting Ireland's position as a small open economy within the European Union and larger world market. The topics were to range from strategic to operational, with an emphasis on the identification of critical issues for competing successfully in international markets.

Several criteria were employed in the choice of material for inclusion in this book. Firstly, the search for suitable material should be as exhaustive as possible to ensure that the collection eventually chosen would be representative of the body of published work and that it would include the best of what was available. Secondly, the search should stretch beyond strictly marketing publications to ensure that relevant material appearing elsewhere should not be missed. Thirdly, the writings should come from the whole of Ireland, North and South, and should provide a showcase for researchers from as many institutions as possible.

A wealth of interesting material was discovered through the search process, far beyond the original expectations of the editors. The final selection was made on the basis of fit within the structure chosen, and on the grounds of clarity and readability. The intention was to present material that would be interesting and readable for marketing practitioners as well as marketing educators and students. For marketing practitioners, this book should provide useful reference material which can be dipped into selectively according to the particular interests of the reader. For marketing educators and students, this book should provide a useful supplement to standard textbooks by providing information and insights on local issues — which is a dimension that is missing from the popular international texts.

The book is structured into ten parts, each incorporating several papers. The first two parts deal with the marketing environment in which Irish firms operate. This topic is further divided to recognise both the supply and demand sides of the environment. In Part I which deals with the supply side, papers by Kieran Kennedy, and Dermot McAleese and Michael Gallagher review the structure of the Irish economy, its growth and export performance. In Part II, on the demand side, two papers by Mary Lambkin review the demographics of the Irish market and trends in consumer spending, saving and credit.

Against this background, Parts III and IV explore the core concepts of marketing as they apply to Irish firms. The concept of customer focus or "consumer sovereignty" which is at the heart of successful marketing is examined in Part III with three papers displaying different, but complementary viewpoints. Jim Ward outlines the fundamentals of good marketing practice which must of necessity focus on the consumer. Tony Meenaghan argues that firms go through cycles in their attitudes towards their customers which vary from warmth to indifference. Audrey Gilmore and David Carson argue the case for customer care and service quality which are the most talked about topics in the marketing discipline today. Finally, Christine Domegan and Bill Donaldson examine the role which information technology has to play in delivering customer service.

The other core issues concern the strategic choices which firms face in their selection of served markets and their positioning therein. The three papers in Part IV focus on strategic questions, particularly from the point of view of small businesses, which represents the majority of Irish firms relative to their international markets. John Murray discusses the key requirements for building a sustainable competitive advantage. Colm O'Gorman and John Murray present research results focusing on growth strategies employed by small- and medium-sized firms, while David Carson and Stanley Cromie examine the marketing planning process employed by small enterprises.

Parts V to IX address marketing management issues, with papers devoted to each of the famous four Ps of marketing: namely, product, price, promotion and place with the further addition of marketing research. Part V, on product management, deals with several distinct issues, all of which are important for Irish firms. The first paper, by Mary Lambkin, Tony Meenaghan and Marie O'Dwyer, explores issues concerned with brand building, which is the subject of considerable debate for Irish industry seeking overseas markets. Brian Fynes and Sean Ennis review the experience of Irish firms with regard to the ISO 9000. A third paper, by Mary Lambkin, presents research evidence with regard to the timing of entry into new markets and its implications for competitive success.

Part VI explores various topics that come under the heading of "promotion" or, what is more appropriately called marketing communications. Tony Meenaghan and Caolan Mannion review the changing nature of marketing communications with particular reference to changes in the media, the audience and the marketing services industry. Kathryn Stewart provides an interesting paper on corporate identity which is an issue addressed by many of Ireland's leading companies in recent years. An article on sponsorship, by Tony Meenaghan, addresses another area of marketing communications increasingly utilised by Irish firms in their quest for access to audiences.

Part VII deals with the interrelated issues of pricing and selling. A paper by Donal Keating provides research evidence with regard to how Irish firms go about pricing their products. Seán de Burca and Mary Lambkin present a review of theory and research on selling and sales management drawing on both Irish and international data.

Part VIII deals with "place" or distribution channels which is a critical issue for virtually every firm involved in the provision of goods or services. A paper by David Shipley, Colin Egan and Scott Edgett examines the important strategic task of selecting distribution channels, while a paper by Emily Boyle discusses the broad strategic options with regard to whether to keep distribution in-house or whether to contract it out. Sean Ennis reviews the dynamics of relationships between buyers and suppliers.

The collection and utilisation of quality information is central to ensuring efficient marketing performance and this is dealt with in Part IX. Tom Harper examines the marketing research industry in Ireland with particular emphasis on quantitative research approaches. Phelim O'Leary focuses on qualitative research which is an increasingly important area of market research.

The final part of the book is concerned with the particular demands of international marketing. In his paper, John Fahy describes the competitive environment facing firms operating within the European Union. Frank Bradley and Sean Ó Réagain provide research evidence concerning successful strategies pursued by small and medium Irish firms in foreign markets, while Bill Clarke presents research on the exporting activities of small firms in Northern Ireland.

It is hoped that readers of this volume will find a number of articles which touch upon their own concerns and which provide some thought-provoking insights that will add to their learning. The editors are conscious also that for every article included in this collection, there are several other equally worthy contributions waiting in the wings, and it is hoped that this first edition will have many successors.

PART I

The Irish Marketing Environment

1
Long-term Trends in the Irish Economy*

Kieran A. Kennedy

THE LONG-TERM RECORD

The economic achievements of the Republic since independence are not inconsiderable. At that time the economy depended preponderantly on agriculture, which directly employed over half the labour force (Table 1.1) and accounted for nearly 90 per cent of merchandise exports (Table 1.2). Manufacturing, the spearhead of development in all prosperous countries, accounted for only 10 per cent of the labour force, and of this two-thirds were engaged in processing of food and drink. The volume of output in manufacturing is now 24 times higher than at independence. This has been achieved chiefly through a remarkable rise in exports since the 1950s, and manufactured exports now account for 70 per cent of total exports, compared with only 7 per cent in 1950.

At independence, over 90 per cent of Irish exports went to the UK. No other European country was so heavily dependent on a single market, and this dependence proved to be a disadvantage given the poor performance of the UK this century. Rapid expansion of Irish exports required diversification not only of the composition of trade but also its destination. By 1991, the proportion of exports going to the UK was down to 32 per cent, and Ireland had carved out major markets in Europe and beyond.

Such developments have helped to raise living standards which are now over three times higher than in the 1920s. The rise in living standards has been accompanied by a substantial improvement in the education, health and housing of the population.

Despite these achievements, however, the Irish record of

---

* This paper was first published in *Irish Banking Review*, Summer 1993, pp. 16-25.

economic development is mediocre when set in a European context. Ireland did little more than keep pace with the UK, which had the worst record in Europe, so that our living standards fell relative to mainland Western Europe. Ireland's income per capita in 1913 was close to the mean of those countries. Now it is just two-thirds of that level, with only Portugal and Greece below it.

An even more demoralising feature of Ireland's economic experience since independence has been the sustained failure to cope with surplus labour. Employment has never grown fast enough to absorb the potential increase in the labour force: uniquely in the western world, the level of employment now is less (by 8 per cent) than it was in the 1920s. Traditionally the surplus was absorbed by emigration, which has amounted to 1.5 million persons since independence. In more recent times, however, emigration opportunities have been curtailed and the scarcity of jobs is manifested chiefly in higher unemployment. In the last 20 years emigration totalled only 115,000 compared with 400,000 in the previous 20 years. In a proximate sense, this accounts for much of the current high level of unemployment. In a more fundamental sense, however, the root cause lies in the sustained deficit in job creation, resulting from long-standing inadequacies in the rate and pattern of economic development.

TABLE 1.1: STRUCTURE OF EMPLOYMENT IN IRELAND 1926 AND 1992

	1926 No. (000)	1926 Share (%)	1992 No. (000)	1992 Share (%)
Agriculture	653	54	150	13
Industry	162	13	316	28
Manufacturing	(120)	(10)	(223)	(20)
Services	406	33	659	59
TOTAL	1,220	100	1,125	100

Source: Kennedy, Giblin and McHugh (1988), Table 7.2 and CSO 1992 Labour Force Survey, Preliminary Estimates October 1992.

TABLE 1.2: COMPOSITION OF IRISH MERCHANDISE EXPORTS (%)

	1929	1950	1991
Commodity			
Food and Drink	86	80	23
Manufactures		7	70
Other	14	13	7
TOTAL	100	100	100
Destination			
UK	92	88	32
Other EC	3	7	42
US	2	2	9
Other	3	3	17
TOTAL	100	100	100
Ratio Exports : GNP (factor cost)	29	20	70

Source: Statistical Abstract of Ireland and Trade Statistics.

It is important to recognise that the twin problems of low income per capita and high unemployment are closely connected, and are both the outcome of the pattern of development. This can be illustrated from Table 1.3 which shows the trend in productivity and income per capita compared with the EC average from 1973 (when Ireland joined the EC) to 1990. Ireland has made spectacular progress in raising productivity, as measured by GDP per worker: Ireland's level rose from 69 per cent of the EC average in 1973 to 89 per cent in 1990. The benefit of this gain, however, has been diluted for two major reasons. First, the growth of GDP in Ireland over this period depended heavily on inward foreign investment and on government borrowing abroad, both of which gave rise to huge income outflows. Accordingly, the rise in GNP per worker, which is a truer measure of the impact on Irish income, was much less. Second, rising unemployment and associated dependency reduced the proportion of the population at work, which is now the lowest in the EU at 31 per cent. The low employment ratio means, for example, that in Ireland every ten workers on average have to support 22 dependants, whereas in Denmark, at the other extreme, every ten workers have to support only 9 dependants. The result is that, as Table 1.3 shows, Ireland has made very little progress in catching up to EC levels of GNP per capita.

TABLE 1.3: PRODUCTIVITY AND INCOME PER CAPITA
IN IRELAND RELATIVE TO THE EUROPEAN COMMUNITY

	1973	1990
	EC 12 = 100	
GDP per Worker	69	89
GNP per Worker	69	80
GNP per Head of Population	59	62

Source: EC Annual Economic Report 1991/92 and OECD Labour Force Statistics, 1970–90.
Note: GNP (gross national product) is the sum of GDP (gross domestic product) and net income outflows to the rest of the world.

SOME LESSONS

Hindsight is often derided as a case of being wise after the event. Yet it is the chief measure of improving foresight. If the focus here is on some of the major mistakes, it is only because we can often learn more from our mistakes than from our successes.

While the protectionist stance in the 1930s can be justified, given the state of the world economy then and the need to establish an industrial base, there were major mistakes in the hasty and indiscriminate way in which the policy was implemented. This has been thoroughly documented recently in an excellent new study by Daly (1992). Furthermore, it was a mistake to persist so long with the policy once it had achieved its limited potential. The underlying defect was the lack of any long-term vision of how the infant industries were expected to mature — something that could not be achieved within the confines of a small home market. The same need for a long-term vision for industrial development still exists. The successes of the last 30 years have been chiefly due to overseas firms, while indigenous industry remains weak and underdeveloped. This was recognised fully in the Culliton Report (1992) which spelled out a new strategy for developing a vibrant export-oriented indigenous sector.

The ill-fated fiscal expansion of the late 1970s was a well-meaning but ill-advised attempt to raise economic activity on the basis of home demand, which left the legacy of a huge debt burden. The basic mistake here was failure to recognise the limits of a small, highly-open economy, for which the key to success lies in the ability to compete effectively in foreign markets — in other words, what matters most is the enterprise and efficiency of the supply side.

The complacent acceptance of emigration was probably a serious mistake also. It is true that, given our relatively poor rate of economic development, emigration acted as a kind of safety valve, and raised living standards more than if the emigrants had remained unemployed at home. In the longer-term, however, it is arguable that the consequences were detrimental. In his recent analysis of Ireland's long-term economic performance, Mjoset (1992) attributes a major role to emigration. In accounting for the vicious cycles he identified, he argues that only if emigration is stemmed can the supply of entrepreneurs be secured. At present, the escape route of emigration has been closed off, at least temporarily. That is very painful in the short term and there is no certainty that the resulting pressure will have a beneficial outcome. Nevertheless, it has led to a greater questioning and created a mood for change, which, if grasped and built on, could prove fruitful.

Finally, our experience should teach us the limits of government in a small, highly open economy with a very democratic tradition. One of the major preconceptions held at independence was that responsibility for regenerating the economy lay with the government, which was assumed to have the necessary power. This preconception has been fed since then by successive governments. It is still so strongly held that when the government does not act, it is blamed for lacking either the competence to recognise the appropriate policies, or the will to implement them. In fact, no government has the power to correct all economic ills, and in a democracy like Ireland the power of government is severely limited by what the electorate will tolerate.

The hard currency stance could form a key element of a long-term strategy where these realities would be recognised. This stance promises an environment of low inflation and, in normal circumstance, lower interest rates. These advantages can only be gained, however, if all parties understand and respect the necessary disciplines. Since monetary and fiscal policy must operate to protect the exchange rate, the defence and expansion of employment falls heavily on the wage bargaining system, and on an adequate entrepreneurial response to improved competitiveness.

While there are some signs that the jobs/income trade-off is now more fully recognised in the exposed sector, the message has not been adequately communicated to the sheltered sector, including the public service. It is to be hoped that some useful lessons in this regard will have been drawn from the recent currency crisis, and, if this happens, the preservation of the new Irish ERM parity will remain the best basis for a long-term strategy.

MAJOR LONG-TERM CHALLENGES

The two major challenges facing the Irish economy are the reduction of unemployment and the raising of living standards towards European levels. In the short to medium term, there is a distinct possibility of conflict between the two, in that aspirations for high pay can limit job opportunities. Of the two, the former is generally said to be the top priority, but this is not often backed up by a willingness to sacrifice immediate pay increases in the interests of enhancing job prospects.

Both the employment and income challenges have to be regarded as long term because of the scale of the problems involved. Ireland faces not only the highest unemployment level in the EU but also the highest natural increase in its potential labour force during this decade. The National Economic and Social Council (NESC) (1991) report on emigration estimated that the potential increase in the Irish labour force during the 1990s (i.e., in the absence of emigration) will remain in the region of 22,000–25,000 a year. If Ireland were to provide jobs for these and, at the same time, reduce unemployment by the year 2000 to the current EU level of about 10 per cent, this would require a growth rate in employment of the order of 3 per cent a year. This is well above anything ever achieved before. ESRI projections suggest that even if Ireland sustained a growth rate of 4 per cent per annum for the rest of this decade, it would give rise, on past experience, to an employment growth rate of little more than 1 per cent per annum. As regards income convergence, the laws of compound interest show that for Ireland to catch up with EU income levels, the growth rate of GNP per capita of 2 percentage points per annum higher than in Europe, which Ireland has achieved since the mid-1980s, would need to be sustained for another 25 years.

These kinds of calculation simply show the long-term nature of our key challenges, but they should not intimidate us or lead us to despair. Because of the rapid decline in the birth rate since 1980, Ireland will experience a considerable alleviation of labour market pressure from the end of this decade onwards. If, therefore,

Ireland could begin to make even modest progress in reducing unemployment in the 1990s, it would enter the next decade in a credible position to effect a much greater impact subsequently. Moreover, to say that a challenge is long term is not to suggest it can be put on the long finger: the sooner we begin the better.

OPTIONS

Whether it would be possible to make progress simultaneously in reducing unemployment and raising living standards towards EU levels depends a great deal on the state of the world economy. In order to pursue both objectives at the one time, Ireland would have to achieve a high rate of growth of both employment and productivity, which would require a sustained high growth of output: it would be necessary to contemplate a GNP growth rate of 6–7 per cent per annum for 10–15 years at least. Rates of growth of this order were achieved by several low income countries of Europe in the period 1960–73 when Europe as a whole was growing at about 4.5 per cent per annum. If similar buoyancy resumed again in the European economy, there is no reason why Ireland could not credibly aim at such a performance.

It would be an altogether stiffer challenge to accomplish a sustained annual growth rate of 6–7 per cent if the EU as a whole were growing at no more than about 2–2.5 per cent per annum, which is the most likely scenario. It would not be impossible, however: the newly industrialising countries of Southeast Asia — Korea, Singapore and Taiwan — have achieved growth rates of that magnitude even in the less buoyant world economy that has prevailed since 1973. A key element in their success has been their extraordinary flexibility and speed of adjustment to changing world market and product conditions. For example, Korean exports to Saudi Arabia rose 37-fold from 1973 to 1977. Later, when the US market was particularly buoyant from 1980 to 1985, the share of Korean exports going to the US rose from 26 to 36 per cent. Korean exports of ships, which accounted for only 4 per cent of its total experts in 1980, had risen to 17 per cent by 1985 (Dervis and Petrie, 1987). The same amazing ability to adapt the product range is found at company level. The World Bank (1987) study cites as typical the case of the Handok Company, a Korean conglomerate employing 3,500 workers: in 1971, 95 per cent of its sales were human-hair wigs; by 1976, paper was the largest contributor to sales; by 1981, watches constituted 85 per cent of sales; and by 1985, while watches were still a major component (at 45 per cent), they were rivalled by computer sales (at 41 per cent).

There is no basis in our past economic experience to justify the hope that Irish firms would exhibit this level of enterprise, or that the workforce and the institutions of the economy would be sufficiently adaptable to support such an effort. If that is so, then in a slowly-growing international economy, it would not be possible for Ireland to make progress simultaneously in regard to both unemployment and income convergence. In those circumstances. there is much to be said in favour of giving priority to employment. The damage caused by unemployment does not end with the poverty and despair suffered by today's unemployed. There is also the danger of creating an enduring dualism in the economy and society through transmission of the same deprivation to the children of the marginalised. The moral legitimacy of a society tolerating "human set aside" on a large scale over a long period is gravely weakened. The upheavals in Eastern Europe in the last four years are a warning that even though societal strains can be contained for a long time, they can eventually and quite suddenly bring about the collapse of the society.

Nor is the traditional safety valve of emigration likely to provide a satisfactory solution. Many of the long-term unemployed, who constitute nearly half of the total unemployed, now lack the resources and skills to enable them to emigrate with confidence. Any substantial increase in emigration would therefore involve a major brain drain, while leaving behind a large substratum with low education and skills. Moreover, modern regional economic theory suggests that labour outflow at a rate involving a reduction in population is likely to reinforce the scale disadvantages of the poorer areas — a conclusion that would find support in Irish economic history. It is unlikely therefore that Ireland could converge to EU income per capita levels unless and until it has begun to address effectively its problem of labour surplus. On the other hand, once the enormous overhang of unemployment has been reduced, Ireland would be better placed to advance convergence.

POLICY PRINCIPLES

The fact that the kind of growth rates needed to make progress simultaneously on unemployment and income convergence may be unattainable does not mean that we should not try to achieve as much growth as possible. There is still enormous scope for economic development in Ireland, and securing that development is a necessary, though not sufficient, means of curbing unemployment.

Without the broad support of the whole community and an adequate entrepreneurial response, no amount of government activity can substitute. Nevertheless, the government has a pivotal role in setting an environment favourable to economic enterprise. It can do so chiefly by maintaining a sound macroeconomic framework; by upgrading the physical infrastructure and the quality of human resources; by attending to the incentive structure of taxation and effectiveness in public spending; and by drawing up and implementing measures to curb restrictive practices. Many of the necessary steps have been outlined in the Culliton Report (1992), and what is important now is that these policies be implemented. The new round of Structural Funds provides support for a higher level of investment in physical and human capital than could be financed from our own resources, but it is vital that these funds be used effectively.

If we are serious about giving priority to unemployment, however, a significant proportion of the extra resources created by economic growth must go in the first instance towards providing jobs for the unemployed, particularly the long-term unemployed, rather than enhancing the income of those actually with jobs. The state has already assumed financial responsibility for supporting the unemployed, but the unemployment compensation system was designed to cushion temporary spells of unemployment — not to deal with unemployment of unlimited duration. It would be open to the state instead to devise measures to provide, or fund the provision of, work for those unemployed beyond one year. There is no shortage of socially useful work to be done, though effective organisation would be challenging. The greater problem, however, is how to pay for it. It would cost more than unemployment compensation and require higher taxes. To minimise the negative effect on the rest of the economy, the remainder of the community would have to be willing to bear this cost without demanding compensation through higher wages, etc. The successful operation of this approach would therefore call for combining a soft heart with a hard head. The community would need to be soft-hearted in its willingness to share income, but hard-headed in insisting that effectively organised work should replace long-term unemployment compensation.*

---

* These and other issues relating to the Irish unemployment problem are discussed in greater detail in Kennedy (1993), recently published.

THE TWO ECONOMIES OF IRELAND

To conclude, we must not overlook the fact that this small island contains two economies which for the most part have gone their separate ways. Both areas, however, are now part of a European Union where economic borders are being dismantled and where a common currency may operate by the end of this decade. Both areas face many common problems: high unemployment, low living standards, peripherality and a weak indigenous manufacturing sector.

It is encouraging that the opportunities for mutual benefit through greater economic co-operation, divorced from any political undertones or overtones, are now becoming more widely recognised in both parts of Ireland. The proposal by Quigley (1992) for a Belfast/Dublin economic corridor has enlarged the focus of potential economic co-operation beyond the notion of greater trade between the two areas. It also highlights the potential for the two economies jointly to encourage production linkages and clustering of industrial activities, which were stressed in the context of the Republic by the Culliton Report.

Quigley emphasised the active involvement of research bodies as one of the prerequisites for the success of his proposals. I am glad to say that the two main applied economic research institutes in the North and South — the Northern Ireland Economic Research Centre in Belfast and the Economic and Social Research Institute in Dublin — are now actively co-operating in a three-year research programme on the two economies of Ireland in an EU context. This programme, which began last autumn, has received significant financial support from the International Fund for Ireland, as well as some private businesses, North and South — including the Northern Ireland Bankers' Association and the Irish Bankers' Federation. It is planned to present the results of the first year's research to decision-makers in the public and private spheres at a conference in Belfast in November 1993.

REFERENCES

Culliton, J. (1992): *A Time for Change: Industrial Policy in the 1990s*, Report of the Industrial Policy Review Group, Dublin: Stationery Office.

Daly, M.E. (1992): *Industrial Development and Irish National Identity 1922–1939*, Dublin: Gill and Macmillan.

Dervis, K. and Petrie, P.A. (1987): "The Macroeconomics of Successful Development: What Are The Lessons?" in S. Fischer (ed.) *NBER Macroeconomics Annual 1987*, Cambridge, Mass.: MIT Press.

Kennedy, K.A., Giblin, T. and McHugh, D. (1988): *The Economic Development of Ireland in the Twentieth Century*, London: Routledge and Kegan Paul.

Kennedy, K.A. (1993): *Facing the Unemployment Crisis in Ireland*, Undercurrents Series, Cork: Cork University Press.

Mjoset, L. (1992): *The Irish Economy in a Comparative Institutional Perspective*, NESC Report No. 93, Dublin: Stationery Office.

National Economic and Social Council (NESC) (1991): *The Economic and Social Implications of Emigration*, Dublin: NESC.

Quigley, W.G.H. (1992): "Ireland – An Island Economy", Address at the Confederation of Irish Industry Annual Conference, Dublin: Confederation of Irish Industry.

World Bank (1987): *Korea: Managing the Industrial Transition*, Washington, D.C.: World Bank.

2
Developments in Irish Trade During the 1980s[*]

*Dermot McAleese and
Michael Gallagher*

As recently as 1981, the balance of payments on current account had registered an alarming deficit equal to 15 per cent of GNP (Table 2.1). A year earlier, the Central Bank Annual Report had opened with the ominous warning that "Ireland is facing a serious balance of payments problem". The deficit, in the Bank's view, was not the result of "exceptional non-recurring factors", nor was there a realistic prospect of its being reduced quickly to more sustainable levels. The consequences of Ireland being forced to resort to official financial agencies for credit was mentioned, with the accompanying possibility of severe economic restrictions being imposed as a condition of such aid. In the context of the early 1980s, the Bank's assessment of the balance of payments problem was by no means alarmist.

Yet, the problem was resolved. In 1985, for the first time since the Second World War, Ireland reported a surplus in merchandise trade, and by 1987 there was an overall current account surplus. A merchandise trade deficit of £1,698 million in 1981 was transformed into a surplus of £2,300 million in 1988. In retrospect, this happened quite quickly and without the array of economic policies which one would normally expect to accompany a balance of payments improvement.

---

[*] This paper was first published in *Irish Banking Review*, Autumn 1991, pp.3–17.

TABLE 2.1: IRELAND'S BALANCE OF PAYMENTS
(Selected Years)

	1980	1981	1985	1987
Balance of Merchandise Trade (£m)	-1,341.7	-1698	137	1,310
Balance on Current Account	-1,037.9	-1,594.7	-650.1	239
% GNP	-12.5	-14.7	-4.1	1.3

	1990e	1993f	1996f
Balance of Merchandise Trade (£m)	2,010	2,294	2,898
Balance on Current Account	667	500	601
% GNP	2.9	1.8	1.9

e = estimate   f = forecast
Source: Central Statistics Office; forecasts from Bradley et al. (1991).

This paper tries to explain why. We begin with an overview of the issue. Ireland's export performance is discussed. This is followed by an analysis of the role of competitiveness and indigenous industry. The part played by import demand is then examined. Our conclusion is that the export sector was the predominant factor in explaining the turnaround. Irish exports have consistently outperformed market growth and, even after allowing for repatriated profits, have generated the large net foreign exchange earnings which have underpinned Ireland's strong current balance of payments position.

REASONS FOR IMPROVEMENT

The current balance of payments consists of four types of transactions:

- Merchandise trade, the largest and best documented element
- Trade in services such as tourism and freight
- Trading and investment income, which includes interest

payments, royalties, profits and dividends paid abroad and received from abroad
- International transfers, the major element being transfers received from the European Community.

There were significant changes in all these components during the decade. However, in absolute terms, developments in merchandise trade exercised the largest net influence. The swing from deficit to surplus involved a foreign exchange saving of £4,000 million.

Assessing the causes of the improvement in the merchandise trade balance is an intrinsically complex exercise. Behind any specific explanation lies much explicit and implicit theorising. An absorption approach emphasises the relation of aggregate demand to aggregate supply and attaches prime importance to excessive demand as a cause of the original deficit. In order to eliminate the deficit, domestic demand must be curbed. Others view the problem as more one of underutilisation of aggregate supply. If the economy is uncompetitive, the deficit will be accompanied by unemployed resources and the need is to find ways of expenditure switching, that is, shifting from imports to domestic substitutes and exports. The policy implication in these circumstances is not to cut domestic demand but to reallocate it towards domestically-produced goods, such reallocation being achieved by measures such as devaluation of the exchange rate, income restraint and improved productivity.

In the early 1980s, the absorption approach was much favoured. As it happened, the budget deficit was about the same size as the current balance of payments. It was tempting to conclude that one caused the other. Fiscal restraint was seen as an essential precondition of solving the balance of payments crisis. (The same assumed linkage appears in contemporary analysis on the US trade deficit.) Irish experience fails to support this analysis. The trade deficit was eliminated by 1985, when the government's budget deficit was still running at £2,015 million or 13 per cent of GNP.

Extensions of this approach to include private sector as well as public sector demand provides some support for the link between aggregate demand and the deficit. The depressed conditions of private demand during the first half of the 1980s restrained the growth of imports. However, a significant feature of the period 1987–90 has been the coexistence of a buoyant domestic demand with a balance of payments position which remained strong. Normally the two variables move in opposite directions. For most of the post-war period, Ireland's balance of payments has improved only with a weakening in economic activity.

If domestic demand does not provide the answer, attention must shift, firstly, to growth of foreign demand and, secondly, to increased competitiveness (arising from some mix of expenditure-switching policies). Recent interpretations draw on both these explanations. National Economic and Social Council (NESC, 1990), for example, refers to "foreign market growth, together with a domestic supply side response, driven by the improvement in competitiveness", as causing a major export expansion (p. 47). Bradley et al. (1991) note that from 1986 onwards "the improvement in Ireland's competitiveness led to a rapid growth in industrial output and exports" (p. 45). The Organisation for Economic Co-operation and Development, on the other hand, downplayed competitiveness as a determinant — "while the improvement in the trade balance since 1981 has been very rapid, it has largely reflected factors other than competitiveness" (OECD, 1987, 72) — and focused instead on structural factors such as the role of overseas companies. The most recent OECD Survey Reports repeats this theme:

> The explanation for the turnaround in the trade balance during the 1980s is to be found in the manufacturing sector, however. The expansion of highly capital-intensive and export-orientated foreign enterprises has resulted in an increasing surplus in high-tech trade, although strong export growth in domestically owned, labour-intensive industries has also contributed to a declining deficit in that sector in recent years (OECD, 1991, 223).

There are, therefore, three contending, and not necessarily exclusive, explanations of the turnaround in the trade balance: overseas companies, competitiveness and import demand. It is worthwhile looking at each aspect in more detail.

EXPORT GROWTH AND OVERSEAS FIRMS

Ireland's export performance represents the continuation of a trend begun in the 1960s when outward-looking policies were developed in an attempt to foster economic growth. The public perception may be that the 1960s represented the era of highest export growth, but in fact the 1980s surpassed the already high figures of the 1960s. The volume of export growth averaged 8.1 per cent per annum, during the period 1961–70, 7.3 per cent during 1971–80 and 8.6 per cent during 1981–90. To have sustained average growth in exports of 8.6 per cent during the 1980s was a considerable achievement. It compares with 3.6 per cent for the United Kingdom and 4.8 per cent for Germany and Denmark. Spain and Portugal were the closest to Ireland within the European Community with growth rates of 8.1 and 8.0 respectively. The EC Commission (1989) singled out Ireland as a country that had attained an "outstanding export performance". In this respect, Ireland has made its mark in Europe; a remarkable achievement given its geographical position on the periphery.

Irish growth is compared with foreign market growth in Table 2.2. The latter is measured as a weighted average of import growth in the markets where Irish goods are sold. These markets grew rapidly during the 1980s, once the recession of 1979–82 was shaken off, yet Irish exports have systematically outperformed market growth. Since 1979, export volume has risen 2.51 times compared with market growth of 2.02. Assuming no relative price change, this translates into an increase in exports of IR£2.71 billion at 1989 prices in excess of a constant market share level.

TABLE 2.2: IRISH EXPORT PERFORMANCE 1979–89*

	Irish Exports	Market Growth*
	% volume increase p.a.	
1979	8.2	9.5
1980	7.6	2.1
1981	0.9	-0.5
1982	7.2	3.9
1983	12.1	7.6
1984	18.3	7.1
1985	6.5	7.4
1986	4.0	6.8
1987	14.2	8.3
1988	7.0	11.0
1989	11.2	9.7(e)
1987–89	251.3	201.5

*   Trade weighted average of non-oil import growth in partner countries.

Source: CSO.

Why did exports grow so rapidly? In order to answer this, we need to look in more detail at the changes in trade patterns during the 1980s. Firstly, the geographical pattern of exports changed. In 1980 exports to the UK, typically the largest market for Irish producers, amounted to 43 per cent of all exports; by 1990 this had fallen to 33 per cent. In the same period exports to the rest of the EC rose from 33 per cent to 41 per cent. The driving force for expansion came from those firms which had developed export markets outside the UK. Secondly, the commodity composition changed. Manufactured goods increased their share of total exports from 54 per cent in 1979 to 69 per cent in 1990. Within manufactured exports themselves, there were remarkable changes. High-tech products accounted for 61 per cent of manufactured exports in 1990 compared with 42 per cent a decade earlier (Table 2.3).

TABLE 2.3: IRELAND'S HIGH-TECH EXPORTS

	£m	As % all High-tech	£m	As % all High-tech
	1980		1990	
Office Machine & Auto-data Processing Machinery	257.9	27.2	2760.3	43.3
Organic Chemicals	254.6	26.8	971.9	15.2
Electrical Machinery	159.3	16.8	728.1	11.4
Professional, Scientific Controlling Apparatus	103.4	10.8	408.9	6.4
Medical, Pharmaceutical Products	80.6	8.5	578.9	9.1
Telecommunications and Sound Recording Equipment	50.4	5.3	181.3	2.9
Photographic Apparatus	22.9	2.4	135.1	2.1
Inorganic Chemicals	19.6	2.1	41.1	0.6
Computer Software	—	—	575.3	9.0
All High-tech Exports	948.7		6381.0	
High-tech as % of all Manufactured Exports	42.2		60.6	
High-tech as % of all Exports	22.9		44.4	

Source: CSO.

Thirdly, the type of firm is relevant; the main activists in the development of industrial exports in new markets were foreign subsidiaries.

All these characteristics were interrelated. Data collection by the Central Statistics Office (CSO) during the 1980s, which distinguished between foreign and indigenous firms, confirmed earlier surveys: overseas subsidiaries exported more than indigenous firms (Table 2.4) and they were heavily concentrated in high-tech goods. High-tech industry, dominated by overseas firms, raised exports tenfold during the decade and increased its share of manufactured exports from 42 per cent to 61 per cent.

TABLE 2.4: IRISH INDUSTRIAL EXPORTS 1983–88

Export/Gross Output Ratio	1983	1988
Overseas Firms	74.4	81.8
Indigenous Firms	38.7	36.3
Share of Exports		
Overseas Firms	61.6	71.2
Indigenous Firms	38.4	27.8

Source: Irish Economy Expenditure Survey, IDA, cited in Foley (1991).

Data-processing equipment accounted for 27 per cent of Irish exports to France and 37 per cent of exports to the Netherlands in 1990. Comparatively new goods such as soft drink concentrates and cream liqueurs entered the statistics. In 1990, soft drink concentrates amounted to over IR£600 million, 50 per cent more than dairy exports, attributable to the Pepsi plant in Cork and the much larger Coca-Cola plant in Drogheda (*Business and Finance*, 13 December 1990). The latter employs 230 people and generates about IR£500 million export sales. Another example is computer software (tucked away modestly under SITC 89, miscellaneous manufactured articles), which now generates £575 million in export revenues from a virtually zero base in 1980.

Although they account for three-quarters of total manufactured exports, not all foreign firms have prospered. UK subsidiaries have done badly, registering a continuous decline in number of firms and numbers employed throughout the 1980s (McAleese 1986; Ruane and McGibney 1991). Given their propensity to export back to Britain, the decline of these subsidiaries has contributed to the rising non-UK share of exports, while at the same time dragging the overall growth rate below what it should otherwise have been.

The considerable "leakage" from overseas plants in terms of direct imports and repatriated profits is now well established. The IDA's Irish Economy Expenditure Surveys show that overseas firms spend only 40 per cent of their gross output on Irish goods and services. (Comparison with the 70 per cent for indigenous firms is invalid given the latter's predominance in the food industry.) Using 1987 data, Foley (1991) shows that the value of gross exports needed to generate £1 of net exports was £3.53 for metals and engineering and £3.16 for chemicals. Too much can be, and perhaps has been, made of the low linkage argument. But it is a necessary qualification in evaluating the significance of Ireland's export boom.

Irish export statistics require careful analysis. Because of the large degree of multinational involvement in trade, the scope for transfer pricing is extensive and some statistical overestimation of export volumes is inevitable. Changes in tax law and the introduction of 10 per cent corporation profits tax, however, have made transfer pricing less attractive. Even after allowing for low linkage, transfer pricing and profit repatriation, foreign firms have made a major net contribution to export performance and net foreign exchange earnings. It was Ireland's good fortune that the IDA was successful in identifying the right firms and the right sectors during the late 1970s and early 1980s, thus laying the foundation of the balance of payments recovery.

INDIGENOUS SECTOR AND COMPETITIVENESS

Indigenous manufacturing industry taken in its entirety performed poorly during the 1980s. Many household names in Irish industry disappeared. There were individual exceptions but often their very success attracted a foreign takeover (in CSO practice, they then cease being indigenous and become foreign). In recent years what have been regarded as quintessential indigenous firms such as Irish Distillers, Carrolls and Jacobs have been acquired by overseas owners. The ambiguity in the definition of an overseas firm creates difficulties for statistical record and no doubt accounts for the considerable discrepancies which arise between different data sources.

Indigenous firms (including the agri-food sector) account for only a quarter of Ireland's industrial exports. Their exports have grown rapidly but not as fast as foreign firms' exports and they are disproportionately concentrated in the UK market. Indigenous firms sell 41 per cent of their exports to the UK compared with 25 per cent for foreign firms (Table 2.5). Indigenous industry's continuing problems in breaking into and developing outside the UK market have long been a theme of discussion.

TABLE 2.5: PATTERN OF EXPORT SALES % 1988

	UK	EC	US	TOTAL £m
Foreign	25.3	48.1	8.5	8,245
Indigenous	41.6	19.8	9.7	2,804

Source: Census of Industrial Production 1988.

The pattern and time profile of Irish sales to the UK during the 1980s merits close scrutiny. Between 1980 and 1985, Ireland's share of manufactured goods imports into the UK fell from 3.21 per cent to 2.88 per cent (Table 2.6).

TABLE 2.6: IRELAND'S SHARE OF UK MARKET IN MANUFACTURES

	1980	1985	1988
	(percentage points)		
Chemicals	3.8	3.5	4.5
Manufactured Goods	2.8	2.7	2.5
Machinery and Transport Equipment	2.8	2.6	2.6
Manufactured Articles (miscellaneous)	4.7	3.7	3.5
All Industrial Exports	3.2	2.9	3.0

Source: CSO.

Share losses were especially severe in traditional clothing and light consumer goods, down from 4.69 per cent to 3.74 per cent, and in textiles down from 8.26 per cent to 4.74 per cent, all within the period 1980–85. These share losses underline the point that export growth was frustrated not just by low UK import growth — in any event UK volume of imports began to pick up after 1982 —

but by the failure of Irish manufacturing exports to retain market share. Closure of UK subsidiaries (which was very severe between 1979 and 1984) and poor performance by Irish-owned companies jointly explain this loss.

There are many reasons why indigenous firms played little part in the geographical diversification of Irish exports. Explanations range from the small size of indigenous firms, to the disadvantage of their being latecomers and considerations such as reluctance to travel abroad and poor command of languages (O'Malley, 1989). Irish exports are determined, as are all exports, by a complex range of variables. While nothing correlates more surely than Irish export buoyancy and buoyancy of world markets, a close study of export performance shows that this is by no means the end of the story. Cost competitiveness also plays a significant role and is likely to be specially important in price-sensitive products which indigenous firms typically sell.

The key elements in the cost competitiveness equation are exchange rates, productivity and factor prices, the last usually approximated by some measure of labour earnings. Sometimes cost trends are inferred by a simple comparison of consumer price increases. On this basis, the loss of competitiveness vis-à-vis those countries participating in the European Monetary System's exchange rate mechanism stands out dramatically. Since the beginning of 1979, Irish prices, after correcting for exchange rate changes, have risen 34 per cent faster than Germany, 41 per cent faster than the Netherlands and 46 per cent faster than Belgium. These figures help to explain smaller Irish firms' difficulties in breaking into the Continental market. Only large companies with resource backing and price-inelastic products were able to shrug it off. Furthermore, the improvement in Ireland's control of costs in recent years has not restored the status quo ante. All that has happened is that the loss of competitiveness trend during the first half of the 1980s has been halted. Relative to the UK there was an improvement in the period 1979–82, mainly due to the appreciation of sterling, followed by a sharp deterioration between 1982 and mid-1986. Since the end of 1986, the position has again improved. The turn for the better was closely associated with the control of inflation, matched by moderate wage demands.

It is not easy to tie these cost/price developments to specific trade performance indices. Thus, the evolution of Ireland's overall export market share reveals a continuing increase in every year since 1979, except for 1985 and 1986. Increased market penetration in these years occurred despite the deteriorating cost trends.

The most cost-sensitive elements in Irish export trade are to be found among indigenous firms' sales to the UK. But the situation is changing. While total UK imports rose by 6 per cent in volume during 1990, Irish exports to the UK performed much better, achieving a 9 per cent volume growth. Alan McCarthy of CTT (now the Irish Trade Board) identified "the strategic positioning by indigenous companies in the less price-sensitive areas of the main markets" as contributing to the resilience of Irish exports in the UK. It appears that Irish exporters have adjusted in time to avoid the worst consequences of the present state of the UK market. In the long run such strategic repositioning is of crucial importance. In the interim, the figures suggest that attention must be focused on economy-wide cost control.

The indigenous sector par excellence is the agri-food sector which has performed much better than other indigenous industries in its penetration of the EC market. Agricultural exports to the EC increased from 29 per cent of all agricultural exports to 39 per cent in 1989. By contrast, exports to the UK fell from 51 per cent to 36 per cent. The share of agricultural exports in total exports, however, has fallen from 37 per cent (1980) to 25 per cent (1989), reflecting the exceptionally rapid growth of industrial exports (up to 3.5 times in the decade) rather than the slow growth of food exports (up 2.5 times). As Riordan (1989) noted, the net impact on the balance of payments is much larger than the export data suggest, given the food industry's low import propensity (10 per cent according to his calculations).

IMPORT GROWTH AND THE TRADE BALANCE

Taken in aggregate, import volume growth has been less than export volume growth. Even in the period of recovery post-1986, the increase of 40 per cent in import volume was exceeded comfortably by the 52 per cent volume increase in exports. The most recent figures have, in fact, revised upwards the trade surplus for 1990 from IR£800 million to £864 million, notwithstanding the 10 per cent fall in agricultural export volume in that year.

Import growth during the 1980s was curbed by a number of factors. The Kinsale Head Gas Field came on stream in the late 1970s and by 1984 was supplying 20 per cent of Ireland's primary consumption. This resulted in a 5 per cent saving in the import bill (IR£417 million) in 1984. In addition. there were considerable savings as a result of the shift from oil to coal. The latter's share of primary energy consumption rose from 10.5 per cent in 1981 to

24.4 per cent in 1989. Some heavily import-intensive projects financed by EMS-related funds came to completion, such as the Moneypoint power station and Dublin Area Rapid Transit System (DART). The oil price decline both in dollar and Irish pound terms, reinforced in the later 1980s by a weaker dollar, further reduced the import bill. Over the five-year period 1983–88, imports of materials for further production rose by only 18 per cent in value. These could be described as "structural" factors, distinct from the effects of depressed private sector demand referred to earlier.

Most Irish imports are non-competitive with domestic suppliers. But a certain proportion fall within the competing import category. Fitzgerald (1987) reported a strong link between competitiveness and import propensity during the period 1960–82. As Table 2.7 shows, there has been a dramatic increase in import penetration in the Irish market across a broad front.

TABLE 2.7: THE RISING IMPORT SHARE OF IRISH CONSUMPTION

	1980	1985	1988
Food, Drink, Tobacco	19.1	23.6	28.3
Food (Excluding Agri-based)	27.9	34.7	37.2
Drink and Tobacco	7.6	9.1	16.3
Traditional Sector	33.5	39.1	49.2
Textiles	46.5	62.2	76.5
Clothing, Footwear	56.6	64.4	70.4
Timber and Furniture	28.4	29.3	43.4
Paper and Printing	33.4	40.3	40.7
Clay Products	12.9	10.3	13.8
Miscellaneous Industries	25.8	33.1	42.3
Metals and Engineering	38.7	45.7	63.3
Modern Sector	56.9	54.1	45.1
Chemicals	59.4	66.3	68.3
Electrical Engineering	53.9	43.4	31.5
TOTAL Manufacturing	34.8	39.9	44.1

Source: Department of Industry and Commerce (1991).

In the case of textiles, the import share of domestic consumption has risen from 46 per cent in 1980 to 76 per cent in 1988; paper and printing from 28 per cent to 43 per cent; clothing from 57 per cent to 70 per cent; and food from 28 per cent to 37 per cent. This last figure is worth pondering over. An agricultural country imports £37 out of every £100 spent on food. A visit to any supermarket provides uncomfortable corroboration of this statistic. Ireland is a significant importer of frozen chips, potatoes, breakfast cereals, frozen food, convenience products and even dairy products such as cheese.

In aggregate, the import share of consumption of manufacturers rose from 35 per cent in 1980 to 44 per cent in 1988. While a high degree of import penetration is to be expected, the extent of this penetration in an economy like Ireland's reflects badly on the cost structure and capacity of import-competing industry. Clearly, the loss of competitiveness referred to earlier had an adverse impact on the import bill. The slow growth of domestic demand, however, ensured that income effects outweighed substitution effects in controlling the size of this bill (currently around IR£3 billion). Since 1988, competitiveness has improved especially vis-à-vis the UK. A survey in *Checkout* magazine (June 1991) confirmed what the macro statistics were indicating. It showed that the Republic was 4.34 per cent cheaper than Northern Ireland for alcoholic drink. For the first time in over a decade, Irish price levels have begun to compare favourably with those of the UK.

SUMMARY OF EVIDENCE

First, a central role is ascribed to the rapid growth of industrial exports as a determinant of Ireland's external surplus. Overseas firms accounted for most of this growth. They increased market share and succeeded in making inroads in Continental and other non-UK markets. Even allowing for their high direct import content and profit repatriation, they made a major net contribution to the balance of payments. Judged by economic performance, the Irish economy benefited from having the right export-oriented firms in the right sectors. There was nothing automatic about this; it happened as a result of successful "targeting" by the IDA.

Second, we differ from others in our assessment of the role of competitiveness factors. As we see it, Irish competitiveness was showing serious disimprovement during the period of major turnaround in the balance of payments. It is hard to see how competitiveness can be invoked as a contributing causal factor in the turnaround. Towards the end of the 1980s, there was a perceptible upturn in competitiveness indicators which may explain why the balance of payments has remained in surplus post-1987, but not how it reached that state.

Third, indigenous industry's performance has not been impressive. However, its exports have only recently been separately measured and the data are subject to distortion. Irish-owned firms have low export ratios and a heavy dependence on the UK market. Both factors limit their dynamism. The price sensitivity of their products made them particularly vulnerable to the adverse price/cost developments of the period 1979–86. Their improved performance in recent years, when Irish competitiveness has begun to improve, adds weight to this hypothesis. Since 1987, indigenous firms have outperformed total exports by one-third.

Fourth, structural change in energy consumption, favourable oil price effects, the exhaustion of "EMS" money and the depressed state of domestic demand restrained import growth through the 1980s. A disturbing feature of the period 1983–88 was the continuing inroads in the Irish market from foreign competition.

Fifth, fiscal policy seems to have exerted little direct influence on the improvement in the balance of payments. A linkage between the budget deficit and the trade deficit has not been evident in Ireland. Thus, the main improvement in the trade deficit occurred between 1981 and 1986. Yet the Public Sector Borrowing Requirement/Gross National Product ratio fell by only 4.7 percentage points and the Exchequer Borrowing Requirement by 3.1 percentage points during that period. We disagree with the view that "severe" fiscal policy brought about the elimination of the deficit (Bradley and Fitzgerald, 1989, 30). However, post-1987 fiscal retrenchment helped to consolidate the balance of payments improvement through its favourable effects on competitiveness.

Sixth, the export expansion had implications for the structure of the trade. A fascinating chapter in a NESC report (1989) shows how intra-industry trade ratios fell in Ireland, contrary to expectations, between 1977 and 1986. One driving force was the accretion of inter-industry specialisation into sectors such as organic chemicals, pharmaceuticals, office and data processing equipment and parts of food processing such as meat and milk products. Another was the specialisation out of traditional industries such as clothing, footwear and travel goods and large indigenous segments of metals and engineering, chemicals and wood and furniture. These changes in trade ratios are consistent with the longer-term perspective of the decade as a whole; exceptionally fast export growth in some sectors and sharply increasing import ratios in others.

WILL THE SURPLUS LAST?

Will the trade and current account surpluses last? Most economic forecasts and projections suggest that it will. The balance of payments is projected to remain in surplus up to the mid-1990s. Bradley, Fitzgerald and McCoy (1991) for example, indicate a growing merchandise trade surplus in excess of IR£2 billion up to 1996 and a current account surplus (inclusive of services and repatriated profits) of almost 2 per cent of GNP. These projections take full account of profit repatriation, high import content and CAP reform and incorporate a respectable 3.5 per cent GNP growth to the mid-1990s. For the first time in many decades the balance of payments constraint appears to be no longer binding.

These projections will only be realised on condition that there is no return to fiscal extravagance, that competitiveness of the economy is maintained and that the personal savings ratio remains high. These are standard macroeconomic preconditions. The rosy outlook for the trade account could also be easily derailed by an adverse movement in the terms of trade. Between December 1989 and December 1990, the index fell from 105 to 95, a deterioration of 10 per cent. The price index of exports fell further, from 106 to 92, a fall of 13 per cent, reflecting severe price cuts in both traditional sectors such as food and the sunrise sectors such as electronics and chemicals. It is ironic that, following a decade of remarkable export expansion, the second absolute decline in the value of Irish merchandise exports (by £260 million) in 30 years should occur in 1990.

A further important proviso would, on the basis of this study, also have to be added. The industrial composition of new firms entering Ireland now and in the recent past must be as judiciously chosen as those which fuelled the export boom in the 1980s. The recent report from the Development Committee supports such an analysis noting that "Ireland is already well positioned in some sectors such as office and EDP, chemicals and electrical engineering, for which demand is expected to grow rapidly over the nineties" (Sectoral Development Committee, 1991). Ireland's export supply capacity must continue to expand not only in manufacturing (indigenous and overseas) but also in the new service industries in the financial sector, in aerospace and tourism, language training, music, video and film, network and communications and consultancy.

REFERENCES

Bradley, J. and Fitzgerald, J. (1989), *Medium Term Review: 1989–1994*, Dublin: Economic and Social Research Institute.

Bradley, J., Fitzgerald, J. and McCoy, D. (1991): *Medium Term Review: 1991–1996*, Dublin: Economic and Social Research Institute.

Commission of the European Communities (1989): *European Economy*, Luxembourg: Office for Official Publications of the European Communities.

Department of Industry and Commerce (1991): *Review of Industrial Performance 1990*, Dublin: Stationery Office.

Fitzgerald, J. (1987): *The Determinants of Irish Imports*, General Research Series 135, Dublin: Economic and Social Research Institute.

Foley, A. (1991): "The Export and Foreign Exchange Contribution of Overseas Industry", in A. Foley and D. McAleese (eds), *Overseas Industry in Ireland*, Dublin: Gill and Macmillan.

McAleese, D. (1986): "Anglo-Irish Economic Inter-dependence: Effects of Post-1979 Changes in the British Economy on Ireland", *Irish Banking Review*, Spring.

National Economic and Social Council (NESC) (1989): *Ireland in the European Community, Performance, Prospects and Strategy*, Dublin: Stationery Office.

National Economic and Social Council (NESC) (1990): *A Strategy for the Nineties: Economic Stability and Structural Change*, Dublin: Stationery Office.

O'Malley, E. (1989): *Industry and Economic Development: The Challenge for the Latecomer*, Dublin: Gill and Macmillan.

OECD (1987): *Economic Survey: Ireland 1986–1987*, Paris: OECD.

OECD (1991): *Economic Surveys: Ireland 1990–1991*, Paris: OECD.

Riordan, E.B. (1989): "The Net Contribution of the Agri-food Sector to Earnings of Foreign Exchange", *Situation and Outlook Bulletin*, Dublin: Teagasc.

Ruane, F. and McGibney, A. (1991): "The Role of Overseas Industry", in A. Foley and D. McAleese (eds), *Overseas Industry in Ireland*, Dublin: Gill and Macmillan.

Sectoral Development Committee (1991): *Report and Recommendations on Ireland's Increasing Share of European Economic and Sectoral Development*, Report No. 15, Dublin: Sectoral Development Committee.

PART II

The Irish Consumer Market

3

Irish Market Demographics*

Mary Lambkin

The size and composition of a market are the most basic determinants of its attractiveness, and are the first variables to be examined by marketing analysts. The small size of the Irish market is frequently mentioned as a limiting factor, particularly for mass market consumer goods which rely on economies of scale in production and marketing for their competitive advantage.

This paper provides information on the demographic variables which determine the size and composition of the Irish market. This information is set in context by showing trends over time and comparisons with other European countries, and by highlighting particular similarities and differences. Vital statistics for the Republic of Ireland are summarised in Table 3.1. Trends in some of the key dimensions are discussed in the following paragraphs.

POPULATION SIZE

The famine which occurred in the 1840s precipitated a century-long decline in the Irish population, reaching a low point of 2.82 million in 1961 (Walsh, 1978). This decline resulted from a combination of factors, most notably heavy emigration, but also included a fall in the marriage rate and an increase in the average age at marriage.

This population trend was reversed during the 1960s and 1970s when a very rapid rate of growth, averaging 1.5 per cent per year, resulted in a peak of 3.543 million in 1986. This growth was partly accounted for by a natural increase in population, averaging 1 per cent per year during this period, brought about by an increase in the number of marriages rather than an increase in family size

---

* Adapted and updated from *The Irish Consumer Market: A Guidebook for Marketing Managers,* Dublin: Marketing Society, 1993.

(Walsh, 1972; Walsh, 1990). However, the most dramatic change at this time was in the pattern of emigration, which declined steadily after 1961 and became a net inflow after 1971 (Walsh, 1978).

TABLE 3.1: VITAL STATISTICS FOR THE REPUBLIC OF IRELAND

Intercensal Periods

Average Rate per 1,000 Population	1966–71	1971–79	1979–81	1981–86	1986–91
Births	21.3	21.6	21.5	19.1	15.7
Deaths	11.2	10.5	9.7	9.4	9.0
Natural Increase (Births–Deaths)	10.1	11.1	11.8	9.7	6.8
Estimated Net Migration Outward–Inward	-3.7	+4.3	-0.7	-4.1	-7.7
Changes in Population	+6.4	+15.4	+11.0	+5.6	-1.0
Total Population (000 End of Period)	2,978	3,368	3,443	3,541	3,523

Source: Statistical Abstract of Ireland, 1993, Central Statistics Office.

In the late 1970s, the Republic of Ireland entered yet another phase in its demographic history. The high rate of immigration which prevailed during most of the 1970s was succeeded by another wave of emigration, which gained momentum as the 1980s progressed, reaching a peak of 46,000 in 1989 (Tansey, 1990; Walsh, 1990). This trend has been reversed yet again in the early 1990s with a net immigration of 2,300 in 1992.

There has also been a very steep fall in the birth rate, from 21.8 per 1,000 in 1980 to 15.1 per 1,000 in 1990, although it is worth noting that Ireland still has the highest birth rate in Europe. By the late 1980s the much smaller rate of natural increase in the population each year was insufficient to offset the increasing emigration, resulting in the first decline in total population in 25 years.

Economic recession is the main explanation for both of these trends (Tansey, 1990). Low incomes and unemployment are believed to have led to a reduction in the marriage rate (from 6.4 per 1,000 of the population in 1980 to 5.0 in 1990), and have also caused many couples to restrict the size of their families. Lack of employment also accounted for much of the emigration trend of the 1980s, which exacerbated the falling birth rate, since most of the emigrants were young adults who would now form their families in countries other than Ireland (Tansey, 1990; Walsh, 1990).

The falling birth rate has also been influenced by social factors, particularly the importation of European norms of behaviour into Ireland. The trend towards smaller families and fewer children which has prevailed in the rest of Europe and the developed world is now occurring in Ireland. An interesting feature of these data is that other countries which traditionally had equally high birth rates, such as Spain, Portugal and Italy, have reduced their rates far more dramatically than Ireland since 1960. The reason for the differing pace of change in Ireland will be explored in later sections, but the main explanation is probably the strength of the influence of the Catholic Church in Ireland.

Some vital statistics for Northern Ireland are shown in Table 3.2 and indicate a pattern of population growth very similar to that in the Republic of Ireland.

TABLE 3.2: VITAL STATISTICS FOR NORTHERN IRELAND

Average Rate per 1,000 Population	1986	1988	1990	1992*
Births	18.0	17.6	16.7	15.9
Deaths	10.3	10.0	9.7	9.3
Natural Increase (Births–Deaths)	7.7	7.6	7.0	6.6
Estimated Net Migration (Outward)	-2.3	-5.0	+1.3	+2.3
Net Rate of Increase	5.4	2.6	8.3	8.9
Total Population (000 End of Period)	1564.5	1578.1	1589.4	1610.3

* Provisional
Source: Northern Ireland Annual Abstract of Statistics, No. 12, 1994, Policy, Planning and Research Unit, Department of Finance and Personnel.

Overall, the population has been growing throughout this century, to its current total of 1.61 million, fuelled by a high birth rate. The birth rate has been falling, however, in the last three decades, particularly in the 1980s, with a trend very similar to that of the Republic. There has also been a steady pattern of emigration from Northern Ireland which accelerated during the 1980s as the recession deepened, reaching a peak of 7,900 people during 1987–88. This trend reversed in the 1990s with a net inflow of 3,600 people in 1992. In line with these trends, the total population of Northern Ireland is expected to grow at a rate of 0.4 per cent per year over the next decade, with a predicted population of 1.73 million by the year 2011.

The total population of the European Union is currently 347 million, which represents 6.5 per cent of the total world population, but this percentage is falling and is expected to reduce to 4.5 per cent of the total world population in 2020 (Table 3.3). If present European trends continue, our vast Common Market will peak in the year 2000, and dwindle to less than 300 million by 2040 (*Business Week*, 6 February 1989).

TABLE 3.3: VITAL STATISTICS FOR THE EUROPEAN COMMUNITY

Average Annual Rate (per 1,000) 1992

Country	Births	Deaths	Natural Increase	Net Migration	1992 Net Increase	1993 Average Population (000)
Belgium	12.5	10.5	2.0	2.5	4.5	10,068.3
Denmark	13.1	11.8	1.3	2.2	3.5	5,180.6
France	12.9	9.1	3.8	1.6	5.4	57,526.6
Germany	10.0	10.9	-0.1	4.3	4.2	80,614.1
Greece	10.1	9.5	0.6	3.4	4.0	10,320.0
Ireland	14.5	8.7	5.8	-1.7	4.1	3,556.5
Italy	9.9	9.6	0.3	1.6	1.9	56,932.7
Luxembourg	13.1	10.2	2.9	10.8	13.7	395.2
Netherlands	13.0	8.6	4.4	3.8	8.2	15,238.9
Portugal	11.6	10.2	1.4	-1.0	0.4	9,850.3
Spain	9.8	8.7	1.1	0.5	1.6	39,114.2
UK	13.5	11.0	2.5	1.0	3.5	57,959.0
EU	11.5	10.0	1.5	2.1	3.6	346,756.3

Source: Eurostat "Rapid Reports: Population and Social Conditions", Population as at 1 January 1993, Number 7, 1993.

Irish Market Demographics 37

There is a clear divide among the EU countries in terms of aggregate population trends. In the south, fertility levels continue to decline, despite low levels already attained. At present, Spain has the lowest birth rate in the community at 9.8 per 1,000 in 1991, while the greatest decline in birth rates in recent years has occurred in Portugal where the current birth rate is 11.6 per 1,000. By contrast, fertility rates in the north have been stable for some years now, with slight increases in Denmark and the Netherlands (13.1 per 1,000, and 13.0 per 1,000, respectively, in 1992). The decline in the birth rates has been offset by immigration in most European countries, resulting in a net increase in population. Ireland and Portugal are the only exceptions, having a net outflow of population through emigration.

AGE STRUCTURE

TABLE 3.4: EUROPEAN COMMUNITY POPULATION BY AGE GROUP

Average % 1991

Country	0–15 M	0–15 F	0–15 Total	15–64 M	15–64 F	15–64 Total	65+ M	65+ F	65+ Total
Belgium	9.3	8.9	18.2	33.6	33.1	66.7	6.0	9.1	15.1
Denmark	8.7	8.3	17.0	34.2	33.3	67.5	6.4	9.2	15.6
France	10.3	9.8	20.1	32.8	32.9	65.7	5.6	8.6	14.2
Germany	8.3	7.8	16.1	34.9	34.0	68.9	5.0	9.9	14.9
Greece	9.5	8.9	18.4	33.5	33.8	67.3	6.2	8.0	14.2
Ireland	13.7	13.0	26.7	31.3	30.5	61.8	4.9	6.6	11.5
Italy	8.5	8.0	16.5	34.2	34.6	68.8	5.9	8.8	14.7
Luxembourg	9.0	8.6	17.6	35.1	33.9	69.0	5.0	8.9	13.9
Netherlands	9.3	8.9	18.2	35.0	33.9	68.9	5.2	7.8	13.0
Portugal	10.6	10.0	20.6	32.3	33.9	66.2	5.4	7.8	13.2
Spain	9.8	9.2	19.0	33.6	33.6	67.2	5.6	8.1	13.7
UK	9.8	9.3	19.1	32.8	32.6	65.4	6.3	9.4	15.7
EU	9.3	8.8	18.1	33.8	33.6	67.4	5.6	8.9	14.5

Source: Eurostat, *Basic Statistics of the European Community*, thirtieth edition, 1993.

The Irish age distribution has traditionally featured a relatively high proportion in the younger age groups, with emigration affecting the population in the middle and older age groups. Ireland has the most youthful population in Europe, with 27 per cent of the population under the age of 15 in 1991 (Table 3.4). By contrast, Germany has only 16.1 per cent of its population in this age group. Ireland also has the lowest percentage of people over 65 at 11.5 per cent, which compares to 15.7 per cent in the UK.

TABLE 3.5: LIFE EXPECTANCY AT BIRTH IN THE EUROPEAN COMMUNITY (YEARS)

Country	1980 Male	1990 Male	1980 Female	1990 Female
Belgium	70.0	72.7*	74.2	79.4*
Denmark	71.4	72.0*	77.2	77.7*
France	70.2	73.0†	78.4	81.1†
Germany W.	71.8	72.2	78.4	78.9
Greece*	72.2	73.6	76.6	78.6
Ireland	70.1	71.0†	75.6	76.7†
Italy	70.6	73.2*	77.4	79.7
Luxembourg	69.1	72.3*	75.9	78.5
Netherlands	72.7	73.7†	79.3	79.8†
Portugal	67.7	70.2*	75.2	77.3
Spain	72.5	73.4*	78.6	80.1
UK	70.2	72.9*	76.2	78.5
EU	70.7	72.8‡	77.4	79.2‡

* Eurostat Estimate
† 1991
‡ 1989

Source: Adapted from Eurostat, "Rapid Reports: Population and Social Conditions", Population as at 1 January, 1992/2; and *Europe in Figures*, fifth edition, 1993; and Statistical Abstract of Ireland 1993, Central Statistics Office.

It is estimated that the youth population of Europe will decline by about 8.6 per cent this decade, with Denmark, Germany, and the United Kingdom most adversely affected (Market: Europe, 1990). In contrast, the number of people surviving to old age is increasing in most countries. By way of illustration, in 1960, life expectancy at birth throughout the Community was 67.6 years for men and 73.4 for women. Three decades later these figures have increased by 3 years for women and 6.3 years for men (Eurostat Rapid Reports, No. 11, 1993). This ageing trend is an important social phenomenon which has serious implications for dependency ratios, and for financing retirement pensions and social welfare budgets.

The ageing trend in Europe and North America is also a feature of the Irish population, although at a slower pace. The median age in Ireland in 1986 was 27.7 years compared to almost 34 years in West Germany. One important factor inhibiting the ageing of the Irish population is the life expectancy level which is still one of the lowest in the EU (Eurostat, 1992/2). The average life expectancy for Irish children born in 1991 is 71.0 for males and 76.7 for females (Table 3.5). In contrast, the average French female born in 1990 can expect to live to the ripe old age of 81.1 years (Table 3.5).

GEOGRAPHICAL DISTRIBUTION

Ireland has traditionally had a very large rural population because of the predominance of agriculture. This rural population has been declining consistently since the middle of the last century, although the rate of decline has been slowing down since 1966. This decline has been significantly influenced by emigration but also by "urban drift" which is similar to the experience of other European countries (Walsh, 1978; Market Research Europe 1989). The vast majority of this urban shift has been toward the Leinster area, particularly Dublin and its hinterland. By 1991, the province of Leinster accounted for 53 per cent of the total population, 60 per cent of which represents the population of Dublin City and County which currently stands at about 1 million (Table 3.6).

Ireland is also following European trends in its pattern of urban settlement (Walsh, 1978). The old metropolitan areas have tended to decline in density while their formerly rural hinterlands have increased, largely due to the spread of car ownership. Recently, this trend has begun to reverse, stimulated by the introduction of tax incentives for urban renewal programmes in the cities and larger towns.

TABLE 3.6: GEOGRAPHIC DISTRIBUTION OF THE IRISH POPULATION

Population (000)	1981	1986	1991
Total	3,443	3,541	3,523
Urban	1915	1997	2,011
% of Total	(56)	(56)	(57)
Rural	1,528	1,544	1,515
% of Total	(44)	(44)	(43)
Leinster (inc. Dublin)	1,790	1,853	1,860
% of Total	(52)	(52)	(53)
Munster	998	1,020	1,008
% of Total	(29)	(29)	(28)
Connaught/Ulster (part of)	655	667	655
% of Total	(19)	(19)	(19)

Source: Census of Population, 1991; and Statistical Abstract of Ireland, 1993; Central Statistics Office.

HOUSEHOLD SIZE AND COMPOSITION

The number of households in Ireland has grown rapidly since the 1960s, reaching over a million today (Table 3.7). This growth has been primarily a response to increasing affluence and population growth, similar to the experience in the rest of Europe. Unlike its European neighbours, however, it has not been influenced to any significant extent by divorce or legal separation (dissolution of marriage without the right to remarry) since the former is prohibited and the latter has not been very much sought until recently.

Irish households are among the largest in Europe, with an average of 3.3 persons (see Table 3.8). This compares with 2.7 in the UK and 2.3 in Denmark which has the smallest households in Europe. The typically large numbers of children in Irish families are the main reason for the large size of households. By way of illustration, the 1991 census showed that 7.1 per cent of family units had 5 or more children, 26.7 per cent had 3–4, 47 per cent had 1–2 and 19.2 per cent had none. As the birth rate falls, of course, the average family size will also fall in the future. It is interesting to note, for example, that the percentage of households having 5 or more children was 24 per cent in 1981, compared with 7 per cent in 1991.

Irish Market Demographics

TABLE 3.7: HOUSING AND HOUSEHOLDS IN IRELAND

	1981	1986	1991
Number of Households (000)	910.7	976.3	1029.1
Average Size	3.9	3.5	3.3
Family Units %	77.7	75.7	73.7
Single Person Households %	17.1	18.2	20.2
Other Households %	5.2	6.1	6.1

Source: Statistical Abstract of Ireland, 1993, Central Statistics Office.

TABLE 3.8: AVERAGE NUMBER OF PERSONS PER HOUSEHOLD

	1980	1992
Belgium	2.95	2.70
Denmark	2.48	2.31
France	2.82	2.64
Germany	2.54	2.32
Greece	3.50	2.86
Ireland	3.90	3.3
Italy	3.22	2.85
Luxembourg	2.87	2.85
Netherlands	2.83	2.43
Portugal	3.35	3.12
Spain	2.88	2.59
United Kingdom	2.82	2.72
EU Average	2.99	2.77

Source: Eurostat, *Europe in Figures*, fifth edition, 1993.

The average number of people in each household is falling in every member state, except Portugal, which has remained stable in recent years. This decline can be attributed to a number of factors including a lower birth rate and changes in social behaviour resulting in fewer adults living with their parents and more elderly people living in old people's homes.

This country is also notable for its small number of single

person households, accounting for 20.2 per cent in 1991. However, the population of single person households is increasing in line with European trends (up from 17.1 per cent in 1981) as the population continues to age and as the incidence of marriage breakdown increases.

SOCIAL CLASS GROUPINGS

Three socio-economic scales are current in Ireland, each developed to address different objectives at different times.

TABLE 3.9: CSO ESTIMATES OF HOUSEHOLD SOCIAL CLASS

CSO (11 Occupational Groups)	
Farmers/Farm Managers	14%
Other Agricultural Occupations/Fishermen	3%
Higher Professional	4%
Lower Professional	5%
Employers and Managers	7%
Salaried Employees	2%
Intermediate Non-manual Workers	12%
Other Non-manual Workers	11%
Skilled Manual Workers	18%
Semiskilled Manual Workers	5%
Unskilled Manual Workers	7%
Unknown	12%

CSO (6 Social Class Groups)		Marketing (6 Groups)	
Higher Professional/Farmers 200+ Acres	10%	AB (Professional/Managerial)	10%
Lower Professional/Farmers 100+ Acres	14%	C1 (White Collar)	20%
Other Non-manual/Farmers 50–99 Acres	17%	C2 (Skilled Working)	25%
Skilled Manual/Farmers 30–49 Acres	22%	DE (Unskilled Working)	30%
Semiskilled Manual/Farmers 30- Acres	14%	F1 (Farmers 50+ Acres)	8%
Unskilled Manual	10%	F2 (Farmers 50- Acres)	7%
Unknown	13%		

Sources: CSO/MRBI Ltd., 1993.

The CSO analyses the Census of Population data into 11 groups based on occupations, and this data is published in Vol. 7 of the Census Reports. In this scale all farmers, since they follow the same occupation, comprise one group, irrespective of farm size.

A working party established under the auspices of the Medico-Social Research Board, developed a social class scale, grouping households and individuals into six groups which the CSO followed for the 1991 census and which is likely to remain the standard model for the future. This scale groups people by occupation and status. The social classes are perceived as essentially "economic groups" within which people can be objectively placed because of their differing resources. Farmers are distributed across the six groups, based on acreage.

The market research industry, when it became established in Ireland in the late 1950s and early 1960s adopted IPA-UK's (Institute of Practitioners in Advertising (UK)) social class groupings, and these continue to be used by marketing people in Ireland, despite the fact that no link exists with the published census data. A best estimate of social class is derived each year by the main Irish market research companies.

Set out above (Table 3.9) are the latest published estimates of household social class on the three scales.

FUTURE DEMOGRAPHIC TRENDS AND EXPECTATIONS

Government projections indicate that the combination of a moderate level of emigration (-10,000 p.a.) and a gradual reduction in the birth rate (1 per cent per annum) would result in a total population of 3.674 million by the year 2001, or a net increase of 0.24 per cent per annum (CSO). The current situation is slightly at variance with these assumptions — emigration is lower and the fall in the birth rate is higher — but these changes are counter-balancing so the aggregate forecast is still reasonable.

The age structure of the population is also expected to alter in the direction of the European norm. The number of people under 15 years of age is projected to decline by about 20 per cent between 1986 and 2001, and the 15–24 age group will decline by about 1 per cent. In contrast, the 25–64 age group is expected in many business sectors, and for government services such as health and social welfare. On the one hand, there will be a significant reduction in demand for all products and services consumed by babies and young children, including education. On the other hand, there will be a sizeable increase in the rate of new household formation by the 25+ age group, with a commensurate benefit for companies marketing consumer durables. There will also be a notable increase in the demand for goods and services appealing to the empty nesters or "free again" category, who will experience increased spending power as their children leave home, often helped by family inheritances (Henley Centre, Ireland, 1992). The market needs of the elderly will attain more prominence too, because of the increasing numbers in this category as people live longer.

REFERENCES

Business Week (1989): "The Greying of Europe", 6 February: 12–16.

Central Statistics Office (1986): *Census of Population*, Dublin: CSO.

Central Statistics Office (1994): *Statistical Abstract of Ireland, 1993*, Dublin: CSO.

Department of Finance and Personnel (1994): *Northern Ireland Annual Abstract of Statistics,* Northern Ireland: Policy, Planning and Research Unit, Department of Finance and Personnel.

Eurostat (1993: *Rapid Reports: Population and Social Conditions*, Luxembourg: EC.

Eurostat (1993): *Basic Statistics of the European Community*, Luxembourg: EC.

Eurostat (1993): *Europe in Figures*, Luxembourg: EC.

Henley Centre Ireland (1992): *Free Again: A Report on the Prospects for the Increasingly Middle-aged Irish Consumer*, Dublin: Henley Centre.

Market Europe (1990): "Six European Trends for the Nineties", 1(1): 1–2.

Market Research Europe (1989): "Housing and Households in Europe", 21(8): 53–64.

Tansey, P. (1990): "Many Young Men of Twenty Said Goodbye", Dublin: *Sunday Tribune*, 21 October.

Walsh, B.M. (1972): "Ireland's Demographic Transformation 1958–70", *Economic and Social Review*, 3(2): 7–20.

Walsh, B.M. (1978): "National and Regional Demographic Trends", *Administration*, 26(2): 162–78.

Walsh, B.M. (1990): *Ireland's Changing Demographic Structure*, Business and Economic Research Series, Dublin: Gill and Macmillan.

4

Consumer Spending, Saving and Credit[*]

Mary Lambkin

INTRODUCTION

Consumer demand is a function of both the size of the market and its spending power. Spending power is determined by the level of disposable income available to the population; that is, income after taxes have been paid. The level of income available, however, does not translate directly into spending. The amount of spending and the pattern of spending is strongly influenced by consumer expectations about the future. When confidence is high, people tend to spend more, often dipping into their savings and increasing their use of credit. In contrast, when confidence is low — as was the case in Ireland for much of the 1980s — people tend to increase their savings and minimise their use of credit. Thus, consumer spending, saving and credit are closely interrelated variables, which are important in explaining fluctuations in sales of virtually all goods and services.

SPENDING POWER

The average per capita spending or consumption levels of all the member states of the European Union are shown in Table 4.1. The levels are expressed in terms of a common measure called a Purchasing Power Standard (PPS) which corrects for variations between currencies and price levels.

These figures show clearly that there is a wide variation in spending power and spending levels among the EU countries, with

---

[*] Adapted and updated from *The Irish Consumer Market: A Guidebook for Marketing Managers*, Dublin: Marketing Society.

the wealthiest countries spending 2–3 times as much as the poorest countries. Germany and Luxembourg show the highest level of spending, while Portugal has by far the lowest. Ireland comes at the lower end of the distribution, close to Greece and Spain.

Combining the relatively low level of spending in Ireland with our small population, it is easy to see that the potential of this market is limited. This is the argument often cited by multinational companies which supply this market by importing products rather than establishing a manufacturing base here, and by Irish companies which go abroad in order to expand their business.

TABLE 4.1: PRIVATE CONSUMPTION PER HEAD, 1990 (IN PPS)*

	Total PPS
Belgium	9,097
Denmark	7,478
France	9,655
Germany	10, 231
Greece	5,081
Ireland	5,878
Italy	9,469
Luxembourg	11,339
Netherlands	8,459
Portugal	3,436
Spain	6,874
United Kingdom	8,987

* **Purchasing Power Standard (PPS):** exchange rates do not necessarily reflect the true purchasing power of a country's currency within its frontiers, and for this reason they cannot be used to give an accurate indication of the volume of goods and services intended for private use in one country or another. Consequently, it is not the ECU which is used as a point of comparison, but the purchasing power standard (PPS) which eliminates the distortions due to different price levels.

Source: Eurostat, *Basic Statistics of the European Community*, thirtieth edition, 1993.

CONSUMER EXPECTATIONS

Because consumer confidence is closely associated with patterns of consumer spending, saving and borrowing, it is useful to review how this variable has changed over time, prior to describing the pattern of consumption.

TABLE 4.2 CONSUMER EXPECTATIONS

	Trough 1981–83		Peak 1988–90		1993	
	Ireland	Euro Average	Ireland	Euro Average	Ireland	Euro Average
Consumer Confidence*	-39	-21	-3	-3	-13	-25
General Economic Situation (next 12 mths)	-48	-35	10	-3	-11	-27
Financial Situation of Household (next 12 mths)	-32	-10	2	10	-5	-9
Likelihood of Major Purchases (next 12 mths)	1	5	5	1	4	-21

* Consumer Confidence represents the arithmetic average of results for five questions, two on the financial situation of the household (last 12 months and next 12 months), two on the general economic situation, (last 12 months and next 12 months) and one concerning the likelihood of major purchases (next 12 months).
Source: European Economy, Supplement B, Business and Consumer Survey Results, Brussels: European Commission, Monthly.

Table 4.2 shows a composite measure of consumer confidence, as well as expectations with regard to the general state of the economy, the financial situation in the household and the likelihood of making major purchases over the next 12 months. These data show that confidence has been low throughout the 1980s and into the 1990s, with very negative scores recorded during the recession in the early 1980s. These figures improved from 1988 to 1990. A negative trend re-emerged in 1991 and continued throughout 1992, exacerbated by the record unemployment levels being experienced at that time, but the figures improved in 1993 providing advance notice of the recovery in 1994 (Central Bank, 1994).

TRENDS IN CONSUMER SPENDING, SAVING AND CREDIT

Table 4.3 provides summary data on consumer spending, saving and credit in Ireland for the 1980s and into the 1990s. Following several years of record growth in consumer spending in the late 1970s, there was a major slump in the early 1980s, with an unprecedented decline of 7 per cent in real terms in 1982. Growth resumed in the ensuing five years but at a sluggish rate, averaging 2 per cent per annum in real terms.

A confluence of several factors caused spending to accelerate from late 1988 through 1989. Increasing consumer optimism seemed to be the main driving force and appeared to occur spontaneously, without any real improvement in the key economic indicators. This increasing confidence released almost ten years of pent-up demand and produced a mini boom in the residential property market, together with increases in sales of new cars and most other consumer goods.

The increased spending was funded from savings and credit in addition to current income. It can be seen from Table 4.3 that the savings ratio (savings as a percentage of disposable income) fell to a record low in 1988 and 1989. There was also a very large increase in personal credit advances, particularly in 1989 (up 31.7 per cent), and housing mortgages accounted for an increasing proportion of this borrowing.

This mini boom in consumer spending was not sustained, however, and in 1990 and 1991 consumer confidence was gradually eroded by rising unemployment and reports of the deepening recession in the UK and elsewhere. The result was slower growth in consumer spending in 1990 and no growth at all in 1991, despite a significant increase in disposable income.

Consumer spending resumed an upward trend in 1992 and 1993 with growth rates of approximately 3 per cent and 4 per cent in real terms (Central Bank of Ireland, 1994). This was fuelled by a growth in incomes of 6 per cent per annum, although not all of this was consumed, resulting in a slight increase in the savings ratio. Personal sector credit increased by only 4.1 per cent in the same period, and most of this growth was accounted for by house mortgages which amount to just over 50 per cent of all personal credit. The slow growth of consumer credit may be attributed to the exceptionally high interest rates experienced in 1993. The scare caused by this phenomenon has continued to constrain the growth of credit in 1994 even now that interest rates have reverted to an unusually low level.

TABLE 4.3: CONSUMER SPENDING, SAVING AND CREDIT IN IRELAND

	1980	1981	1982	1983	1984	1985	1986	1987	1988	1989	1990	1991	1992	1993e
Personal Expenditure (IR£m)[1]	6,012	7,708	8,291	9,012	9,903	11,253	12,100	12,845	13,855	15,214	15,762	16,371	17,268	17,975
% Growth at Current Prices[2]	19.0	22.0	7.0	8.0	9.0	12.0	7.0	5.8	7.9	9.8	3.6	3.9	5.5	3.8
% Growth at Constant Prices[3]	0.4	1.7	-7.1	-1.0	0.0	1.0	2.0	3.0	4.6	6.1	2.0	7.5	2.9	3.8
Consumer Price Index[4]	48.5	58.4	68.4	75.6	82.0	86.5	89.8	92.6	94.6	98.5	101.7	105.0	108.3	110.5
Personal Savings (IR£m)[5]	1348	1,480	2,036	2,044	2,143	2,000	1,588	1,620	1,421	1,213	1,646	2,147	2,381	2,475
Savings % Disposable Income[6]	17.8	16.3	20.1	18.6	17.9	15.7	11.6	11.2	9.3	7.4	9.5	11.6	12.2	12.0
Personal Credit[7]	n/a	n/a	n/a	1,390	1,490	1,659	1,805	2,177	2,526	3,326	3,977	4,262	4,340	4,532
% Credit Growth[8]					7.2	11.4	8.8	20.6	16.1	31.7	19.9	7.2	4.1	4.4

e= estimate

Source:

1,2,3 National Income and Expenditure, Annual Reports, CSO
4 Base, Mid-November 1989 = 100
5 National Income and Expenditure, Annual Reports, CSO
6 Central Statistics Office Calculations, March 1994
7 Central Bank Annual Reports, credit advances from licensed banks, trading institutions and semi-state bodies, recorded in November each year
8 *Central Bank Quarterly Bulletin*, Spring 1994

The performance of the Irish motor industry and the number of new car registrations in a year is acknowledged as being a useful gauge to the state of the Irish economy. The sales slump from 1991 to 1993 was indicative of the economic situation and a general downturn in the market (Table 4.4). However, in line with the general improvement in the economy, car sales are picking up significantly in 1994, with a total of 64,538 new cars registered in the first seven months of the year (Society of the Irish Motor Industry, 1994).

Car sales throughout Europe have shown similar cyclical fluctuations which are a serious problem for an industry estimated to be responsible, either directly or indirectly, for some 12 million jobs or 8–10 per cent of total employment in Western Europe (Euromonitor, 1992). It is worth bearing in mind, however, that car sales are unusually vulnerable to short-term influences, as a large proportion of cars are bought using consumer credit, the cost of which rises with higher interest rates and is often avoided when job security is questionable.

TABLE 4.4: FIRST REGISTRATION OF PRIVATE CARS, 1980–93

1980	91,728
1981	104,645
1982	73,330
1983	61,094
1984	55,893
1985	59,592
1986	58,760
1987	54,341
1988	61,888
1989	78,383
1990	83,407
1991	68,533
1992	67,861
1993	60,792
1994 (July)	64,538

Source: Central Statistics Office, Economic Series, Monthly.

COMPOSITION OF CONSUMER SPENDING

In an earlier section of this paper it was shown that aggregate spending levels differ markedly across the member states of the EU. The information contained in this section shows that these countries also differ significantly in the way they spend their incomes. Apart from differences in retail spending levels, allocations of the consumer's budget on consumer products and services also varies greatly from one member state to another (Table 4.5).

Expenditure on food in Ireland accounts for a relatively large proportion of disposable income (22 per cent). This high proportion is typical of the poorer countries in Europe where incomes are only adequate to cover the essentials, and similar patterns of expenditure on food are found in Greece (28 per cent) and Portugal (33 per cent). In Ireland, this figure is declining, having fallen by about 7 per cent from 1980.

In contrast, people in the wealthier European countries such as France, West Germany and the United Kingdom spend relatively low proportions of their income on food and beverages, although their absolute spending and consumption may actually be higher than that of their less well-off neighbours.

The very high spending on alcohol and tobacco in Ireland reflects exceptionally high excise duties and taxes rather than higher consumption. Similarly, strong sales in Luxembourg is apparently a distortion due to heavy purchases by passengers in transit.

Ireland has the lowest expenditure on housing in the EU which may be explained by a number of factors (Market Research Europe, 1989). One is the high proportion of inherited property in rural areas. A second is that Irish people are far less mobile than other nationals and often stay in one house for their whole adult lives, thereby carrying low mortgages which are paid off at an early age. A third factor is that land and house prices in Ireland have been relatively low by European standards, to the point of attracting purchasers from abroad looking for holiday/retirement homes.

Health expenditure is also low in Ireland, similar to the United Kingdom and Denmark, which reflects the very high proportion of health services provided by the state (35 per cent of the population have medical cards which entitle them to free, state-funded medical care — Department of Health, 1991). This looks set to change, however, as private hospitals are appearing around the country.

TABLE 4.5: CONSUMER EXPENDITURE BY OBJECT, 1992

% of Total Expenditure	Food & Non-alcoholic Drinks	Alcoholic Drinks	Tobacco	Clothing & Footwear	Housing & Household Fuels	Household Goods & Services	Health	Transport & Communications	Leisure	Other
Belgium	17.5	1.4	1.4	7.3	15.5	11.0	11.0	12.5	6.4	16.0
Denmark	15.9	3.2	2.8	5.8	28.7	6.4	2.3	17.4	10.8	6.7
France	15.7	1.9	1.2	6.1	20.4	7.8	10.0	16.3	7.7	12.9
Germany E.	24.0	9.8	2.0	10.1	5.9	5.0	5.2	14.0**	9.3	14.5
Germany W.	14.0	2.5	1.0	7.8	18.9	7.0	14.3	16.0	10.0	8.5
Greece	28.2	2.3	3.6	8.3	11.2	7.6	3.8	13.9	5.7	15.4
Ireland	22.1	11.5	4.1	6.8	10.6	7.1	3.8	12.8	9.5	11.6
Italy	20.8	1.3	1.2	8.7	18.0	9.5	6.3	12.8	8.0	13.6
Luxembourg	15.7	11.0	6.2	7.0	20.0	10.0	7.6	18.1**	4.5	9.5
Netherlands	15.0	1.8	1.6	6.4	18.8	7.1	12.6	10.8	10.4	15.4
Portugal	32.6	1.4	2.0	10.0	8.5*	5.8	2.8	13.1	5.6	18.2
Spain	17.6	1.2	1.5	8.8	14.4	6.4	3.6	18.9	7.4	20.1
UK	12.7	6.5	2.7	5.4	16.4	5.9	1.4	13.2	9.8	25.9
EU Average	16.6	2.9	1.6	7.5	17.6	7.5	8.0	14.8	8.7	15.0

*   Fuels not included
** Communications not included

Source: Adapted from European Marketing Data and Statistics, twenty-ninth edition, Euromonitor, 1994.

Despite the relatively low incomes in Ireland and the high proportion devoted to food and other essentials, Irish people enjoy a reasonably good standard of living, judging by their homes and their possessions. Close to 80 per cent of Irish people own their own homes, which is the highest level of home ownership in Europe (the European average is about 55 per cent) (Market Research Europe, 1989). Irish homes also tend to be relatively large by European standards, with 57 per cent of all houses having five or more rooms.

Irish homes are well stocked with electrical appliances, 99 per cent having fridges/fridge-freezers, 91 per cent washing machines and 87 per cent vacuum cleaners (JNLR, 1991–92). There is also a high incidence of telephones (75 per cent), record players (63 per cent), toasters (53 per cent) and food processors (41 per cent) (See Table 4.6).

Market penetration is also quite high for newer types of electronic and household equipment, such as video recorders (56 per cent), microwave ovens (31 per cent) and compact disc players (17 per cent) (JNLR, 1991–92) (See Table 4.7). In contrast, poorer nations such as Portugal and Greece have not yet reached the same levels of penetration that Irish households have.

Of interest too in the context of consumer spending is the access to and usage of financial services. Recent figures show that 67 per cent of Irish people have bank accounts (54 per cent deposit accounts, 37 per cent chequing accounts), 20 per cent have post office savings accounts, 18 per cent have credit cards, 27 per cent have credit union accounts, 27 per cent have building society accounts, 45 per cent have life assurance, and only 5 per cent own stocks and shares (JNRR, 1991/1992).

PRICING AND CONSUMER REACTIONS

The Consumer Price Index increased very rapidly during the early 1980s, but slowed to an annual rate of increase of 3–4 per cent from 1986 onwards (Table 4.3). The general consumer reaction during the period of high inflation was to reduce spending and increase saving (see Table 4.3 also), which is a common trend in inflationary periods. As the economy resumed a growth trend in recent years, so too did the level of consumer spending and this is likely to effect individual product categories to varying degrees, depending on their relative income elasticity.

TABLE 4.6: OWNERSHIP OF DOMESTIC APPLIANCES, 1990/1991

% of Households	Washing Machine	Dish Washer	Fridge Freezer	Deep Freezer	Fridge	Microwave Oven	Vacuum Cleaner	Food Processor
Belgium	88	26	54	86	53	21	92	91
Denmark	76	26	52	92	56	14	96	83
France	88	33	54	77	50	25	89	83
Germany East	94		99	40			65	
West	88	34	66	73	43	36	96	92
Greece	74	11	70	27	24	2	52	24
Ireland	91	16	54	58	43	31	87	41
Italy	96	18	21	89	83	6	56	48
Luxembourg	93	50	55	91	54	16	88	90
Netherlands	89	12	98	82	60	22	98	84
Portugal	66	14	27	91	87	4	62	37
Spain	87	11	43	55	51	9	29	50
United Kingdom	87	11	98	82	53	48	98	80
EU Average	86	21	61	73	56	24	77	70

Source: Adapted from Euromonitor, *The European Compendium of Marketing Information*, 1992 and JNLR/MRBI Survey.

TABLE 4.7: OWNERSHIP OF CONSUMER ELECTRONICS, 1990

% of Households	Radio	CD Player	Home Computer	Colour/ Mono TV	Video Recorder	Video Camera	Telephone
Belgium	90	26	15	97	42	6	79
Denmark	98	20	14	98	39	5	87
France	98	23	14	94	35	6	89
Germany E.	99			43			
Germany W.	84	24	16	97	42	6	89
Greece	92	5	6	94	37	1	75
Ireland	87	17	12	98	56	2	75
Italy	92	9	12	98	25	4	89
Luxembourg		30	12	98	39	9	75
Netherlands	99	48	25	98	48	7	96
Portugal	60	9	7	92	22	4	52
Spain	95	11	8	98	40	4	66
UK	90	20	22	98	58	4	85
EU Average	91	18	14	94	39	4	83

Source: Adapted from Euromonitor, *The European Compendium of Marketing Information*, 1992 and JNLR/MRBI Survey.

Essential products such as electricity, fuel oils, petrol and food are relatively inelastic, as are alcohol and cigarettes. In contrast, household durables, transport and equipment, clothing and footwear, and discretionary expenses such as holidays and leisure pursuits (services) are strongly price elastic, with sales fluctuating in line with economic conditions (Table 4.8).

TABLE 4.8: ELASTICITIES OF TEN PRODUCT GROUPS [1]

	Price [2]		Expenditure [3]	
Food	-0.55	-0.79	0.48	0.52
Alcohol	-0.12	-0.87	0.62	1.86
Tobacco	-0.34	-0.68	-0.21	0.29
Clothing/Footwear	-0.52	-0.87	1.25	1.93
Fuel & Power	-0.15	-0.22	0.28	0.97
Petrol	+0.06	-0.44	0.96	1.47
Transport & Equipment	-0.82	-1.06	1.00	2.31
Durables	-0.93	-1.43	1.02	1.95
Other Goods	-0.49	-0.73	1.77	2.03
Services	-0.33	-1.38	0.90	1.59

[1] These elasticities were estimated with aggregate, annual data for the years 1958–88. The results vary according to the method of estimation, so a range of estimates are presented here. Readers interested in exploring this topic further should refer to the source.

[2] This should be read as follows: for a 1% increase in price, quantity sold of this type of product is likely to fall by between 0.55 and 0.79%.

[3] This should be read as follows: for a 1% increase in total expenditure, purchases of this product are likely to increase by between 0.48 and 0.52%.

Source: David Madden, "A New Set of Consumer Demand Elasticities for Ireland", Working Paper WP92/13, Department of Economics, University College Dublin, 1992. Used with Permission.

FUTURE TRENDS AND EXPECTATIONS

Economic growth and employment are set to increase strongly over the next two years due to an investment boom and a strong rise in consumer spending, according to a recent forecast by the Economic and Social Research Institute (Cantillon, Curtis and Fitzgerald, 1994). This forecast suggests that confidence should return to the economy as international conditions improve and interest rates remain low. The precise timing of the revival in confidence is hard to judge, but the central forecast sees consumer spending rising by 3.5 per cent in 1994 and accelerating to 6.4 per cent in 1995.

Economic growth is expected to continue at a steady rate throughout the 1990s, with an average growth in GNP of 4–5 per cent per annum, and there is a tentative prediction that the same may hold between 2000 and 2005. These forecasts rely on a continuance of moderate rates of interest and on an exchange rate régime which maintains Ireland's ability to compete in export markets. Any major fluctuations in these key variables would significantly alter the economic forecasts.

Looking to the year 2000 and beyond, the medium-term forecast indicates steady economic growth, rising employment and improved living standards. Specifically, the living standard in Ireland is forecast to improve from 72 per cent of the EU average in 1990 to 83 per cent in the year 2000. A key factor influencing this improvement is the declining birth rate during the 1980s which suggests a reduction in the unemployment rate and in the dependency ratio by the end of the 1990s.

The composition of consumer spending will change in response to general cultural trends and specific demographic factors. The proportion spent on food will continue to decline slowly (from 19 per cent in 1990), and the proportion spent on services and leisure will increase (from 13 per cent in 1990) following the general trends in more affluent countries. There will also be an increase in expenditure on rent and household goods (6 per cent and 8 per cent respectively in 1990), reflecting the increased rate of new household formation.

Successive consumer surveys have shown that Irish consumers consider price to be their dominant concern when shopping (Henley Centre, 1991). Quality is also a major consideration, as are health and environmental considerations, but the evidence indicates that consumers evaluate these factors against price and will only purchase products where the price/value trade-off is in their favour. Marketers, therefore, must continue to aim for positive value for money in any new products they bring to the market.

REFERENCES

Cantillon, S., Curtis, J. and Fitzgerald, J. (1994): *Medium Term Review 1994-2000*, Dublin: Economic and Social Research Institute.

Central Statistics Office (1994): *Economic Series*, Dublin: Central Statistics Office.

Central Statistics Office (1994): *National Income and Expenditure*, Dublin: Central Statistics Office.

Central Bank of Ireland (1994): *Annual Report*, 1993, Dublin: Central Bank of Ireland.

Central Bank of Ireland (1994): *Quarterly Bulletin*, Spring, Dublin: Central Bank of Ireland.

Euromonitor (1992): *The European Compendium of Marketing Information*, London: Euromonitor.

Euromonitor (1994): *European Marketing Data and Statistics*, London: Euromonitor.

European Economy (1994): *Business and Consumer Survey Results*, Supplement B, 1: 9–11.

Eurostat (1993): *Basic Statistics of the European Community*, Luxembourg, EC.

Henley Centre Ireland (1991): *Planning for Social Change*, Dublin, Henley Centre.

Lansdowne Market Research (1992): *Joint National Readership Research (JNRR), 1991/192*, Dublin: Lansdowne Market Research.

Madden, D. (1992): "A New Set of Conusmer Demand Elasticities for Ireland".

Market Research Bureau of Ireland Ltd. (1992): *Joint National Listenership Research (JNLR), 1991-1992*, Dublin: Market Research Bureau of Ireland.

Market Research Europe (1989): "Housing and Households in Europe", 21(8): 53–64.

PART III

Customer Focus

5

Fundamentals of Good Marketing Practice

James J. Ward

Marketing today is not a function, it is a way of doing business. Marketing is not a new ad campaign or this month's promotion. Marketing has to be all persuasive, part of everyone's job description, from the receptionist's to the Board of Directors'. Its job is neither to fool the customer, nor to falsify the company's image. It is to integrate the customer into the design of the product and to design a systematic process for integration that will create substance in the relationship (McKenna, 1991).

This quotation sums up very neatly what marketing means in the 1990s. It also begs a question about the state of marketing in Ireland. How well do Irish companies measure up to the standards implied in McKenna's statement? Is marketing all-persuasive, is it part of everyone's job description, does it integrate the customer into product design?

In an article in the *Irish Marketing Review* (Ward, 1987) this author analysed the background which had led, at that time, to several critical commentaries on the state of marketing in Ireland. The weakness of marketing, as an essential element in business, was identified as a structural problem which resulted from the Irish approach to industrial development. A review of industrial policy revealed a succession of development strategies which omitted marketing as an essential activity. These included the protectionist policy of the 1930s through to the late 1950s, the policy of attracting foreign investment which established production units to provide employment, but left the marketing function to be performed outside the country; and in later years, over reliance on the European Union's intervention system to off-load our food product. All of these policies achieved certain objectives for the economy, but the development of marketing skills was not one of them. They all contributed to the growth of an economy which had a stratum of normal business activity that was absent. Marketing skills are not required in a protected market where industries have monopoly positions, where foreign parents provide the function outside the country or where there is a guaranteed buyer for surplus produce. The result was a lack of opportunity for Irish managers to gain worthwhile marketing experience.

The state of Irish marketing has been addressed more recently than the paper referred to previously in a study sponsored by Co-operation North (College of Marketing and Design and University of Ulster, 1991). The findings of this research are still quite depressing in that the state of the art of marketing was found to be "impoverished", North and South, particularly in the small company sector. Some progress was noticed toward a more professional approach, but the overall view was that the problem largely remains to be solved. Despite this, many Irish companies have succeeded in developing markets based on all-round excellence, including the marketing function.

The purpose of this paper is not to assess the overall quality of marketing in Ireland in the mid-1990s but rather to demonstrate what excellence in marketing means and to provide some examples of it through the performance of Irish companies. In the process it is hoped to counterbalance, to some extent, the general research findings by pinpointing some notable exceptions.

QUALITY MARKETING PRACTICE

What constitutes "quality" marketing practice or how one describes a "marketing oriented company", has been addressed by many authors. Perhaps one of the more interesting treatments of the topic is by Tom Bonoma (1985) who regards good marketing practice as "quality performance in coping with the inevitable execution crises which arise in every firm, and which threaten to short-circuit strategy's impact on the market place".

This "quality performance" is measured by:

1. Marketing effectiveness, "the quality of management's implementation moves as these affect the customers and trade, defined as management's satisfaction with the results of its moves relative to the effort expended", and
2. Marketing efficiency, i.e., "the ability to routinise implementation acts, programmes, systems or policies" in such a way that they demand less effort (Bonoma, 1985).

Peter Doyle (1994) refers to characteristics of marketing-oriented companies, including:

1. Clarity of objectives.
2. Market segmentation.
3. Understanding needs.
4. Creating competencies.
5. Building competitive advantage.
6. Recognising environmental changes.

TEN MARKETING FUNDAMENTALS

In this paper ten fundamentals will be outlined which this author believes characterise good marketing practice and these will be illustrated with examples from Irish companies. The following list represents what this author believes is the essence of good marketing and is a combination of attitude and practice:

1. Improving profit performance (not sales).
2. Understanding customer needs.
3. Seeking customer satisfaction as a central value.
4. Selecting well-focused target markets.
5. Delivering product/service packages designed for target markets.
6. Integrating all company activity around the customer, by having everyone customer focused.
7. Taking a long-term view.
8. Building on strengths and facing deficiencies.
9. Hiring qualified people and investing in them.
10. Developing a good marketing information system.

Improving Profit Performance

Three years ago this author worked with a company in the consumer electronics distribution sector which had 180 customers nationwide. When these accounts were analysed, it was found that half of them could be eliminated and the profits of the company improved because most of the profits came from about 20 per cent of the customers.

This is a well-known phenomenon in business, referred to as the Pareto Principle. It requires companies to analyse their customers to understand where the business is coming from. Without such a systematic analysis incorrect impressions are formed about the value of customers which either undervalue or overvalue their importance. The key point is to focus on generating not just sales, but sales which are profitable. Clearly, in any list of customers there is a top ten and a bottom ten (the numbers could be 20 or 30, the important point is to do the analysis). Most likely, the profit comes from the top, with the bottom perhaps contributing very little or even making a loss. Who should serve these customers from the bottom of a customer list? Surely this is what competitors are for. The only caveat which applies to dropping customers is to assess growth potential, and again this should only mean profitable growth.

UNDERSTANDING CUSTOMER NEEDS

This is the most basic of all marketing fundamentals. However, it is surprising how companies are frequently so out of touch with what their customers' real needs are. Following many years of asking one question, of literally hundreds of companies in Ireland and in a number of other countries, this author has discovered one effective method to sensitise companies to the real needs of their customers. The question is, "What problems do you experience with your suppliers?" The most frequently cited answers are the following:

PROBLEMS EXPERIENCED WITH SUPPLIERS

1. Delivery was late or short.
2. The product did not meet specifications.
3. Poor quality of materials/work.
4. Wrong invoicing.
5. Supplier out of stock.
6. They don't phone back or they use answering machine or play music.
7. Price fluctuations; margins; obtaining prices.
8. Lack of product information and advice.
9. Failure to analyse customer problems.
10. Poor backup.
11. Poor promotion and sales literature.
12. Sales representatives don't inform customer of new products.
13. Inability to make contact with the right person in the supplier company.
14. Long lead times required with customers.

Most people can identify with these problems. What they mean in effect is that suppliers fail to understand that the real needs of their customers concern delivery, correct invoicing, products that meet specifications, etc. Customers are not getting satisfaction from suppliers on these items and until companies are asked to view them from the customer's perspective, they fail to realise their significance.

Irish companies may well be no worse on meeting customer needs than their average counterparts elsewhere. Some Irish companies are outstanding in understanding their customers' requirements. For example, Premier Periclase, a CRH subsidiary, set itself a standard of ensuring that no customer would ever experience any problem or delay in supply due to incorrect documentation. This level of understanding of customers' needs obviously goes far beyond supplying good quality products.

It is interesting to note that most of the items that companies complain about when asked about suppliers relate to customer service. Recent research conducted by Donaldson (1994) in the UK on the relative importance of service activities, confirms the importance of the items on the previous list.

TABLE 5.1: THE RELATIVE IMPORTANCE OF SERVICE ACTIVITIES

(1 = least important, 10 = most important)

Variable	Mean Score	Std. Dev.
Delivery Reliability	7.2500	1.1329
Responsiveness to Requests	6.7667	1.3867
Professional Competence	6.7444	1.4028
Flexibility in Meeting Customer Needs	6.7167	1.4847
Time from Order to Delivery	6.6556	1.5293
Accuracy of Transactions	6.5556	1.6754
Quality of Support Personnel	6.4167	1.5709
Quality of Product Information	6.2611	1.7825
Ease of Contact	6.2389	1.5868
Technical Advice	5.9611	1.9067

These research findings are significant in that they are pinpointing aspects of customer needs that are perhaps missed in the concern of companies for product quality, which is now taken as given, or price, which is important but not the most important issue by a considerable distance. Companies looking for competitive advantage would do well to look to aspects like those listed above before automatically lowering price or spending more on promotion.

SELECTING FOCUSED TARGET MARKETS

Matching competitive advantages or strengths to key target market segments is another critical success factor in marketing. This involves avoiding the temptation to serve all market segments and selecting those customers who are a good fit for company strengths. Small companies need to focus on niche markets where they have some clear advantages over competition.

Selection of target markets begins with collecting good information on potential markets, breaking the markets into manageable segments and then selecting from the segments targets which match companies strengths. When Chanelle Veterinary entered the veterinary pharmaceutical distribution business it did so from this basis — targeting veterinary inspectors, not farmers, offering a level of service which veterinary inspectors needed and were not getting, and playing to strengths which included a knowledge of the veterinary business and personal contracts in that business throughout Ireland.

TAILOR PRODUCTS/SERVICE PACKAGES FOR TARGET MARKETS

Building product/service packages to meet the specific needs of different market segments requires good marketing knowledge. For example, it requires knowledge of what each market segment values and how much they value it. One company discovered recently that 40 per cent of their customers wanted sales calls once a month and the remaining 60 per cent preferred less frequent calls. In the same company some customers wanted a telesales service but others didn't. Being aware of this type of information, which enables a company to tailor a service to each customer, is obviously very important. It also emphasises that you need to know customers very well in order to have this information. The key lesson coming from this is the need to build close customer relationships to enable the company to meet their precise needs.

Earlier we saw the problems which companies experience with suppliers. These problems clearly pinpoint the type of product/service package customers want, but fail to receive.

INTEGRATING ALL COMPANY ACTIVITIES AROUND THE CUSTOMER

The reader may recall the quotation at the top of this paper from Regis McKenna who said that marketing is not a function but a way of doing business. If so, it should permeate the whole company. Whose job is it to serve the customer? The real answer is that it is everyone's, from the first contact point, perhaps on the telephone, to the delivery person. One Belfast company took this aspect of business to heart and realised that their delivery people presented a very poor image of the company. This soon changed when it realised that everyone in the company had an opportunity to represent it. The van fleet livery was changed, delivery workers were provided with uniforms and a more professional image was presented all-round.

Companies should think about how all employees represent them. They can make a positive impression, a negative impression, or no impression. The central massage here is that marketing is *everyone's* job.

Again, reference to the supplier problems listed previously highlights the need to integrate all activities around the customer, from accounts departments, who may send out incorrect invoices, to production and despatch who may cause delivery delays. A marketing-oriented company has a culture in which everyone focuses on the customer under the leadership of the marketing function.

TAKING A LONG-TERM VIEW

Strategic marketing decisions are long term in nature. Their ultimate results come over time. A strong marketing culture cannot be developed in the short term, it may take a number of years. Financial pressures, however, are frequently short term in nature, and if they are not solved quickly, the long term becomes irrelevant. Thus, a balance is required which avoids financial measures that are based on a short-run profit, focus becoming the cause of poor marketing decisions.

What is long term? Perhaps three years or more would do as a working definition. Those who have been in the business for some time will realise that it takes many years to get things working right in most cases. One Irish company which is a good example here is Cashback, the VAT refund company. When Cashback entered the French market three years ago it did not expect to make money in the first year or even two. The development of that market was seen as a long-term venture, requiring a lot of initial investment. Likewise, Japanese companies always invest for the long term and concentrate on building a market position which enables them to be quite profitable after they have become established market players.

BUILDING ON STRENGTHS AND FACING DEFICIENCIES

A critical issue here is knowing what the company's strengths are. What is the company's key skill or competence? What would customers say? Why do the company's top customers buy from it? How is the company seen in relation to competition?

Facing deficiencies means firstly, knowing what they are. Most importantly it means knowing what customers say they are. One Irish company in the footwear sector found recently from a survey that its retail customers wanted to sell their products in their outlets, but the company was not providing enough merchandising support. Competitors were doing much more and as a result getting more prominent in-store positions.

This has now changed and the merchandising deficiency, along with a number of others, has been eliminated. Close customer contact, either through constant talking to or surveying customers (preferably both), was the key to identifying these weaknesses and rectifying them. Companies should guard against illusory strengths which are frequently stated as if they were unique. Very few strengths in business are unique.

Thus, a company which states that it provides better service, has better products or is in business longer and regards these strengths as sufficient, which is frequently the case, had better think again. The really difficult strength to look for and build on is one which competitors can't easily duplicate in the medium term. In other words, what does the company do that is unique to it which can't easily be copied? The answer may be some aspect of service or a strong customer base and loyalty, but it must be specific.

INVESTING IN PEOPLE

One of the real benefits of the large presence of multinational companies in Ireland has been the fact that they have forced suppliers here to raise standards in a total business sense. An example of this is the quality of service provided by companies such as Precision Steel in Galway. Owned and managed by a former multinational manager, this company is a model for companies anywhere. In regard to marketing, all employees know the importance of the customer because they are reminded constantly that "the customer pays the wages". There is a culture focused on the customer in Precision Steel. It permeates the whole company and is driven by the Managing Director, Charles Coughlan. A key factor in the company's success has been the care taken in hiring and the investment made in training. The result is excellence in customer service, a very stable workforce and an order book that is always more than full.

DEVELOPING A GOOD MARKETING INFORMATION SYSTEM (MIS)

Knowing what will satisfy customers in a total sense and monitoring performance in doing so requires information. This doesn't necessarily mean a lot of expensive market research, but it does mean building a good listening culture in the company, training people to listen and to report and then using the feedback. Chanelle from Loughrea, recent winners of the *Sunday Business Post* Small Business of the Year Award, has developed excellent information systems on its customer service. Every customer problem is tracked to its source, the problem is reviewed with the department responsible on a monthly basis and problems are eliminated to the satisfaction of the customer. The Chanelle information system even provides feedback to suppliers on their performance.

A good MIS should provide the raw data to execute much of what has been mentioned already, including segmenting markets, targeting customers and developing product/service packages tailored to precise customer needs.

CONCLUSION

This paper set out to accomplish two objectives:

1. To outline what this author considers to be the fundamentals of good marketing practice.

2. To demonstrate that Irish companies are implementing these fundamentals.

The quality of marketing as practised in Ireland has frequently been criticised, and indeed serious research has found it wanting in many respects. However, it is important to identify excellence where it exists and to demonstrate good role models for others to learn from. In selecting examples here the experience of smaller companies has been relied on rather than that of the better-known ones. In a short paper such as this it has not been possible to deal comprehensively with and to catalogue successes such as the brilliant performance of Waterford Crystal in launching its new Marquis range in the US or the outstanding work of Irish companies such as Bailey's, which are household names.

Given the significance of small businesses to the economy it may be more instructive to show how it is possible for excellence to be achieved on small budgets and to recognise that good marketing practice begins, not with budgets, but with attitudes. Having a strongly customer-focused company is a matter of attitude firstly, and then it becomes a question of implanting this in the myriad activities which constitute the life of the business.

REFERENCES

Bonoma, T. (1985): *The Marketing Edge*, New York: The Free Press.

College of Marketing and Design and University of Ulster (1991): *Marketing Practice: The Republic of Ireland and Northern Ireland*, Belfast: Co-operation North.

Donaldson, B. (1994): "The Competitive Dimension of Customer Service in Manufacturing Industry", Address at Doctoral Seminar, University College Galway, Galway: University College Galway.

Doyle, P. (1994): Address to the International Forum of the Marketing Institute of Ireland, Dublin: The Marketing Institute of Ireland.

McKenna, R. (1991): "Marketing is Everything", *Harvard Business Review*, 69(1).

Ward, J.J. (1987): "Marketing Myopia in Industrial Development", *Irish Marketing Review*, 2: 97–105.

6

Attitude Cycles in Customer Orientation*

Tony Meenaghan

The cornerstone of the marketing gospel is the primacy of the customer. The marketing concept as the discipline's central tenet acknowledges this primacy and asserts that corporate ambitions are met through the satisfaction of customer needs. Marketing education, encouraging the adoption of this orientation, is awash with insights which promote this attitude change. Marketing myopia is held up as a disease to be avoided, while production and product-oriented companies are instanced to show the folly of their ways. The thrust of such education is to create customer-driven organisations — an outcome which will benefit both corporations and consumers alike.

Marketing, having in recent times acknowledged its previous overemphasis on strategy — that is, the external corporate-environment relationship — has now sought to examine those internal factors which affect the quality of strategy implementation. In a society increasingly dependent on the services sector and with technical advancement as the basis of competitive advantage rapidly being eroded, the human element has taken increased importance in marketing. To use Gronroos' (1983) classification, there is an increased emphasis on the "how" factor rather than the "what" factor in terms of differentiating competing market solutions.

The concurrence of these factors in an increasingly deregulated environment has placed emphasis on the human resource factors which affect strategy implementation. Programmes such as service quality, corporate culture, total quality management and

---

* © *Irish Marketing Review*, volume 6, 1993. This article is reproduced with kind permission from Mercury Publications Ltd.

internal marketing involving both marketing and human resources management have as their objective the diffusion of a customer focus to all levels within recipient organisations.

Companies attempting to achieve a customer focus are generally responding to external competitive pressures which necessitate a change in orientation if these companies are to survive (Kanter, 1991; Smith and Kanter, 1991). The purpose of this chapter is to examine the conditions which force a changed corporate orientation and to examine the resultant cycles of attitude in customer orientation within these companies.

THE ERA OF DEREGULATION

In recent times governments worldwide and particularly throughout Europe have increasingly restricted their role to managing the business environment, rather than actively involving themselves in operating state-controlled business. As well as privatising state-controlled industry sectors, governments have sought to deregulate certain industries — the financial services sector being a key example in most developed economies. The widespread acceptance of concepts such as deregulation, privatisation and anti-trust reflects governments' belief in the market as a means of delivering consumer satisfaction.

In essence, these changes, which are also likely to impact upon what were the planned economies of Eastern Europe, represent a significant change in the external environmental context for competing companies. In marketing education, the term "production orientation" is used to describe a company whose primary focus is on its output, rather than on the marketplace. Such an orientation is likely to exist where demand exceeds supply, with the balance of exchange power strongly vested in the producer. The absence of competition facilitates customer disregard and limited reliance on marketing. In market-oriented environments, however, supply exceeds demand, with choice empowering the consumer and necessitating extensive reliance on marketing to ensure continuous focus on customer needs.

The net outcome of increasingly deregulated environments is that companies which were previously state controlled in industries such as aviation, telecommunications, postal communications, transport and even education, as well as those outside direct state control such as financial services, are being forced to take on board rapidly customer-oriented attitudes, in order to survive in previously unknown competitive conditions. They find themselves having to compete with highly skilful competitors from both home and overseas markets. These new environmental conditions necessitate the instillation of a customer focus in highly bureaucratic and production-oriented organisations.

FIGURE 6.1 — ATTITUDES TO CONSUMERS

Stage 1	Customer as saviour
	Customer as mine
Stage 2	Customer as pain
	Customer as necessary pain
Stage 3	Customer as salary payer
	Customer as stream of future earnings
Stage 4	Customer as managed relationship
	Customer as owner/member
Stage 5	Customer as pain
	Customer needs me

CYCLES IN ATTITUDE ORIENTATION

The attitudes held by corporations and their employees are largely a function of the environments within which they must function. As competitive change occurs in their external environment, corporations may undergo a change of attitude to consumers. It is possible to envisage a series or cycle of such changes of attitude along a continuum, with both a positive and negative range. Five basic stages are identified. However, all corporations do not necessarily go through each of the stages. Some companies may go through a number, while in others attitudes to consumers may always be highly positive. But it is more likely that over time corporate attitudes to consumers may oscillate from initially positive or negative or indifferent to perhaps a more neutral state. In order to stay tuned to market needs in highly competitive environments, companies must become positive in their customer orientation. Expressions reflecting the five stages of attitude orientation are outlined in Figure 6.1.

Stage 1: Initial Enthusiasm — "My Livelihood is on the Line"

Many newly established companies are driven by a vision of themselves and their relationship with their markets. Frequently established by entrepreneurs with a deep understanding of market needs, company personnel hold their customers in particularly high regard and are often willing to go to extraordinary lengths to satisfy their needs. This highly positive attitude can be attributed to a number of factors.

The size of the enterprise. This facilitates the recruitment of "like-minds", good internal communications, and the diffusion to employees of the entrepreneur's ethos regarding the customer.

The nature of the entrepreneur. The enterprise is frequently founded by an individual who has gleaned, often elsewhere, an indepth understanding of the market and is spurred on by both a vision and a personal commitment. Difficulties are likely to occur where this positive attitude fails to extend beyond the entrepreneur's active life or becomes diffused with corporate expansion.

Stage 2: Indifferent — Consumer at Corporate Mercy

Over time, often as a result of operating in competitively rarefied environments, companies become production oriented. In such companies consumers are not regarded as the major priority. Market dominance or state-afforded protection will facilitate a cynical and in certain instances even a hostile attitude towards consumers. The provision of the basic product to the consumer is often regarded as dispensing a favour, particularly where demand exceeds supply and the corporate service provider is aware of this. In any dispute regarding the product or service quality, the consumer enjoys limited power. Figure 6.2 contains comments reflecting attitudes towards the consumer. These attitudes will not be the company's official position, but may reflect the practice on the ground among corporate personnel. Furthermore, these attitudes will often be felt rather than articulated aloud.

These comments, often articulated within production-oriented companies, reflect the service provider's belief in the customers' inability to redress this disregard of their needs. The consumer is often seen in a dehumanised manner and regarded as a "pain". This perception of the consumer as a pain may sometimes occur because the company's contact people, aware of customer rights, realise they are forced to defend the indefensible in terms of the service level being delivered.

FIGURE 6.2: SELECTED RESPONSES TO CUSTOMER PROBLEMS

> "I've got your money, so what can you do about it?"
>
> "I'm doing you a favour, you're getting a phone, aren't you?"
>
> "Who the hell do you think you are?"
>
> "So what, let him go, there are plenty more where he came from."
>
> "She's just another account number."
>
> "He doesn't know my name, so what ever he does won't affect me."
>
> "It's not my job, I'm not in marketing."
>
> "This would be a great job, except for the students."

Stage 3: Lukewarm — Customer as Salary Payer

In more competitive environments the consumer is empowered and treated more respectfully. Consumers are regarded as the salary payers and therefore deserving of satisfaction levels ordained by industry pressures. They are still regarded as an external factor in corporate deliberations and probed long distance via market research in order to determine needs which, in the circumstances, must be satisfied. Not only are they important now, but they must be preserved as a stream of future earnings. Despite this recognition of the consumer's position, service levels accorded are often minimalist and begrudging and attitudes could be described as lukewarm rather than positive.

Stage 4: The New Intimacy

In this more positive environment, not only is the primacy of the customer recognised, but the customer becomes the pivotal point around which the company constructs itself. The more extreme version of this customer focus can be labelled "the new intimacy" where customers are regarded more intimately as members and owners, being welcomed and often willingly empowered through corporate advertising. Customers are used to drive and mould the company and its output; in effect, they are taken on board by the company as the architects of their own satisfaction (Reichfield and Sasser, 1990). The company increasingly moves from one-way to two-way communication, giving the consumer a voice in a much more intimate way than is available via traditional research. Customer programmes are established and feedback is encouraged through customer care groups and customer panels, as well as through traditional market research, in an effort to involve consumers in creating their own satisfaction (Boggis, 1991). In reality, as the competitive heat intensifies corporate success will be determined by the intimacy of its relationship with its consumers.

Stage 5: Insincere Sincerity and/or Arrogance

Highly successful companies, which have achieved market dominance with sought-after brands and extremely loyal customers as a result of high quality marketing endeavour and attention to customer care, sometimes begin to take on attitudes more appropriate to production-oriented companies. They start to believe their own hype and providing the consumer with the product often becomes a favour to the "lucky" recipient. Others over time become over formalised in their dealings with consumers. In the case of services, individualism often disappears and the service provided appears staid and clichéd with "insincere sincerity" becoming the order of the day. Organisational enthusiasm and warmth towards the consumer disappears and such companies are as vulnerable to competitive intrusion as are production-oriented companies.

LABELLING THE CUSTOMER

One of the more interesting features of organisations which are either state controlled or enjoy restricted competitive pressures is their perception and labelling of those whom they serve. In many instances they are not afforded the label "customer" with its obvious connotations of control and power. Certain of these labels are contained in Figure 6.3.

The first three labels cloak the consumer in a dehumanising veil, with the result that the service provider is desensitised in their dealings with this abstract figure. In the second three examples the labels given often mask an unwillingness to accord the buyer true customer status because of the nature of the buyer's reliance on the service provider. This is particularly the case with students and patients. This unwillingness to accord consumers their true status often leads to the belief that the customer will tolerate a certain level of dissatisfactions in the exchange because of the nature of the relationship. The net effect is that consumers are often denied their true rights as customers.

Even where the company officially recognises the primacy of consumers and accords them the proper status, this formal perception may differ radically from how consumers are labelled by the workforce. In one telephone company whose mission statement underlines the primacy of the consumer, certain sections of the workforce still label the consumers as "subs" (short for subscribers) while bus personnel in a semi-state transport company know the consumers as "skulls".

FIGURE 6.3: CUSTOMER LABELS

Organisation Type	Customer Label
Banks	Account Holders
Telephone Companies	Subscribers
Television Station	Viewers/Licence Holders
Hospitals/Doctors	Patients
Sports Association	Patrons/Fans
Universities	Students

CUSTOMER FOCUS — LIP-SERVICE OR DEEPLY INGRAINED?

A watershed in the process of customer orientation is the "away from it all think-in or retreat" which results in an articulation of the company core values and a statement of its mission. Such gatherings represent opportunities to acknowledge the primacy of consumers. They are variously regarded as a vital asset or the *raison d'être* of corporate existence. The net result is their formalised enthronement.

The process of reorienting the company to adopt a consumer focus often goes no further than its formal adoption at senior management level. Staff who must encounter customer problems are often deeply cynical of continuing exhortations to adopt a customer focus, from senior organisational figures who isolate themselves from even the merest hint of customer contact. Problems are likely to emerge when the primacy of the customer is institutionalised as a core corporate value, yet corporate staff at the middle and lower echelons continue to regard customers as subs or skulls. A benchmark on the conversion process to a customer focus will occur when skulls become welcomed consumers *à la* new intimacy.

The reality is that the diffusion of customer-oriented attitudes throughout the organisation is difficult, especially for bureaucratically structured organisations emerging from protected environments. Striking jolts of reality therapy via the introduction of competitors to the marketplace are intended to sharpen corporate focus. However, the reaction is often similar to the "boy crying wolf" scenario. Re-education programmes involving internal marketing are intended to effect a consumer orientation. Essentially, internal marketing involves using marketing principles to diffuse consumer-oriented attitudes to all corporate staff as internal consumers (Barnes, 1989). The objective is to bring about a transition from a mere functional to a philosophical/evangelistic view of marketing.

However, internal marketing approaches often falter in the context of organisations with strong representative associations or trade unions. There is a failure to recognise implicitly trade unions as a significant power block in buyer/seller exchanges. Trade unions' orientation is towards their primary constituency, their members, and they are often deeply suspicious of such manoeuvrings with their members. In reality, the surrender of power by a corporation to its consumers may also involve some diminution of trade union power. This is particularly the case in essential service industries which were previously state controlled, where trade union power tends to be a significant factor.

A relevant feature of this reallocation of power is the price extracted by trade unions for industrial harmony. Emerging bureaucratic organisations, poorly equipped to cope with the seepage into the marketplace of highly competitive protagonists, find themselves engaged in a race against time to infuse deeply ingrained rather than superficial pro-consumer attitudes among staff, for which trade unions often extract higher wage rates. The net result is higher cost structures which render such organisations even less competitive in terms of their ability to satisfy consumer needs.

THE CHALLENGE

Competitive conditions in the marketplace — whether prompted by political, economic or technological change — form the catalyst for evolving corporate orientations. As external competitive conditions intensify, companies must undergo a change in attitudes to their customers in order to survive. The resultant cycle in customer orientation will move from a largely indifferent view of the consumer in an environment facilitating a production orientation, to a lukewarm state of consumer cognisance. To survive in a highly competitive environment, companies must adopt an extremely positive orientation towards consumers, involving them as the architects of their own satisfaction.

Too often a customer focus is only superficially adopted and token attitudes are evident. True market and customer-oriented attitudes must be diffused to all levels within the organisation if success is to ensue. Corporations — both those recently released from state ownership and burdened with bureaucratic baggage as well as those in other deregulated industries — must avail of the "window of opportunity" often afforded them, in order to effect deeply ingrained customer-oriented attitudes prior to the arrival of highly effective competitors.

REFERENCES

Barnes, J. G. (1989): "The Role of Internal Marketing: If the Staff Won't Buy It, Why Should the Customer?", *Irish Marketing Review,* 4(2): 11–21.

Boggis, F. (1991): "Customer Care: A 'Bottom-Up' View of a 'Top-Down' Policy", *European Journal of Marketing,* 24(12): 22–34.

Gronroos, C. (1983): *Strategic Management and Marketing in the Services Sector,* Bromley, England: Chartwell-Bratt.

Kanter, R. M. (1991): "Even Closer to the Customer", *Harvard Business Review*, 69(1): 9–10.

Reichheld, F.F. and Sasser, W.E. Jr. (1990): "Zero Defection: Quality Comes to Services", *Harvard Business Review*, 68(5): 105–11.

Smith, R. and Kanter, R.M. (1991): "Championing Change", *Harvard Business Review*, 69(1): 119–30.

7

Quality Improvement in a Services Marketing Context[*]

*Audrey Gilmore and
David Carson*

INTRODUCTION

Quality is a much abused term throughout aspects of business and by marketers in particular. Historically, when marketers talk of improving quality, the focus has been on improving the features of the product or service. While this is a wholly acceptable objective, alone it displays a myopic view of the "total marketing effort". That is, marketing is not just concerned with the product dimension, it must maintain a balance with decisions on price, promotion and distribution.

Equally, when improving any aspect of marketing quality it is not enough to focus only on the prescriptive aspects of improvement, but consideration must be given to the implementation of quality improvement. Thus, this paper is concerned with two main issues, the full spectrum of "quality improvement" in marketing and the implementation dimensions of decision-making on quality. This discussion uses conceptual models to develop both themes.

Many authors (Morgan and Piercy, 1991; Schmalensee, 1991; Witcher, 1990) argue that marketing practitioners' and academics' response to the quality issue has been unremarkable. Indeed, they go so far as to say that the existing literature on the nature and focus of the interface between marketing and quality has been wholly inadequate.

---

[*] This paper was first published in *Journal of Services Marketing*, Vol. 7, No. 3, pp. 59-71.

IMPROVING PRODUCT QUALITY

Most of the literature which exists on the relationship between quality and marketing focuses primarily on the tangible aspects of quality improvement and deals with product quality in particular. Indeed, even this literature on product quality has been deemed inadequate. A recent article (Morgan and Piercy, 1991) quotes Phillips et al.'s comment in 1983 that "in view of the importance of product quality it is surprising that so little attention has been paid to it by marketing scholars", and add that there has been little evidence in the literature since to change that opinion. There has been scant attention given to the quality improvement of any other functions of marketing activity. There is evidence that this is the case in practice also. Using the example of recession-hit fast food marketers, Bonoma (1991) describes how they go about improving the quality of their marketing activity by adding more product features, rather than giving better service, changing the restaurant sites or improving the value for money.

TOTAL QUALITY MANAGEMENT AND MARKETING

To date, academics and practitioners in both services and physical goods marketing have focused on the "product" aspect of the marketing mix when improving quality. Many of the recent developments in this quality improvement have been as a result of Total Quality programmes which in many cases concentrate on improving systems and processes which then impact on product quality. Total Quality Management (TQM) has also attempted to improve employees' perceptions pertaining to the performance quality of the systems and procedures, and thereby the product offering. Examples of private companies in the USA which have adopted this philosophy are Hewlett-Packard, McDonnell-Douglas and Ford. In these companies TQM has been described as the managerial philosophy which entails the involvement of the entire organisation in the quest for continual improvement (Juran, 1988).

THE FULLY EXTENDED PRODUCT AND QUALITY

However, improving the product offering is not sufficient to improve quality throughout the whole of the marketing function. Consider the fundamental concept of marketing in relation to the marketing mix function. This concept requires that marketing variables must be fully integrated for maximum impact and effect.

If this is not so, the marketing effort may be wasteful.

The marketing mix is essentially a balance of interrelating activities and techniques which must come together for proper efficiency and impact. If one component of the marketing mix is changed, then it will have an effect on the other variables. Any changes made to the components of the marketing mix should be carried out with the total marketing picture in view. Each variable should be seen in the context of the other variables. A good product poorly distributed may never reach the market, or a good product which is either priced too high or too low may have a limited appeal for its intended target market. Similarly, a change in promotional activity on its own will probably be counterproductive. Increasing promotional activity alone could create a mismatch through having insufficient stocks to meet customers' demand, or using different promotional offers for the same product may confuse the customer.

Thus, if the quality of one component (the product) is substantially improved, then one should naturally expect compatible improvement in quality in all other components of the mix. These issues sharpen considerably in the context of services marketing. In services at least theory has learned to accommodate the notion of the "fully extended product". This will improve the overall service quality by considering all aspects of the product by taking into account and making improvements in a balanced co-ordinated way. The concept of the fully extended product tries to take account of this need. A company's marketing offerings can be identified by detailed consideration of the fully extended service product; that is, the company's total offer to the customer. This can be described by taking account of the pre-purchase, during purchase and the post-purchase experience.

Figure 7.1, a model of "The Fully Extended Product",[1] serves to illustrate some of the key components of the purchase stages, although naturally these may vary according to the particular situation.

---

[1] The term "model" as used throughout this paper stems from Kuhn's (1962) description that a model is a "simplified representation of a concept, system or process" and that to be of value it must "bear some measure of similarity to the structure or process being modelled" (George, 1968). Therefore the model must be suited to its purpose. The models described in this paper were designed to show the interactions and integration of marketing concepts and management functions.

Pre-purchase experience incorporates all those factors that lead customers toward a decision of choosing and using the product/service. This may include their exposure to any advertising and promotional activity.

Purchase experience encompasses everything that happens during the transaction or use of a product. Examples of this may include the current availability of the product/service, staff accessibility and the quality of the information and advice given.

Post-experience involves all post-purchase motivations and company contact to which the customer may be subjected. Direct customer contact, such as the use of mailshots and customer loyalty schemes, may be included at this stage.

FIGURE 7.1: FULLY EXTENDED PRODUCT

```
                         Fully Extended Product
         ┌───────────────────────┼───────────────────────┐
    Pre-purchase            During Purchase          Post-purchase
  (product choice)       (pre-boarding and         (repeat purchase)
                          on-board experience)
```

Promotional Activity	Brochures/Leaflets	Physical Facilities	Product Features	Advertising	Direct Promotional Activity	Customer Loyalty	Complaint Handling
	Advertising Message	PR Activity	Ease of Booking		Maintaining Contact with Customer	Mailshots/Direct Mail	After Sales Service/Spares
Availability (of product, staff information/advice)	Physical Facilities	Choice/Range of Products	Accessibility		Special Promotions/Offers	Value for Money	Complaint Handling

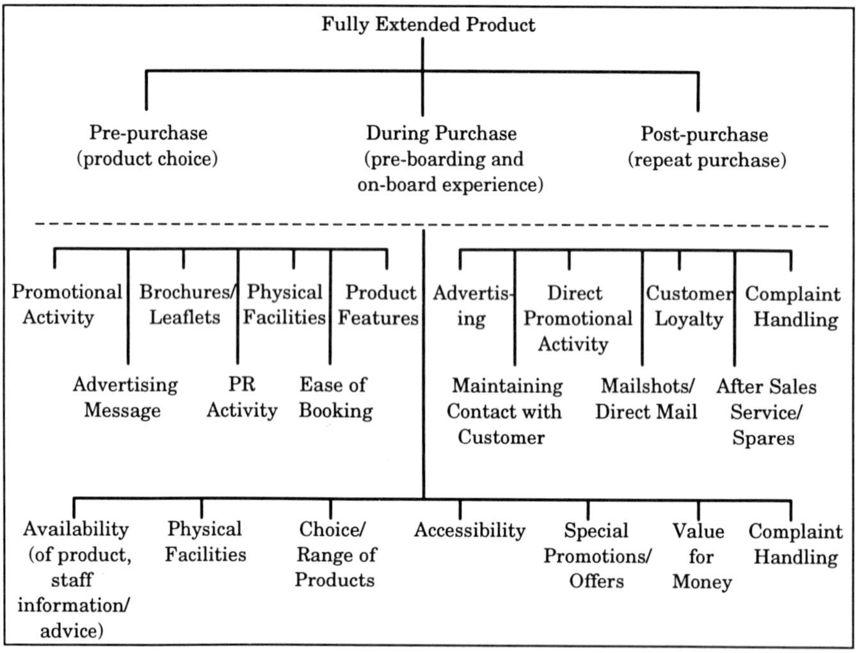

The contention here is that in order to improve the quality of marketing it is vital to pay attention to detail in all aspects of a company's marketing offerings. The marketing mix concept needs to be expanded and adapted to suit the particular service situation. It is marketing management's task to determine how the component parts of the marketing mix may be brought together to make a complete whole, through committing itself to a thorough decision-making process. The design and management of the marketing mix will depend on how the company perceives its strengths and weaknesses in relation to the threats and opportunities in the market and environment in which it is to compete.

THE MARKETING CONCEPT AND QUALITY

So far the discussion has focused on the tasks with which marketing is involved, though the marketing function is not necessarily the same as the marketing department's task. The marketing function is spread over a large part of the organisation outside the marketing department and all the activities which have an impact on the current and future buying behaviour of the customer cannot be taken care of only by marketing specialists. Many staff and support functions include an element of marketing as well. In most firms a large number of employees have something to do with marketing. These people perform inter-firm functions which require a service orientation similar to customer-contact functions. People involved in support functions such as production, technical servicing and invoicing have been called "part-time marketers" (Grönroos, 1990). Often these people do not know they have this role as well as their functional tasks, and management may also fail to understand this dual role responsibility. However, because marketing is spread all over the organisation it has been argued that marketing specialists can only take care of part of the total marketing function, and therefore the nature of the marketing cannot be only that of a specialist function (Grönroos, 1990). The concept of marketing is market-oriented management rather than a separate function and this is particularly so in a services marketing situation. Thus, it is important to recognise that the marketing concept transcends all management functions and the whole organisation.

CUSTOMER RELATIONS AND QUALITY

Consequently, there is clearly a need for management to take account of all marketing functions and related activity when considering quality improvement. Therefore, a deeper understanding of the marketing function based on the customer relations and marketing situations which actually exist is required in order to improve the quality of the company's marketing activity. It has been argued that the most important issue in marketing is to establish, strengthen and develop customer relations where they can be commercialised at a profit and where individual and organisational objectives are met (Grönroos, 1990).

The size and shape of the marketing function depends on the nature of customer relations. Each service company should ensure that its company functions are organised in such a way as to maximise its customer relationships. The essence of customer relations is represented by the interaction points between a company's staff and its customers. These interaction points can happen obviously at the personal interface between individuals but also, and less obviously, at the intangible/impersonal interaction between company communication and customers. Thus, all company communication techniques including advertising, direct mail, public relations, etc., serve to contribute to customer relations. All these interactions need to be fully integrated if they are to be effective. The effectiveness of total service quality will depend on the quality of customer–staff interactions in all areas of marketing activity. The key generic marketing functions for a service situation are shown in Figure 7.2. These functions can be subdivided and extended according to the type of business activity in which a company operates and its company structure.

FIGURE 7.2: SPECTRUM OF KEY MARKETING MANAGEMENT FUNCTIONS FOR QUALITY IN CUSTOMER RELATIONS

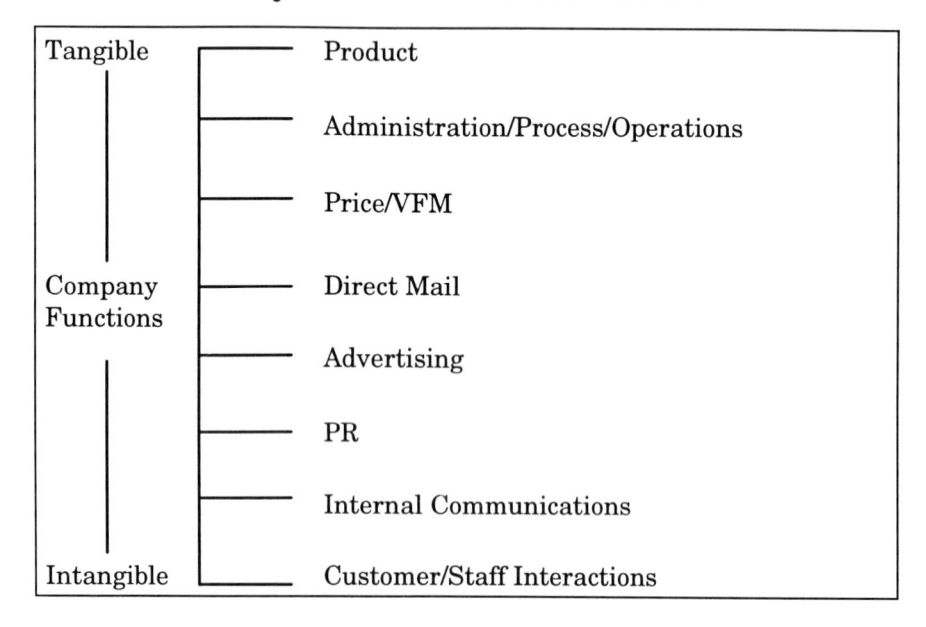

Company Functions	
Tangible	Product
	Administration/Process/Operations
	Price/VFM
	Direct Mail
	Advertising
	PR
	Internal Communications
Intangible	Customer/Staff Interactions

This model (Figure 7.2) recognises the need to focus managers' attention on improving the quality of all marketing activity and related functions. It can be related to any business circumstance and service as a "descriptive" framework on this issue. However, for the purpose of more penetrative understanding in a specific situation it is then necessary to elaborate on this simple framework in order to arrive at a more comprehensive picture. Some of the description so far acknowledges the activity of quality in the service context. Therefore, to examine and develop this model in improving the quality of marketing in a services context it will be important to take account of the fundamental characteristics of services.

SERVICE QUALITY CHARACTERISTICS AND QUALITY

The multidimensional nature of the quality construct is found in much of the services marketing literature. Various studies (Carson and Gilmore, 1988/90; Grönroos, 1982; Kuhn, 1962) identify and describe some dimensions of service quality. It is generally accepted that quality is about consistent conformance to customer expectations (Crosby, 1979) and "fitness for purpose" (Juran, 1988). Principally, customers have both instrumental and psychological expectations about a product or service performance (Swan and Combs, 1976), where expectations relate to both quantifiable hard data and qualitative soft data. Hard data have been described as relating to performance and reliability standards or any tangible dimensions, whereas soft data are those concerned with descriptions of and knowledge about customers' feelings, perceptions and requirements (Smith, 1987). These are more difficult to measure because they are intangible.

The important elements of this issue are brought together in a conceptual model of the "Dimensions of Service Quality" by Carson and Gilmore (1989/90). The scope of these dimensions ranges from the hard, tangible, relatively easy to measure and evaluate aspects such as packaging and product range, to the soft, intangible, more difficult to measure and evaluate aspects such as the degree of courtesy and consideration experienced by the customer. A focus on both tangible and intangible dimensions of marketing offerings is necessary in order to improve the quality of these aspects of the marketing mix. Considering these elements from the perspective of marketing management, the same continuum with its hard and soft, tangible and intangible, criteria can be used to produce a continuum as illustrated in Figure 7.3. This model shows that in order to implement a market-led initiative successfully, emphasis must be placed on the intangible aspects of the total offering, as well as dealing with the tangible aspects.

Consequently, there is a need for an integrated approach to quality improvement in marketing management functions which needs to focus on the quality of the tangible and intangible aspects of the marketing offerings, in addition to focusing on the quality of all marketing activity and related functions. In order to do this we must therefore bring Figures 7.2 and 7.3 together in an integrated way. This is shown in the matrix model in Figure 7.4.

FIGURE 7.3: MARKETING MANAGEMENT DIMENSIONS OF SERVICE QUALITY

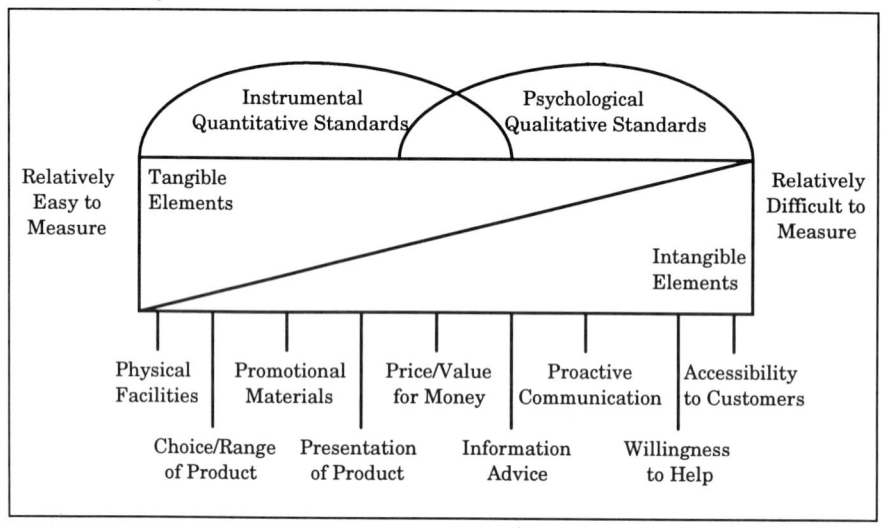

```
                    Instrumental              Psychological
                Quantitative Standards    Qualitative Standards

Relatively    Tangible                                          Relatively
Easy to       Elements                                          Difficult to
Measure                                                         Measure
                                                Intangible
                                                Elements

        Physical    Promotional    Price/Value   Proactive      Accessibility
        Facilities  Materials      for Money     Communication  to Customers

            Choice/Range   Presentation   Information    Willingness
            of Product     of Product     Advice         to Help
```

The quality improvement model serves to match marketing functions with the service quality dimensions, showing how the marketing function and activity are influenced by the tangible and intangible nature of the service elements. Some of the company functions and activities have more tangible aspects than others. For example, product management focuses on issues such as the physical facilities and choice and range of products available. People and staff management functions are made up of predominantly intangible aspects such as being accessible and customer friendly.

Quality Improvement in a Services Marketing Context 89

FIGURE 7.4: A HOLISTIC MODEL FOR QUALITY IMPROVEMENT

The main benefit of the matrix is twofold. First, the matrix format shows the inter-relationships of the company functions with the service quality dimensions, and as such demonstrates the importance of addressing both the tangible and intangible aspects of service quality improvement in an integrated way. Second, in illustrating that service quality is both tangible and intangible; it particularly emphasises the intangible dimensions and it enables the specific components of tangible and intangible to be positioned within the overall service quality concept.

To explain further, it serves to emphasise the folly of only improving the product aspect of the marketing mix as has been the focus of many quality improvement programmes in the past. The product aspects of the marketing activity such as the physical facilities, layout of the service area, choice and range of product, are shown in the top left quadrant of the matrix model. When illustrated in this way it emphasises how the tangible product aspects are only a fraction of the company's total marketing activity to be taken into account in order to improve overall service quality. Any quality programme which focuses on the product aspects alone neglects many of the more intangible aspects shown in the bottom right quadrant. These are aspects of marketing activity which impact strongly upon the internal and external communication dimensions and are the foundation stone of good marketing performance.

It is vital to recognise that all the dimensions on the model have an important role to play and are all interactive. An over-concentration on one area to the neglect of the others may cause a serious imbalance of marketing activity and therefore result in a waste of resources and only minimal improvement.

OPERATIONALISATION OF THE MODEL FOR QUALITY IMPROVEMENT IN A SERVICES CONTEXT: A CASE EXAMPLE

The remainder of this paper will focus on illustrating the model in practice by using the example of a car ferry ship company; that is, a description of the development of a quality improvement which is currently being implemented in the largest ferry ship company in the world, Stena, with a particular focus on the company's Irish/Scottish route. Stena's ships all have a variety of products and services on board. These include a restaurant/cafeteria, a bar with live entertainment, a video lounge/cinema, a children's play area, a snack bar, and a comfortable lounge for each of the customer segments: foot passengers, motorists and freight drivers.

The impetus for improvement in the quality of its marketing activity stems from the Stena company's recent acquisition of Sealink British Ferries in the United Kingdom. Quality is the basis of Stena's management philosophy. This quality dimension is so important to Stena that the company has a main board director with responsibility for quality and also a functional department solely for monitoring quality improvements. The Stena philosophy requires all staff, regardless of function, to seek to improve the quality of the Stena service. The philosophy is translated to practice through the "cruise ship" concept, whereby guests are encouraged to enjoy a cruise ship atmosphere while travelling. Quality "standards" are set by performance ratings from guests using the service. The emphasis is always on striving to increase or improve the standards of the quality of service. In contrast, this philosophy would have been generally considered alien to Sealink's activities before the acquisition, hence there is a considerable challenge for the new company's management to implement a programme of quality improvement.

The first steps in improving the quality of services marketing began with an analysis of customer perceptions of the company's current service quality using the dimensions of service quality as seen in the model in Figure 7.4, and further identifying how management could improve the performance of the overall service. The analysis focused on the customers' perceptions and also took account of the opinions and perceptions of travel agents who acted as the company's distribution and sales network.

The analysis highlighted the quality dimensions, illustrated in Figure 7.3, which required immediate attention and were thought to be indicative of other factors which would emerge in the future and thus needed to be tackled through appropriate mechanisms.

While the results of the comprehensive analysis showed a clear dissatisfaction with a wide range of marketing activity, the underlying problem lay with functional management decision-making and staff performance. Both these dimensions would need to be addressed before significant improvement could be made in the actual quality of service.

The aim now was to enhance Stena Sealink's overall marketing performance by focusing on the key functions of the company's operations as defined in the model, and improving the quality of each employee's contribution to the marketing activity.

The holistic model shown in Figure 7.4 is the conceptual foundation framework used to guide specifically the operationalisation and implementation of such a quality programme. The matrix can be used to identify the issues to be addressed and shows the responsibility of each particular company function in relation to each of the dimensions of service quality. The responsibility of each company function is identified, and those issues requiring improvement can be allocated to the individual operators concerned. Each problem area can be examined and specific tasks identified.

FIGURE 7.5: QUALITY IMPROVEMENT IN OPERATION

	Personnel	Issues to Address	Tasks
Product Management Physical Facilities Choice/Range of Products Presentation of Product	Chefs /Stewards	New Items for Menu Presentation of Food	Create Variety Lighter Meals/Snacks Special Needs Customers Items for Lower Price Range Freshness Hotness Menu Displays Serving Presentation
Advertising Management Promotional Materials Proactive Communication	Advertising, Direct Mail and PR Customers	Passenger Communication	Improve/Standardise Messages Promote Offerings Creativity
Pricing Management Price/Value for Money	Managers/ Cashiers/ Chef	Pricing/Value for Money	Investigate Costs/Margins Special Offers Family Meals

Figure 7.5 illustrates how the matrix (Figure 7.4) can be used as the mechanism for triggering action. Each company function's problem area to be addressed is shown in the context of the dimensions of service quality. Thus, the choice or range and presentation of product dimensions are the responsibility of product management, the promotional materials and activity are the responsibility of advertising management and the price/value for money dimensions are the responsibility of the pricing management

team. The physical facilities and layout dimensions of the product management responsibility are not included in this operationalisation model because they incur capital expenditure and are improved on an annual basis when the ferries are in dry dock. The other columns show the personnel within each company function who have responsibility for that activity, the issue or problem to be addressed and the tasks involved.

Improving quality in marketing involves recognising that quality is about continual change. In a service organisation change is predominantly about behaviour. Changing behaviour involves a learning process and it is evident that adults learn because they want to learn (Quimby et al., 1991). Employees need to be involved in improving quality so that involvement will encourage motivation and lead to individuals taking an active role, so teamwork and participation at all levels needed to be encouraged. Developing and implementing a quality strategy demands the support not only of top management but also of managers and staff at all levels in an organisation.

In implementing the quality model the principles of implementing the marketing concept were applied; that is, key staff were involved in confronting the problem/task and in subsequent decision-making.

Responsibilities and accountability were delegated widely to the operational and implementation staff who previously had not been given responsibility for decision inputs. Thus, the objective was that teams of staff involved in the delivery of that job function would have responsibility for improving the quality of their performance where previously they had simply been directed to do. Staff were encouraged to form "self support teams" consisting of those individuals who had an influence on the quality outcome of a given issue. The teamwork aspect is considered crucial to the implementation of quality improvement, and as such it is worthwhile to take a moment to emphasise the teamwork issue. What are the foundations of this importance? Any staff development programme should enable each individual and team to learn through their work, recognise their current level of competence, develop new competencies and be able to interpret them effectively in their job situation. Teamwork and participation are better ways to solve problems because knowledge, information and skills are distributed among a number of people (Revans, 1984). The involvement of those people who have the relevant knowledge, information and skills about the particular area requiring change are essential to real improvement. Teamwork is an integral part of this "action learning" method of achieving company development which is strongly advocated by Revans (1984). He writes that team meetings provide an opportunity for teams or individuals to seek help from other teams, they serve as an internal source of pressure on members of each team to keep their individual work moving, and they provide mutual encouragement and support. Because learning is a social process managers learn more from their exchanges with each other than from an outsider (1984). Consequently the involvement and participation of all staff concerned will lead to a consensus of opinion and agreement on necessary tasks. This results in a uniformity of tasks and everyone working toward the same goal.

IMPLEMENTING ACTION LEARNING

An intensive training workshop was set up. The aim of this workshop was to discuss the issues raised from the findings of the market research study. This workshop involved all the key personnel in Stena's Irish/Scottish route whose day-to-day responsibilities revolved around the actual management, planning and operational aspects of their functional roles in the company. These staff worked in close contact with customers and they agreed that the issues outlined in the analysis of customers' perceptions of current service quality were indeed the major causes of customer complaints. They were in the best position to determine what could be done to overcome these problems and raise the quality of on-board services.

These key personnel readily accepted and indeed were motivationally stimulated by the responsibility for developing and building on the quality of service they already provided. This contributed to maintaining the commitment and enthusiasm of staff, particularly the key personnel, so that the quality improvement process could maintain momentum.

The staff organised themselves according to the key functions of the company's quality improvement operations denoted in the Operationalisation of Quality Improvement Model (Figure 7.5). The emphasis of these decisions was twofold:

(1) To improve the quality of the tangible aspect of their particular area/issue; thus, the product management team would seek to improve the menu in the ship's restaurant and the presentation of the food;

and most importantly,

(2) To improve the quality of the intangible aspect of these particular areas/issues. This meant taking account of all the intangible issues considered under the heading of internal communication and customer/staff interaction. These can be found in the bottom right quadrant of the Holistic Model for Quality Improvement (Figure 7.4).

That is, the product management team incorporated all personnel who were involved in decisions relating to any aspects of the product, such as hotel managers, stewards and chefs. The advertising management team involved the PR and advertising managers, and the pricing management team involved cashiers, chefs and managers. Each of these functions involved management teams of 2–6 in number. Within this context each group addressed an identified and appropriate problem area, focusing on issues to address and the tasks involved. These groups involved as many other staff from their functional area as possible in discussions charged with the responsibility of producing suggestions and solutions to problems. The counterpart groups from each service area would communicate with each other to compare ideas and agree which were the most feasible suggestions for implementation. It was crucial that as many staff as possible felt involved and participated in the service development process. Each group was responsible for coming up with realistic ideas and plans for improvement, without incurring any capital or additional manpower expenditure, within a specified time period. All groups agreed to formulate ideas for improvement and present them to the whole team.

The outcomes and agreements reached at these meetings were recorded on a single sheet of paper under the headings: "Tasks", "Action to be Taken", "Responsibility", "Completion Date".

At the next meeting this record sheet was produced with each completed item checked off and in so doing highlighted any task which had not yet been resolved. This encouraged further discussions and plans for completing those tasks in relation to the progress they had made, problems they were encountering and the next stage in the way forward.

A key component of an effective programme was a co-ordinator/facilitator who could monitor the developments and ensure that progress was being made from one meeting to the next. This role was carried out by an independent consultant. Good planning, communication with the people involved and co-ordination played an important part in the development process, preventing pitfalls and poor participation. One of the vital priorities was to maintain close contact with the key decision-makers in order to ensure continued support for the quality improvement process and commitment to the goals.

SUMMARY

The quality improvement model has been used in the Stena Sealink Company as the basis of gradual and systematic improvement. The quest for continual improvement was maintained by means of discussions, team meetings and regular feedback sessions. Feedback from each of these planning workshops was important in order to monitor the progress of each team and measure the effectiveness of the quality improvement process over the longer term. This feedback accentuated any further changes that needed to be made and identified any group needing more encouragement or some outside advice before progressing to the next stage of development.

The monitoring of all suggestions was continuous and the responsibility of all team members. Staff involvement and responsibility for improving the tangible offerings of the company clearly encouraged and indeed necessitated increased internal communication in the planning and execution stage.

At the stage of performing and delivering the service product to customers, external communication was an integral part of monitoring customer perceptions of the new offerings. The measurement of results required staff to communicate proactively with customers. When new ideas had been implemented, customers were made aware of these new products and services through announcements, posters and point-of-sale material.

Ongoing observation studies continued to monitor how customers responded to the new products and services on board. Many new ideas were refined to suit any observed or requested customer preferences. In addition to observing customers, members of each team were encouraged to talk proactively to customers more frequently throughout their visits on board and particularly when customers were using the new services and products offered.

This provided useful and immediate feedback to the staff who were involved in the creation and evolution of offering improved services. Praise and appreciation from customers also provided encouragement to the staff who were initiating and implementing their new suggestions on board. This first-hand communication with customers led to a more pleasant atmosphere on board overall and a closer understanding of customer likes and dislikes than had been experienced prior to the changes on board.

MANAGERIAL IMPLICATIONS AND RECOMMENDATIONS

The Holistic Model (Figure 7.4) and the Operationalisation Model of Quality Improvement (Figure 7.5) serve to emphasise all the issues involved in quality improvement. There are a number of significant benefits of using these models, principally in relation to structure, focus, balance, consistency and organisation:

(1) Structure — these models offer a systematic and structured approach to the enormous task of managing service marketing quality improvement.
(2) Focus — the use of the models can provide a clear focus on the key aspects of service quality which require attention and also focuses on how those aspects affect and interact with each other. As the quality programme progresses it can be expected that the developments will impact upon activities leading to further improvements and additional initiatives in other areas of the service marketing function. The Operationalisation of Quality Improvement Model lends itself to refinement and adaptation as a result of these developments. Indeed, refinement and development of the model will help target main areas of quality weakness, and in so doing contribute to the aim of achieving an overall level of quality on a consistent basis.
(3) Balance — by using these models marketing managers can ensure that quality improvements are made in a balanced way across the key marketing functions by recognising the tangible/intangible nature of these functions, particularly in a services operation. The value of using this model to measure and improve the overall quality is to ensure that it happens in a cohesive way.
(4) Consistency — in order to improve and maintain marketing quality it is important to recognise that it is a continuous and ongoing process. The main purpose must be continually to develop and improve all marketing activity and all dimensions of the service to customers.

(5) Organisation — as marketing quality improvement involves change and changing behaviour of staff in particular, it is vital to involve all staff in the changing process. Participation and involvement as shown in the Operationalisation Model will contribute to the commitment and co-operation of staff in the evolving work environment.

In the light of this dynamic environment, the Holistic Model and the Operationalisation Model for Quality Improvement in a services context serve to provide a stable framework from which to work and, since stability is a most desirable management circumstance, this can only be of significant value to the management of marketing services.

REFERENCES

Bonoma, T. (1991): "How Are We Doing? Not Too Bad Overall", *Marketing News,* 25(20): 17.

Carson, D, and Gilmore, A. (1989/90): "Customer Care: The Neglected Domain", *Irish Marketing Review,* 4(3): 49–61.

Christopher, M., Payne, A. and Ballantyre, D. (1991): "Relationship Marketing: Bringing Quality, Customer Service and Marketing Together", Address at the Marketing Educators Conference, Cardiff: Marketing Educators Conference.

Crosby, P. (1979): *Quality is Free, The Art of Making Quality,* London: McGraw-Hill Books.

George, F.H. (1968): "The Use of Models in Science", in R.J. Chorley, and P. Haggett (eds), *Models in Geography,* London: Methuen.

Gronroos, C. (1982): "A Service Quality Model and its Marketing Implications", *European Journal of Marketing,* 18(4): 36–44.

Gronroos, C. (1990): *Service Management and Marketing. Managing Moments of Truth in Service Competition,* Lexington, M.A.: Lexington Books.

Gronroos, C. (1990): "Relationship Approach to Marketing in Service Contexts: The Marketing and Organisational Behaviour Interface", *Journal of Business Research,* 20(1): 3–11.

Hammons, C. and Maddux, G.A. (1990): "Total Quality Management in the Public Sector", *Management Decision,* 28 (4): 15–19.

Juran, J.M. (1988): *Juran on Planning for Quality,* New York: The Free Press.

Kuhn, A.H. (1962): "Complex Interactive Models", in R.H. Frank, A.H. Kuhn and W.F. Massey (eds): *Quantitative Techniques in Marketing Analysis,* Homewood, Illinois: Irwin.

Morgan, N. and Piercy, N. (1991): "The Interface of Marketing and Quality: Research Propositions for Market-led Quality Strategy", Address at the Marketing Association Summer Educators Conference, Chicago, Illinois: American Marketing Association.

Parasuraman, A., Zeithaml, V. and Berry, L. (1985): "A Conceptual Model of Service Quality and its Implications for Future Research", *Journal of Marketing,* 49(4): 41–50.

Phillips, L.W., Chang, D.R. and Buzzell, R.D. (1983): "Product Quality, Cost Position and Business Performance: A Test of Some Key Hypotheses", *Journal of Marketing,* 47(2): 26–43.

Quimby, C., Parker, L. and Weimerskirch, A.M. (1991): "How Exactly Do You Communicate Quality?" *Quality Progress,* June: 52–4.

Revans, R. (1984): *The Sequence of Managerial Change,* Bradford: MCB University Press.

Schmalensee, D.H. (1991): "Marketers Must Lead Quality Improvement or Risk Becoming Irrelevant", *Services Marketing Newsletter,* 7(1): 1–3.

Smith, S. (1987): "How to Quantify Quality", *Management Today,* October: 86–8.

Swan, J.E. and Combs, L.J. (1976): "Product Performance and Customer Satisfaction", *Journal of Marketing,* 40(2): 25–33.

Witcher, B.J. (1990): "Total Quality and The Marketing Concept", *The Quarterly Review of Marketing,* 15(2): 1–6.

8

Customer Service and Information Technology[*]

*Christine T. Domegan and
Bill Donaldson*

INTRODUCTION

Customer Service (CS) and Information Technology (IT) are widely accepted as valuable resources in gaining a competitive advantage. Essentially, CS is viewed as a differentiating tool to gain an advantage over competitors. Although we may not clearly recognise it, our society is experiencing its third great wave of change. The first wave of change was the agricultural revolution, the second was the rise of industrial civilisation, the third and current wave of change is information. As in the earlier instances, this "Information Revolution" will significantly impact society and the way in which economic activity is conducted. Clearly, the rate at which information can be created has greatly accelerated, which in turn has expanded the demand for efficient, timely, and accurate information.

> Managers perceive that Information Technology (IT) is having a significant impact on business, government and organisational life now. They increasingly agree that IT has become a strategic resource as it brings about or facilitates major changes in industry sectors, in competitive behaviour and in organisations' own strategy, structure and functioning. (Earl, 1989).

---

[*] This research was part of an EC COMETT sponsored study, 1990–91. The paper was first published in *Journal of Information Technology*, Vol. 7, pp. 303–12.

This paper reports on a study which examined some of these issues by researching leading edge companies and IT consultants in the UK, Ireland and France. The report also addresses the differences between leaders and followers in the adoption of IT in the area of CS for competitive advantage.

INFORMATION TECHNOLOGY AND MARKETING

While many people have heard of the term IT, fewer know what it means precisely . It is difficult to offer a simple definition of IT, but it is essential to explain how IT is defined for the purposes of this study. IT incorporates three avenues of technology: computing, microelectronics and telecommunications. It is through the use of these technologies that information, in all its forms (words, numbers, pictures, for example), is acquired, processed, stored, presented and transmitted (Liebster and Horner, 1989). Therefore, anyone who deals with information is a potential user of IT. Coupled with this, marketing managers are particularly reliant on accurate, timely and efficient use of information in directing the interaction between the firm and its market environment (Aaker and Day, 1986). Without information, marketing managers would not be able to make meaningful decisions and to monitor the consequences of these decisions (Kotler, 1991).

Despite the numerous examples of firms improving competitive positioning by implementing IT systems, the adoption level of IT by marketing managers has remained relatively low (OASIS, 1989). Studies have shown that there is a clear correlation between a strong market orientation, extensive use of information sources (internal and external to the firm), and exploitation of IT (Butler Cox, 1984, 1987; OASIS, 1989). The pressures which motivate a company to adopt IT in CS are the need to reduce costs, increase efficiency and the opportunity to create or maintain a competitive position (Fletcher, 1990).

WHAT IS CUSTOMER SERVICE?

In the area of marketing management, increasing attention has been paid to service-related aspects which are seen to increase added value and enhance customer satisfaction. Managers of businesses across many industries have identified CS as an area of significant importance. CS has moved from a descriptive and reactive activity of the 1970s to proactive management activities of the 1990s. More so than before, evidence shows that improving the quality of service to customers is a key to competitive success, particularly for European firms faced with more open markets and increased competition from 1992 (Humble, 1991). As a result, it comes as no surprise that firms are cultivating CS as a valuable asset in strategically differentiating their products and services from the competition (Kyj and Kyj, 1987).

As in the case of defining marketing, people frequently mean different things when discussing CS. As a result, there is no one universally accepted understanding of the term. In operationalising any marketing variable within a research framework, the meaning ascribed to that variable must be clear and unambiguous. In exploring a definition of CS, four distinct streams of thought can be identified. First, many of the definitions readily available describe CS as the "net result of all logistical efforts" (Ballou, 1971). This is understandable as the area of CS historically evolved as an element of the firm's logistics or distribution system. Secondly, a wider description of CS views it as an operationalisation of the marketing concept and as the fifth and "missing" element of the marketing mix (Donaldson, 1986). Defined as such, CS can be managed as a measurable and identifiable process (Christopher, 1983). Thirdly, CS is a strategic concept embedded in the corporate philosophy and mission of the business. This is an approach which sees CS as a philosophy similar to a marketing orientation (Peters and Waterman, 1982; Payne, 1988). Finally, CS can be understood from a service industry perspective, where it is a function of perceptions and quality (Horovitz and Cudennec-Poon, 1990).

The principal benefits of CS to the firm are enhanced profitability and customer satisfaction which in turn positively affect corporate image. An additional benefit of CS is that it may provide firms with a competitive advantage because of its inherent unique qualities. That is, where product, price, place and promotional programmes cannot offer lasting advantage, or are readily imitated, CS may not be so easily duplicated or short-lived. This is achieved by protecting the customer base, by enhancing the saleability of the product and generating income as a separate benefit.

For the purposes of this study, CS assumes the marketing approach and is viewed as a process, both identifiable and measurable, between the buyer and the seller. "Ultimately, Customer Service is determined by the interaction of all those factors that affect the process of making products and services available to the buyer" (Christopher, 1983). Thus, CS is viewed in the broad context of the marketing mix, whereby CS has utility for product, price, place and promotion. As can be seen from the description above, CS can cover a broad area of a firm's operations. Naturally, how firms define CS may differ greatly from one firm to the next. Even how an individual firm deals with individual market segments may vary.

RESEARCH OBJECTIVES

IT and CS are now accepted by large organisations as necessary resources against competitive threats, especially by multinational enterprises. Many small- to medium-sized European firms are still significantly weak in the strategic and tactical exploitation of IT in many spheres of their business, and in particular, in the area of CS. As succinctly expressed by Peter Keen (1991) in his latest book, *Shaping the Future: Business Design Through Information Technology*: "Customer Service, operations, product and marketing strategies, and distribution are heavily, or sometimes even entirely, dependent on IT".

Against this background, this research study investigates how an organisation may strategically employ IT in CS to gain a competitive advantage. The research objectives were therefore:

(1) To highlight trends and developments within the areas of IT and CS;
(2) To assess how firms employ IT, particularly in CS, to gain a competitive advantage; and
(3) To determine the pressures driving the use of IT in CS.

THE RESEARCH METHOD

Research was conducted in three European countries — the UK, Ireland and France. The study was conducted in four sequential phases and is descriptive in nature.

Phase 1: Literature Review

A comprehensive review of IT and CS literature was undertaken to identify issues pertinent to the areas of IT and CS. In addition, information gathered from this literature review served as an input into the design and implementation of the empirical research.

Phase 2: Survey of IT Software Suppliers and Management Consultants

In-depth personal and postal surveys were conducted with the leading IT software suppliers and management consultants within the three countries. The top 15 software suppliers and management consultants from all three countries were selected on the basis:

(1) That they had assisted or been directly involved with the analysis, design and implementation of IT systems in the sphere of marketing and CS;
(2) Sales and turnover levels;
(3) Performance rankings with respect to sales, profits, assets, stockholders' equity and employee numbers within their respective countries; and
(4) Reputation and perceived expertise as judged by a panel of experts from the academic and business communities.

The software suppliers and management consultants were also asked to identify small- and medium-sized enterprises (SMEs), within Ireland, France and the UK which were pioneering the use of, and/or which had a competitive advantage with respect to, IT in the area of CS.

Phase 3: Survey of Firms Using IT in the Area of CS

A postal survey was conducted of firms identified in phase 2 which had a competitive advantage with respect to IT in Customer Service. A total of 166 questionnaires were sent with an overall response rate of 40 per cent. This method was chosen since the interest was in the successful application of IT in CS rather than the general practice at the time. By carefully selecting a segment of firms which are sensitive to CS and IT issues, rather than a random survey of firms in general, it was intended that the findings would point out future direction and not simply describe "average practice". As a result, the findings of the survey represent "cutting edge companies" rather than "average practice".

Phase 4: Examples of "Best Practising Firms"

In addition to the personal and postal surveys, 20 firms were selected as examples of "best firms". From these examples, case histories were developed to illustrate specific areas of IT and CS applications.

RESEARCH FINDINGS

Use of IT in Marketing and CS

Similarities among the three countries were strong and, as expected, large firms lead in the application of IT in marketing and CS. In all three countries, American companies were perceived as prominent in using IT in CS, with indigenous firms appearing to lose ground in Ireland and France.

The leading sectors in the use of IT in CS were, not surprisingly, the service industries, where the basis of differentiating products and services by offering superior CS appears to be well established. Financial services was the leading sector in all three countries, with banking common to Ireland and France, travel services common to Ireland and the UK, followed by insurance in France and retail services in the UK. The industry sectors which lag behind tend to be those which produce highly tangible goods. These sectors included textiles, furniture and clothing in all three countries, which traditionally are known for their "marketing myopia". In Ireland and the UK, construction and engineering are seen to be slow to adopt IT, while in France, the food, drink, tobacco and paper, printing and publishing industries were ranked the last to use IT in marketing and/or CS.

The main findings of the study show that the use of IT in marketing has increased over the past three years. More significantly, respondents expect that this trend will not only continue, but accelerate over the coming three years.

Table 8.1 shows that this use of IT by the marketing and CS function is still at an early stage of development. The high figure for applying IT to CS in Ireland is to be expected, as, to date, minimal use of IT has been made by Irish firms, whereas in the UK, sales and distribution functions have already benefited from IT tactical applications.

IT, MARKETING AND CS DEFINED

Participants were asked to identify the currently accepted definition and scope of IT within their firm. The survey also asked respondents to identify the currently accepted definitions and scopes of Marketing and Customer Service. Again, strong similarities are evident among all three countries. Large firms consistently defined IT, marketing and CS in their broadest terms. That is, IT was seen to include "all forms of electronic processing and transmission of data to facilitate strategic and operational business purposes". Marketing meant "placing major emphasis on market needs, adapting products and services where necessary" and CS was defined as "a total corporate philosophy aimed at a continuous relationship between the firm and its customers". However, the practices of these large firms suggests that they are not as sophisticated in applying IT, marketing or CS as their comprehension of these terms would suggest. The results also highlighted a significant gap when comparing large firms with small- and medium-sized firms, and their understanding of the concepts. SMEs view IT as a tactical tool to facilitate routine operations while CS is viewed as order processing, delivery and billing activities. It appears that a vast majority of European firms are in an evolutionary process in terms of their sophistication in utilising IT in CS. Larger firms are further down this road than most SMEs, but large organisations and SMEs alike are not as sophisticated as they could be.

TABLE 8.1: PREDICTED PERCENTAGE INCREASE OF IT USAGE WITHIN THE FIRM OVER THE NEXT THREE YEARS

	Ireland (%)	France* (%)	UK (%)
Marketing	9	7	5
Customer Service	22	7	6
Sales	6	9	3
Distribution or Delivery	8	2	2

Note: Non-response rate for France was high and so the results may be biased.

BUSINESS PLANS WITH REFERENCE TO IT AND CS

To examine whether this strategic understanding of IT translates into practice, respondents were questioned on their business plans. Large firms were more likely to have formalised IT and marketing plans, with over 50 per cent of respondents claiming to have a written IT plan with specific reference to CS. Small firms relied more on informal IT guidelines, with fewer still having written CS plans. The number of SMEs with a written IT plan containing CS issues was negligible. Ireland, in comparison with the UK and France, demonstrated a noticeable lack of formalised IT and CS plans, as Table 8.2 shows.

The results also showed that large firms currently view IT in CS as having a medium-to-high strategic and operational impact on their businesses, whereas SMEs perceived the impact as low-to-medium. All firms, regardless of size, expect the future strategic and operational impact of IT in CS to be substantial. The expectations were highest in Ireland, with the UK and France somewhat behind. This could be attributed to different positions on the evolutionary scale of IT, marketing and CS. For all organisations, in all three countries, the future strategic use of IT in CS far outweighs the operational applications.

TABLE 8.2: THE PERCENTAGE USE OF FORMAL BUSINESS PLANS

	Ireland		
	Yes (%)	No (%)	Don't Know (%)
Formal IT Plan	83	13	4
Formal Marketing Plan	83	10	7
Formal CS Plan	59	34	7
Formal IT Plan w.r.t. CS	50	43	7

	United Kingdom		
	Yes (%)	No (%)	Don't Know (%)
Formal IT Plan	88	12	0
Formal Marketing Plan	94	6	0
Formal CS Plan	81	19	0
Formal IT Plan w.r.t. CS	81	19	0

	France*		
	Yes (%)	No (%)	Don't Know (%)
Formal IT Plan	84	16	0
Formal Marketing Plan	89	11	0
Formal CS Plan	88	12	0
Formal IT Plan w.r.t. CS	81	19	0

* *Note:* Non-response rate for France was high and so the results may be biased.

BUSINESS OBJECTIVES WITH REFERENCE TO IT AND CS

In developing their business plans, survey participants were asked to identify their firm's top three business objectives for the next two years. Findings were strikingly similar among the three countries (see Table 8.3), with CS being the number one business objective. The need to increase market share and reduce costs reflects a number of forces at work in the business environment, for example, increasing competition and the depressed economic climate. It is interesting to note that a conflict does not appear to occur for firms which are aiming to improve CS and reduce costs at the same time.

To assess further the linkage between the value of IT and CS as essential features in business objectives and plans, participants were asked whether their firms viewed IT and CS as a means to gain a competitive advantage, and whether their major competitors used IT and CS to gain a competitive advantage in the marketplace. Responses from all three countries were clear: firms and their major competitors employ IT and CS as competitive tools. However, in Ireland competitors do not yet appear to be using IT to gain an advantage. This may be due to firms having insufficient information regarding competitive actions.

TABLE 8.3: FIRMS' TOP THREE BUSINESS OBJECTIVES OVER THE NEXT TWO YEARS

	Ireland	United Kingdom	France*
(1)	Customer Service	Customer Service	Customer Service
(2)	Reducing Costs	Increasing Market Share	Increasing Market Share
(3)	Increasing Market Share	Reducing Costs	Reducing Costs

* *Note:* Non-response rate for France was high and so the results may be biased.

These findings show that CS is crucial to firms' progress. Essentially, CS is viewed as a differentiating tool to gain an advantage over competitors. The trends prevailing in Irish, UK and French firms, highlighted in the previous tables, can be summarised as follows :

(1) Improving Customer Service is a top business objective for the coming two years.
(2) IT currently plays a significant role in improving CS.
(3) Firms and their competitors view the application of IT in CS as a means to gain a competitive advantage.

PRESSURES DRIVING THE USE OF IT IN CS

The top pressures which drive companies to pay more attention to the use of IT applications in CS, as identified by this research, are:

(a) CS provides a competitive edge
(b) Management vision
(c) Customers are more demanding
(d) Cost structure improvements.

When asked to comment on the factors essential to the successful implementation of IT applications in CS, the highest ranking factors in the three countries were:

(a) Awareness of customer needs
(b) Management commitment
(c) Clear definition of requirements aligned to the firm's business objectives.

These findings demonstrate that European managers are well aware of the strategic relevance of CS and IT in today's competitive environment. Yet, few managers appear to have a clear picture of exactly how CS and IT can be exploited. While such managers may possess a "business vision", a lack of management commitment implies no true opportunity or drive to capture a competitive advantage. This management deficit, coupled with more sophisticated, demanding consumers and fierce competition, will see many firms with a competitive disadvantage rather than a competitive edge.

IT TECHNOLOGIES FOR 1991 AND 1995

IT applications currently in operation tend to be staff operated (80 per cent). Future applications in all three countries are expected to be more customer oriented, that is, to involve the customer directly. Personal computers, Electronic Data Interchange (EDI), Local Area Networks (LAN) and Point of Sale (POS) were noted as the most important of these applications for current and future operations. This further supports the pronounced trend towards more direct customer involvement with IT, which should lead to decreased customer costs, increased customer loyalty and enhanced company–customer relationships (Table 8.4).

Lismona Wear Plc is one such example of a company using EDI and, as we will see below, illustrates how such a development can give the smaller firm an opportunity to position itself strategically, through the use of IT in CS.

TABLE 8.4: TOP THREE IT TECHNOLOGIES FOR 1991 AND 1995

	Ireland	
	Currently in Operation	**Planned to be in Operation**
(1)	Personal Computers	Point of Sale (POS)
(2)	Point of Sale (POS)	Electronic Data Interchange (EDI)
(3)	Local Area Networks (LAN)	Local Area Networks (LAN)
	United Kingdom	
	Currently in Operation	**Planned to be in Operation**
(1)	Point of Sale (POS)	Point of Sale (POS)
(2)	Electronic Data Interchange (EDI)	Electronic Data Interchange (EDI)
(3)	Local Area Networks (LAN)	Local Area Networks (LAN)
	France*	
	Currently in Operation	**Planned to be in Operation**
(1)	Point of Sale (POS)	Electronic Data Interchange (EDI)
(2)	Personal Computers	Local Area Networks (LAN)
(3)	Electronic Data Interchange (EDI)	Personal Computers

* *Note:* Non-response rate for France was high and so the results may be biased.

EDI SYSTEM CONNECTING LISMONA TO ITS CUSTOMERS

Lismona Wear Plc (Lismona) is involved in the design, manufacture and marketing of children's outerwear to a range of customers in the UK and Ireland, principally chain stores, such as British Home Stores (BHS) and Mothercare. The garments are manufactured at the company's factory at Portadown (Co. Armagh, N. Ireland), where 200 people are currently employed.

The company has installed a direct computer link with BHS for "call-off orders", and similar links are being developed with other key customers. This facilitates a very fast turnaround of call-offs and the company has a very high level of success with immediate fulfilment of call-offs (i.e., four-day turnaround). Feedback from Lismona's buyers indicates that, in terms of deliveries and customer service, Lismona is one of the best suppliers in the market. Such a link with customers has given Lismona an advantage in the market, enabling the firm to provide superior customer service which results in enhanced customer loyalty.

The primary objective of the EDI system connecting Lismona to its buyers was to expedite deliveries (i.e. turnaround time). Benefits accruing to Lismona were: improved delivery performance, reduced manufacturing lead times, reduced administration costs and improved stock control.

IT TECHNOLOGIES IN OPERATION AND PLANNED FOR THE NEXT TWO YEARS FOR CS

A number of important issues arise from Table 8.5. Firstly, in the near future the emphasis will continue to move from the currently staff operated IT applications to more customer operated applications. Secondly, the IT applications in the future will be less tactical and more strategic in nature. This suggests increasing confidence in IT investments, more demanding customers and in the long term, a more strategic use of IT than that which currently exists. The planned future use of on-line databases indicates that companies are beginning to recognise the value of information about industry trends, customers and competitive moves. Avonmore Foods demonstrates how the use of a customer information file and sales information can reduce sales administration costs while increasing sales.

AVONMORE FOODS
— A CUSTOMER INFORMATION SYSTEM

Avonmore Foods is one of the largest dairy co-operatives in Ireland and the UK. The Kilkenny-based co-operative dairy society has expanded continuously since its establishment in 1967.

TABLE 8.5: CURRENT AND PLANNED IT TECHNOLOGIES FOR CUSTOMER SERVICE

	Ireland	
	Currently in Operation	**Planned to be in Operation**
(1)	On-line Database Access	Electronic Transmission of Customer Paperwork
(2)	IT Support for Sales Administration	Customer Tracks Order via IT Telemarketing
(3)	Staff Use of IT to Support CS	
(4)	Sales Performance Monitoring System	

	United Kingdom	
	Currently in Operation	**Planned to be in Operation**
(1)	Staff Use of IT to Support CS	Electronic Transmission of Customer Paperwork
(2)	On-line Database Access	Customer Enters Order via IT
(3)	Telemarketing	Customer Uses IT to Obtain Product Information
(4)	IT Support for Sales Administration	
(5)	Electronic Transmission of Customer Accounts	

	France	
	Currently in Operation	**Planned to be in Operation**
(1)	Telemarketing	Customer Enters Orders
(2)	IT-based Delivery Service via IT	Staff Operated Applications
(3)	Customer Tracks Order via IT	Customer Uses IT to Obtain Product Information
(4)	Sales Performance Monitoring System	IT Support for Communications between Head Office and Field

* *Note:* IT applications are listed in order of priority and received a rating of at least 70 per cent.

Its main activities in the consumer market include the production of a variety of spreads, cheeses and milks. This is complemented by its pigmeat range from Roscrea, giving Avonmore a significant share of Ireland's supermarket shelf space. In addition to the consumer markets, Avonmore has a grain and feed division, as well as a large liquid milk division, with a turnover in excess of £60 million.

As expected of such a large organisation, Avonmore operates a number of IT systems, such as EDI link-ups with major supermarkets, stock and inventory control systems, a payment and billing system, as well as a customer information system (known in Avonmore as CIS).

In developing CIS, Avonmore knew that it wanted to develop more accurate and detailed client profiles. It also wanted to ensure that the system was sufficiently flexible to allow various divisional or departmental managers to access and manage the data in forms appropriate for their individual operations. Given these guidelines, Avonmore consulted prospective CIS users (sales representatives, branch, divisional and senior managers, etc.) as to what features they sought in such a system. Although such consultation was time consuming and occasionally tedious, the payback came in the form of a significant adoption rate by potential users. However, problems did arise in developing CIS.

For example, upon delivery of CIS, users (i.e., managers) realised that they wanted the system to do more than it was originally designed for. Avonmore learned that users are good at expressing current needs, yet may lack sufficient vision to predict future needs.

Unlike a system which is developed for a given department which then claims ownership of the system (e.g. accountancy), CIS did not belong to any one specific department or functional area. Consequently, in the early stages, maintenance of the database system was poor. This was quickly corrected by appointing an official CIS "champion" to manage and update the system's database.

What follows is one example of how Avonmore is using CIS to increase existing customer loyalty and to expand market share. Avonmore discovered that its sales representatives were operating on the basis of the "80/20 rule". That is, 80 per cent of the customers whom the sales representatives visited were only providing 20 per cent of Avonmore's sales. To remedy this situation, a local branch manager conducted an experiment whereby he selected from CIS 120 customer names and accompanying profiles to give to a sales representative. The sales representative was put on an incentive scheme and was given sole responsibility for these 120 customers and asked to maximise the profitability of these accounts. The 120 customers were categorised as follows:

(a) 20 were key Avonmore customers
(b) 60–80 were customers doing 50 per cent or less of their business with Avonmore
(c) 20–30 were potential Avonmore customers (i.e. were currently not doing any business with Avonmore).

The result of the experiment was a resounding success. In the first year, sales nearly doubled from £350,000 to £670,000 per annum. Over a three-year-period, sales increased from £2.8 million to £4 million. One factor contributing to this success was that the client profiles, accessed by the sales representative from the CIS, detailed the clients' buying patterns and requirements. Such information enabled him to target customers more accurately and time his visits to match individual client needs.

CS ACTIVITIES THAT IT MAY FACILITATE

Survey participants were given a range of CS activities, and were asked, with reference to their firm's operations, firstly, to rank them in terms of high versus low IT current usage (Table 8.6); and secondly, to rank them in terms of high versus low (expected) IT future usage (Table 8.7).

Regardless of country or firm size, a large proportion of IT applications are in the planning stage, although larger companies had a greater proportion of IT applications in the experimental stage. These findings also confirm that mechanistic operations such as order entry, processing delivery and invoicing are the starting point of IT applications in marketing, and in particular, in CS. Reasons for this might lie in the argument that benefits in labour saving and accuracy are obvious. Managements take comfort in the visibility and cost justifications of their actions. It is also suggested that the areas using IT now, and those that will use it in the future, are more difficult to appraise, with a need for creative and proactive use of innovative IT applications. It is easy to record information but difficult to use it effectively and harder still to yield it as a strategic weapon. Large multinational firms seem to lead this movement. Many small- and medium-sized enterprises, especially in the UK and Ireland, may be left behind.

TABLE 8.6: CURRENT USAGE OF IT IN CUSTOMER SERVICE

Ireland

	Low Current Usage	High Current Usage
(1)	Pattern Design	Customer Entry Orders
(2)	Merchandising	Product Differentiation
(3)	Quality Circles	Delivery of Products

United Kingdom

	Low Current Usage	High Current Usage
(1)	Quality Circles	Delivery of Products
(2)	Packaging	Delivery of Service
(3)	Pattern Design	Lowering Customer Costs

France

	Low Current Usage	High Current Usage
(1)	Sales Support Administration	Promotion Effectiveness
(2)	Quality Circles	Delivery of Products
(3)	Delivery of Products	Including Customer Loyalty
(4)	Pattern Design	Lowering Customer Costs

* *Note:* CS activities are listed in order of priority and received a rating of at least 65 per cent.

INDEX OPTICAL COMPANY AND A TOTAL CS PACKAGE[*]

The Index Optical Company was established in 1986 and trades as an optical manufacturer and wholesaler. The company manufactures lenses, frames and completed spectacles for opticians in central Scotland. The company evolved from the wish to gain strategic advantage by fully exploiting new technology.

Market research shows that 89 per cent of the opticians in central Scotland would use a modern laboratory in preference to those currently providing this service. The company identified four key areas in which they could gain competitive advantages:

---

[*] *Source*: Chris Connolly as adapted from Keith Fletcher (1990, pp. 122–3).

(a) Accuracy of service
(b) Speed of service
(c) Feedback of information
(d) Price.

TABLE 8.7: EXPECTED FUTURE USAGE OF IT IN CUSTOMER SERVICE

	Ireland	
	Low Expected Usage	**High Expected Usage**
(1)	Lowering Consumer Costs	Customer Paperwork
(2)	Pattern Design	Sales Support Administration
(3)		Sales Forecasting
(4)		Delivery of Services
(5)		Delivery of Products
(6)		Customer Entry Orders
(7)		Service–Product Information
(8)		Point of Sale

	United Kingdom	
	Low Expected Usage	**High Expected Usage**
(1)	Packaging	Measuring CS Activities
(2)	Quality Circles	Sales Support Administration
(3)	Merchandising	Customer Query Handling
(4)	Pattern Design	Marketing Information

	France	
	Low Expected Usage	**High Expected Usage**
(1)	Lowering Customer Costs	Marketing Information
(2)	Pattern Design	Sales Forecasting
(3)	Sales Support Administration	Sales Support Administration

* *Note:* CS activities are listed in order of priority and received a rating of at least 80 per cent and low expected usage received a rating of at least 40 per cent.

The accuracy of service would be achieved by the use of a modern, well-maintained computer-driven plant, as well as by an atmosphere on the shop floor which was conducive to quality and efficiency. The other key areas were also achieved with the use of an IT system. A tracking system enabled any job within the laboratory to be located instantly, progress monitored and priority jobs actioned, thus enabling a speedier service and good feedback.

The second part of the system covered the management accounts, job pricing, stock control and customer profit analysis. The third part was telex communications with the suppliers for stock orders. The company's use of IT has resulted in radical changes. The initial target turnover was surpassed by 300 per cent. Within the first year, four out of eight competitors went out of business, because of Index's ability to improve CS.

In the marketplace there have also been substantial improvements. The percentage of spectacles being returned by an optician due to inaccuracy or errors was reduced from an average of 30 per cent to 2 per cent. The completion time for spectacles was reduced from an average of 6 working days to an average of 1.5 working days. The system also generates a list of jobs outstanding for each account which is more than one day in the laboratory and provides reasons and expected delivery dates. Customers are thus continuously informed of any delays, pre-empting customer complaints.

The computerised manufacturing standardised the cost of manufacture, regardless of type of lenses, allowing a standardised pricing policy to be followed. This simplified purchasing, while reducing the price to the majority of customers. The system also allowed Index Optical to supply all the currently available products. The result of the use of IT was that Index could offer the best all-around package of customer service (i.e., delivery times, accuracy, price, and feedback in the event of delay). This gave Index a substantial competitive advantage over other suppliers.

BARRIERS IN IMPLEMENTING IT IN CS

The main barriers in utilising IT in CS were identified by respondents across all three countries as the same: implementation time (of systems), actual costs and perceived costs (in terms of an effective return on investment).

Companies which pursue a cost-driven IT probe may risk the possibility of alienating customers. Management clearly cannot afford to be negligent as regards the time and cost involved in improving the application of IT in CS. Such action inhibits further growth in this area.

Competition, lack of a company vision, and customer resistance were rated as the three minor barriers to be contended with in using IT in CS.

A limiting factor in all of the above is the effectiveness of such future use of these technologies. A lack of integration of these tools into a common system, to give a strategic focus to all strategic, marketing and CS activities would result in a fragmented approach to IT. Such a development could leave firms which are "stuck" in the evolutionary process of using IT in either marketing or CS, in a less than satisfactory position.

CONCLUSION

The intention of this study and the case histories was to reveal "best practice" companies with respect to using IT in CS. The findings did identify important differences between "leading edge" firms and others. Leading edge companies utilising IT in CS, were found to exhibit all, or most of the following six characteristics:

(1) They are marketing oriented.
(2) They view CS as part of their corporate philosophy.
(3) They have written plans for IT and marketing, both with specific reference to CS.
(4) These plans reflect customer needs.
(5) The prime drivers are customers and the need to develop competitive advantages in their markets.
(6) IT and CS are viewed as having strategic implications on the way business is conducted and driven in the future. IT and CS are clearly not seen as administrative or operational activities.

REFERENCES

Aaker, D.A. and Day, G.S. (1986): *Marketing Research,* third edition, New York: Wiley.

Ballou, R.H. (1971): "Developing Definitive Statements of the Customer Service Function", Address at the National Council of Physical Distribution and Management Conference, Oak Brook, Illinois: National Council of Physical Distribution and Management.

Butler Cox (1984): *Information Technology and its Impact on Marketing and Selling*, London: Butler Cox.
Butler Cox (1987): *Information Technology and the Consumer*, London: Butler Cox.
Christopher, M. (1983): *The Strategy of Distribution Management*, London: Gower.
Donaldson, B. (1986): "Customer Service — The Missing Dimension in Marketing Management" *Journal of Marketing Management*, (2)2: 133–44.
Earl, M.J. (1989): *Management Strategies for Information Technology*, New York: Prentice-Hall.
Fletcher, K. (1990): *Marketing Management and Information Technology*, Herts: Prentice-Hall.
Gattora, J. (1988): "What is Customer Service?", "How Do We Develop Customer Service Strategies?" and "What Does an Appropriate Level of Service Cost?", *International Journal of Physical Distribution and Materials Management*, 18(2/3).
Horovitz, J. and Cudennec-Poon, C. (1990): "Putting Service Quality into Gear" *Quality Progress*, 24(1): 54–70.
Humble, J. (1991): *Service, the New Competitive Edge, A Survey of Executive Opinion of Senior Managers in Ireland*, Dublin: Digital (Ireland) and the Marketing Institute of Ireland.
Keen, P.G.W. (1991): *Shaping the Future: Business Design Through Information Technology*, Harvard: Harvard Business School Press.
Kotler, P. (1991): *Marketing Management Analysis, Planning, Implementation and Control*, seventh edition, Englewood Cliffs, N.J.: Prentice-Hall.
Kyj, M.J. and Kyj, L.S. (1987): "Customer Service Competition in Business to Business and Industrial Markets: Myths and Realities", *The Journal of Business and Industrial Marketing*, 2(4): 45–52.
Liebster, L. and Horner, C. (eds): *The Hamlyn Dictionary of Business Terms*, London: Hamlyn.
OASIS in Association with the Chartered Institute of Marketing (1989): *A Report on the Management of Marketing Information*, Berks: Organisation and Systems Innovations Ltd.
Payne, A.F. (1988): "Developing a Marketing-Oriented Organisation", *Business Horizons*, 31(3):46–53.
Peters, T.J. and Waterman, R.H. (1982): *In Search of Excellence: Lessons from America's Best-Run Companies:* New York: Harper and Row.

Part IV

Strategic Marketing in Irish Companies

9

Competitive Advantage: The Vital Edge[*]

John A. Murray

In general, marketing has concentrated much of its effort on understanding customers and customer needs and behaviour in great depth so as to align the products and services of companies with market demands. This became the very essence of the so-called "marketing concept". Marketing, in many companies, is given the responsibility for ensuring market-orientation and for driving the message of serving customer needs into the heartland of strategy-making. In the heartland of strategy-making, however, the needs of customers have always been weighed in combination with the capabilities and resources of the company and with the competences and ambitions of competitors. As markets become more intensely competitive, understanding this triangular relationship becomes ever more critical to effective strategy. Marketing has changed as a result. Effective marketers are still the corporate windows onto customer needs and market behaviour, but in addition they have also had to take much more responsibility, firstly, for a genuine understanding of company competences and secondly, for market-based strategies to outperform competition. The game is not about serving customers. It is about serving customers by creating and leveraging distinctive company capabilities in a manner which critically outperforms competing companies in a sustained manner.

---

[*] This paper was first presented at the National Marketing Conference, Dublin, 8 November 1991.

FIGURE 9.1: WE SPEND A LOT OF TIME UNDERSTANDING...

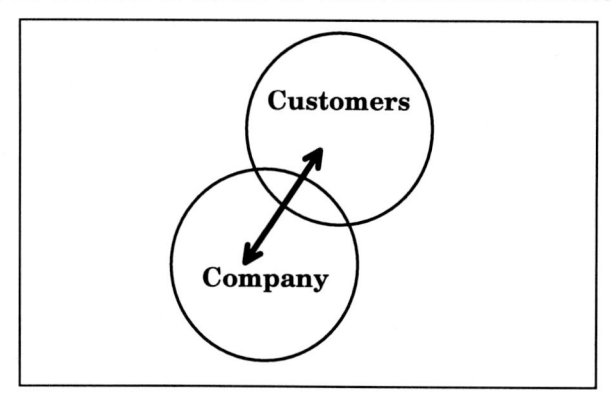

FIGURE 9.2: IT'S CRITICAL THAT WE ALSO UNDERSTAND...

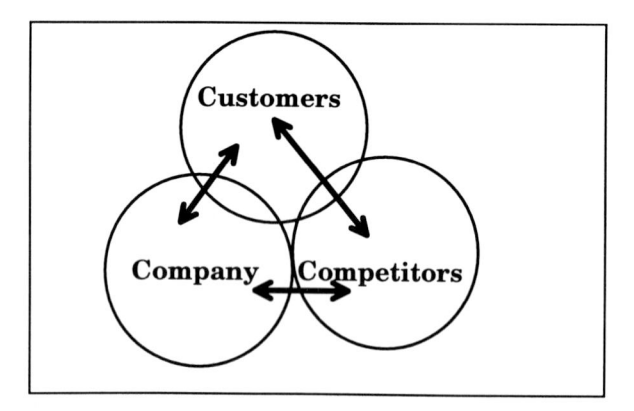

THE NATURE OF COMPETITIVE ADVANTAGE

Outperforming competitors is the result of building a meaningful competitive advantage. And competitive advantage in blunt terms means being better than anyone else at some things that matter to customers. If one cuts the origins of competitive advantage to their barest essentials, it is clear that companies win in the marketplace because they offer the customers more value than others do or because they can offer the customer an acceptable product or service at lower cost. In the crudest terms, you can be better or cheaper. If you are neither, why should anyone buy?

To reduce competitive advantage to "better" or "cheaper" is to oversimplify. We should preferably refer to "better" in terms of "higher in perceived value" — the reality of being better lies in the eyes of the customer. Similarly, the reality of being cheaper lies in providing a service or product at "lower delivered cost" to the user. This concept of "cheaper" stresses cost-in-use to the customer as distinct from production cost. What matters to the customer is the overall cost of purchase and use. Japanese car companies built their cost advantage not just on their extraordinary successes in manufacturing, but also on the reliability of their vehicles which resulted in lower life-cycle costs to the owner.

A third basis for competition which is now changing the shape of markets is speed. In intensely competitive markets where customer needs shift ever more quickly and where competitive imitation catches up ever more relentlessly, getting to market faster has become a significant source of competitive advantage. It yields the advantages of surprise, of establishing early market share and leadership status and of adding months or years to the profitable life of a company's product.

FIGURE 9.3: COMPETITIVE ADVANTAGE LIES IN BEING ...

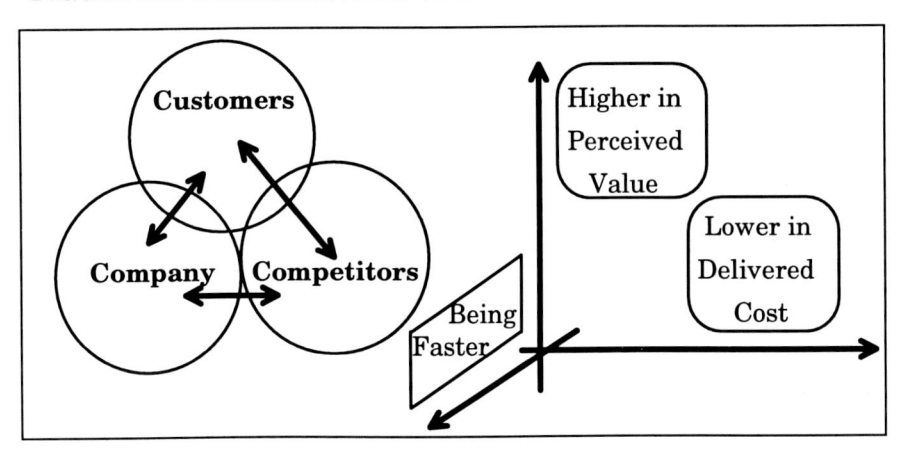

We might therefore view the basic competitive game-plays as being based on strategies which result in the company being better, cheaper or faster than competitors. This view underscores the essential point of competitive strategy — it is a relative notion. Better, cheaper, faster are all relatives which can only be calibrated if we already understand the value, the cost and the speed-to-market of competing companies' products. Each basis for outperforming is in turn rooted in customer knowledge — value is embedded in customer perceptions; cost is embedded in the cost-in-use to the customer, and speed is embedded in customer preferences with regard to time. Curiously, marketing professionals seem to have been rather slow to broaden their view of their marketing task to encompass some of these competitive imperatives and one might be forgiven in looking around the corporate world for suggesting that those responsible for manufacturing and operations management have been more creative and aggressive about putting customer needs together with competitive necessities. The three most commonly cited measures of effectiveness in manufacturing or operations management are probably quality, cost and time, and a major revolution in the way in which we make things and deliver services is emerging from this focus in manufacturing.

FIGURE 9.4: THE COMPETITIVE GAME PLAYS ...

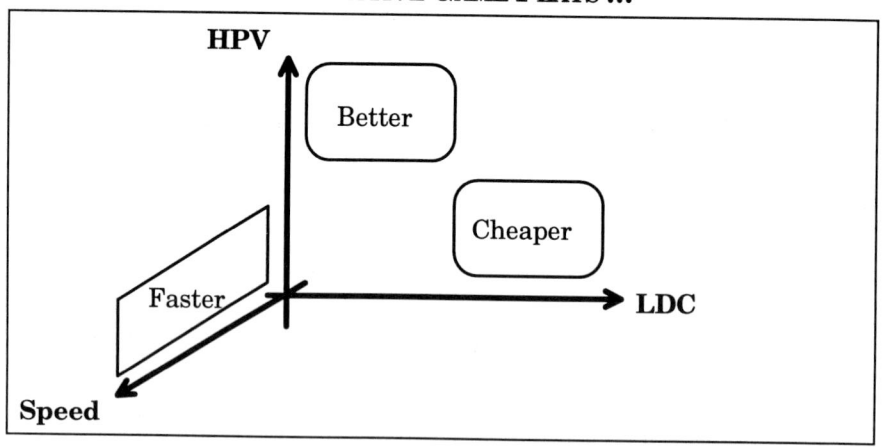

FIGURE 9.5: AND THE "IDEAS" OF "LEAN MANUFACTURING" ARE STEALING MARKETING'S HIGH GROUND!

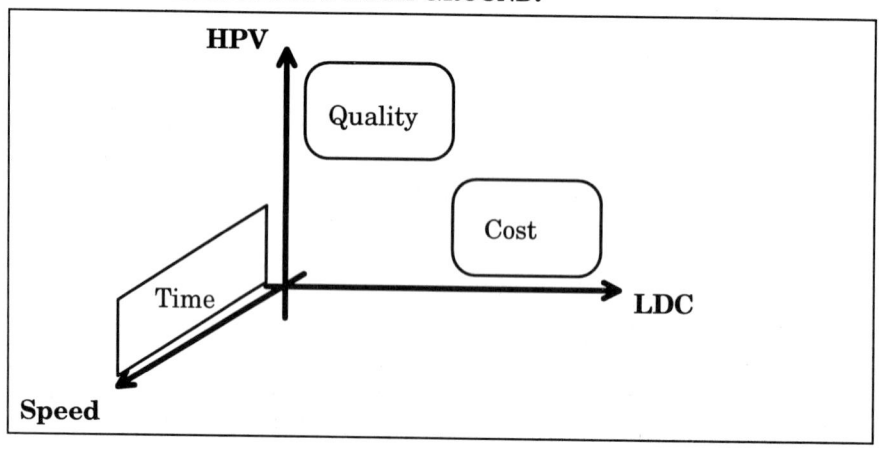

Starting to some substantial degree with the development of the so-called Toyoda system at Toyota, and in Japan in general in the late 1950s, this revolution has led to what is now called "world class manufacturing" or "lean manufacturing" in the west.

Looking at and listening to manufacturing and operations managers who are at the forefront of "lean manufacturing" methods, it is easy to believe that they have stolen marketing's clothes. Standing in the very heartland of company competencies — where things are made — their concern is to engineer methods and systems that yield customer-defined levels of quality, cost and timeliness while using the standards of "best-in-class" competitors as the benchmarks they seek to outperform. Marketing has a lot to learn from manufacturing and it remains one of the great failures of many companies that they cannot integrate the work of marketing and operations management in the most fundamental manner. Companies which continue to manage through controlled border skirmishes between these two areas — in the tradition of what Americans refer to as "silo management" — are doomed to failure.

COMPETITIVE SUPREMACY

While competitive advantage may be based on superior value, cost or speed, true competitive supremacy lies in a combination of all three. Combining all three bases of advantage demands exceptional managerial competence but leads to a winning and sustainable advantage in most market conditions. Because it is a difficult managerial task it is of course also hard to imitate.

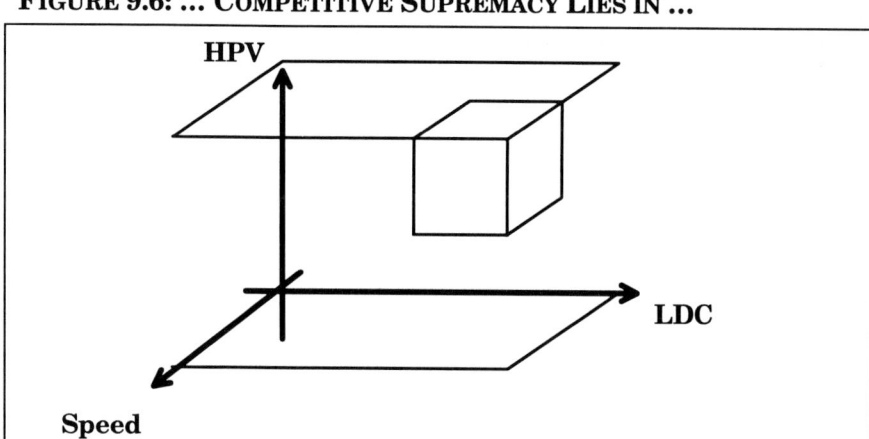

FIGURE 9.6: ... COMPETITIVE SUPREMACY LIES IN ...

World class companies such as Sony manage this competitive positioning through their investment in technology, miniaturisation, and branding for customer value; through manufacturing systems to deliver superior quality at low cost and through new product development methods that bring products to market faster than rivals.

Building and maintaining a competitive advantage demands that marketers fashion a strategic relationship between customers, competitors and their company. Customer needs and competitor strengths and weaknesses in the marketplace must be matched with the core competences of the company. The core competences of the company are the essence of its competitive ability. They are resources or skills which give it access to a variety of market needs, rather than limiting it to one market segment or application area. They directly generate perceived customer benefits. They are difficult for competitors to imitate when their importance becomes known. While marketers have long-established skills in exploring customer needs in the marketplace, they have surprisingly limited skills in exploring the vitals of their own organisation. Yet without intimate knowledge of the core competences of the company — whether these lie in R&D, production processes, personnel practices, or distribution arrangements — it is impossible to develop well-grounded competitive strategy for the market.

Competitive advantage is therefore fashioned from deep knowledge of the market (customers, market structures, the key factors for success in the market); knowledge of the competition (who they are and who will be the new competitors, their strategies, their strengths and weaknesses); and knowledge of the company (core competences, the competences which are distinctive to the company and therefore confer a competitive edge, the intent it pursues over the long term).

FIGURE 9.7: SO COMPETITIVE ADVANTAGE IS FASHIONED FROM...

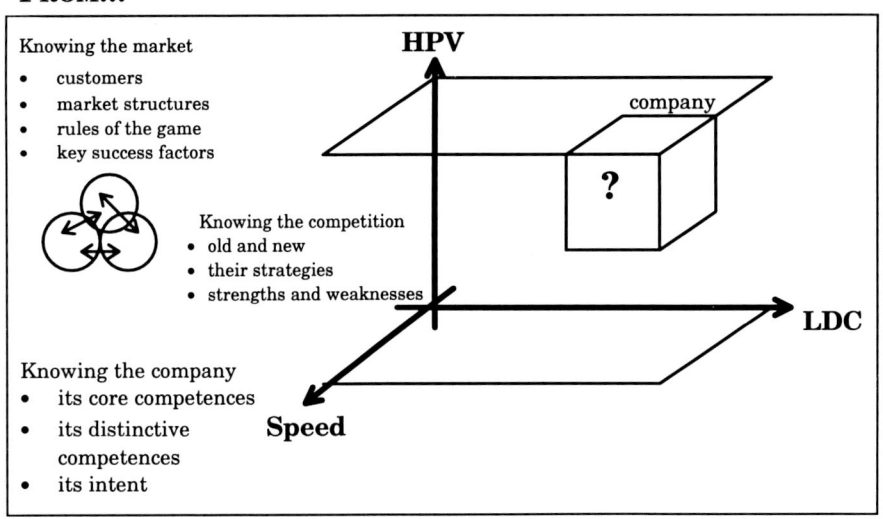

Knowing the market
- customers
- market structures
- rules of the game
- key success factors

Knowing the competition
- old and new
- their strategies
- strengths and weaknesses

Knowing the company
- its core competences
- its distinctive competences
- its intent

HPV

Speed

LDC

company

?

SUSTAINABLE COMPETITIVE ADVANTAGE

Competitive advantage is strategically valuable only if it is sustainable over time because only in sustained advantage will we find adequate and defensible margins and long-term profitability. Having a competitive advantage is one thing, but keeping it is by far the most difficult task. Sustaining advantage is not a matter of static defence but rather a matter of continuous upgrading as market needs shift and as competitors improve their competitiveness. Those who have cost advantage therefore face a continuous necessity to improve cost structures and lower their delivered cost still further. The pressure to build greater customer value is also continuous as customer expectations increase and as competitors add value through service or product enhancement, through better distribution or through brand investment. And just at the moment many companies are struggling to add time-based advantage to traditional strengths in customer value and delivered cost. The process of sustaining advantage is therefore one based in continuous exploration of the various bases for advantage and of adding layers of advantage. Success lies in many layers of advantage built up over years, not in a one-dimensional strategy. The task is therefore to maintain existing sources of competitiveness while simultaneously adding new sources in a creative fashion.

FIGURE 9.8: HOW DO WE BUILD ADVANTAGE ... AND KEEP IT?

COMPETE OR CO-OPERATE?

While the notion of competitive advantage suggests an all-out drive to deal with competitors through direct competition, experience clearly shows that it is often more effective to co-operate selectively with competitors. The late 1980s in particular saw an upsurge in strategic alliances and joint venture arrangements and in the use of shared resources among competing firms (reservation systems among airlines; information networks among insurers etc.).

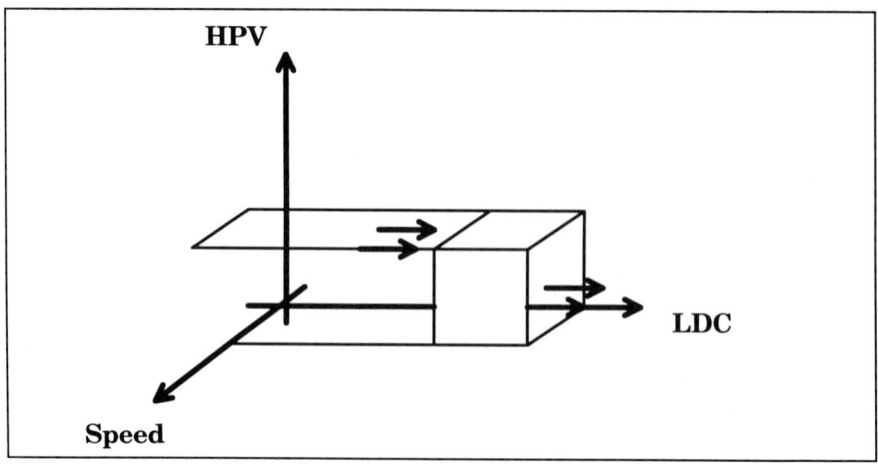

FIGURE 9.9: KEEPING IT IS A WAR OF MOVEMENT ....

Competitive Advantage: The Vital Edge 131

FIGURE 9.10: ... BASED ON BUILDING LAYERS OF ADVANTAGE ...

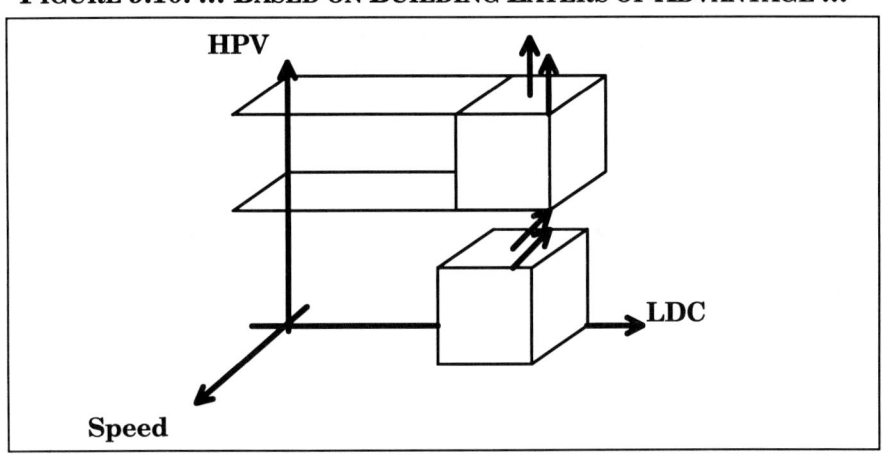

FIGURE 9.11: DEFEND BY CO-OPERATING ....

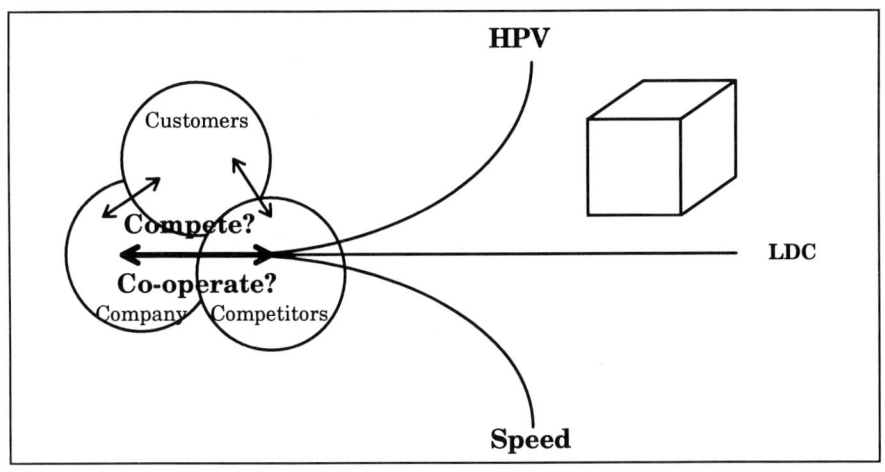

Co-operation may yield access to markets on a reciprocal basis; access to necessary technology in a world of spiralling R&D costs; access to competences that the firm cannot hope to build organically; enhanced ability to enter markets rapidly; and in a world of increasingly global markets it may be the only means of acquiring the necessary critical mass in financial and distribution terms to take on international markets.

IN CONCLUSION

Overall, however, the best source of competitive advantage lies in the ability (or occasionally the good luck!) to rewrite the competitive "rules-of-the-game" for the market. European companies like Benetton in clothing, Ikea in furniture, ABB in the electrical sector, BA in airlines, Tetrapak in packaging, Lego in toys, have succeeded largely because they changed the traditional rules of how to compete and left their competitors — warmly wrapped in the conventional wisdom of how to compete — at a long-term disadvantage. The ability to change the rules springs from deep insight (often intuitive rather than rational) into underlying customer needs and in new competences which have not been previously used in the market. It is therefore a creative ability and is most often associated with one or a small number of entrepreneurs or managers. The role of creative and committed leadership should never be forgotten in the search for competitiveness.

FIGURE 9.12: BEST OF ALL, REWRITE THE RULES ....

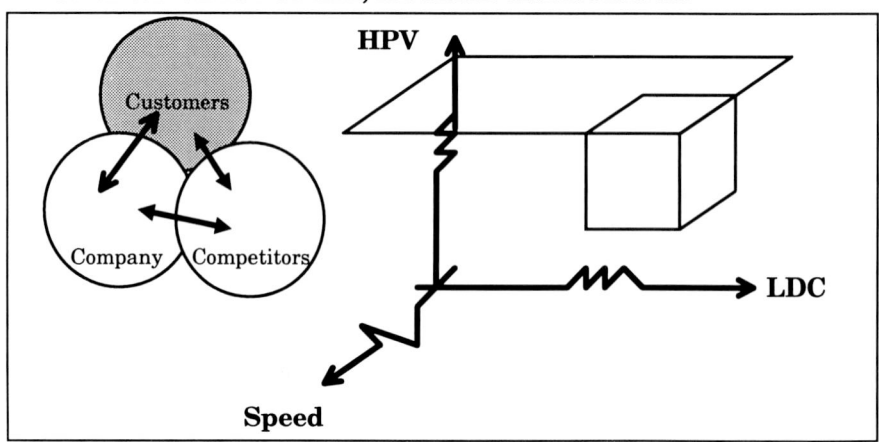

If there is one general feature distinguishing many of the competitive winners of the past decade, this author would suggest that it has been their ability to craft new delivery systems ... new ways of getting to market that produce major shifts in both value and cost for the customer. Benetton's restructuring of the business system — from raw material sourcing to outsourcing most of their manufacturing, to the rapid dyeing of grey garments, to their information technology infrastructure, to their unique form of controlled but independent retailing — effectively industrialised the

Competitive Advantage: The Vital Edge 133

fashion business, producing high perceived value at low delivered cost for the target markets and creating a huge barrier to imitation in a market with very low barriers to entry.

FIGURE 9.13: SUSTAINING ADVANTAGE IN THE 1990S ...

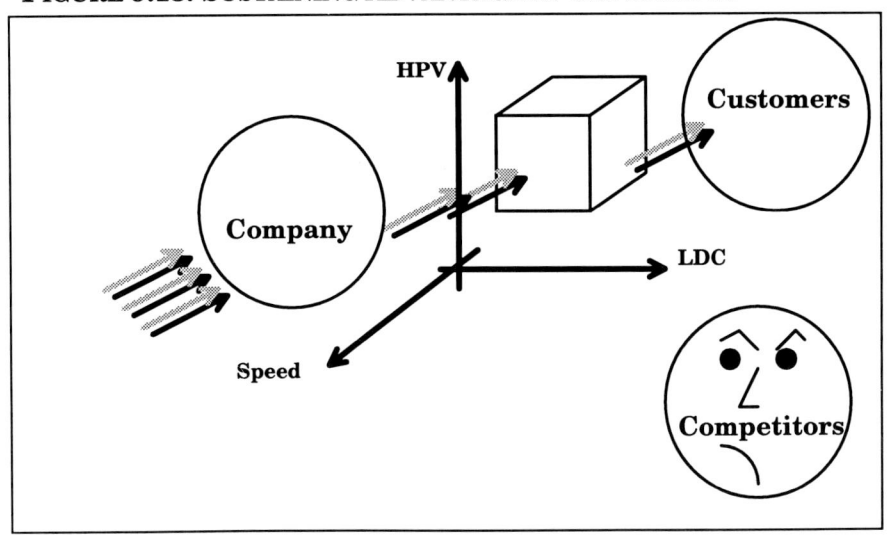

(Diagram: Three axes labeled HPV (vertical), LDC (horizontal right), and Speed (diagonal). A "Company" circle on the left with arrows directed through a cube at the origin toward a "Customers" circle in the upper right. A frowning "Competitors" face in the lower right.)

... THE INNOVATIVE DELIVERY SYSTEM

Most industries are locked into the conventional industry wisdom of how to move from raw material to final customer service and support and in this lies the greatest barrier to building significant and sustainable advantage. If everyone operates by the same rules, based on the same assumptions, is it any wonder that competitiveness becomes ever more marginal and profits become ever more pressured? Is it any wonder that many of the competitive surprises that occur are caused by entrepreneurial firms and by managers of a rather iconoclastic character? Imitation is never the source of sustained advantage: innovation is.

10

Going for Growth: Strategies of High Growth Small Businesses

*Colm O'Gorman and
John A. Murray*

INTRODUCTION

Growth remains one of the more puzzling aspects of organisations. Why do some firms grow and others not? Is it a matter of luck in the choice of market and technology and means of transacting business? If so, why is it that within the same industry and market context one firm grows and another does not? Is this difference in behaviour due to differentials in the aspirations or past experience of the managers? Is it due to different choices in organisation structure or process? Is it due to the different strategies chosen by the managers of the different firms? This paper documents the findings of a study which set out to explore the importance of the last explanation suggested. Clearly, there is more to growth than the choice of a particular strategy. However, it was felt that, given the traditional difficulty that surrounds our ability to explain growth, a focus on one of the possible explanations — difference in the nature of strategy — was justified. In particular, it was hoped to establish what strategies distinguished high growth firms from their low or no growth colleagues.

The findings of a study of 131 small and medium-sized firms (US$10 million–$2 billion turnover) indicates that those which were growing rapidly and successfully were characterised by two critical features: they had positioned themselves in growing markets and they pursued distinctive growth-oriented strategies. The study suggests that those small companies that wish to grow must pay special attention to the decisions they make with regard firstly, to market choice (industry, sector, segment), and secondly, to strategic positioning and resource allocation within the chosen arena of competition.

WHAT THE LITERATURE TELLS US ABOUT GROWTH

The puzzle of organisational growth has always been a theme of writing and research in the strategy and the business policy literatures (Ansoff, 1958; Chandler, 1962; Christensen, Andrews and Bower, 1965; Andrews, 1971). Chandler (1962) used the concept of strategy to describe the growth of the firm. He described growth in terms of pursing strategies of volume expansion, geographic expansion, vertical integration, and diversification. Ansoff (1965) suggested a growth matrix which described the growth of a firm in terms of the relationship between existing products and markets and new products and/or markets. Within the organisational development literature Child and Kieser (1982) discussed firms' growth in terms of a change and/or extension to the firm's domain. Product life-cycle literature, in general, argues that a product develops through a number of discrete stages and that each stage requires different competitive strategies (Rumelt, 1979; Porter, 1980).

A survey of the normative and empirical literature on strategy suggested several common themes which appear to be associated with high growth in companies. The most pervasive of these themes are:

- High growth companies are characterised by a *focus strategy*. This means that they concentrate on a limited number of market segments (Anderson and Harris, 1978; Porter, 1980; Kuhn, 1982; MacMillan, Hambrick and Day, 1982; Cavanagh and Clifford, 1983).
- High growth companies compete using *differentiated* strategies (Abannatt, 1967; Porter, 1980; Kuhn, 1982).
- The outcome of a focused differentiated competitive strategy should be a *dominant* market position (Kuhn, 1982; Anderson and Zeithmal, 1984; Buzzell and Gale, 1987). Interestingly, the literature suggests that the success of a growth strategy should be measured in terms of the achievement of a leading market share position in the target market.
- The source of the uniqueness which drives the firm's differentiation strategy is *innovation* (Abannatt, 1967; Scherer, 1980; Hambrick, MacMillan and Day, 1982; Cavanagh and Clifford, 1983; Buzzell and Gale, 1987).

- This innovation is manifested by an *emphasis on the company's products,* with successful high growth companies emphasising product quality, customer service, product brand name, and product value to customers (Kuhn, 1982).
- High growth companies are characterised by superior performance on a *number of competitive devices* such as product quality, premium prices and the introduction of new products (Hambrick, MacMillan and Day, 1982; Anderson and Zeithmal, 1984; Day, 1986; Buzzell and Gale, 1987).
- High growth companies have a propensity to invest in *future-orientated expenses,* such as marketing, the building of distribution channels, product R&D, product availability, and in capacity increases through new plant and equipment (Hambrick, MacMillan and Day, 1982; Anderson and Zeithmal, 1984; Buzzell and Wiersema, 1981).
- High growth companies grow by building on existing strengths and by emphasising *corporate relatedness* in products and businesses (Channon, 1973; Rumelt, 1974, 1979; Woodward, 1976).
- The choice of market position and competitive strategy is the result of *corporate flexibility* — an ability to change market position and/or competitive strategy when necessary (Abbannat, 1967; Katz, 1970; Cohn and Lindberg, 1972; Kuhn, 1982).

THE RESEARCH

These themes were translated into a list of strategic attributes which it was hypothesised would characterise high growth companies. The research therefore attempted to test the propositions that high growth companies:

(1) Focus on market segments.
(2) Compete on the basis of differentiation and on the basis of the uniqueness of their product and company.
(3) Are characterised by innovation (where innovation is a measure of the percentage of a company's sales that comes from new products).
(4) Are flexible (flexibility is a measure of a company's ability to change market focus and to introduce new products).
(5) Are characterised by superior competitive devices relative to their competitors (they have superior product quality, superior customer service, a higher percentage of new products, and can charge premium prices).

(6) Are product orientated (they emphasise product quality, customer service, and product branding).
(7) Spend more than competitors on future-orientated expenses (they spend on market development, product development, new plant and equipment and on capacity expansions).
(8) Grow by building on their existing strengths and grow in related areas of business.
(9) Dominate their market niche in terms of their market share ranking.

These nine propositions were tested on a sample of small and medium-sized indigenous industrial Irish companies. The size range of the companies studied was a turnover of between IR£6 million (US$10 million) and IR£1.2 billion (US$2 billion), though the sample was skewed towards the lower size restriction. Within this size range there were 317 indigenous companies in the manufacturing, distribution, wholesaling, retailing, farming cooperative and service sectors (with the exception of companies operating in financial services). A questionnaire was sent to these 317 companies and 131 valid responses were received, a response rate of 41 per cent. This response rate achieved the necessary representativeness of the population in terms of company size and growth rates (Table 10.1).

TABLE 10.1: SIZE RANGE OF POPULATION AND OF RESPONDENTS

1989 Sales (IR£m)	No. of Companies in Population	No. of Responses in Sample	Percentage of All Responses
>50 to 1,371	79	31	24%
>21 to 50	80	23	18%
>10.5 to 21	79	39	30%
>6 to 10.5	81	37	28%
	319	130	100%

The respondent companies were divided into four growth quartiles on the basis of growth rate of the core business for the 1984–89 period (Table 10.2). The high growth quartile of sample companies was compared to the low growth quartile.

TABLE 10.2: SAMPLE DIVIDED INTO QUARTILES BASED ON GROWTH RATE

	Core Business Growth Rate	No. of Companies
Bottom Quartile	-50% to 22%	32
Lower Middle Quartile	24% to 49%	31
Upper Middle Quartile	50% to 100%	32
Top Quartile	112% to 2,000%	32

FINDINGS

High growth companies focus on market segments.

The mean size of served market for high growth companies was IR£226 million. This compares to a mean for low growth companies of £486 million and a sample mean of £357 million. The smaller size of the market competed in is interpreted as an indication of a market focus strategy. A surprising result was that Irish growth companies were more likely to have a wider product range. This result was unexpected because it was thought that as part of their focus strategy high growth companies would be characterised by a narrow product range (as suggested by Hambrick, MacMillan and Day, 1982). A possible explanation for this is that the small size of the Irish market requires Irish companies to cover all product options in their niche.

High growth companies compete on the basis of differentiation and on the basis of the uniqueness of their product and company.

High growth companies were more likely to have products that were differentiated from their competitors'. Forty-five per cent of the high growth companies had products that were "somewhat different", "substantially different" and "radically different", compared to 16 per cent for low growth companies. Customer differentiation was measured by having the respondents compare the "kind of customers" to whom they sold with those of their competitors. High growth companies were not different from low growth companies on this measure.

The results did, however, suggest that high growth companies differ in terms of their personnel policies. Sixty-seven per cent of high growth companies claimed "radically different", "very different" and "somewhat different" policies compared with their competitors, while 33 per cent of low growth companies did so. The other functional areas — marketing, production, finance, R&D, and distribution – did not differentiate between the two groups.

High growth companies are characterised by innovation.
Innovation was measured as the percentage of a company's sales that came from new products. Relative to their competitors and compared to low growth companies, high growth companies had a higher percentage of new products. The mean percentage of sales coming from new products in high growth companies was 38 per cent compared with 15 per cent for low growth companies and a total sample mean of 23 per cent. Relative to low growth companies rapid growers had a core product that was, on average, much younger — by a factor of 25 years! Seventy per cent of high growth companies responded that they had a "much higher" or "higher" percentage of sales from products introduced within the previous five years compared with their competitors, while 36 per cent of low growth companies said the same.

High growth companies are flexible.
Flexibility was measured as the firms' ability to change market focus and to introduce new products. As already noted, the high growth companies were characterised by a higher percentage of sales coming from new products as compared to low growth companies. As a measure of the firms' ability to change focus, their "growth direction" was considered. For both the high growth and the low growth group over 50 per cent of the respondents choose either "expansion in the domestic market" or "retrenchment in the domestic market" as their primary growth direction, for the period 1984–89 (59 per cent for the low growth group and 53 per cent for the high growth group). However, further analysis indicates that in the low growth group, 50 per cent were not involved in any change of focus, compared to 19 per cent for the high growth group.

High growth companies are characterised by superior competitive devices relative to competitors in terms of having superior product quality, superior customer service, a higher percentage of new products, and premium prices.
Product quality, customer service and the percentage sales attributable to new products each discriminated between the high

growth and low growth groups. Relative to competitors, high growth companies were more likely to sell higher or much higher quality products than the low growth companies. Competitively, high growth companies were also more likely to have a higher customer service reputation, (91 per cent "much higher" and "higher" compared to 54 per cent for low growth companies). As already noted, new product activity differentiated between the high growth and low growth groups. Selling prices did not discriminate between the high growth and low growth groups.

High growth companies are product orientated — in terms of emphasising product quality, customer service, and product branding.

As already noted, product quality and customer service discriminated between the two groups. Brand-name profile was not a statistically significant difference. Overall, however, the proposition of product emphasis seems supported.

High growth companies spend more than competitors on future-orientated expenses in terms of market development, product development, new plant and equipment, and capacity expansions.

Of these four expense areas, two discriminated between the high growth and low growth group. Relative to competitors, high growth companies had a much higher percentage growth in capacity over the previous five years — 88 per cent of high growth companies were "much higher" and "higher", compared with 28 per cent for low growth companies. Relative to competitors, high growth companies had newer plant and equipment. The measure used to test for product development was the ratio of R&D expenditure to sales. This did not successfully discriminate between the two groups, though the outcome of R&D expenditures — new products — did discriminate between the two groups. Market development expenditure was measured by the advertising and promotion to sales ratio, the stocks to sales ratio, and the number and penetration of distribution channels used. None of these factors discriminated between the two groups. The evidence is that high growth companies spend more on capacity expansions and new plant and equipment, but that their spending on market and product development is no different.

High growth companies grow by building on their existing strengths and grow in related areas of business.

Each company was asked about its growth path between 1984 and 1989. High growth companies grew by "expansion in the domestic market", by "related new product diversification", and by "expansion in overseas markets". Low growth companies described their growth direction as "retrenchment" and "related new product diversification".

High growth companies do not necessarily dominate their market niche in terms of market share ranking.

It is of interest that market share ranking did not distinguish high growth from low growth companies.

In addition to these findings about factors the study set out to explore, it became clear from the analysis that *high growth companies compete in markets with higher growth rates*. The mean growth rate of high growth companies' served markets was approximately three times that of low growth companies (Table 10.3).

TABLE 10.3: MEAN PERCENTAGE SERVED MARKET GROWTH RATE

Year	High Growth Companies	Low Growth Companies	All Companies
1987–88	9.8	3.4	5.1
1988–89	11.5	3.2	6.8
1989–90	11.5	2.3	8.1

Another surprising fact was that relative to their competitors *high growth companies were more likely than low growth companies to have a higher percentage return on sales*. Seventy per cent of high growth companies believed they had "much higher" and "higher" return on sales than competitors, compared to 38 per cent for low growth companies. Moreover, mean return was at least 80 per cent higher for high growth companies (Table 10.4). There is some limited evidence in the data that profits and growth are correlated — something which is a little unexpected since it is normally anticipated that growth strategies are costly and dilute profitability during growth.

TABLE 10.4: CORE BUSINESS PROFITS AS A PERCENTAGE OF SALES*

Year	High Growth Mean	High Growth Std.D	Low Growth Mean	Low Growth Std.D	Total Sample Mean	Total Sample Std.D
1989	10.7	8.1	5.9	4.9	7.7	6.9
1988	9.7	7.7	5.3	4.3	6.8	6.6
1987	9.2	7.0	4.0	2.8	6.1	6.4
1986	8.2	6.0	4.2	3.3	5.8	5.3
1985	8.3	5.9	4.6	3.6	5.6	6.6

Note: One company indicated a loss which is not included in the above.

IS GROWTH DRIVEN BY THE MARKET OR BY MANAGEMENT?

To test whether the choice of market was a key determinant of growth, the companies were classified into market sectors using the classification scheme used by the Irish Central Statistics Office. This initial analysis suggested that the choice of broad industrial sector was not a determinant of growth rate. However, when the industrial subsectors in which the companies competed were examined, high and low growth companies were found in different competitive arenas. The sample of respondent companies was split into two on the basis of percentage growth in core business sales for the 1984–89 period. The companies in each half of the population were then classified into two-digit industrial subsectors. It then became apparent that the companies from the high growth half of the sample were in different subsectors from those of the low growth half of the sample.

DISCUSSION

Overall, many of the various strategies associated in the literature with growth were confirmed for the case of small and medium-sized Irish businesses. Some divergences and unexpected features of growth in this population were also observed. The literature had suggested that market-dominance might be a characteristic of high growth companies. Market share ranking and growth are both outcomes which the literature normatively prescribes as organisational goals. Further analysis of the data suggested that one set of strategic attributes characterises companies when they are pursuing a growth strategy — that is, when they are "getting growth" — and another set of attributes characterises companies when they have successfully achieved penetration of their market — that is, when they "have growth". The survey companies included companies at both of these stages. Companies which have achieved a dominant position in their market may still achieve high growth if the market continues to grow at a high rate. Alternatively, they may stop growing and not choose any new market arenas in which to recommence growth.

The cases highlighted the importance of the choice of market in determining the growth rate of a company — the choice of a high growth market resulting in a high growth rate and the choice of a low growth market resulting in a low growth rate. In addition, the competitive strategy which the company develops to penetrate its chosen market affected the success of the company and its ability to achieve a dominant position in its market. It appeared that neither explanation was sufficient and that it is necessary to combine both if growth is to be explained completely.

It is therefore suggested that the first key managerial choice is "where to compete" but that this is followed by key choices about "how to compete". It appears to be the combination of these that results in growth, in market dominance and in sustained growth. Some important implications flow from this:

(1) Market choice is a critical managerial decision, though as the literature on strategic change would suggest, it is not a choice that is, or can be, subject to frequent change (Miller and Friesen, 1980; Mintzberg and Waters, 1982). Furthermore, market selection will always be constrained by previous choices made by the organisation.
(2) The choice of market determines the likelihood of further growth: if the "wrong" market is chosen, then growth will be limited or unachievable.
(3) The choice of a growing market is not a sufficient condition for successful growth. Other decisions will influence whether an organisation achieves a dominant position in its market and whether it continues to grow after the market growth rate has slowed. The survey suggests that the choice of a growing market is a necessary but insufficient condition for growth.

REFERENCES

Abbannat, R.F. (1967): "Strategies For Size", PhD dissertation, Harvard University.

Ackoff, R.L. (1974): *Redesigning the Future*, New York: Wiley-Interscience.

Anderson, C.R., and Zeithmal, C.P. (1984), "Stage of the Product Life Cycle, Business Strategy, and Business Performance", *Academy of Management Journal*, 27: 5–24.

Andrews, K.R. (1971): *The Concept of Corporate Strategy*, Homewood, Illinois: Dow-Jones-Irwin.

Ansoff, H.I. (1958): "A Model for Diversification", *Management Science*, 4.

Ansoff, H.I. (1965): *Corporate Strategy*, New York: McGraw-Hill.

Buzzell, R.D. and Gale, B.T. (1987): *The PIMS Principles*, New York: The Free Press.

Buzzell, R.D. and Wiersema, F.D. (1981): "Successful Share-building Strategies", *Harvard Business Review*, 53(1): 35–44.

Cavanagh, R.E. and Clifford, D.K. (1983): "Lessons from America's Mid-sized Growth Companies", *The McKinsey Quarterly*, Autumn 3: 2–23.

Chandler, A.D. (1962): *Strategy and Structure*, Cambridge, Mass.: The M.I.T. Press.

Channon, D. (1973): *The Strategy and Structure of British Enterprise*, London: Macmillan.

Child, J. and Kieser, A. (1981): "Development of Organisations Over Time", in P.C. Nystrom and W.H. Starbuck, *Handbook of Organisational Design*, Oxford: Oxford University Press.

Christensen, C. Roland, K.R., Andrews and Bower, J.L. (1965): *Business Policy, Text and Cases*, Homewood, Illinois: R.D. Irwin.

Cohn, T. and R. Lindberg (1972): *How Management is Different in Small Companies*, New York: Harper & Row.

Day, G. (1986): *Analysis for Strategic Market Decisions*, St Paul: West Publication Company.

Hambrick, D.C., MacMillan I.C. and Day, D.I. (1982): "Strategic Attributes and Performance in the BCG Matrix — a PIMS-based Analysis of Industrial-Product Business", *Academy of Management Journal*, 25(3): 510–31.

Hammermesh, R.G., Anderson, M.J., and Harris, J.E. (1978): "Strategies for Low Market Share Businesses", *Harvard Business Review*, 56(3): 95–102.

Katz, R.L. (1970): *Cases and Concepts in Corporate Strategy*, Englewood Cliffs, N.J.: Prentice-Hall.
Kuhn, R. L. (1982): *Mid-Sized Firms: Success Strategies and Methodology*, New York: Prager Press.
Miller, D. and Freisen, P.H. (1980): "Momentum and Revolution in Organisational Adaptation", *Academy of Management Journal*, 23(4): 591–614.
Mintzberg, H. and Waters, J.A. (1982): "Tracking Strategy in an Entrepreneurial Firm", *Academy of Management Journal*, 25(3): 465–99.
Murray, J. (1984): "A Concept of Entrepreneurial Strategy", *Strategic Management Journal*, 5(1): 1–13.
Porter, M.E. (1980): *Competitive Strategy*, New York: The Free Press.
Rumelt, R. (1974): *Strategy, Structure and Economic Performance in Large American Industrial Corporations*, Boston: Harvard University Press.
Rumelt, R. (1979): "Evaluation of Strategy Theory and Models", in D.E. Schendel, and C.W. Cooper (eds), *Strategic Management: A New View of Business Policy and Planning*, Boston: Little Brown.
Scherer, F.M. (1980): *Industrial Market Structure and Economic Performance*, Chicago: Rand McNally.
Sommerhoff, G. (1969): "The Abstract Characteristics of Living Systems", in F.E. Emery (ed.), *Systems Thinking*, Middlesex: Penguin.
Woodward, H. (1976): "Managerial Strategies for Small Companies", *Harvard Business Review*, 54(1): 113–21.

11

Marketing Planning in Small Enterprises: A Model and Some Empirical Evidence[*]

*David Carson and
Stanley Cromie*

INTRODUCTION

Much of the literature on small firms, particularly that which examines marketing in small organisations, indicates implicitly and explicitly that small firms are different from large companies. In an effort to add to the growing volume of knowledge on the marketing activities of smaller ventures, this paper will note the characteristics of small firms and then review the marketing planning literature in an attempt to establish appropriate techniques for assessing the marketing planning activity of smaller businesses. A model for marketing planning in small ventures will be used to report on how 68 small, young firms actually do their marketing planning.

THE CHARACTERISTICS OF SMALL FIRMS

The term "small firm" is used frequently in business literature and practice, but before we examine its characteristics it is important to say what we mean by this term. Definitions of small firms range from numbers of employees and size of revenue, to type of business and size of premises. A comprehensive general definition is offered by the Committee for Economic Development (1978).

---

[*] This paper was first published in *Journal of Consumer Marketing*, Vol 7, No. 3 Summer 1990, pp. 5-189.

A small firm is one which possesses at least two of the following four characteristics:

(1) Management of the firm is independent. Usually the managers are also the owners.
(2) Capital is supplied and the ownership is held by an individual or a small group.
(3) The area of operations is mainly local, with the workers and owners living in one home community. However, the market need not be local.
(4) The relative size of the firm within its industry must be small when compared with the biggest units in the field. This measure can be in terms of sales volume, number of employees or other significant comparisons.

However, of all the variables used in defining small enterprises, relative size is used most frequently: indeed it is often the only variable used. For example, any firm can be considered small when its sales volume, total employees, capital investment, and so forth are much smaller than the corresponding figures for the largest firm in its field (Steinhof, 1978). But just how important is this issue of relative size? Is it, in fact, the small business characteristic that has the most significance for the practice of marketing in these organisations?

It is widely accepted that small enterprises have characteristics different from those of larger companies, but the most significant differences relate to the business objectives, management style, and marketing practice of these enterprises rather than their relative size (Leppard and McDonald, 1987). In support of this contention, several qualitative characteristics which differentiate small from large concerns have been emphasised: the scope and the scale of operations, the independence and the nature of their ownership arrangements, and their management style (Scholhammer and Kuriloff, 1979).

Several authors emphasise the importance of management style in contributing to the success of small organisations. For example, there have been comments on the "limited formal business education" of owner managers (Tate et al., 1975) and suggestions that small business problems and failures occur because of a "lack of managerial skill and depth, and personal lack and misuse of time" (Broom et al., 1983).

It is apparent, therefore, that small firms have distinctive quantitative and qualitative characteristics which differentiate them from large ones, but a question arises as to the impact of these characteristics upon their marketing attributes.

MARKETING CHARACTERISTICS OF SMALL FIRMS

Several authors have identified a number of areas in which small business owners and managers differ from professional marketing managers in large companies. They note that the former tend to have negative attitudes towards marketing, perceive marketing as a cost, treat distribution and selling as uncontrollable problems, and, most significant, believe that each case is so specific that it cannot be approached using general rules (Carson, 1985; Cohn and Lindbore, 1972).

In addition, there have been observations of a general weakness in marketing by small firms and suggestions that this may arise because the firms have difficulty in attracting and affording qualified personnel (Broom et al., 1983). In a similar vein, owners of small firms need to be, or become, their own "expert" in many areas because, unlike the manager in a large company, they are not usually in a position to employ experts (Gaedeke and Tootelian, 1980). In view of this need to be a "general specialist", it has been noted that essential differences in managing small and large firms arise because in the former the focus is on the pragmatic use of techniques as aids to problem solving, whereas in the latter it is on achieving "high co-ordination and control of specialists" (Scholhammer and Kuriloff, 1979).

We have argued that the characteristics of small firms are many and varied and that they tend to be different from large company attributes. When viewed from a marketing perspective, many small firms' features and characteristics can be described as constraints. For example, there are three broad constraints on small firms' marketing activity (Carson, 1985):

(1) *Limited resources,* such as limitations on finance, marketing knowledge, and time, may contribute to limited marketing activity relative to large competitors.

(2) *Specialist expertise* may be a constraint because managers in small businesses tend to be generalists. Traditionally, the owner/manager is a technical or craft expert who is unlikely to be trained in any major business disciplines. In addition, marketing expertise is often the last of the business disciplines to be acquired by an expanding small company. That is, finance and production (if the company is a manufacturing

unit) experts usually precede the acquisition of a marketing counterpart.

(3) *Limited impact* on the marketplace may be a constraint because small businesses have fewer orders, customers, and employees than large companies. Consequently, the impact of a small firm's presence in an industry or geographic area is likely to be limited because of its size alone. Similarly, because of limited resources and lack of marketing expertise, the impact on the media through advertising and publicity will often be negligible in relation to large company activities.

What then are the issues that arise out of this discussion? It is obvious that the distinctiveness of small firms is compounded when marketing in them is taken into consideration. That is, small firms' marketing is shaped by the peculiarities of small firms and may well be constrained by them.

MARKETING PLANNING ADAPTED FOR SMALL FIRMS

What impact do the issues raised above have on the ability of small firms to plan their marketing activity? Can and do they use standard marketing planning approaches when organising their marketing activity? The debate to date would suggest that they may require an approach that is unique to their own requirements and capabilities.

THE MARKETING PLANNING PROCESS

The purpose and value of planning in marketing are well documented in the literature. For example, "effective marketing planning lies at the heart of a company's revenue-earning activities" (McDonald, 1984). In general, marketing planning is extremely valuable in clarifying management thinking and giving a sense of direction to managers in other functions, both subordinates and superiors. Marketing planning often allows the marketing profile to permeate a firm's activities and instils a marketing perspective into activities such as setting objectives, motivating, and directing staff, establishing priorities, and improving the quality of market information. All this can lead to a greater awareness and acceptance of change and may promote general business success.

Let us elaborate on the nature of marketing planning. It is described as a process that "explores what marketing actually does — the actual process by which marketing operates" (Mandell and

Rosenberg, 1981). But how precisely is marketing planning described and explained? The literature is awash with descriptions and explanations as to what is involved. For example, most texts in marketing management include at least one chapter on marketing planning processes, but they are often variations on a theme.

The principal stages in the process involve conducting an internal audit, conducting an external audit, devising a strategy, and implementing and controlling the marketing activities. This definition suggests that planning is a formal process, although the possibility of conducting informal marketing planning should not be overlooked, especially in small organisations.

Where in an organisation does planning occur and in what ways is it integrated with other activities? In other words, how does marketing management apply it? "The problem is not that the philosophy of marketing is not believed, rather it is that most companies just cannot make it work" (McDonald, 1984). Planning is often regarded by middle managers as a sophisticated, elitist activity carried out solely by specialists or very senior management. But where does or should planning actually occur in an organisation and how does it integrate across an organisation's managerial structure?

The nature of planning can vary according to the complexity of an organisation. Strategic planning in a simple organisation is an "evolutionary" process, through which major decisions are reached on objectives, policies, and strategy. "These determinations, made definitely and in writing, might be adequate for [such] a fledgling firm as the basis for detailed plans. This may suffice for a small and homogeneous type of business. That is, it has only its corporate level of planning" (Lorange and Vancil, 1977).

However, other writers (Assael, 1985; Guiltinan and Paul, 1985; Kotler, 1984; Lorange and Vancil, 1977) suggest that planning must occur throughout an organisation's decision-making structure. This logic can sensibly be applied to marketing planning. That is, all aspects of marketing activity must be co-ordinated and integrated through careful planning. Indeed, an understanding of this issue is fundamental to sound marketing planning activity. As Kotler (1984) states, "In order to plan effectively, marketing managers must understand the key relationship between types of marketing mix expenditures and their sales and profit consequences".

It is clear, therefore, that marketing planning must permeate the whole of the marketing function in any organisation if it is to operate effectively, and the concept of the marketing planning process is fundamental to such effectiveness.

The importance of marketing planning is a point that is well made in most of the literature. However, as was intimated earlier, there are few descriptions of marketing planning that correspond with each other. It is possible, of course, to identify the common threads in the process. But why the variations? Cynics might suggest that marketing authors offer their own "unique" description of a well-established process merely to enhance their self-esteem. More kindly it could be argued that variations are simply a case of semantics and that different authors express the same ideas using slightly different terminology. It is an interesting exercise to explore some of the descriptions of the marketing planning process given by the authors cited above.

One author (Greenley, 1986), aware of this plethora of definitions, has attempted to produce a composite model of the marketing planning process. His model incorporates both strategic and functional marketing planning. He justifies this structure by stating that "in practice companies tend to include both marketing strategy and tactics within the same marketing plan document".

FIGURE 11.1: THE STAGES OF MARKETING OPERATIONAL PLANNING

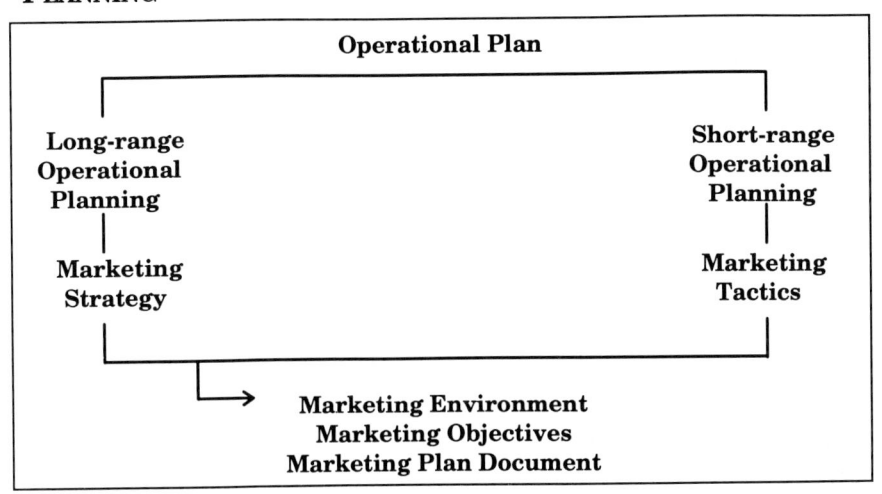

```
                        Operational Plan

    Long-range                              Short-range
    Operational                             Operational
    Planning                                Planning

    Marketing                               Marketing
    Strategy                                Tactics

                → Marketing Environment
                  Marketing Objectives
                  Marketing Plan Document
```

Source: Gordon E. Greenley (1986), *The Strategic and Operational Planning of Marketing*, New York: McGraw-Hill.

The Greenley model "has been synthesised from major texts by writers such as Cravens, Jain, Kotler, Luck and Ferrell, and McDonald" (1986). Greenley also puts this model into the context of a broader "planning framework" which shows the relationship between the strategic and operational planning processes (Figure 11.1 above).

A DIFFERENT PERSPECTIVE REQUIRED

The fundamental concept of marketing planning is well documented, but there can be, and is, a plethora of approaches to describe its scope and function.

There is little doubt that there are many ways of implementing the marketing planning process and we have seen that the idiosyncrasies of small firms can have a significant influence upon its implementation, but there are many other factors that may equally influence marketing planning practice in small firms. Two are of particular significance in this debate: the "evolution" of marketing practice, and the dominating influence of the owner/manager's beliefs and values upon marketing activity. Let us consider briefly these two issues.

The foundation for the marketing "evolution" of a small firm lies in the widely documented concept of the business life cycle. Some writers put much store on the significance of this life cycle to small business success. For example, the business life cycle acts as a guide to small firms as they work through different stages of business life (Justis, 1981). More specifically, attention is drawn to the need for an awareness of the changing role of top management as the organisation grows (Scholhammer and Kuriloff, 1979). Essentially they see the role changing from one of task-oriented activities and line responsibility to one of co-ordination, strategic planning, and public relations.

This life cycle and the resulting shift in managerial orientation, as it relates to marketing in growing ventures, can be anticipated: ... a company passes through a four-stage marketing development process. In the initial stage, entrepreneurs sell customised products to friends and contacts. They must then exploit a larger marketplace through the stages of opportunities marketing, responsive marketing and finally diversified marketing (Tyebsee et al., 1983).

Others also believe that firms progress through four stages starting with a reactive phase and moving towards a proactive one. More precisely, firms engage in initial marketing activity, then progress to reactive selling, then go to the DIY marketing approach, and finally move towards integrated proactive marketing. As firms evolve, "a different perspective is required". They argue that the development and role of marketing planning can be attributed to the influence of the "culture carrier" within an organisation (Leppard and McDonald, 1987).

Let us say a little more about cultural carriers. If we regard organisational culture as a set of inherited ideas, values, and norms which are more or less shared by the members of the enterprise and which influence member behaviour, then the cultural carrier is the person who plays a dominant part in the process of acquiring culture. It is noted that in small firms owner/managers, because of their visibility, power, and influence, will play a dominant role in moulding organisational culture. The proprietor's influence will extend to the acceptance of marketing planning, as identified by four levels of acceptance: owners may deliberately ignore it, treat it unthinkingly and merely pay lip service to it, treat it moderately seriously, or treat it very seriously. In support of this proposition these authors state:

> The acceptance of marketing planning is largely conditioned by the stage of development of the organisation and the behaviour of the corporate culture carriers. Thus it is that different modes of marketing planning become more appropriate at different phases of the company's life.
>
> While the marketing planning process itself remains more or less consistent throughout, how that process is managed must be congruent with the current organisational culture. (Leppard and McDonald, 1987)

Because of the predominating influence of the proprietor, it is possible that an organisation and its owner/manager will progress through the levels of acceptance of marketing planning depicted without acquiring additional cultural carriers. An execution may occur, however, in the final level of development when a measure of technical expertise may be required to devise and implement complex marketing planning.

What then is the outcome of our discussion? Taking account of all the issues addressed so far, it would appear that marketing planning must "fit" the circumstances of the organisation. It may not be enough to take elaborate models of marketing planning and attempt to apply them to different companies at different levels of marketing development and evolution. In fact, marketing approaches:

... concentrate almost exclusively on the "medicine" itself and show relatively little concern for the "patient". That this should happen makes about as much sense as a doctor dispensing the same drug to every patient he sees, irrespective of his or her condition. (Leppard and McDonald, 1987)

We acknowledge the need for "fitting" the marketing approach to suit the circumstances and characteristics of small firms. We accept also that the management style and culture of a small firm will influence the character and nature of marketing planning activity. Consequently, we consider that a "simplistic" approach to the marketing planning process may be suitable for small firms.

MARKETING PLANNING BY SMALL FIRMS: SOME EMPIRICAL EVIDENCE

To discover the validity of our literature review and subsequent conclusions, we investigated the process by which small young firms actually do their marketing planning. The 68 firms in our study are approximately four years old, are small — mean employment is 4.8 persons — and have a median turnover of £600,000. Seventeen firms provide industrial services, 16 supply consumer services, and 35 are engaged in manufacturing. Most firms are located in the Greater Belfast area and some in rural locations in Ireland.

Given this profile, it is most likely that this sample is in the initial stage of marketing development as outlined above. Their marketing planning is most likely the product of reacting to situations, paying lip service to good marketing practice, and certainly being simplistic in terms of the models reviewed above. In this approach the marketing planning concepts may well be inherently sound but they are sufficiently broad and elementary to be both workable and attractive to the small business owner/manager.

Firms at an early stage of evolution may merely consider the most basic approach to the marketing planning process. This incorporates two fundamental components: external considerations — those issues that are outside the firm's influence or control — and internal considerations — those issues that are within the organisation's control. A small firm may examine external and internal matters either in a very elementary way or with varying degrees of complexity and sophistication. The factors determining the actual approach are manifold and the depth of the marketing process may well depend upon the firm's resources, background expertise of the entrepreneur, commitment to success, and marketing effectiveness. We used the simple model shown in Figure 11.2 as the basis for our investigation.

FIGURE 11.2: A FRAMEWORK FOR THE MARKETING PLANNING PROCESS IN SMALL FIRMS

Marketing Issue	Marketing Approach		
	Non-marketing	Implicit Marketing	Sophisticated Marketing
External considerations e.g., market knowledge, customers			
Internal Considerations e.g., promotion, price			

We decided to restrict our investigation to the following external points of interest: market knowledge, competitors, customers, market information, significant happenings in the market, and competitive advantage. The internal considerations of interest are promotion, price and service.

Other crucial elements of the marketing mix, such as product and distribution, are considered to be implicitly contained within the framework. Small firms will automatically take account of the product when considering issues such as competitive advantage, price, and promotion, and similarly distribution will be an inherent part of service, product, and promotion.

To the purist, our approach may suggest poor marketing. But purists may well view the topic entirely from the logical framework of the stages of the marketing planning process, and disregard the characteristics of the small business owner/manager, the company, and market circumstances. "Bad marketing" as defined by a marketing analyst may represent marketing which stretches a proprietor to the limits of their capabilities at that point in time. It may also be part of the process of "learning" through which the manager must pass before being able to develop further.

In Figure 11.2 we can see that under each of the marketing issues, we envisaged respondents taking a non-marketing approach, an implicit marketing approach, or a sophisticated marketing approach. In order to generate some data on these issues, we asked respondents the following questions during tape recorded personal interviews:

(1) Could you tell me something about the market(s) for your product(s)/service(s)?
(2) Tell me something about your competitors.
(3) Why do your customers buy from you rather than from your competitors? What advantage do you offer them that competition cannot meet?
(4) Could you tell me something about your customers? How many do you have? Who are your key customers?
(5) Where do you gather information that lets you know what is happening in your markets? How do you keep in touch with changes in your markets?
(6) What do you consider to be the most important event in your market over the past few years?
(7) What methods do you use to promote your products or services?
(8) Tell me about your communication with customers after you have supplied them with goods or services.
(9) Could you tell me how you go about setting the price(s) for your goods and services? What are the principles underlying your pricing?

The interviewers adopted a non-directive approach with very limited prompts in an attempt to discover how the sample really "did their marketing". If respondents had very little to say on an issue, they were encouraged to be more forthcoming but no attempt was made to lead them into making statements. The interview data were analysed in two ways. In the first instance, all 68 responses to each of the questions were played back on a tape recorder and each classified as a non-marketing, implicit marketing, or sophisticated marketing response. Then, on the basis of the responses to all nine questions, each person was categorised into one of the three groups. This qualitative analysis was shared among three researchers who had frequent discussions to ensure that the assortment process was not unduly biased.

To make the model operational, let us present a portrait of a non-marketing and an implicit-marketing firm. The former defines its markets in very general terms such as middle class people, reacts to customer inquiries, has little or no idea who customers are or where they come from, uses few or no sources of market information, and feels that no significant event occurred in the market over the four years of its experience. It describes competitive advantage in terms of the benefits its service/product bestows on customers without relating this to the competition; it uses few methods of promoting its enterprises, uses cost-plus pricing strategies, and responds to complaints rather than thinks positively about customer service.

A firm with implicit marketing is seen as one which describes its markets in terms of market segments, size, or location; which mentions the number of customers it has and is able to distinguish between key customers and normal customers; has several complementary sources of information about markets and understands the key events that occurred in its market together with their impact on the firm; and can describe its competitive advantage in terms of the benefits accruing to customers, although it does not detail exactly how it defeats the competition. An implicit marketing firm uses several proactive promotion methods; it sets its price on the basis of what the market will bear and what the competition charge, and it proactively contacts customers to make sure that its product/service is meeting customer needs.

We will not present a portrait of sophisticated marketers since few of our sample can be defined in this way. However, some firms practise sophisticated marketing in some of the nine marketing planning sections of the model and we will draw attention to them as we report the results.

SUMMARY OF RESULTS

Our primary purpose here is to discuss the marketing planning process as it operates in small enterprises and to verify the validity of our arguments using the results of an empirical study. To avoid unnecessary detail we will merely present a summary of our research and ask those readers who require a detailed knowledge of the empirical data to consult an additional source.[1]

Table 11.1 presents a summary of our findings. Note that very few of the sample are classified as sophisticated marketers and that, on the majority of issues, there are more non-marketers than implicit ones. Rather than giving a description of the findings for each of the nine component parts in the model, we will present a composite overview of the way in which non-marketing, implicit marketing, and sophisticated marketing companies performed in relation to external and internal factors.

---

[1] See Cromie, Carson and Ayling, 1987.

TABLE 11.1: THE CLASSIFICATION OF THE SAMPLE INTO MARKETING PLANNING CATEGORIES ON EACH COMPONENT OF THE MARKETING PLANNING MODEL

Factor	Non f	Non %	Implicit f	Implicit %	Sophisticated f	Sophisticated %
External						
Market Knowledge	31	46	33	48	4	6
Competitor	39	57	29	43	0	0
Customers	35	51	30	44	3	5
Market Information	30	44	36	53	2	3
Significant Event	45	66	23	34	0	0
Competitive Advantage	45	66	23	34	0	0
Internal						
Promotions	42	62	26	38	0	0
Price	40	59	28	41	0	0
Service	44	65	24	35	0	0

External Factors — Non-marketing Firms. These firms typically have little knowledge of their markets, will react to demand from anywhere, and have only a vague impression of their customer profile. They feel they have few, weak, or no competitors and that their products are unique, when in fact they may not be. Generally these companies do not view their products in the context of competitive advantage; any competition they are aware of they feel is only in their immediate locality. Similarly, these non-marketing firms do not know much about their customers; indeed several talk of having a huge number of customers and are essentially order-takers. Others merely react to consumer demands (their customers come to them).

The paucity of the sources of information and the haphazard manner in which market data are gathered suggest that many firms devote little serious attention to the issue. Equally, many are unable to record what is happening in their markets or describe important episodes as something initiated by themselves. Many were unaware of key events, even though independent observers felt that their markets were experiencing significant change.

Internal Factors — Non-marketing Firms. These non-marketing firms tend to use few or none of the normal techniques and are rather dubious about the benefits of promotion. Indeed many question the cost effectiveness of the activity. On pricing, non-marketers use predominantly cost-plus pricing and do not alter their charges when dealing with patrons. Indeed, some of the sample stated openly that it is immoral to charge too much. As for after-sales services, these firms display a product orientation and believe that after-sales service is unnecessary or unimportant.

External Factors — Implicit Marketing Firms. In contrast to non-marketers, implicit marketers know their markets in ways such as geographical boundaries and areas for future expansion. While market segmentation is not fully developed, many of this group are able to target sectors such as "small specialist knitwear and Irish shops in the United States" in the pursuit of sales.

These firms also know the competition in terms of the number of competitors they face and where they are located, and they have some detail on how the competition threatens their business. For example, a clothing manufacturer said that she "has five competitors in the Belfast and Bangor areas and three of them are larger than ourselves". This woman is aware of the competition and has some views on her competitors' strengths and the threats they pose.

Knowledge of the market is also defined more precisely. These firms rely on several sources of information ranging from trade and media publications to competitors and customers, and they use this information in an informal but balanced manner. Information about customers is implicitly combined with identifying the needs of customers. Typically, these firms will discuss important issues with competitors; for example, some owners invite customers to say how products/services might be modified to meet their needs more fully. Many of these firms use the information gathered to establish a competitive edge.

Internal Factors — Implicit Marketing Firms. The significant feature of the implicit marketers is that they attempt to use the internal factors for marketing their products/services and often "mix" them skilfully. For example, for promotion they may combine advertising and direct mail as a means of generating customers. They use pricing according to what the market will bear, taking account of competitive prices and individual customer perceptions of value. They also stay in fairly close contact with clients and encourage repeat business through after-sales service.

Sophisticated Marketers. As Table 11.1 shows, there were very few of the sample that could be described as sophisticated marketers, and indeed none used internal factors in a positively proactive and meaningful way. A few firms did, however, show a sophistication in relation to information and knowledge about both customers and their markets.

SUMMARY AND GENERAL CONCLUSIONS

If we take account of the inherent characteristics of small firms, the empirical data generated by this study, and the subsequent interpretation and evaluation, some general conclusions about marketing in new small firms can be made. Small firms have a "distinctive marketing style". There is little or no adherence to formal structures and frameworks. Because of their limited resources, the marketing activity of small firms is inevitably restricted in its scope and activity. This restriction manifests itself in marketing which is simplistic, haphazard, often responsive and reactive to competitor activity.

Small firms, particularly those in the early stages of development, are inherently product oriented, so it is not surprising that much of their marketing is also product oriented. Similarly, their marketing is oriented around price, possibly because they have an inherent feeling of vulnerability on price, particularly in relation to large competitors. Perhaps the most significant factor contributing to small firms' marketing style is the omnipresence of the owner/manager. The business proprietor is naturally involved in all aspects of the business, and this is no less so in marketing. Consequently, the marketing style can be described as an "involved" one which relies heavily on intuitive ideas and decisions and, probably most importantly, on common sense.

Marketing theorists should be careful not to criticise small firms' marketing for not being properly structured and not adhering to classic marketing approaches. Just as a company must conform to the needs of the marketplace if it is to be successful, so should marketing conform to the capabilities of the practitioner if it is to be effective. Such is possibly the case in our sample. The owners are doing marketing, but marketing according to their own terms and requirements and not some theoretical framework. Whether such marketing can lead to a rapid growth of income is more problematic, but it is "their style" and it may well suffice until the proprietors decide that they want to expand and perhaps move from the entrepreneurial stage of development of their businesses to a managerial phase.

If small firms' marketing activity is to be assisted and improved, what can trainers and advisors do to help? First, recognise that small firms do have a distinctive marketing style as outlined above. Acceptance of the features of this distinctive style will ensure that unrealistic marketing advice and guidance will be avoided. Drawing analogies with physical activities such as learning to swim or run long distances serves to illustrate the point. For example, in the beginning it is enough to float rather than swim correctly and effectively and to jog rather than maintain a sustained running pace. In marketing it may be enough to do what is in the bounds of reasonableness and capability, because to do any "better" may be beyond such bounds.

A second significant issue in advising and guiding small firms is to recognise that any improvement in marketing performance can happen only over time and as a result of experience. Timescales will of course vary according to the individual, the firm and its products, and market conditions, but certainly "new and better" marketing is unlikely to be adopted before learning has been gained through the firm's natural growth period. Equally, until an owner/manager has experienced the impact of marketing, no matter how simplistic, that owner/manager is unlikely to accept ultra-sophisticated and "correct" marketing.

In short, if small firms are to be assisted effectively in improving their marketing, it is incumbent upon advisors to adapt the marketing approach to suit the level of simplicity required by small organisations, and to recognise that improvement cannot occur overnight. It needs an investment in time and careful monitoring. Small ventures need step-by-step help as they develop their marketing from a very simplistic approach to a more sophisticated one.

REFERENCES

Assael, H. (1985): *Marketing Management: Strategy and Action,* Boston: Kent Publishers.

Broom, H.N., Longenecker, J.G. and Moore, C.W. (1983): *Small Business Management,* Cincinnati, Ohio: South Western Publishing Co.

Carson, D.J. (1985): "The Evolution of Marketing in Small Firms", *European Journal of Marketing,* 19(5): 7–16.

Cohn, T., and Lindbore, R.A. (1972) "How Marketing is Different in Small Companies", An American Management Association Management Briefing, New York: American Management Association.

Committee for Economic Development (1978): in D. Steinhoff, *Small Business Management Fundamentals.* Maidenhead: McGraw-Hill.

Cromie, S., Carson, D. and Ayling, S. (1987): "The Marketing Planning Process in Small Firms". Address to the Tenth UK Small Business Policy and Research Conference, Cranfield School of Management: UK Small Business Policy and Research Conference.

Gaedeke, R.M., and Tootelian, D.H. (1980): *Small Business Management,* California: Goodyear Publishing Co.

Greenley, G.E. (1986): *The Strategic and Operational Planning of Marketing.* Maidenhead, McGraw-Hill.

Guiltinan, J.P. and Paul, G.W. (1985): *Marketing Management: Strategies and Programs.* Maidenhead: McGraw-Hill.

Justis, R.T. (1981): *Marketing Your Small Business.* Englewood Cliffs, N.J.: Prentice-Hall.

Kotler, P. (1984): *Marketing Management: Analysis Planning and Control.* Englewood Cliffs, N.J.: Prentice-Hall.

Leppard, J., and McDonald, M. (1987): "A Reappraisal of the Role of Marketing Planning", *Journal of Marketing Management,* 3(2): 159–71.

Lorange, P., and Vancil, R.F. (1977): "Strategic Planning Systems" in D.F. Abell and J.S. Hammond (eds), *Strategic Marketing Planning.* Englewood Cliffs, N.J.: Prentice-Hall.

Luck, D.J., and Ferrell, O.C. (1979): *Marketing Strategy Plans.* Englewood Cliffs, N.J.: Prentice-Hall.

McDonald, M.H.B. (1984): *Marketing Plans: How to Prepare Them; How to Use Them.* London: Heinemann.

Mandell, M.I., and Rosenberg, L.J. (1981): *Marketing,* Englewood Cliffs, N.J.: Prentice Hall.

Mendham, S., and Bannock, G. (1982): "Small Business and Economic Change", Address at the International Congress on Small Business, Malaga, Spain: International Congress on Small Business.

Scholhammer, H., and Kuriloff, A. (1979): *Entrepreneurship and Small Business Management.* New York: John Wiley.

Steinhoff, D. (1978): *Small Business Management Fundamentals.* Maidenhead, McGraw-Hill.

Tate, C.E., Megginson, L.C., Scott, C.R., and Trueblood, L.R. (1975): *Successful Small Business Management,* Dallas: Business Publications.

Tyebsee, T.T., Bruno, A.D. and McIntyre, S.D. (1983): "Growing Ventures Can Anticipate Marketing Styles", *Harvard Business Review*, 61(1): 64–6.

PART V

Product and Brand Management

12

International Brand Strategy: Its Relevance for Irish Marketing

*Mary Lambkin,
Tony Meenaghan and
Marie O'Dwyer*

INTRODUCTION

It has long been recognised that intangible assets such as brand names and corporate goodwill are particularly valuable and are frequently of more significance to corporations than the physical assets which support them. The main value of brands derives from the loyalty which they engender among their consumers, which translates into a steady and enduring revenue and profit stream. These benefits are inevitably magnified for brands which sell in international markets, and the highest premiums accrue to global brands such as the many household names with which we are all familiar (see Table 12.1 for a list of the world's Top 20 brands).

Strong international brands represent the cumulative outcome of a large and sustained marketing investment, often stretching back over 50 years or more. Obviously, companies launching new products and brands face a major competitive disadvantage in comparison with large, successful brands already established in their markets. This problem is particularly acute for small companies coming from small and peripheral markets, such as Ireland. Indeed, debate on the question of whether Irish firms can or should invest in brand development often concludes that it is an impossible task, and that a more attractive option is to become a sub-supplier, thereby passing the responsibility for branding to the custodian of the brand who has access to both financial and marketing power. The production of private label food products or food ingredients for onward processing represent instances of the latter option.

TABLE 12.1: TOP 20 MOST VALUABLE BRANDS WORLDWIDE

Brand	Product	Company	Current 1992 Value ($m)	Sales ($m)	Operating Margin (%)
1 Marlboro	Cigarettes	Philip Morris	39,469	10,688	45
2 CocaCola	Soft Drinks	CocaCola	33,446	9,090	30
3 Intel	Microchips	Intel	17,810	3,969	55
4 Kellogg's	Cereals	Kellogg	9,678	5,391	18
5 Nescafé	Coffee	Nestlé	9,174	5,073	19
6 Budweiser	Beer	Anheuser Busch	8,243	5,332	19
7 Pepsi	Soft Drinks	PepsiCo	7,502	5,881	14
8 Gillette	Razors	Gillette	7,147	1,978	35
9 Pampers	Nappies	Proctor Gamble	5,924	4,300	16
10 Bacardi	Rum	Bacardi	5,494	1,360	40
11 Winston	Cigarettes	BJR Nabisco	5,229	2,689	31
12 Levi's	Jeans	Levi Strauss	4,881	3,400	18
13 Newport	Cigarettes	Loews/Lorillard	4,590	1,288	45
14 Motorola	Microchips	Motorola	4,134	1,330	30
15 Kodak	Films	Eastman Kodak	4,122	2,660	17
16 Camel	Cigarettes	BJR Nabisco	3,674	1,813	28
17 Nike	Sports Shoes	Nike	3,497	2,829	16
18 Campbell	Soup	Campbell Soup	3,447	2,933	17
19 L'Oréal	Cosmetics	L'Oréal	3,403	882	15
20 Hennessey	Cognac	LVMH	3,398		42

Source: Frazer, Ian (1992), "Is it the End of the Road for Brands?", in *Media International*, September, pp. 28–30.

This question of whether to brand or sub-supply, while generating considerable debate, has not yet been subject to rigorous analysis or research. The purpose of this paper is to begin such an analysis by identifying the important questions involved and by conducting a preliminary review of the evidence available both in Ireland and internationally.

The paper commences by defining the concept of a "brand" and goes on to explore the commercial rationale for building brands. It then reviews pertinent issues concerning international brands, in order to provide the context for a discussion of Irish brands. The final sections discuss the prerequisites for building successful brands and outline some options for Irish firms which may help them to leverage their limited resources.

THE "BRAND" CONCEPT

In his best-selling marketing management text, Philip Kotler defines a brand as "a name, term, symbol or design, or a combination of them, which is intended to identify the goods or service of one seller or group of sellers and to differentiate them from those of competitors" (Kotler 1992: p. 442).

Most writers agree, however, that a brand is far more than a name. It is the sum total of the attributes — both real and perceived — which the brand name conjures up in the customer's mind and which causes an enduring preference for one product over another. De Chernatony (1989) has listed several functions performed by brands. A brand serves:

- As a piece of legal property in which a manufacturer can invest and which is protected from competitive attack or trespass.
- As a differentiating device, in that it helps the consumer to identify the product and therefore to specify, reject or recommend it.
- As a shorthand device for consumers to avoid having to embark on a lengthy choice process with each purchase.
- As a promise of consistent quality.
- As a means of projecting self-image.

Many commentators focus on the last of these points, emphasising the idea of a brand "personality". This refers to the idea that a brand is a unique combination of physical, aesthetic and emotional elements which consumers can describe in as much detail as they would if they were talking about a human person.

For the purpose of analysis, brands are often examined along two dimensions: *functionality* and *representationality* (de Chernatony and McWilliams, 1989). Functional attributes refer to features of the product such as its size, capacity and performance specification, as in the case of a car. Representative attributes refer to the image and symbolism of the product and other intangible features that convey to the consumer the intended or, perhaps, unintended image, such as expensive or cheap, exclusive or common, masculine or feminine, and so on. These latter symbolic factors are particularly evident in the case of cars, as instanced by examples such as the Citroën 2CV, Volkswagen Beetle, Jaguar XJ6 and BMW 525 i.

At the centre of the brand/consumer relationship is a set of beliefs about the attributes manifest in the brand. These attributes or "core values" are the sum of the emotional and rational appeals of the brand and are developed over time based on the consumer's brand experience. As such, the values believed to exist in the brand form the basis of the brand/consumer relationship. A brand represents certain values to the consumer; therefore, "Cadbury is luxury and indulgence; Kellogg's is taste, variety and quality — 'the best to you each morning', while Persil is bright and white but in a caring family context" (Clarkin, 1991: p. 10).

FIGURE 12.1: ANATOMY OF A BRAND: AVONMORE

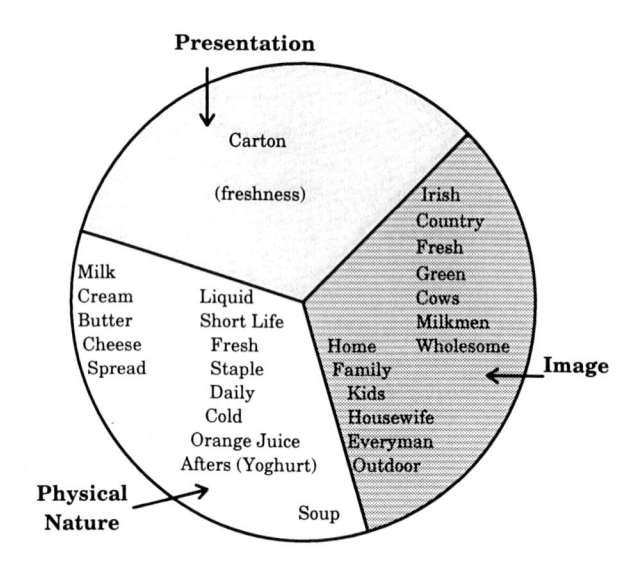

Source: Adapted from Clarkin, Eamon (1991), "What's in a Name?", *Checkout,* May, p. 10.

Research conducted jointly by Irish International Advertising Agency and Lansdowne Market Research (Clarkin, 1991) suggests that the perception of brand values derives from certain key elements of brand identity, notably physical product components, presentation aspects of the product and image components. The physical components such as being bulky or slender, fresh or frozen etc., affect consumer perceptions of the brand. Presentation aspects such as package size, shape and materials and other presentation features, either in shop display or advertising, further affect perception. Finally, the brand image components are those values which consumers associate with the brand and which are driven by the profile of the brand user and other communicated values such as freshness, goodness etc. An example, using the Avonmore brand, is presented in Figure 12.1 above, showing the physical nature, presentation aspects and image components as the major sources of brand image.

CORPORATE BENEFITS OF BRANDING

As indicated, branding is an important influence on marketplace transactions, being especially relevant in the consumer goods market. Brands help to simplify consumer decision-making by giving a sense of security and consistency to the consumer. Furthermore, brands also carry "images", or symbolic meanings which may provide social value, especially for socially visible products, as in the case of clothing, cars, home furnishings, etc.

As well as performing certain functions on behalf of consumers, companies engage in brand building to build brand equity. Today, brand equity is regarded as the manufacturer's most valuable asset. It is the financial value placed on the guaranteed flow of corporate income deriving from loyal consumers. In a general sense, brand equity can be defined in terms of the marketing effects which are uniquely attributable to the brand; that is, those outcomes which result from the brand that would not occur if the same product or service did not conjure up that aura for the consumer (Keller, 1993).

Brand equity is a function of the customer's familiarity with and perceptions of the brand. Therefore, the emphasis in building brand equity is on improving customers' knowledge of the brand (Keller, 1993). The relevant dimensions which distinguish brand knowledge and affect consumer response are the awareness of the brand (in terms of brand recall and recognition) and the favourability, strength and uniqueness of the brand associations stored in the consumer's memory. Figure 12.2 summarises the various dimensions of brand knowledge.

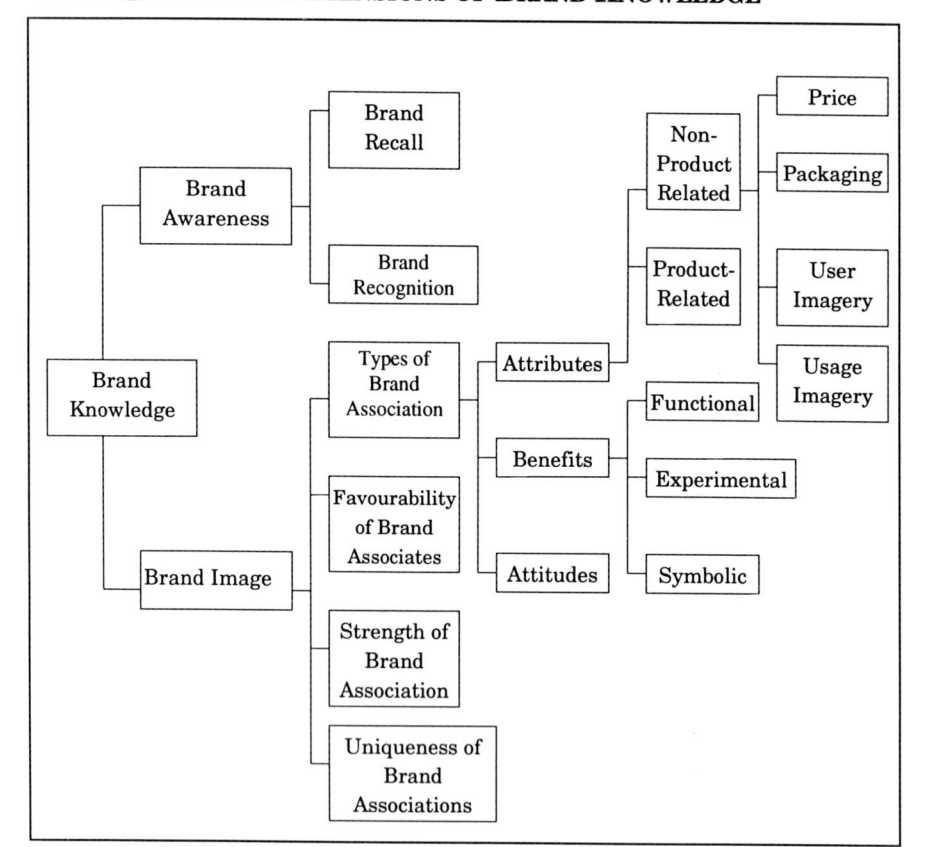

FIGURE 12.2: THE DIMENSIONS OF BRAND KNOWLEDGE

```
Brand Knowledge
├── Brand Awareness
│   ├── Brand Recall
│   └── Brand Recognition
└── Brand Image
    ├── Types of Brand Association
    │   ├── Attributes
    │   │   ├── Non-Product Related ── Price, Packaging
    │   │   └── Product-Related ── User Imagery, Usage Imagery
    │   ├── Benefits
    │   │   ├── Functional
    │   │   ├── Experimental
    │   │   └── Symbolic
    │   └── Attitudes
    ├── Favourability of Brand Associates
    ├── Strength of Brand Association
    └── Uniqueness of Brand Associations
```

Source: Kevin Lane Keller (1993), "Conceptualising, Measuring and Managing Customer-Based Brand Equity", in *Journal of Marketing,* Vol. 57, p. 1–22.

The benefits accruing to corporations from owning strong brands may be summarised as follows:

(1) *Customer Loyalty*

The core strength of a brand rests with the customers who favour that brand and continue to purchase it in preference to competing alternatives (Keller, 1993). The more customers who prefer the brand and the greater their loyalty to it, the stronger the brand. That age-old advertising ploy of asking consumers whether they would swap their favourite brand of detergent for Brand X is rooted in a clear realisation of this concept of brand equity.

(2) *Price Premium*
Because successful brands are perceived by their loyal consumers to be better than the alternatives, the customers are normally prepared to pay more for them. It would generally be expected, therefore, that strong brands command a price premium over their weaker competitors (Doyle, 1989).

(3) *Market Share*
A successful brand is one which consumers want to buy and retailers want to stock — thereby achieving a higher market share. Furthermore, brands with a high market share are much more profitable. The well-known PIMS research findings showed that on average, products with a market share of 40 per cent generate three times the return on investment of those with a market share of only 10 per cent (Doyle, 1989).

(4) *Economies of Scale*
The large market share enjoyed by strong brands facilitates the attainment of economies of scale in production, marketing and distribution. The resultant cost advantage together with the price premium that strong brands command, results in the higher operating margins revealed by the PIMS research when compared to smaller and weaker competitors.

(5) *Overcomes Barriers*
A strong brand can help to overcome barriers to entry for new product additions. A strong brand can provide leverage in the distribution channel. Like customers, the trade has less uncertainty dealing with a proven brand name that has already achieved recognition and associations. As such, a strong brand can provide an edge in gaining both shelf facings and co-operation in implementing marketing programmes.

(6) *Brand Extensions*
A strong brand can be extended into related product categories and subcategories. Strong brands can provide a platform for growth via brand extensions, e.g., in the US Proctor and Gamble's Ivory soap product has been extended into several cleaning products, facilitating business opportunities which would have been much more expensive to enter without the Ivory name. Similarly, in Europe, Vanish as a clothes soap, has been extended to a powder detergent and more recently, to a carpet cleaner.

(7) *Competitive Advantage*
   Today corporations can quickly emulate advances in technology or product formation. But what cannot be copied is the personality of a brand, thus the existence of a strong brand provides a competitive advantage which often presents a real barrier to competitors.

Therefore, brand owners benefit from the leverage and loyalty which brands engender. Strong brands support premium prices, facilitate distribution and lead to improvements in sales, market share, customer loyalty, trading profitability and earnings per share. All these corporate benefits derive from consumer propensity towards long-term brand loyalty or repeat purchase.

INTERNATIONAL BRAND BUILDING

The concept of global brands has engendered much controversy. One side of the debate has been taken by Levitt who suggests that world markets are being driven "toward a converging commonality" (Levitt, 1983). In Levitt's new world order, "homogenisation" of wants is driven by new technology, mass communication and travel. The result is a new commercial reality — the emergence of global markets for standardised consumer products on a previously unimagined scale of magnitude. Levitt argues that segmenting international markets on political boundaries and customising products and marketing strategies for country markets or on national or regional preferences is not cost effective. The company of the future, according to Levitt, will be a global company which views the world as one market to which it sells a global product (Levitt, 1983).

Many marketing professionals remain sceptical about the claims for global marketing. Observers agree that for products aimed at the very affluent market in many countries, global marketing might be an advantage since these highly affluent and mobile consumers could be thought of as living in a global village. Products included might be some brands of whiskey, perfume and some very expensive watches (Arnold, 1992).

Authors such as Reisenbeck and Freeling (1991) have raised practical questions as to how far international marketing may be standardised. They have pointed out various exceptions and argued the merits of localisation. For example, the French eat four times more yoghurt than the British, the British consume eight times more chocolate than the Italians, and so on. Their conclusion is that a mixed strategy is most appropriate, standardising the core aspects of the brand — that is, those which provide competitive advantage, but allowing local adaptation of secondary aspects.

Because of the many local differences which become evident in creating a global marketing strategy, marketers remain dubious about the prospect for large-scale global marketing. Instead, indications are that more regionalised approaches, such as branding for Europe or for Asia, might be more appropriate at this time than adopting the global approach.

> Certain emerging commonalities in the Euromarket will accelerate a diffusion of products and brands across national borders and beyond traditional preferences. Increasing urbanisation and attendant lifestyles of travel and cosmopolitanism are likely to broaden interests in Europroducts and Eurobrands, established or new (Beldo, 1991: p. 6).

The creation of the Single European Market has led many leading marketers such as Unilever, Nestlé, American Express and Ford — to mention but a few — to concentrate their efforts on the creation of Europroducts and Eurobrands. With trade barriers officially dismantled throughout the European Union, manufacturers and retailers now have a golden opportunity to expand. Ogilvy & Mather predicts that many established brands, initially designed and promoted to match the needs of one country, will slowly be replaced by "Eurobrands", thereby developing recognition on a wider scale. Such brands will be resisted successfully only by locally-produced specialist or value-added "niche brands", able to exploit local knowledge and contacts. Therefore, the Single European Market is seen to lead to a bipolarisation in the marketplace between large Eurobrands and small specialist or local niche products. This is not necessarily seen to mean fewer in number, but fewer types of brands. The mass market regional brands selling in one or two countries will have to compete head-to-head with strong international ones (Roberts, 1989).

In the European detergent market, for example, Proctor and Gamble seized much of the initiative in the 1980s with pan-European brands, such as Ariel, which achieved leadership in many countries. The issue now seems to be not whether to engage in global branding, but how much standardisation is appropriate, where and when. The quest for global brands is high on the management agenda for most leading-edge companies. The

Japanese in particular are vigorously pursuing global brands (Barwise and Robertson, 1992).

The advantages of building and holding an international brand can be summarised as follows (de Chernatony, 1993, a):

(1) *Economies of Scale*

   Eurobranding is seen to hold out the promise of economies of scale through centralised production, distribution and advertising. The production of much larger volumes worldwide may aid in driving down costs and may lead to the use of one advertising strategy across many countries.

(2) *Economies of Scope*

   The printing and packaging of products in several languages may lead to logistical benefits, allowing stock to be rapidly shifted from one country to another.

(3) *Greater Bargaining Power*

   Larger production volumes provide brand owners with greater power when negotiating with suppliers.

(4) *Greater Control*

   International branding may lead to a reduction of duplicated internal effort with greater co-ordination from headquarters.

(5) *Similarities between Consumers*

   As people become more mobile and adventurous in their buying, similarities between countries increase and international brands can better meet these similar needs.

(6) *New Opportunities*

   Slow growth in the home market may be overcome by the development of international brands which can be sold in many other countries.

Many companies are likely to continue to strive towards the creation of international or Eurobrands in the future. However, there is still no evidence that the long talked of and much sought after Eurobrand can become a market leader in all countries, according to market analyst Euromonitor. The *European Directory of Consumer Brands* shows little if any evidence of the same brand appearing in the top-three ranking (by market share) in all four of the largest European markets (UK, Germany, France and

Italy). Despite the breakdown of tariff and non-tariff barriers, many barriers to international branding, such as the wide spectrum of tastes, customs and languages, still exist (*Irish Marketing Journal*, 1992).

So far, only one brand, CocaCola, is on the top of the consumers' tongues worldwide. A survey of 3,000 consumers split equally between Japan, America and Europe shows that Coca-Cola is not only the most powerful brand name in the US, but also second in Japan and sixth in Europe (see Table 12.2). None of its eight closest rival brand names — IBM, Disney, McDonald's, Honda, Sony, Toyota, BMW and Porsche — made the top 50 in all three areas. Landor Associates, a firm of image consultants which organised the survey, judged brand power on two criteria: first, "share of mind" or the consumer's familiarity with the brand; and second, their "esteem" for the product — in other words, how good they thought it was. The survey is seen to give some clues as to how distant the prospect of the global market is. Perhaps companies are rushing to create international or pan-European brands which may be impossible to create in the time frame and to the degree envisaged (*The Economist*, 1988).

TABLE 12.2: A RANKING OF WORLD BRANDS

Ranking	America	Japan	Europe
1	CocaCola	Takashimaya	Mercedes-Benz
2	Campbell's	CocaCola	Philips
3	Pepsi-Cola	National	Volkswagen
4	AT&T	Matusita	Rolls-Royce
5	McDonald's	Sony	Porsche
6	American Express	Toyota	CocaCola
7	Kellogg's	NTT	Ferrari
8	IBM	Japan Air Lines	BMW
9	Levi's	All Nippon Airlines	Michelin
10	Sears	Seiko	Volvo

Source : Landor Associates (1988), in "It's the Real Thing", *The Economist,* 19 November, p. 80.

Branding in the Irish market represents a situation similar to that existing in markets worldwide, with a mixture of both indigenous local and international brands in most product sectors. In the consumer products sector, brands such as Barry's Tea, Harp Lager, Bachelors, Time Out, Tayto, Ballygowan, etc., are highly successful examples of local brands competing against international brand competition.

A similar situation pertains in the services sector where there has been a major growth in brand building in recent times. The Irish retail banks and other financial institutions continue to dominate their sector, while Dunnes and Superquinn represent very distinct and successful examples of Irish service brands. While the success of Irish service companies can be attributed to functional factors such as company size, trade relationships etc., there is no doubt but that the brand imagery developed over time has provided an important barrier to denying aspiring competitors.

Despite some evidence of successful local branding and the advantage of a favourable image in foreign markets, Ireland has not been particularly successful in creating major international brands. In fact it is a source of some concern that, apart from some notable examples, the number of internationally recognisable marks and brands of superior quality products to come out of Ireland, are disappointingly few (Purgavie, 1989; Linane, 1993).

While Waterford Crystal represents a successful example of continued investment in global branding, Bailey's Irish Cream is a more recent example of this phenomenon. Launched in 1974, Bailey's is now the world's number one selling cream liqueur by a large margin, and is sold in 130 countries around the world. Guinness is another internationally recognised and highly rated brand currently engaged in a major effort to capitalise on this fact in both European and North American markets. The Kerrygold label launched by the Irish Dairy Board is a further example of a success story abroad, being variously positioned in the markets of Europe. While there are few examples of internationally branded Irish services, U2, the Irish rock band, hold a dominant position in their industry, while Campbell Catering and its Bewley's brand are an example of Irish brand building abroad, Thermo King Europe represents a powerful example of industrial branding.

IMPEDIMENTS TO BRAND DEVELOPMENT IN IRELAND

While cognisant of the asset value delivered by strong brand franchise, many companies, particularly in Ireland, regard international brand building as a highly expensive exercise, difficult to quantify in tangible terms and best left to those multinational giants who can afford such intangible luxuries.

The reasons suggested for Ireland's failure to engage in brand building and to create more than a handful of international brands are varied. These reasons include the high costs and risk involved, restrictions on investment and a lack of adequate marketing expertise in this area. Geoff Read of Ballygowan Spring Water argues that the population here is too small to generate sufficient cash to invest in building an international brand. The pertinence of this point is particularly evident when one considers that the population of the Greater Birmingham area, represents a greater market volume than the Republic of Ireland as a whole. In addition, Ireland traditionally lacks good research and development into consumer products and does not have an enormous pool of management resources in terms of export-oriented people. Jim Moran of Moranco Strategic Marketing argues that Irish firms lack many of the marketing skills necessary to launch and maintain global brands (Sedgwick, 1993).

The creation of international brands involves high costs and equally high degrees of risk. For instance, at the top end of the scale, it has been estimated that it costs $60–100 million to launch a new international brand, such as a fragrance product, in the main markets of the world (Linane, 1993). Michael Campbell, Director General of RGDATA states that:

> it could cost anything up to £20 million to launch an international brand, depending on the type of impact you want to make. And this does not guarantee that the brand will "take off". Twenty million pounds is seen as a conservative estimate, but few enough Irish companies could even afford that (Linane, 1993: p. 10).

The reality is that these suggested investments greatly underestimate the funding needed to create an international brand, particularly when the costs of developing a brand against ingrained competition are likely to far exceed the funding necessary to maintain an established brand. The scale of investment in established brands can be seen by reference to Table 12.3 which indicates television advertising expenditure for well-known brands across major European markets.

TABLE 12.3: TELEVISION ADVERTISING EXPENDITURE FOR WELL-KNOWN BRANDS ACROSS MAJOR EUROPEAN MARKETS.

Rank 1992	Brand	Product	Total $m	Germany $m	Spain $m	France $m	UK $m	Italy $m	Neth. $m
1	Kellogg's	Breakfast Cereal	208	20	26	30	109	23	<1
2	Kinder	Confectionery	205	20	16	11	2	155	1
3	Renault	Cars	196	8	106	34	24	24	<1
4	Barilla	Baked Goods, Pasta	194	3	2	2	—	187	—
5	L'Oréal	Cosmetics	187	35	43	34	19	54	2
6	Fiat	Cars	186	7	25	4	7	142	1
7	Ariel	Detergent	181	35	59	19	47	15	6
8	Citroën	Cars	154	4	87	18	9	35	1
9	Ford	Cars	143	22	42	11	49	18	1
10	Peugeot	Cars	126	10	40	26	12	37	1
11	Opel	Cars	100	28	42	14	-	15	1
12	Danone	Dairy Products	95	7	54	20	3	11	<1
13	Dash	Detergents	89	9	19	8	-	52	1
14	Philips	Electronics	86	6	13	11	10	44	2
15	McDonald's	Fast Food	83	28	11	14	28	-	2
16	Nestlé	Confectionery	80	8	25	23	16	7	1
17	CocaCola	Soft Drinks	77	9	37	3	6	21	1
18	Persil**	Detergent	76	28	<1	3	43	—	2
19	Fairy	Dish Washing	76	20	76	20	14	—	—
20	Seat	Cars	76	2	42	3	1	28	<1

** Persil is marketed by Henkel in Germany, Spain and the Netherlands. Unilever markets Persil in the UK and France. A pan-European brand is defined as a product which is advertised on TV in three or more countries.

Source: Euromarketing (1993), "Top 100 Brands Boost Spend", in *Euromarketing*, Vol. VI, Issue 33, May.

Two particular points with regard to the accompanying table are instructive. Firstly, the quoted figures refer only to television advertising and not to all marketing communications expenditure, let alone marketing expenditure, which together are likely to be several times the quoted figures. Secondly, the figure quoted for the No. 1 television advertised brand, Kellogg's, across the six key European markets was $208 million, which is approximately equal to two-thirds of the entire expenditure on all advertising in all media in Ireland for all products and services in the equivalent year.

While the scale of investment is obviously a prohibitive factor, a further difficulty is posed in the case of public companies whose shareholders may express concern at the idea of investing large amounts of money in the creation of international brands which may not have a return for many years. The heavy outlay of cash is a problem for many companies which are already highly geared and this is compounded by the long pay-back period typically involved (often 5–8 years). Accounting regulations which require marketing expenditure to be expensed in the profit and loss account, rather than capitalised (in contrast to investment in plant and machinery), also acts as a constraint, particularly to public companies concerned about stock market reaction to their short-term financial results (Linane, 1993).

OPTIONS FOR DEVELOPING IRISH BRANDS INTERNATIONALLY

The options facing indigenous Irish companies seeking to develop markets overseas for their output can be categorised under two broad headings, namely sub-supply and brand development. The first such option is to sub-supply either primary or secondary processed output to an international marketing company which controls all responsibility for marketing and branding of the ultimate product abroad. This sub-supply option incurs limited marketing costs, and yields no control over the brand franchise in foreign markets. It is the route most commonly employed by Irish companies seeking markets overseas. An example of this strategy is the manufacture of food ingredients by Erin Foods for the Gerber brand of baby food products in the French market.

Branding represents the second option available to indigenous Irish businesses seeking to develop overseas markets. As indicated earlier, the ability to exploit this option is a function of financial capability. Under this branding option a variety of approaches can be pursued. In the case of Waterford Crystal, two different branding options have been used in recent years. One such option was the acquisition of the Wedgwood company, thereby providing control of this notable brand, while more recently international growth has been achieved through developing and launching the Marquis brand which now holds the number 6 position in the US premium crystal market (O'Donoghue, 1994).

The majority of Irish businesses seeking international markets do not possess the financial/marketing capability of a multinational such as Waterford Crystal and therefore are forced to consider other branding options. One such option is to sell out to a multinational corporation, an example of which is provided by Irish Distillers which was taken over by Pernod Ricard. The net result of this option is greater market access for the purchased brands which are now controlled by a foreign multinational, rendering somewhat mute the notion of being an Irish brand. Similar examples of the takeover route to international markets are provided by Cantrell & Cochrane's acquisition of Ballygowan and Northern Food's acquisition of Green Isle. While these examples represent the acquisition of Irish brands by foreign companies, indigenous Irish companies have also been involved in acquiring overseas companies. Examples under this heading include Bord na Móna, Waterford Foods and Avonmore. Such a strategy generally provides a distribution bridgehead for developing the Irish brand in the overseas market, rather than ownership of foreign brands per se.

Forming a strategic alliance with a foreign-based company represents a further method of developing the brand abroad. This can be concluded with a major distributor who provides access to targeted markets. This option which retains some degree of brand control is often chosen as a low investment route to international brand building as media expenditure requirements are offset by below-the-line and shelf-space opportunities presented by the strategic alliance. Similarly, a strategic alliance can be formed with a multinational corporation whereby, under a licensing deal, the brand achieves access to foreign markets.

A further variation on the strategic alliance option is evidenced by the Kerrygold example whereby the brand is developed and controlled under the auspices of a marketing organisation, such as the Irish Dairy Board, established to represent producers in a specific industrial sector. Similar strategies have been adopted by other national producers, particularly in the area of food marketing, as evidenced by the Danish approach to marketing its food produce abroad.

The reality with regard to brand building by Irish business is that there has been an extreme unwillingness to embark on the road to developing branded business overseas. The food sector wherein Ireland has considerable competitive advantage is a case in point, in that constituent companies in this highly branded industry adopt a dual strategy of branding in the home market and sub-supply in foreign markets. With regard to what are perceived to be successful Irish brands abroad, it is interesting to note the results of a recent survey of overseas business travellers with regard to their awareness of Irish brands (McNulty, 1994). The top six Irish brands in terms of spontaneous awareness were (percentages in brackets) Guinness (63), Jameson (30), Bailey's (18), Waterford (16), Kerrygold (14) and Ballygowan (7). Of these brands, four are controlled by foreign multinational corporations. Waterford Crystal, while Irish in identity and location is increasingly foreign in terms of sourcing of product and finance, while Kerrygold represents the fruits of continued investment by a government-sponsored marketing organisation rather than a single Irish indigenous product.

CONCLUSION

The value of brands as corporate assets is increasingly recognised. Nowhere is this more true than in international marketing where multinational corporations seek the benefits which accrue from global branding. The brand marketplace is increasingly populated by strong international brand names, regionally focused brands servicing two or possibly three national markets and niche brands developed locally. Inevitably, the rewards in branding are commensurate with the volume markets served, and therefore the path to corporate growth lies in brand building. However, the investment which is required to develop and maintain an international brand is significant and beyond the financial capability of the owners of strong local brands seeking growth.

A number of strategies are available to Irish companies seeking to grow their brands in international markets. Inevitably, all such strategies require some degree of relinquishment of control to a strategically chosen partner who will offset the deficiencies in finance, market power and marketing skills which hitherto limited the brand's development. In a peripheral economy such as

Ireland, companies attempting to build their brands internationally must seek accommodation with strategic partners to realise their brand ambitions.

REFERENCES

Arnold, D. (1992): *The Handbook of Brand Management*, The Economist Books: London.

Barwise, P. and Robertson, T. (1992): "Brand Portfolios", *European Management Journal*, 10(3), 277–85.

Beldo, L. (1991): "Outlooks on Euromarket 1992", *Applied Marketing Research*, 31(1): 3–7.

Clarkin, E. (1991): "What's in a Name", *Checkout*, May: 10–11.

de Chernatony L. (1993)(a): "Ten Hints for EC Wide Brands", *Marketing*, 11 February: 16.

de Chernatony L. (1993)(b): "The Seven Building Blocks of Brands", *Management Today*, March: 66–8.

Doyle, P. (1989): "Building Successful Brands: The Strategic Options", *Journal of Marketing Management*, 5(1): 77–95.

Economist. The (1988): "It's the Real Thing", 17 November: 80.

Euromarketing (1993): "Top 100 Brands Boost Spend 28%", 6(33).

Frazer, I. (1993): "Is it the End of the Road for Brands", *Media International*, September: 28–30.

Irish Marketing Journal (1992): "Eurobrands Not Certainties", September: 11.

Keller, K.L. (1993): "Conceptualising, Measuring and Managing Brand Equity", *Journal of Marketing*, 57(1): 1–22.

Kinsella, S. (1989): "Where Branding is King", Address at the National Marketing Conference, Killarney: National Marketing Conference.

Kotler, P. (1992): *Marketing Management — Analysis, Planning, Implementation and Control*, seventh edition, Englewood Cliffs, N.J.: Prentice-Hall.

Levitt, T. (1983): "The Globalisation of Markets", *Harvard Business Review*, 83(3): 92–102.

Linane, Carmel (1993): "The Economics of Creating a Brand", *Checkout*, May: 12.

McWilliam, G. and de Chernatony, L. (1989): "Branding Terminology — The Real Debate", *Marketing Intelligence and Planning*, 7(7/8): 29–32.

Murphy, J. (1990): "Assessing the Value of Brands", *Long Range Planning*, 23(3): 23–9.

O'Neill, P. (1989): "To Brand or Not to Brand", Address at the National Marketing Conference, Killarney: National Marketing Conference.

Purgavie, B. (1989): "Irish Branding", Address at the National Marketing Conference, Killarney: National Marketing Conference.

Riesenbeck, H. and Freeling, A. (1991): "How Global are Global Brands?", *McKinsey Quarterly*, 4: 3–8.

Roberts, J. (1989): "Advertising the European Way", *Europe*, November: 30–32.

Sedgwick, L. (1993): "Losing the Brand Game", *Management*, 40(6): 8–11.

13

Quality Standards and ISO 9000: Do the Results Meet the Expectations?[*]

*Brian Fynes,
Sean Ennis and
Gerard Ryan*

INTRODUCTION

Over the past decade many commentators have highlighted quality and the management thereof as being of fundamental importance in the attainment of a competitive advantage (Feigenbaum, 1983; Ishikawa, 1985; Oakland, 1989; Atkinson, 1990; and Witcher, 1992). Scheuring (1992) has made the observation that the combination of mature, highly competitive markets and the pressure on companies to become low-cost suppliers whilst at the same time maintaining consistently high levels of quality has resulted in the emergence of quality as a "strategic imperative" for many organisations. He defines quality as a "conformance to customer requirements from an internal and external perspective".

The early part of this paper attempts to trace the evolutionary development of quality from being simply an inspection exercise towards playing a strategic role in the formulation and implementation of business strategy. More specifically, the middle section examines the characteristics of the ISO 9000 series of standards, and examines the rather limited research which has been undertaken on its adoption and effectiveness. The final part reports on the findings of a survey on the experiences of a number of Irish companies which have recently adopted this standard.

---

[*] This paper was first presented at the IMP Conference, 1993.

THE DEVELOPMENT OF QUALITY AS A MANAGEMENT FUNCTION

While the techniques and tools of quality management have emerged in an evolutionary fashion, their development can be categorised into four distinct "quality eras" (Garvin, 1987). Figure 13.1 identifies these stages in greater detail. The essential message to be learned from this representation is that the management of quality has moved from a reactive, tactical exercise with a narrow focus, to an essential element of business strategy, embracing all functions, from purchasing through production, marketing and customer feedback.

FIGURE 13.1: THE FOUR LEVELS IN THE EVOLUTION OF QUALITY MANAGEMENT

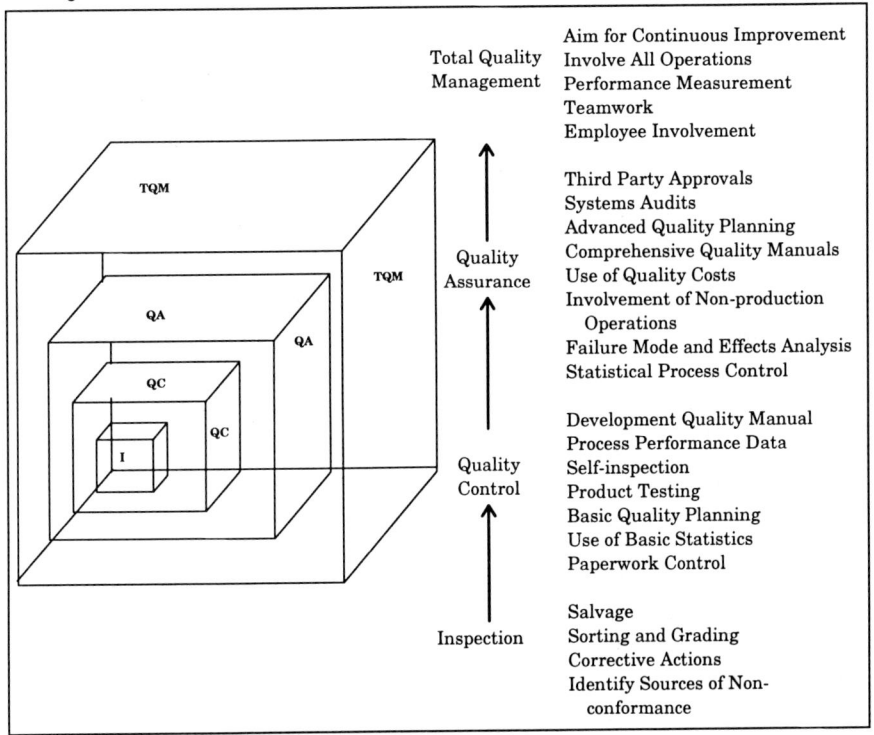

Total Quality Management	Aim for Continuous Improvement Involve All Operations Performance Measurement Teamwork Employee Involvement
Quality Assurance	Third Party Approvals Systems Audits Advanced Quality Planning Comprehensive Quality Manuals Use of Quality Costs Involvement of Non-production Operations Failure Mode and Effects Analysis Statistical Process Control
Quality Control	Development Quality Manual Process Performance Data Self-inspection Product Testing Basic Quality Planning Use of Basic Statistics Paperwork Control
Inspection	Salvage Sorting and Grading Corrective Actions Identify Sources of Non-conformance

Source: Dale and Plunkett (1990).

INSPECTION

Formal inspection procedures were introduced as part of the development from the single lot production methods of the artisans and skilled craftsmen to the mass production methods experienced during the heyday of scientific management and Fordism. As mass production methods developed using special-purpose machinery to produce interchangeable parts followed by a pre-established sequence of assembly operations, manufacturing needs began to change. The specific need for inspection during manufacturing occurred initially in the armaments industry (Hounshell, 1984; Taylor, 1919) where a seminal application of the principles of scientific management included the assignment of inspection as one of the eight functional "bosses" for effective production management. Radford (1922) also linked inspection activities directly with the ability to control the quality of output. As such, it was established formally as a key management responsibility within the sphere of quality control for a number of years until the development of statistical quality control which emerged from innovative research at Bell Laboratories.

STATISTICAL QUALITY CONTROL

In 1924, landmark experiments took place at the Hawthorne plant of Western Electric in the United States. The researchers involved with the experiments included Walter Shewhart and later, Joseph Juran, and were largely responsible for what is now referred to as statistical quality control (Shewhart, 1931; Juran, 1951). They reported that variations exist in every facet of manufacturing and that these variations could be understood through the application of simple statistical tools such as sampling and probability analysis. Later still, the advent of the Second World War created the need to produce large volumes of product, especially in the munitions sector, to an acceptable quality level. In order to ensure such a consistent, acceptable level of quality, the United States War Department set up a committee to draft standards in this area (Dodge, 1969). As these standards dramatically improved the quality of output, the 1940s witnessed a significant growth in the number of training courses on quality control.

QUALITY ASSURANCE

Based on the experience gained from managing quality in a mass production environment, the focus of quality management changed from that of simply inspecting product to managing process quality. In essence this broadened the area of responsibility from that of simply quality control to the other business functions directly involved in influencing the product in the organisation. While problem prevention remained the primary goal, four elements emerged as part of this quality assurance movement:

(1) A *cost of quality* focus — including prevention, appraisal and failure.
(2) An emphasis on *total quality control* — from product design right through to placing it in the hands of the customer.
(3) Use of *reliability engineering* — the probability of a product performing a specific function without failure for a given period of time under specific conditions.
(4) The pursuit of *zero defects* — a programme designed to promote a constant, conscious desire to do a job right first time (Crosby, 1979).

While these developments contributed in no small measure to reducing defects in manufacturing, the goals of the quality department were still essentially defensive in nature and focused on defect prevention. Quality was viewed in a narrow, negative perspective and treated as a device to avoid inadequate levels of performance which in turn, could damage company performance.

STRATEGIC QUALITY MANAGEMENT

A number of factors in the external environment began to exert increasing influence on the behaviour of firms in the 1970s and the early part of the 1980s. Abernathy et al. (1981) pinpointed the superior quality and reliability of Japanese manufacturers as being the main reasons for the loss of market share and profitability of American firms. Empirical evidence of this phenomenon was provided from the automobile, semi-conductor and colour television markets (Magaziner and Reich, 1982; Juran, 1978 and Porter, 1983). Government agencies in the United States also pursued a policy of stricter policing of product quality. In addition, product liability suits began to rise dramatically, growing at an annual rate of 28 per cent between 1974 and 1978 (Mallot, 1983). These forces combined to increase sharply the costs of producing defective products which, in turn, forced the issue of quality management very firmly on the agenda of senior management. Hagan (1984) notes that the definition of what was meant by quality, shifted from an internal perspective of quality represented by quality specifications, to an external standpoint as defined from the customer's point of view.

The key features of this re-definition include:

- It is not those who offer the product but those whom it serves — the customers, users and those who influence or represent them — who have the final word on how well a product fulfils needs and expectations.
- Satisfaction is related to competitive offerings.
- Satisfaction, as related to competitive offerings, is formed over the product's lifetime, not just at the time of purchase.
- A composite of attributes is needed to provide the most satisfaction to those whom the product serves.

This attempt to refocus quality represents a critical change of emphasis, by defining quality relative to the competition rather than against fixed internal standards. Thus, marketing research on the customer's perception of the product becomes an active part of the quality value chain (Ishikawa, 1984). The landmark study instigated by the Strategic Planning Institute (Buzzell and Gale, 1987) also provided strong empirical evidence of the link between quality and profitability. As companies began to match the competition's existing quality levels, the opportunity arose for exceeding those levels — in essence, establishing the concept of continuous, never-ending improvement (or what the Japanese call *kaizen*) as opposed to the established acceptable quality levels (AQL) concept.

THE DEVELOPMENT OF QUALITY STANDARDS

The influence which Japan has had on the evolution of quality as a strategic weapon has already been referred to and cannot be understated. Concurrent with the focus on quality in Japan during the 1940s and 1950s was the development in the early 1950s, by the national standards association, of Japanese Industrial Standards (JIS). Two and a half thousand of such standards were in place by 1952. Because of the unique role played in industry by the Japanese government, and in particular the Ministry of International Trade and Industry, many companies felt compelled to achieve JIS certification. In essence, the procedures adopted for auditing such companies became the blueprint for the subsequent process adopted more recently in Europe. Garvin (1987) argues that the JIS mark played a pivotal role in bringing legitimacy and co-ordination to Japan's quality movement. It is also worthwhile pointing out that this happened at least 20 years before the concept gained any impact in the US and Europe.

THE DEVELOPMENT OF QUALITY STANDARDS IN EUROPE

Britain developed the BS 5750 Quality System Standard in 1979 in response to the proliferation of quality standards used by companies when evaluating the performance of their suppliers. This standard shows the company how to establish, document and maintain an effective quality management system, thereby enabling it to demonstrate a commitment to supplying goods which conform to the quality needs of its customers.

In 1979 the International Organisation for Standardisation (ISO), based in Geneva, formed a technical committee to develop a single standard for the operation and management of quality assurance. In 1987 the quality standard ISO 9000 was formally adopted throughout Europe as the basis for quality systems and was based predominantly on the BS 5750 model. It consists of a series of five standards which set down the minimum standards for the management and control of quality assurance. The National Standards Authority of Ireland (NSAI) administers the standards within the Republic of Ireland.

THE EXPERIENCE SINCE 1987

In a survey of 20 companies in the UK (Rayner and Porter, 1990), 35 per cent of the firms which received accreditation claimed that the reason for seeking certification stemmed from "actual customer pressure". Only 10 per cent cited the improvement of product quality as being a justifiable reason. No evidence was demonstrated that firms sought to put in place a system of quality assurance as a basis for future quality improvement initiatives. This survey is clearly based on a very small sample and, as a consequence, considerable caution must be exercised when attempting to use it as a basis for making meaningful observations which can be applied to companies in general.

COSTS AND SAVINGS ASSOCIATED WITH ISO 9000

Rayner and Porter (1990) in the same study also attempted to compare the relevant costs and benefits and to develop a financial model of how the possible savings resulting from the implementation of ISO 9000 compared with the likely costs of implementation, assessment and maintenance. Table 13.1 represents the analysis for the "average" firm which participated in the survey. On the basis of their calculations, they estimate that the installation of

ISO 9000 would pay for itself during the third year of operation. This will clearly vary, however, depending on the size of the firm and the nature of the product.

TABLE 13.1: FINANCIAL MODEL FOR ISO 9000 COST SAVINGS

Initial Quality Costs	5.0%				
Discount Rate	14.0%				
Savings:					
Turnover	2,690,000	2,690,000	2,690,000	2,690,000	2,690,000
Total Quality Costs (% of Turnover)	5.0%	4.4%	3.8%	3.2%	2.5%
Total Quality Costs	134,500	118,360	102,220	86,080	67,250
Total Savings	0	16,485	32,280	48,420	67,250
Costs:					
Internal Development Effort	17,900				
Consultancy Assistance	2,100				
External Costs	5,200				
Internal Maintenance Effort (QM)		12,500	12,500	12,500	12,500
External Reinspection Costs		2,200	2,200	2,200	2,200
TOTAL COSTS	25,200	14,700	14,700	14,700	14,700
Net Savings	-25,200	1,785	17,850	33,720	52,550
Discount Factor	100.0%	87.7%	76.9%	67.5%	59.2%
Present Value of Net Saving	-25,200	1,565	13,519	22,761	31,109
Cumulative NPV	-25,200	-23,635	-10,116	12,645	43,754

Rayner and Porter concluded that:

> the survey provided conflicting evidence on the value of BS 5750 as a tool for improving the overall profitability of the business. Some respondents expressed themselves to be strongly in favour of BS 5750, and wanted to extend the principles of quality management systems throughout the company. Other respondents took the more jaundiced view that the BS 5750 simply documented their usual business practices which were sometimes "lacking in quality". The results indicated that, overall, BS 5750 Certification has been a valuable and worthwhile exercise for the majority of firms.

While this study does pose some reservations, it is clear that the further diffusion and development of ISO 9000 is assured. This is primarily due to the completion of the Single European Market which is expected to consolidate the adoption of such a system, and moreover, will put pressure on those companies from outside Europe who wish to sell within the European Union. Bodinson (1991) supports this view and argues that it will be virtually impossible to sell products in this market after 1993. Similarly, O'Toole (1992) concludes that achieving ISO 9000 accreditation is merely a stepping stone in the development of a total quality strategy, while Kendrick (1990) indicates that American companies are also gearing up to comply with the standard.

In summary, a good quality assurance system provides a necessary base from which firms can gain the benefits from introducing a wide range of quality improvement techniques (Voss and Blackmon, 1993; Dale and Plunkett, 1990). Initiatives such as statistical process control, just-in-time and total quality management can provide benefits such as those which Japanese counterparts have achieved, only if an effective Quality Assurance System is in place. The literature on ISO 9000 does little to publicise this fact. It is also the main reason why we have treated this topic as part of the *evolutionary process* of quality management from a narrow internal inspection exercise to that of a strategic part of business strategy, and why we believe the topic merited further research as outlined below.

RESEARCH METHODOLOGY

Prior to undertaking primary research, an examination of the literature provided by NSAI indicated that the benefits fall into two broad categories:

(1) **The Supplier** (i.e., the firm). Independent assessment and registration by NSAI gives authoritative verification to the quality claims of a company. The National Register of Certified Products and Companies is increasingly used as a primary source of procurement by national and local government agencies. Inclusion in the register provides evidence of effective quality control procedures now demanded for grant-aid by state agencies. By meeting the requirements for ISO 9000, the Irish supplier saves time and money by cutting down on multiple assessments and factory inspections.

(2) **The Customer.** ISO 9000 provides a guarantee that the customer's needs are being met. It eliminates the need for their own supplier assessment and drastically reduces receiving inspection costs. It creates confidence in their suppliers because endorsement by the NSAI allied to its perceived integrity, independence and expertise is recognised and accepted worldwide. It makes decisions on buying easier: the National Register of Certified Products and Companies simplifies the selection of an acceptable supplier.

It is perhaps worth noting that these benefits are, to all intents and purposes, marketing-related benefits with the possible exception of "drastically reducing incoming inspection costs".

An initial examination of the Register established that as of June 1992, 416 firms had received accreditation for ISO 9000 (this has since risen to in excess of 1,000); 320 of these firms were in the manufacturing sector, representing the primary target population of the research.

The research design included had two major objectives:

(1) To identify the main motivating factors which led companies to seek ISO 9000 accreditation.
(2) To examine the experiences of those companies since they introduced the ISO 9000 system to their operations.

A mailed questionnaire was used as the primary method of data collection. Prior to sending this questionnaire, a pilot version was sent to four practising Quality Assurance Managers currently working with firms which had received ISO 9000. This helped to establish whether the main issues were being addressed and if not, which additional issues would need to be covered in the final version of the questionnaire. It also served to fine-tune question semantics and validate the reliability of the research instrument.

In addition, it was felt that some non "quality" personnel perspectives and viewpoints should be incorporated into the construction of the final questionnaire. As a consequence, two company visits were undertaken and in-depth interviews were carried out with two marketing managers, three production managers and four engineers.

One hundred questionnaires were randomly mailed and 34 valid responses were received for part 1 of the questionnaire (which examined the main motivating factors), and 33 valid replies were received for the second part (which examined the main experiences of the respondents). This represented approximately

10.6 per cent of all manufacturing firms which have received ISO 9000 in the Republic of Ireland.

RESULTS: ISSUES OF MOTIVATION

Respondents were asked to rate the degree to which the following factors represented their motivation to seek ISO 9000:

- Retention of existing customers
- Gain new customers
- Entry to new markets
- Fewer dissatisfied customers
- Greater internal discipline
- Reduce scrap and waste.

A five-point rating scale (as depicted on the x-axis) was used: 0 = "no part played" to 5 = "played a very significant part" and the results are presented in Figure 13.2. This section of the survey demonstrates that the motivation to seek ISO 9000 is the result of a combination of factors such as market pressures and the desire for internal improvement, and a range of other additional issues, depending on the firm's circumstances. Such additional issues include those of complying with customer requirements, the desire to be the first to achieve ISO 9000 in the industry sector and the desire to achieve international recognition. The longer term issue of quality playing a part in business strategy was also mentioned.

Specifically, three broad conclusions can be drawn from these responses:

(1) Market pressures such as the retention of existing customers or awareness of competitor's moves are the main influencing factors in the decision to seek ISO 9000 status. This is in line with research results in the UK (Rayner and Porter, 1990). However, entry to new markets was not seen as very significant.
(2) A desire for internal improvement is a very significant factor in Irish industry. This is in marked contrast to the results of the British survey.
(3) Four of the firms interviewed cited that the acquisition of ISO 9000 was viewed as being part "of a long-term quality strategy". This again contrasts with the experiences of the companies surveyed in the UK.

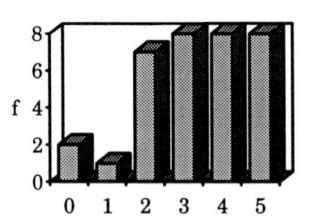

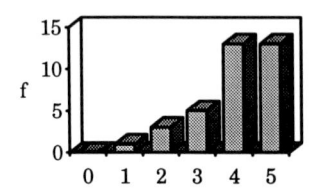

FIGURE 13.2: ISSUES OF MOTIVATION

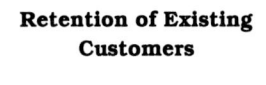

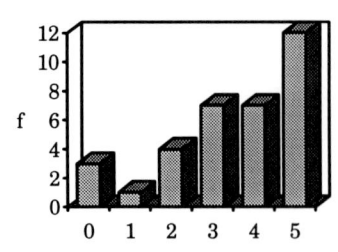

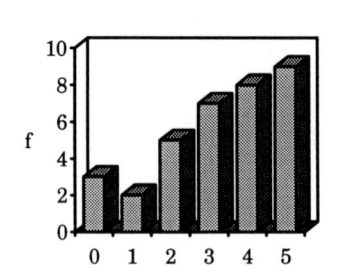

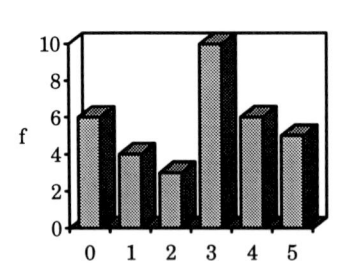

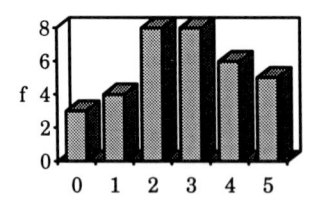

RESULTS: BENEFITS FROM ISO 9000 IMPLEMENTATION

Respondents to this section of the questionnaire were asked to gauge the percentage change which occurred under five main headings: Marketing, Quality, Productivity, Human Resources

Quality Standards and ISO 9000 197

and Vendor Relationships. This paper examines two of these areas: marketing and vendor relationships. Respondents were asked to indicate percentage increase or decrease in performance levels across a selection of relevant measures. The respondents were acquainted with the fact that it was difficult to attribute any performance change to any one particular factor, and were asked to take this into account in their responses. Thirty-three valid responses were received with regard to these issues.

MARKETING CONSIDERATIONS

A number of important observations can be made in relation to these results. Firstly, none of the respondents reported adverse marketing results: this may indicate that even in difficult economic and market circumstances (as was the case during the period under investigation), firms were still able to maintain their market position. The results are summarised in Figure 13.3.

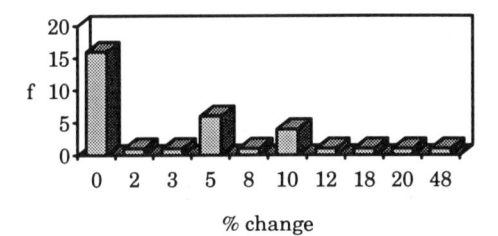

FIGURE 13.3: IMPACT ON MARKETING PERFORMANCE

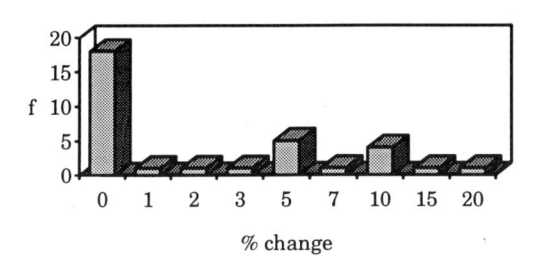

Market Share

Marketing Turnover

FIGURE 13.3 (CONTD.): IMPACT ON MARKETING PERFORMANCE

No. of Customers

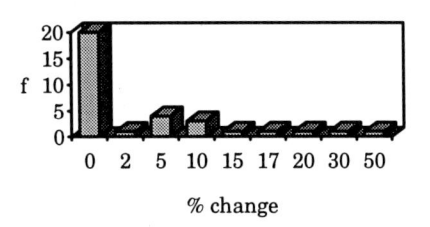

% change

Fifty-four per cent of the companies indicated that there was no change in their firm's market position as a result of implementing ISO 9000. This was to be expected as 27 per cent reported that improved marketing performance was not a factor in influencing their decision to seek accreditation. Also, some of the participating firms were subsidiaries of multinationals and did not have any responsibility for marketing. Fifty-two per cent reported an increase in turnover with the average increase amounting to 10.6 per cent. Forty-five per cent reported an improvement in market share, the average being 7.5 per cent while 39 per cent experienced an increase in the customer base with an average being in the region of 13.1 per cent.

These results indicate that there is a reasonably sound basis for firms to expect an improved market performance, if that was their motivation in seeking ISO 9000. This improvement is more likely to show itself in increased turnover and increased market share. Emphasis was given to seeking new customers, which could be interpreted as firms being more concerned with improving their present position within present markets. It also may indicate a preoccupation with the shorter-term, as opposed to viewing ISO 9000 as a contributor to long-term competitive performance.

VENDOR RELATIONSHIPS

One of the major developments in Total Quality Management is the changes which can occur in the relationship between a firm and its vendors. This is generally reflected in a movement away from a traditional, adversarial approach to that of a co-operative arrangement, placing particular emphasis on long-term "win-win" relationships.

Quality Standards and ISO 9000 199

In relation to the number of vendors, the results indicate that 39 per cent experienced no change, 43 per cent a decrease and 18 per cent an increase. The expected result would be a decrease in the number of vendors — moving towards longer-term, closer relationships. However, where a decrease was indicated, it proved to be substantial, averaging 18.6 per cent. The results are summarised in Figure 13.4.

FIGURE 13.4: VENDOR PERFORMANCE

Number of Vendors

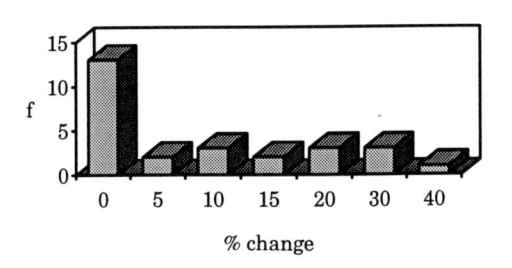

Vendor Quality Performance

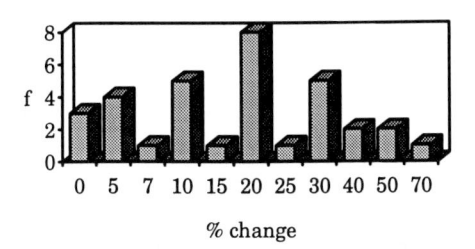

Quality of Relationship

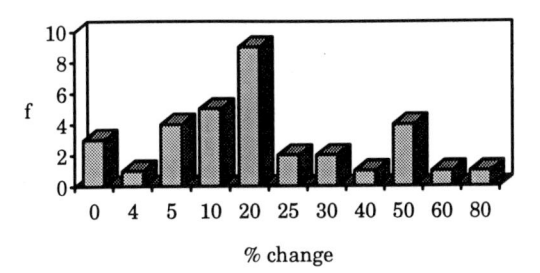

The quality performance of the vendor base is critical to the achievement of an overall improvement in a firm's product quality. As a consequence, an improvement would be expected in this case, where a firm implements an effective QA system. This expectation was confirmed in the results. Ninety-one per cent of the respondents indicated an improvement in vendor quality performance, the average being 22.6 per cent. This provides very strong evidence to support the belief that ISO 9000 leads to significant improvements in this area. More specifically, it provides for benefits resulting from reduced defects, reduced returns from vendors, less administration and increased certainty of meeting orders on time.

Ninety-one per cent of the respondents indicated that they experienced an improvement in the quality of vendor relationships, the average being 24.8 per cent. None of the respondents experienced a disimprovement. This result confirms the view that ISO 9000 improves working relationships with vendors, leading to a greater appreciation, on the vendor's part, of the real needs of the firm. In particular, such an improvement allows both parties to work together effectively to eliminate raw materials problems.

CONCLUSIONS AND RECOMMENDATIONS

The selective results presented in this research indicate that the participating firms broadly achieved the marketing- and vendor-related benefits which initially motivated them to seek ISO 9000 accreditation. In contrast to other studies in Britain and America, many of the companies did not reduce their vendor base.

A worrying feature of this survey is that many of the firms are more focused on the immediate day-to-day concerns and tend to view ISO 9000 as an end in itself rather than as a component of a broader quality strategy. This is evidenced by their concern with present markets and present customers and the retention of existing customers, as opposed to any market opportunities which might present themselves elsewhere. While a small core of companies did view quality in a strategic context, there is clearly a need to educate Irish managers to view quality and ISO 9000 in a broader context.

This survey adds weight to the suggestion that Irish companies view the ISO 9000 accreditation as an end in itself rather than as a means towards the achievement of a continuous improvement strategy which will place total quality management at the forefront of business strategy. This creates a further suspicion that the ISO 9000 exercise is perceived as a tactical, inspection function. Further research (possibly of a qualitative nature) is needed to expand on this aspect of the findings.

REFERENCES

Abernathy, W.J., Clark, K.M. and Kantrow, A.M. (1981): "The New Industrial Competition", *Harvard Business Review*, 59(5): 68–81.

Atkinson, P.E. (1990): *Creating Cultural Change: The Key to Successful Total Quality Management*, Kempson: IFS Publications.

Bodinson, G.W. (1991): "Warning: Ignoring ISO Standards May be Harmful to Your Company's Future", *International Management*, 46(3):. 11–12.

Buzzell, R.D. and Gale, B.T., (1989): "Market Perceived Quality: Key Strategic Concept", *Planning Review*, 17(2), 6–15.

Crosby, P.B. (1979): *Quality is Free*, New York: McGraw-Hill.

Dale, B.G. and Plunkett, J.J. (1990): "The Process of Total Quality Management", *Total Quality Management*, Reading, M.A.: Addison-Wesley Publishing Company.

Dodge, H.F. (1969): "Notes on the Evolution of Acceptance Sampling Plans, Part 1", *Journal of Quality Technology*, 1(2): 77–88.

Feigenbaum, A.V. (1983): *Total Quality Control*, New York: McGraw-Hill.

Garvin, D. A. (1987): *Managing Quality*, New York: The Free Press.

Hagan, J.T. (1984): "The Management of Quality: Preparing for a Competitive Future", *Quality Progress*, December: 21–22.

Hounshell, D.A. (1984): *From the American System to Mass Production, 1800–1932*, Baltimore: John Hopkins Press.

Ishikawa, K. (1984): "Quality and Standardisation: Program for Economic Success", *Quality Progress*, January: 18–19.

Ishikawa, K. (1985): *What is Total Quality Control? The Japanese Way*, Englewood Cliffs, N.J.: Prentice-Hall.

Juran, J.M. (1951): *Quality Control Handbook*, New York: McGraw-Hill.

Juran, J.M. (1978): "Japanese and Western Quality: A Contrast", *Quality Progress*, December: 10–18.

Kendrick, J.J. (1990): "Certifying Quality Management", *Quality*, August: 38–40.

Magaziner, I.C. and Reich, R.B. (1982): *Minding America's Business*, New York: Harcourt Brace Jovanovich.

Mallot, R.H. (1983): "Let's Restore Balance to Product Liability Law", *Harvard Business Review,* 61(3): 67–8.

Oakland, J.S. (1989): *Total Quality Management,* London: Heinemann Professional Publishing.

O'Toole, G. (1992): "The ISO 9000 — Is it worth the Effort?", Unpublished MBS Dissertation, Department of Marketing, University College Dublin.

Porter, M.E. (1983): "The US Television Set Market" in *Cases in Competitive Strategy,* New York: The Free Press.

Radford, G.S. (1922): *The Control of Quality in Manufacturing,* New York: Ronald Press.

Rayner, P. and Porter, L.J. (1990): "BS 5750/ISO 9000 — The Experience of Small and Medium-Sized Firms", *International Journal of Quality and Reliability Management,* 8(6): 16–28.

Taylor, F.W. (1919): *Shop Management,* New York: Harper and Brothers.

Scheuring, E.E. (1992): "Purchasing and Quality — Keynote Address", in *Proceedings of the First Purchasing and Supply Education and Research Group (PSERG) Conference,* University of Strathclyde: Purchasing and Supply Education Research Group.

Shewhart, W.A. (1931): *Economic Control of Quality of Manufactured Products,* New York: Van Nostrand Company.

Voss, C.A. and Blackmon, K.,L. (1994): "BS5750, ISO 9000, EN 29000 and Quality Performance; The British Experience", Working Paper, London: London Business School.

Witcher, B. (1992): "TQM and the Creation of a Market Responsive Organisation". in M.J. Baker (ed.) *Perspectives on Marketing Management,* Chichester: Wiley.

14
Timing Market Entry*

Mary Lambkin

The importance of timing of entry into new markets is an implicit assumption in many of the concepts and models which are used in strategic decision-making. This includes such well-known ideas as those of barriers to entry and mobility (Bain, 1956; Porter, 1980), the experience curve (Boston Consulting Group, 1973; Day and Montgomery, 1983), and portfolio analysis (Day, 1977; Wensley, 1982). In general, all of these concepts rest on the premise that to be an early entrant and, in particular, to be a pioneer, confers a long-term competitive advantage arising from the opportunity to build scale, to accumulate experience, and to achieve product differentiation ahead of competitors. These advantages, in turn, are expected to result in long-term market share leadership and in a superior level of profitability.

This tendency for pioneers to outperform later entrants has already been demonstrated in several research studies covering different industries and different types of businesses (Bond and Lean, 1977; Whitten, 1979; Robinson and Fornell, 1985). What is not so well understood, however, is how later entrants fare in their entry attempts and, in particular, whether it is better to be an early follower of the pioneer into a still-growing market than a late entrant into a more mature market situation. A related question is whether there are particular combinations of resources and competitive strategy which can allow businesses to overcome the disadvantages of late entry.

RESEARCH STUDY

The research study described in this paper was undertaken in order to obtain answers to some of those questions. The evidence

---

* © *Irish Marketing Review,* volume 4, 1990. This article is reproduced with kind permission from Mercury Publications Ltd.

was obtained by studying two samples of businesses, both of which were drawn from the PIMS (Profit Impact of Marketing Strategies) database. One sample contained 129 start-up ventures which had been in operation for a minimum of four years, while the other contained 187 "adolescent" businesses which had been in business for approximately eight years (Biggadike, et al., 1978). The reason for including two samples of businesses in this study was mainly to ensure that any trend observed in the start-up sample remained consistent over time. Another precautionary measure was to use four-year averages in studying both samples so as to reduce the effects of year-to-year fluctuations. Thus, the results for the start-up sample refer to the average achieved during their first four years of operations, while the results for the adolescents refer to their second four years.

The research methodology used was to compare the mean values of the businesses in different timing of entry categories within each sample and to test for statistically significant differences among these means. Three timing of entry categories for which measures are available in PIMS were used for this purpose, namely, pioneers, early followers and late entrants. These categories are defined as follows:

(1) The first business or one of the *pioneers* in developing a product or service.
(2) An *early follower* of the pioneer in a still-growing, dynamic market.
(3) A *later entrant* into a more established market situation.

Prior to discussing the results obtained from the analysis of these businesses, it is necessary to point out some other features of the data which may influence their interpretation. Firstly, all of the businesses in these samples are subsidiaries or divisions of large, established corporations, the majority being in the Fortune 500. They do not reflect, therefore, the experience of independent new ventures started by individual entrepreneurs. Secondly, all of these businesses survived their entry attempts — they would have been eliminated from the database otherwise — and, consequently, nothing can be said about the relative rates of survival or failure among different types of businesses. Thirdly, since this study analysed the pooled experience of a wide range of industries, it is possible that the averaging process conceals some variations which are specific to particular industries. Finally, although the comparison between start-up and adolescent businesses gives some impression of trends over time, it cannot be considered as a true reflection of the historical performance pattern of a single sample of businesses tracked over a long period of time.

Even allowing for these caveats, however, the results obtained in this study are sufficiently strong to suggest the presence of some genuine differences in the performance experience and in the competitive strategies of the businesses studied which would seem to be important enough to merit consideration by managers involved in market-entry decisions.

TIMING OF MARKET ENTRANCE AND PERFORMANCE

Market Share

Consistent with previous studies, Table 14.1 shows that pioneers enjoy a substantial market share advantage over all later entrants. Furthermore, a comparison of the results for the start-up and adolescent samples suggests that the advantage of pioneers' increases over time, both in terms of absolute and relative market share. This supports the widely held view that it is easier to build market share in the early stages of the market's development before competitive pressures become very intense (Aaker and Day, 1986).

TABLE 14.1: TIMING OF ENTRY AND MARKET SHARE: START-UP AND ADOLESCENT SAMPLES

Variable	Mean	Pioneers	Early Followers	Late Entrants
		Start-up Sample		
No. of Observations	129	46	40	43
Market Share	14.76	23.96	9.63	9.70*
Relative Market Share[†]	35.79	66.16	17.84	20.02*
		Adolescent Sample		
	Mean	Pioneers	Early Followers	Late Entrants
No. of Observations	187	63	61	63
Market Share	21.45	32.56	18.75	12.95*
Relative Market Share[†]	55.10	99.56	39.11	26.13*

*   Differences are significant at the 1% level.
†   Relative Market Share is the share of the business divided by the combined share of the three largest competitors.

This argument would also account for the market share pattern exhibited by the late entrant categories. From a position of virtually identical levels of market share in the start-up sample, early followers manage to achieve a six percentage point advantage over late entrants in the adolescent phase. Some of this difference may accrue from variations in the composition of the two samples, but it seems unlikely that this is the only explanation. Given that early followers increase their share by nine percentage points from the start-up to the adolescent stage while late entrants increase by only three percentage points, it seems reasonable to argue that some factor in the competitive environment must be influencing the relative differences between the two categories. The fact that it is very difficult to build market share upon entry into mature markets has already been shown in another PIMS study in which a sample of 69 entrants gained, on average, only four percentage points in share over an eight-year period (Yip, 1982).

TABLE 14.2: TIMING OF ENTRY AND PROFITABILITY: START-UP AND ADOLESCENT SAMPLES

Variable	\multicolumn{4}{c}{Start-up Sample}			
	Mean	Pioneers	Early Followers	Late Entrants
No. of Observations	129	46	40	43
Return on Sales	-23.71	-40.6	-12.72	-16.23*
Return on Investment	-19.35	-22.96	-16.95	-16.64
Cash Flow/Investment	-40.29	-46.48	-37.22	-36.53
	\multicolumn{4}{c}{Adolescent Sample}			
	Mean	Pioneers	Early Followers	Late Entrants
No. of Observations	187	63	61	63
Return on Sales	6.91	10.57	6.20	3.95*
Return on Investment	15.8	20.65	17.58	9.22*
Cash Flow/Investment	-6.79	-7.37	-6.96	-6.05

* Differences are significant at the 1% level.

PROFITABILITY

The relative profit performance of the three entry groups, shown in Table 14.2, varies substantially between the start-up and adolescent samples. Taking the start-up sample, it can be seen that pioneers experience more negative results than any of the later entrants across the three measures of financial performance (return on sales, return on investment and the ratio of cash flow to investment), although the differences are statistically significant only for return on sales. This pattern is consistent with the product life cycle model which suggests that the earliest entrants have to bear high costs in developing new markets and that these costs are unlikely to be offset by sufficient sales volume to prevent large losses and large negative cash flows (Levitt, 1965). The same logic would suggest, however, that the losses incurred by pioneers in their early years would soon be replaced by profits as they begin to reap the benefit of a quickly established leadership position. This is borne out in the adolescent sample which shows pioneers to have achieved substantial profit levels during their second four years of operation.

PERFORMANCE WITHIN ENTRY CATEGORIES

These aggregate performance differences were examined in greater detail by comparing businesses which were more and less successful within each of the three categories. Success was determined on the basis of market share because this variable was more highly correlated with order of entry than any of the measures of financial performance. The mean level of market share for the entry group provided the dividing line for assigning businesses to high-share and low-share subgroups.

The number of observations in these subgroups as well as their relative performance in terms of market share and profitability are shown in Table 14.3. The first point to note from these results is that not all pioneers achieve high market shares. There is actually considerable variation on this measure, with more businesses having market shares below the mean than above it. Thus, while on average pioneers outperform later entrants, to be a pioneer is no guarantee of continued market leadership. In fact, it appears from this evidence that considerable numbers of pioneers find their initial leadership positions unsustainable under the pressure of competition from later entrants. This simultaneous occurrence of success and failure may be further illustrated by reference to the financial performance of the different entry groups. The financial performance of the pioneers shows significant variation across the three measures (return on sales, return on investment and the ratio of cash flow to investment). The high share pioneers clearly take the greatest risk in terms of the size of their initial cash outlays and the extent of losses which they are prepared to sustain during their start-up phase, even though they are rewarded by a high level of return in adolescence.

TABLE 14.3: ORDER OF ENTRY AND PROFITABILITY: WITHIN GROUP COMPARISONS

Variable	Start-up Sample			Adolescent Sample		
	Mean	High Share	Low Share	Mean	High Share	Low Share
Pioneers						
Market Share	23.96	54.69	5.94	32.56	55.97	18.15
No. of Observations	46	17	29	63	24	39
ROS	-40.26	-54.48	-31.92	-10.57	13.25	8.92
ROI	-22.96	-40.45	-14.30	20.65	28.33*	15.93*
Cash Flow/Investment	-46.48	-61.18†	-37.48†	-7.37	-1.03*	-11.27*
Early Followers						
Market Share	9.63	19.51	4.32	18.75	32.72	9.69
No. of Observations	40	14	26	61	24	37
ROS	-12.72	-8.10	-15.21	6.20	13.00†	1.78†
ROI	-16.95	-1.98	-25.00	17.58	31.39†	8.63†
Cash Flow/Investment	-37.22	-35.00	-38.42	-6.96	-2.43	-9.90
Late Entrants						
Market Share	9.70	22.25	4.26	12.95	23.06	5.84
No. of Observations	43	13	30	63	26	37
ROS	-16.23	0.48*	-23.47*	3.95	4.65	3.46
ROI	-16.64	19.92†	-32.48†	9.22	10.65	8.22
Cash Flow/Investment	-36.53	16.54*	-45.19*	-6.05	-4.20	-7.35

*   Differences are significant at the 5% level.
†   Differences are significant at the 1% level.

The performance pattern of the early followers is quite different from that of the pioneers. High-share early followers experience only marginally negative profits in their first four years, while low-share early followers experience substantial losses. For the high-share businesses, this would seem consistent with the possibility of entering the market at a lower point on the experience curve than pioneers, allowing direct costs to be more in line with prices from the commencement of operations. The low-share pioneers, in contrast, do not seem to benefit from such effects, perhaps because of a lack of knowledge of the relevant manufacturing process.

The weak starting position of the low-share early followers continues to dog their performance in the adolescent stage when these businesses are shown to earn lower returns than any of the other groups or subgroups. This evidence points to the conclusion that a weak follower position is the least desirable of all competitive positions. On a more positive note, these results also indicate that the profit levels of the high-share early followers can actually match or even exceed those of high-share pioneers. This finding is particularly remarkable in view of the lower share base of the early followers (the average share of the high-share pioneers is 56 per cent while that of the early followers is 33 per cent in the adolescent sample). Given the rule of thumb which has evolved from PIMS research that every 10-point difference in market share converts to approximately a 5 per cent difference in return on investment, a much larger differential would have been expected between these two groups (Buzzell, et al., 1975).

The absence of such a differential in these results complicates the interpretation of the overall performance pattern. These results do not support the constant relationship between scale and performance which is widely believed to typify most markets (Buzzell, 1981). Perhaps the most likely interpretation of this instance is that the classic pattern is distorted by the intervention of a particular configuration of structure and strategy which enhances the performance of the medium-sized businesses.

The experience of the late entrants in this sample provides yet another profile. The most notable finding is that late entrants which achieve a relatively high market share seem to enjoy positive profits from the outset, or, at least, for the average of their first four years. They also experience significantly less negative cash flow/investment ratios than the low-share late entrants. These findings are consistent with the concept of a segmentation or "niche" strategy in which the risk of making a late entry into a highly competitive market is offset by the low costs of a small-scale manufacturing operation with minimal overheads.

In sum, this simple comparison of performance within the three entry groups demonstrates the presence of substantial variation among the constituent businesses and provides quite a few insights into the reasons underlying this variation. The next section explores these factors in more detail by comparing the structures and strategies of the high and low subgroups.

STRUCTURE AND STRATEGY WITHIN ENTRY CATEGORIES

The variables examined in this section fall into three fairly discrete groups which have been given separate labels. The first group, labelled "relationship to parent", contains variables describing the levels of resources which a start-up business has available to it by virtue of its ownership characteristics. This includes the opportunity to share production facilities, distribution channels and brand names/corporate reputation, the possibility of buying materials or selling output internally, and the benefit of inheriting manufacturing and marketing results.

The second group of variables, labelled "entry strategy", encompasses factors which describe the competitive stance of the business at its point of entry. This includes such items as whether the mode of entry was via internal development or acquisition, the extent to which the product being launched was a significant advancement over existing products, the presence or absence of patent protection, the breadth of the product line being offered, and the scale of entry (including production capacity and market coverage) relative to competitors.

The third group of variables, labelled "competitive strategy", covers factors reflecting the ongoing competitive position of the business. It reflects such management decisions as how much money to spend on marketing, what level of product quality and support services to offer, what price to charge, and what level of direct costs to seek — all measured relative to competitors.

Some of the variables in these groups are indices made up of several components and others are measured in brackets representing ranges of values; so the absolute values are not interpretable in many cases. The value of these results, therefore, is to indicate trends and patterns rather than absolute differences in structure and strategies of the businesses examined.

Tables 14.4, 14.5, 14.6 show a comparison of the high and low share subgroups within each entry category on all of these structure and strategy variables. The results of these analyses are discussed separately for each of the entry categories.

PIONEERS

As shown in Table 14.4, variables in the relationship to parent

Timing Market Entry

category seem relatively unimportant in distinguishing between high and low share pioneers, indicating perhaps that the resources which a firm brings to the market are not as important as the strategy it uses to compete in that market.

TABLE 14.4: HIGH- AND LOW-SHARE PIONEERS: ANALYSIS OF STRUCTURE AND STRATEGY

Variable	Start-up Sample Mean Share = 23.96		Adolescent Sample Mean Share = 32.56	
	Low Share	High Share	Low Share	High Share
Mean Share	5.94	54.69	18.15	55.97
No. of Observations	29	17	39	24
Relationship to Parent				
Parent Co. Size	1618.600	2543.500	1492.400	1107.100
Parent Co. Diversity	0.762	0.715	0.893	0.799
% Sales Internal	4.975	2.718	1.231*	4.458*
% Purchases Internal	14.378	11.583	6.846	9.375
Shared Facilities	1.690	1.882	1.667	2.000
Shared Customers	2.207	2.000	2.128	2.375
Shared Marketing	1.793	1.765	1.897	1.625
Brand Names/Goodwill	0.345	0.235	n/a	n/a
Familiarity Manufacturing	2.241	2.206	n/a	n/a
Familiarity Marketing	2.000	1.863	n/a	n/a
Entry Strategy				
Breadth Product Line	1.586*	2.118*	2.231	2.167
Scale Market Entry	1.690†	2.098†	2.154	2.181
Capacity/Market	16.300†	185.300†	27.300†	76.670†
Patent Protection	0.362	0.324	0.385	0.354
Origin	2.621*	2.059	n/a	n/a
Rel. Product Advantage	3.897	4.177	n/a	n/a
Competitive Strategy				
Rel. Marketing Expenditure	2.026†	2.980†	2.829	3.028
Rel. Product Quality	40.250	57.060	37.10‡	52.250‡
Rel. Customer Services	3.526	3.779	3.487	52.250
Rel. Price	112.510†	100.430†	107.059†	102.479†
Rel. Direct Costs	126.840	113.59	100.338	98.258

*   Differences are significant at the 5% level.
†   Differences are significant at the 1% level.
‡   Differences are significant at the 10% level.

The importance of an appropriate strategy is certainly borne out by the differences which are evident in the entry and competitive strategies of more and less successful pioneers. In the case of entry strategy, it appears from the results obtained on the start-up sample that the achievement of high market share for market pioneers is positively associated with a broad product line, a large market entry scale, a high investment in production capacity and a tendency to enter markets by internal development rather than by acquisition. The fact that some of these results are not significant in the adolescent sample suggests perhaps that these variables are most important in helping businesses to become established initially. With regard to competitive strategy, high-share pioneers appear to spend substantially more than low-share pioneers in promoting their products, and to offer lower prices than their competitors — evidence perhaps of a conscious attempt to build up sales volume so as to exploit experience effects. All of these characteristics reinforce the conclusion which has already been suggested elsewhere (Biggadike, 1979), that the more successful pioneers in the PIMS database are those which follow an ambitious market leadership strategy from the outset, reflected in a heavy investment in production scale and an aggressive promotional strategy.

EARLY FOLLOWERS

As in the case of the pioneers, the results in Table 14.5 show that the market share of early followers is not strongly influenced by any of the variables in the relationship to parent category. These results, therefore, do not indicate that early synergistic benefits arise from having other businesses in related areas. In fact, the main differences between the high- and low-share early followers also relate to their entry strategies and, particularly, to their scale of entry. High-share early followers tend to have a broader product line, a wider market distribution and a larger production capacity than low-share followers, although on a lower base than the high-share pioneers.

The high-share early followers also display some advantages in competitive strategy, particularly in their direct production costs. The lower costs of the high-share group are consistent with their larger scale and demonstrate, perhaps, why a scale advantage is a necessary prerequisite for a successful early follower strategy. These results also show that such a scale advantage may be enhanced by having a relatively high quality product and a superior level of customer services.

In sum, these results indicate that the most successful early followers are those which manage to "leap-frog" their markets on a relatively large scale with good quality products, which allows them to achieve low costs from the outset and, therefore, an early and high return on their investment. The less successful early followers, in contrast, have none of these advantages, which is reflected in their inordinately poor profit performance.

TABLE 14.5: HIGH- AND LOW-SHARE EARLY FOLLOWERS: ANALYSIS OF STRUCTURE AND STRATEGY

Variable	Start-up Sample Mean Share = 9.63		Adolescent Sample Mean Share = 18.75	
	Low Share	High Share	Low Share	High Share
Mean Share	4.32	19.51	9.69	32.72
No. of Observations	26	14	37	24
Relationship to Parent				
Parent Co. Size	2370.000	976.000	1531.460	1480.250
Parent Co. Diversity	1.038	1.050	0.988	1.058
% Sales Internal	6.165	1.434	3.162	5.458
% Purchases Internal	13.870	9.933	17.135	9.292
Shared Facilities	2.115	2.286	1.784	1.875
Shared Customers	2.385	2.500	2.405	2.500
Shared Marketing	1.731	2.143	2.000	1.917
Brand Names/Goodwill	0.385	0.571	n/a	n/a
Familiarity Manufacturing	2.192	2.143	n/a	n/a
Familiarity Marketing	1.974	2.214	n/a	n/a
Entry Strategy				
Breadth Product Line	1.462	1.714	1.588†	2.083†
Scale Market Entry	1.410	1.595	1.613†	2.181†
Capacity/Market	7.820*	65.270*	13.240†	47.550†
Patent Protection	0.231	0.321	0.257	0.271
Origin	2.500	2.429	n/a	n/a
Rel. Product Advantage	3.192	3.571	n/a	n/a
Competitive Strategy				
Rel. Marketing Expenditure	2.093	2.405	2.214	2.497
Rel. Product Quality	17.144	24.361	12.390*	27.670*
Rel. Customer Services	3.039‡	3.643‡	2.845	3.130
Rel. Price	100.650	98.511	102.297	102.371
Rel. Direct Costs	124.000	100.840	106.889†	101.079†

*   Differences are significant at the 5% level.
†   Differences are significant at the 1% level.
‡   Differences are significant at the 10% level.

LATE ENTRANTS

The late entrant category differs from the previous two, as shown in Table 14.6, in that here the parent firm characteristics do seem to influence performance.

TABLE 14.6: HIGH- AND LOW-SHARE LATE ENTRANTS: ANALYSIS OF STRUCTURE AND STRATEGY

Variable	Start-up Sample Mean Share = 9.70		Adolescent Sample Mean Share = 12.95	
	Low Share	High Share	Low Share	High Share
Mean Share	4.26	22.25	5.84	23.06
No. of Observations	30	13	37	26
Relationship to Parent				
Parent Co. Size	1170.000†	3729.000†	2570.500	1671.600
Parent Co. Diversity	0.964	0.704	1.241†	0.581†
% Sales Internal	6.915	6.325	4.297	2.346
% Purchases Internal	16.306	22.132	14.838‡	5.115‡
Shared Facilities	1.667	1.692	1.460*	1.769*
Shared Customers	2.200†	3.462†	2.541	2.695
Shared Marketing	1.633	2.000	1.730*	2.154*
Brand Names/Goodwill	0.433	0.462	n/a	n/a
Familiarity Manufacturing	2.033	2.346	n/a	n/a
Familiarity Marketing	2.189	2.462	n/a	n/a
Entry Strategy				
Breadth Product Line	1.433	1.231	1.378†	1.769†
Scale Market Entry	1.678	1.641	1.658‡	1.859‡
Capacity/Market	11.610‡	22.450‡	8.620†	30.590†
Patent Protection	0.233	0.269	0.189	0.231
Origin	2.700	2.385	n/a	n/a
Rel. Product Advantage	3.300*	3.846*	n/a	n/a
Competitive Strategy				
Rel. Marketing Expenditure	2.344	2.481	2.480‡	2.862‡
Rel. Product Quality	12.300‡	33.020‡	19.635	21.254
Rel. Customer Services	3.158	2.904	3.318*	3.731*
Rel. Price	101.587	106.892	102.727	104.204
Rel. Direct Costs	108.567	116.435	103.130	104.704

* Differences are significant at the 5% level.
† Differences are significant at the 1% level.
‡ Differences are significant at the 10% level.

In particular, the parent firms of high-share late entrants

appear to concentrate on closely related businesses which permits them to share production facilities, customers/distribution channels and marketing programmes. These characteristics benefit late entrants by allowing them to overcome the barriers to entry that are likely to be a feature of mature markets. It also appears that high-share late entrants benefit from a relatively large-scale assault on their markets, although, in this instance, the base is very much lower, suggesting that large scale is necessary to achieve critical mass rather than to obtain a competitive advantage.

Another important finding in the entry strategy section is that the more successful late entrants have significant product performance advantages over their low-share peers. Unfortunately, this measure is unique to the start-up sample and therefore cannot be validated by comparison with the adolescents. However, the evidence on competitive strategy which shows successful late entrants to have a product quality advantage supported by good customer services and substantial marketing expenditure lends further weight to the product performance difference.

In sum, these variables suggest that the opportunity to build a viable level of market share for late entrants rests on two main criteria: first, the ability to overcome barriers into the market and, second, the possession of a competitive advantage in terms of product performance and/or customer services.

SUMMARY AND CONCLUSIONS

The study discussed in this paper was undertaken with the objective of obtaining a more detailed understanding of the relationship between timing of entry and performance than has hitherto been available. The results of this study confirm that timing of entry is strongly related to performance, as has been known for some time, while they also demonstrate that the aggregate differences between entry categories conceal a considerable degree of variation, both in the performance and in the strategies of the constituent businesses.

More specifically, these results show that the businesses which are likely to earn the highest long-term returns are market pioneers which commence operations on a large scale and use heavy marketing promotion to accelerate their descent down the experience curve, resulting in a virtually unassailable competitive position. Well-known companies which are accredited with such a strategy include CocaCola, Campbell's, Bird's Eye, Hallmark and

Wrigley's in consumer markets, and Du Pont, John Deere and Xerox in industrial markets. Closer to home, Waterford Glass, Kerrygold and Baileys would also seem representative of this category.

The only other entrant group which can hope to approach the level of profitability enjoyed by market pioneers is that of the early followers who enter their markets on a relatively large scale with a high quality, differentiated product and a low level of direct costs, enabling them to reach profitability at an early stage in their operations. The most notable example of this strategy is IBM which was an early follower both in mainframe computers and in microcomputers. Other examples include Texas Instruments in calculators, Fairchild in semiconductors and Matsushita in video-recorders.

Contrary to expectations, perhaps, the results also show that late entrants which can circumvent the barriers to entry into mature markets and have a competitive advantage in terms of price or product performance can earn a satisfactory level of return on their investment, even though they cannot hope to match the market share of earlier entrants. The microcomputer market has several examples of this strategy including Compaq and Amstrad. Examples may also be found in many other markets such as Canon in photocopiers and Honda in cars.

The one position which is particularly unattractive according to these results is that of the early follower which suffers from the dual disadvantages of small scale and poor quality or undifferentiated product. Businesses in this situation earn the lowest returns of all and probably face the greatest likelihood of being forced out of the market. The early withdrawals of many of the diversified electronics companies from the mainframe computer industry (including General Electric, RCA and Xerox) is one case in point and, curiously, their experience has been repeated in microcomputers where Xerox, Texas Instruments and Ericsson have already acknowledged defeat and withdrawn.

These findings clearly have implications for management decision-making. At a general level, they highlight the importance of timing as a variable which needs to be actively considered in making market-entry decisions while, more specifically, they offer guidelines for managers faced with particular timing options. First, for those who are fortunate enough to have the opportunity to pioneer new markets, they indicate the desirability of following an ambitious strategy from the outset to pre-empt the possibility of later entrants usurping their leadership position. Second, for those who are not pioneers but who wish to exploit the apparent opportunities in fast-growing new markets, these results point to the necessity of having a genuine competitive advantage on which to base an assault on the market to avoid the risk of becoming "stuck-in-the-middle" (Porter, 1990) with low market share and low profitability. Finally, these results indicate that profitable opportunities can exist even in mature markets for companies which can identify small segments of demand which they can serve uniquely well.

REFERENCES

Aaker, D.A. and Day, G.S. (1986): "The Perils of High Growth Markets", *Strategic Management Journal,* 7(5): 409–21.

Bain, J.S. (1956): *Barriers to New Competition*, Cambridge, M.A.: Harvard University Press.

Biggadike, E.R. (1979): "The Risky Business of Diversification", *Harvard Business Review,* 57(3): 103–11.

Biggadike, E.R., Tetlow, P., and Swire, S.J. (1978): *The Start-up Business Report: A Strategic Planning Tool for Making Decisions about New Ventures*, Cambridge, M.A.: Strategic Planning Institute.

Bond, R.S. and Lean, D.F. (1977): "Sales Promotion and Product Differentiation in Two Prescription Drugs Markets", Economic Report, US: US Federal Trade Commission.

Boston Consulting Group (1973): "History of the Experience Curve", *Perspective,* 125.

Buzzell, R.D. (1981): "Are there Natural Market Structures?", *Journal of Marketing,* 45(1): 42–51.

Buzzell, R.D., Gale, B.T. and Sultan, R.C.M. (1975): "Market Share — A Key to Profitability", *Harvard Business Review,* 53(1): 97–106.

Day, G.S. (1977): "Diagnosing the Product Portfolio", *Journal of Marketing,* 41(2): 29–38.

Day, G.S. and Montgomery, D.G. (1983): "Diagnosing the Experience Curve", *Journal of Marketing,* 47(2): 44–58.

Levitt, T. (1965): "Exploit the Product Life Cycle", *Harvard Business Review,* 43(6): 81–94.

Porter, M.E. (1980): *Competitive Strategy: Techniques for Analysing Industries and Competitors,* New York: The Free Press.

Robinson, W.T. and Fornell, C. (1985): "The Sources of Market Pioneer Advantages in Consumer Goods Industries", *Journal of Marketing Research*, 22(3): 305–17.

Wensley, R. (1982): "PIMS and BCG: New Horizons or False Dawn?", *Strategic Management Journal*, 3(2): 147–58.

Whitten, I.T. (1979): *Brand Performance in the Cigarette Industry and the Advantage of Early Entry, 1913–1974*, Washington D.C.: Federal Trade Commission.

Yip, G.S. (1982): *Barriers to Entry: A Corporate Strategy Perspective*, Lexington, MA: Lexington Books.

Part VI

Marketing Communications

15

The Changing Face of Marketing Communications

*Tony Meenaghan and
Caolan Mannion*

INTRODUCTION

The term "marketing communications" is an umbrella term used to describe the various methods of communications and persuasion available to the marketing manager. It includes elements such as advertising, sales promotion, public relations, and selling. It supplants, yet simultaneously incorporates, the older classification "above-" and "below-the-line" advertising, but is more broadly based in that it highlights both the importance of the public relations function and the role of personal selling in the marketing process. Given the scope of marketing activity under this heading and the multiplicity of factors impacting upon it, the term incorporates a field of marketing activity that is both diverse and evolving.

The purpose of this paper is to review, as the title suggests, the changing face of marketing communications. It will attempt to do so by examining changes in a number of interrelated sectors of the communications industry, namely, changes in the media, changes in the audience, and changes in the supply/production industry. It will, where appropriate, refer to evidence from both the Irish and larger international marketplace.

Figure 15.1 provides a research-based snap-shot of the various elements which currently constitute the marketing communications industry (excluding personal selling). It illustrates the relative emphasis accorded to the individual components of marketing communications, in that the figures under each heading represent the value of that activity in the UK market for the year 1992.

FIGURE 15.1: THE MARKETING COMMUNICATIONS MAP

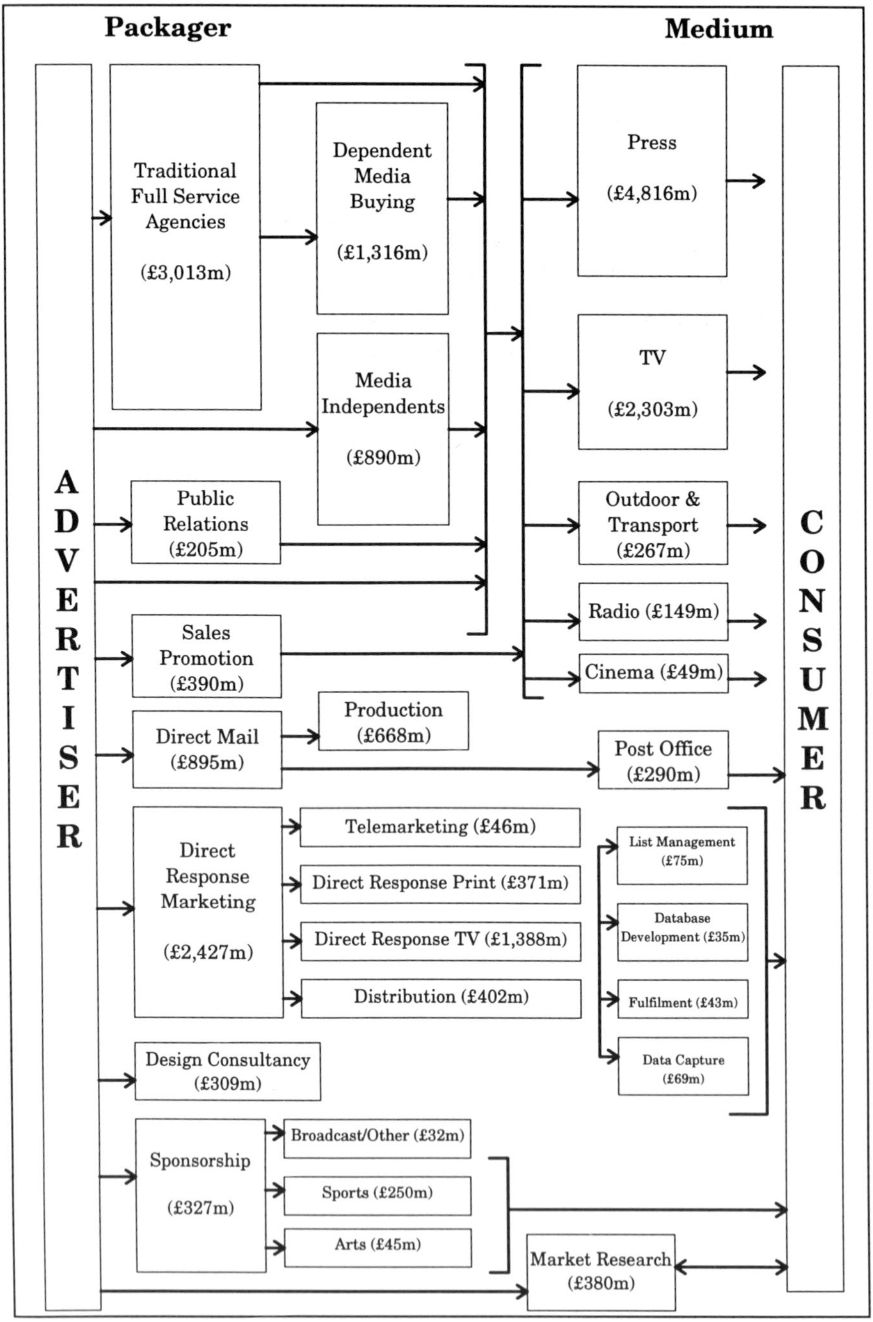

Source: Adapted from Snowden, Suzanne (1992), "The 1992 Marketing and Communications Map", *Admap*, October, p. 51.

CHANGES IN THE MEDIA

Above-the-Line Activity

There has been little evidence of major change taking place in the traditional above-the-line media in Ireland. Table 15.1 below, which portrays the allocation of expenditure to the various above-the-line media between 1988 and 1992 shows an increasing market-share in this sector for both the national and regional press, and radio. This fact reflects an increased number of national press titles now serving the Irish market and the developments in radio under the auspices of the Independent Radio and Television Commission (IRTC). A declining percentage of above-the-line expenditure is currently allocated to both the magazine and outdoor sector, while temporary changes to television are largely attributable to the effects of the 1990 Broadcasting Act, which is discussed more fully below. The level of cinema advertising, though small in percentage terms, continues to grow as it does in most developed economies. Expenditure on media advertising in Ireland for 1993 showed an 8 per cent increase over 1992 estimates with the share held by each medium remaining static (Hayden, 1994).

TABLE 15.1: ESTIMATES OF IRISH ADVERTISING EXPENDITURE IN IRELAND, 1988–92

Year	1988		1989		1990		1991		1992	
Medium	£m	%	£m	%	£m	%	£m	%	£m	%
National Newspapers	45.0	33	56.0	36	63.0	38	64.0	37	70.5	37
Regional Newspapers	4.5	3	5.5	3.5	6.0	4	6.5	4	7.5	4
Magazines	10.0	7.5	10.5	7	10.0	6	9.0	5	9.0	5
Television	48.0	36	51.0	33	51.0	31	56.5	32	64.5	35
Radio	14.5	11	18.0	12	20.0	12	24.0	14	24.5	13
Outdoor	12.0	9	12.5	8	13.0	8	13.0	7.5	14.0	7.5
Cinema	0.5	—	0.5	—	0.8	0.5	1.0	0.5	1.0	0.5
Total	134.5		154.0		163.8		174.0		191.0	

Source: Advertising Association of Ireland, based on Central Statistics Office, National Newspapers of Ireland, and Advertising Statistics of Ireland data.

Above/Below-the-Line Expenditure Reallocation

One of the most significant changes in the world of marketing communications in recent times has been the reallocation of marketing communications expenditure from above- to below-the-line media outlets. The extent of this reallocation is evident in the following examples. In the US market, traditional media advertising in 1992 accounted for 25 per cent of all advertising expenditure compared to 42 per cent in the mid-1970s (Shergill, 1993). In the US packaged goods industry consumer and trade promotions now account for 70 per cent of communications expenditure (Donnelly, 1992). Less dramatic, though no less significant, evidence of this reallocation of expenditure is available from the Irish market. Research carried out by the Marketing Development Programme (MDP) at UCD on behalf of the Advertising Association of Ireland in 1993 showed that non-media advertising (NMA) accounted for 38 per cent of total advertising expenditure with the total estimated value of non-media advertising for 1992 given as £117 million. Arising from this study, the breakdown of expenditure to various forms of non-media advertising is shown below in Table 15.2.

TABLE 15.2: BREAKDOWN OF NMA EXPENDITURE, 1992

Non-Media Activity	1992 Expenditure (£ million)
Point of Sale	34
Direct Mail	19
Exhibitions	18
Competitions	15
Added Extra	10
Extra Product/Money Off	8
Demonstrations	7
Sampling	6

Source: A Report on the Extent and Trends of Non-Media Advertising in Ireland (1993), UCD Marketing Development Programme for the Advertising Association of Ireland.

Given the diversity of opportunities presented by non-media advertising, the subcategories are variously employed by different industry sectors to achieve their particular objectives. This is evident from Table 15.3 which indicates the extent to which the food sector relies on competitions, point-of-sale and money off/ extra product deals to boost sales, while the financial sector is heavily reliant on direct mail and point-of-sale activity for the fulfilment of their corporate ambitions.

TABLE 15.3: EXPENDITURE ON NMA ACTIVITY BY SECTOR, 1993

Activity	Food	Household	Industry	Finance	Other	Total
Direct Mail	3	4	14	33	26	16
Exhibitions	1	14	29	6	17	15
Point of Sale	22	35	23	33	33	29
Demonstration	12	5	7	2	2	6
Sampling	8	14	2	—	1	5
Added Extra	10	11	5	11	9	9
Extra Products/ Money Off	16	10	7	1	—	7
Competitions	28	7	5	4	12	13

Source: A Report on the Extent and Trends of Non-Media Advertising in Ireland (1993), UCD Marketing Development Programme for the Advertising Association of Ireland.

TABLE 15.4: BREAKDOWN OF NMA BUDGET BY SECTOR, 1992

Industry Sector	% of Budget Allocated to Trade	% of Budget Allocated to Consumer
Food	23.0	77.0
Household	48.8	51.2
Industrial	39.8	60.2
Finance*	43.5	56.5
Other	36.6	63.4
Overall	38.0	62.0

*   The financial sector allocates a high proportion of its NMA spending on promotions to brokers.

Source: A Report on the Extent and Trends of Non-Media Advertising in Ireland (1993), UCD Marketing Development Programme for the Advertising Association of Ireland.

As is the case with above-the-line expenditure, the NMA budget is variously allocated to a combination of trade or consumer promotions with a reported 62 per cent of NMA expenditure allocated to final consumers and 38 per cent to the trade sector (MDP, 1993). However, this general pattern varies quite widely by industrial sector, as shown in Table 15.4 above. The food sector directs 77 per cent of its non-media advertising to the end consumer while the household sector directs some 50 per cent of its NMA budget to the trade.

A Media Explosion

From the development of the printing press to the creation of radio and television, technological advance has always been the catalyst for the development of new media. This is evident in the recent utilisation of satellite for broadcast purposes and will again prove true with the advent of the much heralded "super-highway" as technological advance continues to provide alternative access routes to consumers. The current explosion in media access to consumers is apparent in both the fragmentation of traditional media and a developing range of new media opportunities.

Fragmentation of traditional media. Media fragmentation, brought about by technological advance, increased leisure time availability and other life-style changes is significantly altering access routes to target markets. In the case of the more traditional media opportunities the extent of this fragmentation is particularly evident. With regard to the press, the following examples are indicative. In the UK market, BRAD (British Rate And Data) indicate that there has been a 53 per cent increase in the number of magazines available in 1993 compared to 1984, with 694 more consumer and 1,746 more business and professional titles (*Magazine News*, 1994a). In the category, women's magazines, the Audit Bureau of Circulation (ABC) now audits 45 different magazine titles in this category alone (ABC, 1993). The extent of fragmentation in the German market is indicated by the fact that there are 8,000 magazines available in that marketplace (*Magazine News*, 1994b).

In the Irish print media an expanding range of indigenous Irish productions has had to compete with UK imports. This is particularly evident in the newspaper market where the traditional titles, the *Irish Press, Irish Independent*, and *The Irish Times*, have had to compete with new Irish titles launched in the 1980s, such as the

Star, Sunday World, Sunday Tribune, and *Sunday Business Post.* These home-grown titles in turn have to compete with imported British tabloid and quality titles, a situation which has led to some concern in the Irish media.

In the case of radio there has also been a vast expansion of media opportunities with the Independent Radio and Television Commission (IRTC), established in 1988, granting licences to 26 independent radio stations, not all of which currently survive. It is perhaps in the area of television that technology is having the greatest impact on media developments. There are now an estimated 157 stations currently servicing the European market compared with 67 in 1980 (Perry, 1994), while the number of broadcast hours on European television has trebled since 1985 (Antenna, 1993).The more specific situation with regard to television penetration in Ireland is indicated in Table 15.5. While the penetration of the main terrestrial stations is largely unchanged in recent times, the situation with regard to the satellite stations is indicative of the proliferation of television audience access possibilities. Essentially, now that these satellite stations are once more available on the main cable networks, the penetration rates reported for 1992 are again largely applicable in 1994.

TABLE 15.5: TELEVISION STATION PENETRATION, 1988–93

Year	RTE	BBC 1	BBC 2	UTV	HTV	CH4	S4C	Sky	Sky
1988	100	58	58	50	9	49	8	31	—
1989	100	61	61	53	10	52	7	30	4
1990	100	64	64	54	11	57	8	32	23
1991	100	63	63	53	12	53	10	34	31
1992	100	65	65	53	12	53	9	37	33
1993	100	66	66	57	10	57	7	16	15

Base: All TV Homes = 100%.

Source: AGB TAM.

New media developments. As marketers continue to seek alternative access routes to target markets, new media opportunities have developed. While certain of these, such as cable and satellite broadcasting, result from technological advance, others stem more strongly from the desire for more cost-efficient access to markets.

Notable amongst these is commercial sponsorship which is valued at $10 billion worldwide (SRI, 1994). The explosive growth in this medium is graphically illustrated by the fact that the UK sponsorship market was valued at £4 million in 1970 (Buckley, 1980), but by 1993 the UK market was valued at £400 million (Mintel, 1993). On a pro-rata basis, the Irish market would currently be valued at approximately £20 million. These estimates of direct spending do not include the support spend necessary to promote the sponsor's association with an event. Industry suggestions are that a figure at least equivalent to the direct costs must be invested in support promotions, which greatly increase the marketing investment in this medium. The percentage of total advertising expenditure going to sponsorship in the UK is 4.3 per cent, in the USA 3.3 per cent, and in Italy 7.0 per cent (ISL Marketing, 1992).

Product placement is another example of advertisers seeking alternative routes to markets. Product placement is the inclusion/presentation within programmes — normally television or film — of goods and services as part of realistic scene creation. In effect, programme or film producers offer, for monetary return, to show particular products or services in their productions which ultimately are seen by consumers. Its recency, growth, and primary location are indicated by the fact that 35 placement agencies were established in the US between 1982 and 1990 (Swain, 1990). Its potency can be seen by the fact that a brand such as Ray Ban sunglasses increased its sales from 18,000 units to over 4 million units as a result of being placed in over 160 movies per year, such as *Risky Business* and *Top Gun*. Its impact on conventional advertising is indicated by the report that only £370,000 was spent advertising sunglasses in the main British media in 1989, less than half the figure for 1985, even though sales were worth £43 million (Lees and Rayment, 1990).

The development of cable and satellite broadcast linkages, and interactive media, as well as other new media such as sponsorship, product placement, the advertorial, represent new additions to the continuing explosion in media possibilities. Meanwhile, advertising through electronic mail via the Internet, a computer-based medium, has passed from futuristic possibility to everyday reality, with highly targeted advertising to self-selecting subscribers (Steinberg, 1994).

Increased Clutter

One of the inevitable consequences of the explosion in media opportunities is increasingly cluttered channels of communication to selected audiences. A recent Marketing Society publication (*Perspectives*, 1994) suggests that by the age of 20, the typical North American has seen 800,000 ads on television. Were one also to include advertising in media other than television, the net result is an incredibly cluttered, noisy environment with obvious consequences for attempts to gain the attention of selected audiences and ultimately persuade them to behave as suggested. Recent commentary on this cluttered advertising environment would indicate that viewer recall of advertising has fallen (Micklethwait, 1990). A further development among all consumers of advertising, inevitably linked to clutter, is consumer attitudes to advertising. Recent research indicates that consumers are becoming more hostile towards advertising in general, and that they increasingly fail to see the benefits of the exercise at all (Pollay and Mittal, 1993; Mittal, 1994).

Media Inflation

TABLE 15.6: ADULT CPTS INDEXED ON THE EUROPEAN AVERAGE

Country	TV All-time	Newspaper Mono	Newspaper Colour	Radio All-time	Cinema
Belgium	153	84	101	60	92
Denmark	155	135	101	204	117
Finland	124	111	130	225	95
France	68	206	86	89	104
Germany	124	106	117	50	62
Greece	29	117	152	21	237
Ireland	52	114	262	61	137
Italy	109	76	67	—	—
Netherlands	69	64	96	44	129
Norway	233	114	136	210	62
Portugal	52	66	92	—	—
Spain	121	65	63	52	125
Sweden	172	87	173	—	100
Switzerland	173	143	394	589	144
UK	76	34	77	65	93
Europe	**100**	**100**	**100**	**100**	**100**

Source: Marsh, Frances (1991), "Irish TV Half European Average", *Irish Marketing Journal*, December, pp. 10–11.

Media costs, measured on the cost of reaching 1,000 members of the targeted population (CPT), show Ireland generally to be a reasonable cost environment in which to mount an advertising campaign. This is evident from Table 15.6 which indicates the relative costs of European media. As indicated, television costs in Ireland are approximately half the European average, while colour press advertising costs are some two-and-a-half times the European average. A comparison of costs across all media with our nearest market, the UK, is instructive, showing media costs in Ireland generally to be above those available in that market.

Whilst these figures may appear attractive from a relativist perspective they are unlikely to provide much solace to domestic-focused Irish marketers who have witnessed substantial media inflation in recent years. The level of media inflation which has affected the Irish media market is indicated in Table 15.7.

TABLE 15.7: FIVE-YEAR INDEX OF IRISH MEDIA COSTS

Year	Consumer Price Index*	RTE TV	RTE Radio 1	2FM	Cinema
1989	100.0	100	100	100	100
1990	101.7	105	114	135	127
1991	105.0	138	123	147	120
1992	108.2	160	154	166	124
1993	109.8	161	147	175	122
	Sunday	Mornings	Evenings	Regional	Magazines
1989	100	100	100	100	100
1990	111	112	105	107	107
1991	118	115	125	109	130
1992	121	124	138	134	125
1993	125	132	136	132	127

*   Annual averages.

Source: McConnells, Media Facts, 1994.

Media inflation associated with RTE TV can be attributed to the Broadcasting Act introduced in 1990. This Act, which had the objective of forcing the placing of advertising in other media, particularly the developing local radio sector, through the capping of RTE revenue, had the effect of boosting the advertising revenue to spill-over media such as UTV and Channel Four and, more importantly for Irish advertisers, driving up media rates (AAI, 1992; DKM, 1991; DKM, 1992). Whilst the rate of inflation in television has been minimal between 1992 and 1993, the reality is that, over the period 1989–93 in the case of broadcast media, advertisers have been facing media costs between six and eight times the consumer price index.

CHANGES IN THE SUPPLY/PRODUCTION INDUSTRY

As a result of the fusion of various pressures such as technological advance, increased consumer sophistication, and the changing regulatory environment, as well as increasing client pressure for value, the supply/production industry which services marketing communications is the subject of fundamental adjustment. A number of specific changes can be identified.

The Growth of Specialist Agencies

An inevitable consequence of the shift in expenditure to below-the-line is the increased reliance by advertisers on the services of specialist agencies. As such, the communications industry is now serviced by specialist agencies in the fields of direct marketing, promotions, and sponsorship amongst others. While traditional agencies have attempted to minimise the income loss by either establishing or taking over specialist service agencies, the net outcome is increased servicing of client needs by specialist agencies, either as independents or advertising agency subsidiaries.

The Growth of Media Specialists

Whilst the expansion/contraction of services has long been a feature of the history of advertising agencies worldwide, oscillating from the full-service/one-stop-shop to the "hot shop" concentration on core advertising, one of the most notable trends in recent times has been the emergence of the media specialist, who increasingly has taken on one of the key services offered by traditional advertising agencies.

Advertisers, driven by a demand for efficiency in expenditure, are increasingly utilising the services of media specialists to place advertising created by the traditional agency. This emerging trend is more evident in the case of the multinational brands wherein the advertising is often produced in one market — the US, for example — and then circulated for media placement in each national market, either through an international media buying specialist, or its local equivalent. In Western Europe in 1990 it was estimated that 34 per cent of media buying was handled by media specialist companies — that is, those not integrated into the team at a full-service agency. Media specialists can be of three types:

(1) Genuinely independent specialist companies such as Carat International.
(2) Agency-owned media "dependants", such as Zenith and Initiative, owned by Saatchi and Lintas respectively.
(3) Media buying clubs such as the Media Partnership in the UK which buys on behalf of several traditional agencies such as JWT, Ogilvy and Mather, BBDO, and DDB.

The relative shares of media buying by both media specialists and traditional agencies is shown in Table 15.8.

TABLE 15.8: MARKET SHARE OF MEDIA SPECIALISTS, 1990

Country	Specialists %	Clubs %	Agencies/Others %
Austria	8	19	73
Belgium	13	36	51
Denmark	17	—	83
Finland	37	—	63
France	40	32	28
Germany	20	4	76
Greece	2	40	58
Italy	27	12	61
Netherlands	25	17	58
Norway	42	—	58
Portugal	24	39	37
Spain	72	19	9
Sweden	60	—	40
Switzerland	4	6	90
UK	30	—	70
Total	34	13	53

* Including agency owned and independents.

Source: Green, Andrew (1992), "Death of the full-service ad agency", *Admap*, January, 1992, p. 22.

The penetration of media specialists in the Irish market is apparent from a recent IAPI study which indicates that 16 per cent of major Irish advertisers place their media buying with a media independent, compared to 3 per cent five years earlier (IAPI, 1994).

The Traditional Advertising Agency

While advertising agencies have long been faced with changing environmental conditions, the variety of factors and the speed of change currently impacting on the advertising industry have serious consequences for the traditional advertising agency. Squeezed between value-seeking, marketing-oriented clients, better educated and more sophisticated consumers, and a variety of niche competitors offering specialist services, the traditional advertising agency is reassessing its position in the marketing communications industry.

The challenge for the traditional advertising agency is to redefine its role in an increasingly changing industry. The extent of its dilemma is obvious. Media advertising, the preserve of the traditional agency, is falling as a percentage of all marketing communications expenditure. In 1991, expenditure on media advertising in the UK accounted for 1.47 per cent of gross domestic product (GDP), its lowest level since 1985 (Briggs, 1993). Between 1987 and 1992 media advertising rose by five-year historical growth of 6.5 per cent, while the specialist activities of public relations and direct marketing rose by 12 per cent and 11.2 per cent respectively (Briggs, 1993). With media independents often undertaking the placement of advertising at a commission level of 2–3 per cent, traditional full-service agencies are being undercut in this aspect of service. The result is declining agency profitability with the Institute of Practitioners in Advertising (IPA) in the UK indicating that industry net profit (before interest) fell from 2.2 per cent in 1988, to 1.9 per cent in 1989, and to 1.55 per cent in 1990.

Furthermore, there is evidence that agency/client relationships are increasingly of shorter duration. Media International estimates that 10 years ago 50 per cent of major accounts stayed with the agency for 10 years or more. Today that percentage is less than 25 per cent (Briggs, 1993). A recent IAPI survey of major advertisers reported that 28 per cent of respondents were unlikely to stay with a full-service agency, while a further 13 per cent were not sure (IAPI, 1994).

Faced with an increasingly turbulent marketplace the traditional full-service agency must undergo fundamental adjustment in order to survive (Byles, 1992; Feldwick, 1992). The onus is now on the traditional agency to move from a product orientation to being more customer responsive — in effect to introduce the values sought by clients such as flexibility, speed, and accountability allied to the ability and willingness to suggest solutions outside the agency's traditional area of service (*Marketing*, 1994). Given the importance of delivering on these objectives in order to survive, the organisational focus is on "re-engineering" the agency by introducing project managers in a less hierarchical structure with an emphasis on out-sourcing the requisite talents. A recent commentary on advertising had this to suggest concerning the traditional agency:

> To survive in the next decade, a new breed of agency will have to emerge. The new agency will be half the size of the old agency, more flexible and with the ability and desire to work across twice as many areas and be more cost-efficient. Agencies will need to change their attitude, become more client focused and learn to empathise with client needs. (Cawley Nea Ltd., 1993)

Production Costs

While technological advance has benefited many aspects of advertising creation such as computer-aided design, film and television production, as well as all aspects of press advertising, the reality is that the production costs of advertising are escalating. In fact, in many economies they are outstripping the previously discussed media rates. In the UK market, media rates in press display advertising increased by 24 per cent between 1981 and 1991, while production costs increased by 59 per cent. This escalation is even more marked in the case of television where advertising production costs increased by 97 per cent over the decade to 1991 against increased media costs of 55 per cent over the period (Henry, 1993). Increased production costs are a major concern for indigenous Irish advertisers whose advertising costs must be allocated over smaller audience numbers relative to their counterparts in other European and international markets, who allocate production costs over much larger audiences.

Globalisation

As client companies have altered their focus from individual markets to contemplate the global consumer, the support industry that is communications has similarly felt the need to readjust. This is evident in the development of global advertising agencies which now are selected to service clients on an all-market basis (Turnbull and Doherty-Wilson, 1990). It follows from this development that campaigns are planned with a global consumer in mind in terms of creative advertising work and media planning, as well as the range of subsidiary services.

In this regard, Irish advertisers increasingly tend to focus beyond the Republic of Ireland market with 34 per cent of all major advertisers having an all-Ireland (i.e., Republic of Ireland plus Northern Ireland) focus to their advertising, compared to five years ago (IAPI, 1994). Forty-four per cent of major Irish advertisers expect that, by 1999, their campaign focus will be on an all-Ireland basis, while 41 per cent expect their campaign to have a joint British and Irish focus (IAPI, 1994).

CHANGES IN THE AUDIENCE

The audience, which is the fulcrum of all marketing communications activity, is changing in several key ways.

Audience Control of Media

Increasingly, technology is delivering greater control of the media to the audience. While increased media opportunities afford the consumer greater choice, other developments also empower the audience. In the case of televisions, video recording machines (VCRs) enable the consumer to decide what programmes will be seen and the time of viewing, with in-built facilities to "zip" advertising. In 1988, VCR penetration in Ireland was 26 per cent of households while multi-set penetration was 16 per cent. By 1993, VCR penetration had increased to 58 per cent with multi-set penetration increasing to 29 per cent (Harper, 1994). In a similar manner, the advent of remote control units has led to greater audience control of the broadcast media, with penetration of units in Irish homes increasing 5 per cent in 1981 to 56 per cent in 1991 (Irish Tam Establishment Survey, 1992).

The advent of the "super-highway", which uses the in-home personal computer as a central data point will further empower consumers who can already access the *Irish Times* via E-mail, and whom, it is suggested, will soon be able to determine their preferred evenings viewing, bypassing the offerings of the local broadcast station, cinema, and video outlet. The net result of these changes is the surrender of control of media to the audience, who will then decide to download the output of these media on their terms, and not that of the media owner.

Increased Audience Sophistication

While early theories of advertising effects tended to view the audience as "passive palsies" (Bauer, 1971), who would succumb to persuasion through repetition of communication, modern advertising theory tends to regard the consumer in a more positive light, as educated, confident, and mature (King, 1991). In effect it is now fashionable to refer to the "sophisticated consumer" as an integral part of the communications process (Lannon and Cooper, 1983). Much of modern advertising tends to presume an intelligent, sophisticated audience as a party to the communication process — a consumer complete with predispositions, intellectual, as well as financial, who is advertising literate and plays an active, rather than a passive or submissive role in modern communications. This recognition has had a dramatic effect on the creation of modern advertising. A particularly important section of the audience is the youth market who are the recipients of volumes of commercial messages unparalleled in previous generations. One marketing consultant specialising in this market sector suggests that:

> People under 25 feel disenfranchised by politics, but empowered by consumer choice. They are more sussed, more ad literate, marketing literate, and they know more about brands, they have more information. Today's teens are well versed in participating in the commercial world. Probably their only area of power is as a consumer. (From Benson and Armstrong, 1994)

In a similar vein, research conducted in the UK by J. Walter Thomson, the Henley Research Centre, and Millward Brown has led to the description of the 1990s consumer as the "thoughtful butterfly" (*Marketing Week*, 1993). This consumer is more sceptical and thoughtful about the choice of brand, willing to consider the merits of own label alternatives, and concerned with quality and benefits other than mere badge status. From a communications point of view, the thoughtful butterfly represents a more difficult target. Being literate, sceptical and even dissatisfied about advertising techniques, this consumer can no longer be relied upon to absorb the mass media used to deliver the brand message. Such consumers manifest less stability in absorbing marketing output, being apt to switch between many modes of purchasing and consumption behaviour inside short periods, thereby bringing chaos to attempts to reach markets defined using traditional segmentation approaches.

Audience Fragmentation

Audience fragmentation represents one of the inevitable consequences of media proliferation as audience sizes diminish with increased media opportunities. Research conducted into the effects of television station proliferation (Buck, 1989) shows that there is a threshold point beyond which greater channel choice does not lead to more viewing. In effect, the total pool of audience viewing tends to remain stable, with newer channels cannibalising audience from existing stations. Between 1970 and 1989 the share of audience held by the three major US networks has fallen from 90 per cent to almost 60 per cent, with the share of audience held by cable networks increasing from 3 per cent to 22 per cent over the period.

As the situation pertaining in the US market unfolds in European broadcasting, there is likely to be a move from conventional broadcasting to *narrowcasting*, with both methods of access to audiences competing side by side over time for audiences which will increasingly exhibit loyalty to programmes and life-style reflections, rather than stations *per se*.

While this may result in less wastage in targeting more tightly defined audiences, the major side effect is higher costs for diminished audiences. A McKinsey report (1992) shows that the average cost of a prime-time spot in the US market had risen four-fold between 1970 and 1990, while average ratings for shows had fallen by 20 per cent. Advertisers in that market had to increase advertising at nearly twice the rate of inflation to maintain a given level of audience impact.

SUMMARY

Marketing communications is currently undergoing fundamental change in all aspects of this industry. Changes in the media have led to a diversity of access routes to targeted consumers, with advertisers increasingly turning to non-media advertising, because of the escalating cost of both producing and placing traditional media advertising. Consumers of advertising are now perceived as better educated and more mature than previous generations. This sophisticated consumer has led to increased reliance on research as the basis for strategy development in both marketing and advertising. Audiences are increasingly fragmented, capable of being reached more cost-effectively through specialist media in an environment which is increasingly cluttered.

Today's marketers are better informed, and increasingly manage their marketing communications actively rather than relying on their agency to handle this activity on their behalf. Driven by corporate desire for increased profitability, modern advertisers are increasingly demanding of the agencies operating on their behalf. This has had major ramifications for the traditional agency which, faced with competition from highly efficient specialist agencies and media independents, is experiencing a breakdown in traditional methods of remuneration, allied to demands for greater accountability and quality in the service provided.

REFERENCES

Advertising Association of Ireland (1992): *Report and Review*, Dublin: Advertising Association of Ireland.

Antenna Report on Broadcasting (1993): London: Nomad Productions.

Audit Bureau of Circulation (1993): *Consumer Press Circulation Review*, Hertfordshire: Audit Bureay of Circulation.

Bauer, R.A. (1971): "Games Profile and Audience Play", in *Innovative Behaviour and Communication*, London:Holt, Rinehart, and Winston.

Benson, R. and Armstrong, S. (1994): "These People Know What You Want", *The Face*, July: 52–7.

Briggs, M. (1993): "Why Agencies Must Change", *Admap*, 28(1): 20–22.

Buck, S. (1989): *The Future for Old and New Television Channels in the UK, Some Clues from Around the World*, London: AGB Research.

Buckley, D. (1980): "Who Pays the Piper?", *Practice Review*, Spring: 10–14.

Byles, D. (1992): "Full-Service Agencies Effectiveness and Evaluation", *Admap*, 27(5): 35–7.

Cawley Nea Ltd. (1993): *The New Order in Irish Advertising*, Dublin: Cawley Nea Ltd..
DKM Ltd. (1991): *Economic Impact of the Broadcast Act, 1990*, Dublin: DKM.
DKM Ltd. (1992): *Issues in Irish Broadcast Policy*, August, Dublin: DKM.
Donnelley Marketing Inc. (1992): *Fourteenth Annual Survey of Promotional Practices*, New York: Donnelly Marketing.
Feldwick, P. (1992): "Full-Service Agencies — Coherence and Fragmentation", *Admap*, 27(5): 37–9.
Green, A. (1992): "Death of the Full-Service Ad Agency", *Admap*, 27(1): 21–4.
Harper, T. (1994): "The Changeable Irish TV Audience", *Admap*, 29(4) 40–42.
Hayden, F. (1994): Director, Assoication of Advertisers in Ireland (AAI), Personal Discussion, August.
Henry, H. (1993): "How Production Costs have Outstripped Media Rates", *Admap*, 28(1): 15–8.
IAPI (Institute of Advertising Practitioners in Ireland) (1994): *A View from the Top*, Address at IAPI Conference, April, Dublin: Behaviour and Attitudes.
Irish Tam Establishment Surveys (1992): Dublin: AGB/TAM.
ISL Marketing (1992): *Annual Estimates of Sponsorship Markets*, London: ISL Marketing.
Lannon, J, and Cooper, P. (1983): "Humanistic Advertising — A Holistic Cultural Perspective", *International Journal of Advertising*, 2(2): 195–213.
Lees, C. and Rayment, T. (1990): "Shade Wars: How Big Money Goes Riding on a Film Star's Nose", *The Sunday Times*, 22 July: 5.
Magazine News (1994a): "Datafile", February (25): 26–7.
Magazine News (1994b): "Datafile", April (26): 10–11..
Marketing (1994): "Trouble in Adland, Part I", 5(4): 18–21.
Marketing Development Programme (1993): *A Report on the Extent and Trends of Non Media Advertising in Ireland*, Dublin:UCD.
Marketing Society of Ireland, (1994): *Perspectives*, June, 1(2): 1.
McMurdo, L. (1993): "Chasing Butterflies", *Marketing Week*, 21 May: 28–31.
Micklethwait, J. (1990): "Assault on the Heartland — The Fight for Marketing Budgets in America" in "Survey of the Advertising Industry", *The Economist,* 9 June: 3.

Mintel (1993): *Special Report on Sponsorship*, London: Mintel.

Mittal, B. (1994): "Public Assessment of TV Advertising: Faint Praise and Harsh Criticism", *Journal of Advertising Research*, 34(1): 35–53.

Perry, J. (1994): "European Lessons about TV's Future", *Admap*, 29(6): 18–23.

Pollay, R.W. and Mittal, B. (1993): "Here's the Beef: Factors, Determinants, and Segments in Consumer Criticism of Advertising", *Journal of Marketing*, 57(3) 99–114.

Shergill, S. (1993): "The Changing US Media and Marketing Environment: Implications for Media Advertising Expenditures in the 1990s", *International Journal of Advertising*, 12(2): 95–115.

Snowden, S. (1992): "The 1992 Marketing and Communications Map", *Admap,* 27(10): 50–51.

SRI (Sponsorship Research International) (1994): *Annual Estimates of Sponsorship Expenditure*, London: Sponsorship Research International.

Steinberg, S. (1994): "Travels on the Net", *Technology Review*, 97(5): 20–31.

Swain, G. (1990): "Cue the Coke", *Daily Mirror*, June, 16–7.

Turnbull, P. and Doherty-Wilson, L. (1990): "The Internationalisation of the Advertising Industry", *European Journal of Marketing*, 24(1): 7–15.

16
Corporate Identity: A Strategic Marketing Issue[*]

Kathryn Stewart

INTRODUCTION

Corporate identity has grown in importance during the 1980s. This is illustrated by the rate of growth of the design industry in the United Kingdom: during the five years to 1988 the annual growth rate is reckoned to have been in the region of 22–30 per cent (Croft, 1990). Much of the revenue of these companies is derived from the design of corporate identities. Although corporate identity is obviously of concern to marketing practitioners, a review of current marketing texts and journal papers would suggest that academics are not devoting to it any degree of attention. Most mainstream marketing texts mention corporate identity only as an item on the communications mix checklist. Southgate (1990) suggests that the market research industry has been similarly remiss in its less than sophisticated approach to researching design. Olins (1989), one of the design industry's gurus, argues that corporate identity's importance has to do with its symbolic values. He is at a loss to explain why the power of symbolism should be "so little detailed and so little understood".

This paper attempts to provide some understanding as to what corporate identity is and to explain its relationship with corporate image. It argues that corporate identity is a strategic issue and that it has a powerful role to play in financial services marketing. A case example illustrates how one bank has grasped the corporate identity nettle.

---

[*] This paper first appeared in *International Journal of Bank Marketing*, Vol. 9 No. 1.

CORPORATE IDENTITY: TOWARDS AN UNDERSTANDING

Kennedy (1977) noted the emergence of questioning the "distinction between a company's visual identity — the letter headings, corporate symbol, and all the forms which identify the organisation visually — and the total corporate image". Indeed, the terms "corporate image" and "corporate identity" do appear to be used interchangeably. Abratt (1989) recommends clarification of three concepts: corporate personality, identity and image. The corporate image management process which he models (Figure 16.1) attempts to do this.

FIGURE 16.1: THE CORPORATE IMAGE MANAGEMENT PROCESS

Corporate Personality	Corporate Identity	Corporate Image	
Corporate Philosophy ↓ Core Values Corporate Culture ↓ Strategic Management ↓ Corporate Mission ↓ Business Objectives ↓ Strategy Formulation ↓ Strategy Implementation	Organisation's Communication Objectives and "Game Plan" Functional Communication Objectives Development of Structures and Systems	IMAGE INTERFACE	ORGANISATIONS PUBLICS
			Customers Government Bankers Influential Groups General Public The Media The Trade Internal
↑_____	Feedback	_____	

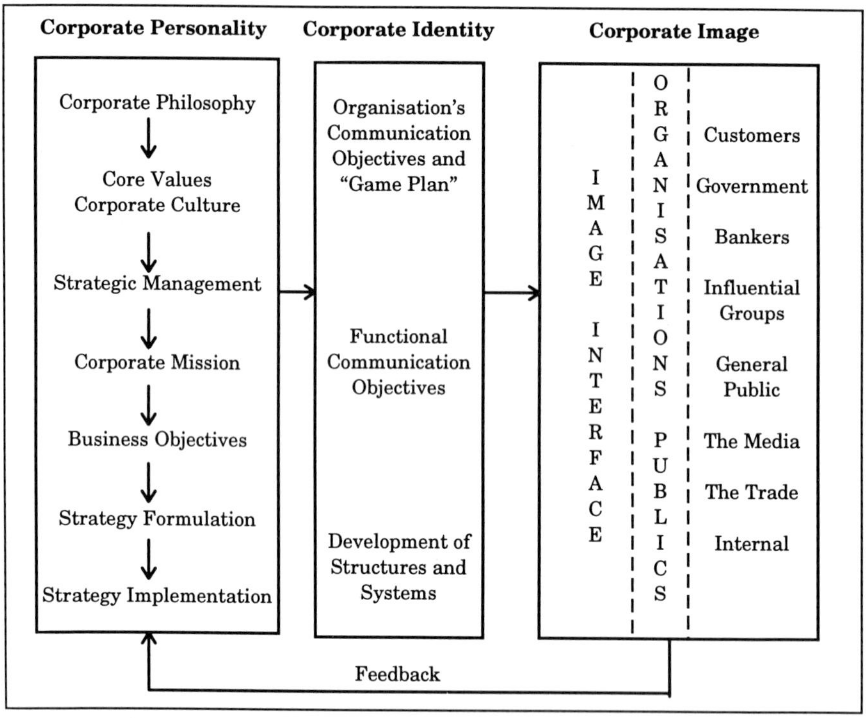

Source: Abratt, R. (1989).

He asserts:

> Every company has a personality, which is defined as the sum total of the characteristics of the organisation. These characteristics — behavioural and intellectual — serve to distinguish one organisation from another. This personality is projected by means of

conscious cues which constitute an identity. The overall impression formed by these cues in the minds of audiences constitutes an image.....

Most writers on corporate identity describe it in terms of cues, as will be shown throughout the paper. Olins (1989) views corporate identity as being affirmed by a company's products, buildings, communications materials and by how the organisation behaves. It is expressed by the names, symbols, logos, colours and rites of passage which the organisation uses to distinguish itself, its branded products and constituent companies. These expressions, Olins states, "serve the same purpose as religious symbolism, chivalric heraldry or national flags and symbols: they encapsulate and make vivid a collective sense of belonging and purpose. At another level, they represent consistent standards of quality and therefore, encourage consumer loyalty".

Corporate image is a complex construct which develops on the basis of our experiences, whether direct or indirect, with an organisation. Some of those experiences are of the organisation's corporate identity. Howcroft and Lavis (1986) see corporate image as a function of the following interdependent levels: corporate identity, public relations, advertising, design of distribution and delivery systems and product features. In relation to the banks, Sinkula and Lawtor (1987) conclude that image is made of four constructs. These are traditional service, convenience, competence and visibility. Anspach (1983) helps to provide the point of distinction between corporate identity and image. He describes corporate identity as the total presentation of the organisation. Presentation uses many media and the resulting image is cumulative.

Gray and Smelzer (1985) provide a taxonomy of the potential means of corporate image communication. Its principle components are nomenclature, formal statements, organisation, imagery and graphics, permanent media and promotional media. It is this taxonomy which is employed in the case study which concludes this paper.

It can be concluded that corporate identity and corporate image are closely bound together. Identity, as projected by the organisation, contributes to the shaping of people's perceptions such that an image of the organisation is formed.

Retail banking may illustrate the distinction between corporate identity and corporate image.

FINANCIAL SERVICES EXAMPLES

Slogans

Now, what can we do for you?   Bank of Ireland.
The listening bank   Midland Bank.
The friendly bank   National Westminster Bank.

Branch Design

Traditional: teller windows, counters, queuing systems dominate.
Contemporary: open-plan, less screens and shutters, plants, seated waiting areas.

Logos and Symbols

Three arrows: National Westminster Bank.
Griffin: Midland Bank.
Black horse: Lloyds Bank.

These projections of identity seek to shape an image, in the minds of financial services customers, of customer-oriented businesses, rather than that of patronising institutions. Smith and Harbisher's (1989) research suggests, however, that banks are still not considered to be as approachable, but are seen to be more efficient and businesslike than building societies.

Abratt's (1989) model illustrates how corporate identity relates to corporate image.

CORPORATE IDENTITY: THE RATIONALE

The debate regarding the importance of corporate image and identity as management tools (Kennedy, 1977) would seem to be resolved. They are part of the strategy agenda, to be managed and designed to competitive advantage. Gray and Smelzer, (1985) cite examples of businesses whose images were an inaccurate representation of the reality. The consequences can be summarised as below-par performance. In 1987 they developed the notion of corporate image having strategic import. They argued that

> a well-conceived corporate image programme can provide a company with the kind of individuality necessary to prosper in today's competitive environment. A positive image accomplishes this by communicating the company's unique best qualities to its various

Corporate Identity: A Strategic Marketing Issue

publics. The programme should also reflect the particular mission and strategies of each company.

If corporate image is, in part, the child of corporate identity, then the purpose of corporate image promotion must be examined. Kennedy (1977) rightly asserts that "it is not sufficient to say that a good image is a valuable asset for any company to have". Her literature review reveals 14 objectives for promoting corporate image. In general, these relate to encouraging favourable behaviour towards an organisation by its publics.

The notion that organisations operate in an environment which is composed of a variety of actors or publics is well established in the marketing and management literature (see, for example, Kotler, 1988). In many respects the organisation's prosperity lies with these publics. This is apparent when one considers their composition. Typically, companies are concerned with customers, distributors and retailers, financial analysts, stockholders, government, the general public, special interest groups and employees. The impact that each may have varies in direction and force. Similarly, the perception that each of these groups has of an organisation may vary. What is of interest, for example. to shareholders is not automatically of interest to customers.

Communications may be targeted to particular groups. In-house magazines are designed for the employee public, annual reports for the financial publics, public relations and sponsorship for the general and consumer publics, and so on.

Despite targeting, non-targeted publics will also have access to many of these communications. This implies that consistency of message should concern the organisation. Gray and Smelzer (1985) argue that failure to achieve consistency and reinforcement of messages can result in a blurred or negative image. Thus, while each public has different communication needs, there is an underlying requirement for consistency. This has obvious implications for corporate identity. Howcroft and Lavis (1986) argue that without the signal of corporate identity there is nothing for either staff or customers to respond to in a coherent way. Presumably the coherence of the response is related to the coherence of the message.

A question arises as to the extent to which corporate identity can be targeted. At one end of the spectrum is the same name, symbol, message and media for all audiences; at the other end is product-market related name, symbols, messages and media. Gray and Smelzer (1987) offer four approaches to the targeting question. The "single entity" approach views the product and the entire corporation as one and the same. The opposite relationship is brand dominance, with mixed and equal dominance falling in between. Whichever option is appropriate, and this is a function of corporate structure and style (Olins, 1989), the consistency and coherence criteria still hold.

The underlying, and often implicit, rationale for corporate image and identity is that being familiar with an organisation leads to a more favourable disposition towards it. This logic is upheld by research. Worcester (1986) found an almost perfect correlation "between how well a company is known and how favourably it is regarded". The link between favourability and behaviour is not so straightforward. Worcester (1986) found that the actions people take with respect to a company depend on far more than whether or not they like or dislike the company. He also notes, however, that where the facts of the situation contradict the image, it is the company which suffers the consequences.

Given that all organisations project an identity, whether managed or not, the bottom line is that a company should not confuse or deter its audiences. In addition, those audiences should be clear about what the organisation does and its values. After that, a well-managed programme may relate the organisation to the audiences, facilitate differentiation, positioning, attraction and retention of customers, employees, shareholders and so on.

CORPORATE IDENTITY DEVELOPMENT PROCESS

The importance of corporate identity means that it warrants attention during the strategic planning process. Organisations should formulate answers to questions such as that posed by Levitt (1960) — what business are we in? The outcome of the process is that the organisation has a clear mission for its business, its objectives and strategies. These are the touchstones for tactical decisions.

The issue addressed here is how corporate identity decisions are incorporated within the planning framework. Topalian (1984) asserts that their place is within the strategic planning process: "to communicate effectively with a genuine and individual voice, there has to be a clear understanding within organisations as to what they are and what they stand for".

Likewise, Abratt (1989) affirms that corporate identity decisions should be an integral part of the strategic process. Anspach's (1983) approach suggests that once the major strategic decisions have been made, identity should be examined to determine whether there is need for a change. He provides a list of eight signals which occasion identity change. These are rapid growth, new geographic markets, new products, mergers and acquisitions, changing product mix, seeking larger market share, confusing key audiences in terms of understanding the organisation or making other competitive moves. Both Anspach's and Abratt's frameworks provide the structure for developing corporate identity.

CORPORATE IDENTITY IN THE FINANCIAL SERVICES SECTOR

The financial services sector demonstrates differences in the marketing of services. The importance of corporate identity has already been stressed. It has further consequences in service industries. This arises because of the nature of services and the characteristics which distinguish them from goods. Bateson (1989) notes that while existing concepts and methods are applicable to services as well as goods, there may be problems in their application. He suggests that this is a difference of degree or level.

This is illustrated in the communications mix of service companies. Rathmell (1974) notes that service promotion differs from promotion of goods, primarily in terms of the relative importance assigned in the total marketing programme and in the media mix. This difference in emphasis is corroborated by Zeithaml et al. (1989). Their research found that service firms emphasise the usage of personal selling and image: "overall, (service) firms appear to emphasise designing facilities to achieve specific marketing or image objectives, dressing customer contact personnel in a certain way, and gearing much of their marketing to projecting a specific company image".

Rushton and Carson (1985) show that service intangibility has implications for customers, product-benefit marketing and marketing techniques and practices. They argue that since a service does not have an appearance, there is a need to create an appropriate provider image. The service encounter is one location where image is formed, reaffirmed or adapted. Given that it is much more cost-effective to retain, rather than create, customers, (Clutterbuck, 1989 and Liswood, 1989), management of this encounter is a critical marketing task (Czepiel et al., 1985). The role of the service employee in this context is much enhanced and internal marketing therefore is appropriate (Berry, 1989). Corporate identity programmes can be seen as integral to both customer retention and internal marketing.

It has been further contended that financial services companies also have additional special characteristics which influence their approach to marketing. McIvor and Naylor (1980) assert that the marketing style of a financial services organisation can never be as uninhibited as that of a manufacturer of fast-moving packaged goods. The reason for this inhibition is the fiduciary responsibility imposed on the industry. In a similar vein, Zavoos (1989) cautions that the vital role of customer confidence in the financial services industry must be respected.

Many changes have occurred over this past decade in the environment of financial services organisations. These have made the use of marketing necessary in an industry which had been slow to adopt a marketing orientation, Hooley and Mann (1988) conclude that "financial institutions have moved substantially towards the adoption of a marketing orientation in the last five years; there is, however, some way to go".

In this instance, one aspect of marketing — corporate identity — is the focus. It is somewhat disappointing that in the texts available on financial services marketing, little attention is paid to this issue. One exception is *Retail Banking: The New Revolution in Structure and Strategy* by Howcroft and Lavis (1986). One chapter, albeit brief, is devoted to image issues. The authors' research finds that an emotional gulf exists between customers and banks which embodied British qualities of security, probity, reliability and coldness: virtues which were deemed critical to the functioning of a financial system were damaging in many other respects.

Further analysis revealed that banks were being used as providers of money transmission services, rather than as unique suppliers of financial packages. In addition, bank services were perceived as difficult to use. Howcroft and Lavis (1986) conclude that communication is the key to overcoming the impersonality, authoritarianism, arrogance and patronising effect of the banks. With respect to using image to achieve competitive differentiation, they suggest that the banks have failed. Likewise, Morello's (1988) research shows that while Dutch banks are seen as positive institutions they all could enhance the effectiveness of their understanding of image formation. Watkins and Wright (1986) go further and suggest that developing a suitable corporate image is a prerequisite for success in the personal financial services market. Smith and Harbisher (1989) investigated the importance of corporate image in financial services. Although using a limited sample, they found that building societies and banks are attempting to project their identities. The research also suggests that, so far, this projection of identify has failed to create distinct corporate images in consumers' minds.

Corporate identity programmes are not, however, a "new product" for banks. Sullivan (1981) reports that in the US, programmes became popular in the late 1960s. He predicted that corporate identity programmes would again have an emphasised role, with the rise in mergers and acquisitions and the consequent need for banks to develop a consistent image for their disparate entities.

Olins (1989) shows how banks, from as early as the 1920s and 1930s, used architecture, graphics and related materials to try to develop an image which was strong, rich, responsible and conservative. When their environment began to change, the banks went through a period of uncertainty with regard to style. The result was the development of "me-too" or generically styled banks.

It is clear then, that the banks have work to do. If banks are organisations different from those of a few years ago, then their identities, and therefore their images, need to reflect this new reality. In the following example, Allied Irish Banks plc, illustrates how one bank/financial services organisation has grasped the corporate identity opportunity.

ALLIED IRISH BANKS: 1966–90

Allied Irish Banks Ltd was formed in 1966 by the merger of three Irish banks, The Munster and Leinster Bank, The Provincial Bank of Ireland and The Royal Bank of Ireland. It became a public limited company (plc) in 1980. The figures in Table 16.1 illustrate its growth.

TABLE 16.1: BANK GROWTH

	1964	1990
Assets	IR£270 million	IR£16 billion
Employees	2,600	14,000
Branches	430	650

Growth has arisen with new geographic markets (Britain and the USA), but also through new product markets. A range of companies exist under the parenthood of Allied Irish Banks plc, providing different financial services to different markets.

By the late 1980s, Allied Irish Banks plc had surpassed the humble origins to which its name referred. Likewise, it had also moved with the changing environment which has already been discussed. This led the company to take stock of who it was and where it was going — that is, to the strategic planning process. In 1987 the company embarked on a programme which it entitled "Marketing Action Programme". This involved a marketing audit, facilitated by external consultants but emphasising the participation of staff at all levels in the company. This identified areas where the organisation needed to change. The new business mission emerged. It reads:

> Value and service are at the heart of our business. We aim to provide real value to every one of our customers and to deliver the highest standards of service in banking and financial services.

Delivery of service remains the thrust, and the company recognises its Irish base. However, it now has an international focus, and this must be reflected in its operations, structure and style.

Corporate Identity 1966–89

With that in mind, Allied Irish Banks plc decided in 1989 to examine its corporate identity, and the services of a specialist consultancy, Wolff Olins, were retained. Marketing research revealed certain problems with the corporate identity. These can be analysed using part of the taxonomy of corporate identity provided by Gray and Smelzer (1985):

Nomenclature. The name "Allied Irish Banks plc" was meaningful to the personal markets, especially in Ireland, though it was often abbreviated to AIB. In the non-Irish personal market it implied that it was first and foremost an Irish bank. This denied its international focus and the many other financial services it provided. In the capital markets, the name did not yield a cohesive identity. Thus, each subsidiary company was seen as a completely separate entity. Although each subsidiary's name was prefixed by "Allied Irish", these titles did not give the impression of a cohesive group of subsidiary companies.

Organisation. The lack of cohesive identity meant that staff in one subsidiary did not identify with those in another.

Imagery and graphics. A number of inadequacies were found with the existing imagery and graphics. The corporate logo was originally designed to reflect the coming together of the three banks. It was based on a roundel with three spokes whose hub encapsulated the letter "A". The meaningfulness of this was lost with the passage of over 20 years since the merger. It was also unfortunate that the logo bore a remarkable similarity to the one used by Mercedes Benz. Blue was the dominant colour and this did not provide distinctiveness in an industry where blue is *de rigueuer*.

Permanent media. All signs, stationery, forms and business cards were uniformly branded with the three-spoked roundel. "Allied Irish Bank" also featured heavily. Branch facilities adhered to this uniformity.

Promotional media. All advertising copy was concluded with "Allied Irish Banks: You bring out the best in us". Since undertaking the marketing action programme, advertising has been emphasising the new direction and the commitment to the provision of quality service to customers. Typical copy read:

> At Allied Irish Bank, we have chosen a new direction. We see our goal clearly: we intend to be the best. But ambition alone is not enough. We must provide our management and staff with the skills, systems and supports necessary to reach this goal. The beginning of this process was the simple recognition that our customers are the most important people in our organisation and to fully satisfy their needs, nothing less than the best will do.

The company was signalling to its publics that it was changing. The examination of its corporate identity was a part of that change.

Overall, the old identity was found to have served its purpose when the message to be communicated was that the company was, indeed, an Allied Irish Bank. The decision, therefore, was taken that the company required a new identity.

Allied Irish Banks plc:
Corporate Identity Development Process

A corporate identity project team and steering committee were established, composed of staff from throughout the organisation. They, along with the consultants, were charged with creating an identity which reflected changes in shape, structure and philosophy. At the same time it also needed to convey the cohesion of the organisation and its customer friendliness, reflect its Irish heritage and be recognisable. These messages emanated directly from the marketing action programme.

Draft logos were designed and researched with customers and staff. Once a choice was made, the process was started of producing some 50 different print items, communicating with staff and preparing for a launch. The company chose to have a high-profile launch before all materials were prepared. It was anticipated that implementation would take two years to complete: the momentum of the project, therefore, was not dissipated, nor was confidentiality breached.

On 8 January 1990 the new identity was unveiled to the public, by a live telecast on the national television station, RTE. Staff were informed of the new identity one week before the public launch and given watches, featuring the new logo, to commemorate the event. Promotional literature was widely distributed to increase awareness and understanding of the new identity.

Using some components from Gray and Smelzer's (1985) taxonomy, the new identity can be described:

Nomenclature. The new company name is AIB Group, "AIB" prefixes the specialist areas of business, AIB Bank, AIB Investment Managers, AIB Group Treasury and so on. The one exception to this is the wholly owned First Maryland Bancorp which keeps its name, simply because it remains meaningful in that marketplace.

Imagery and graphics. The corporate symbol is inspired by one of the earliest known Celtic images of the Ark. The new colours are purple, gold, green and red. AIB states:

> The Ark is a symbol of our heritage, of security, and of the many communities we serve. Our new corporate colours express the warmth and friendliness of the Irish which is an integral part of AIB's character. These three elements — name, symbol and colour — sit within the framework of an overall style which expresses how we wish to serve and communicate with all our customers, with clarity, warmth and professionalism.

Permanent media. All documents and signs were redesigned to express the new identity. Corporate identity guidelines were to be applied to the interior design of all aspects of branch merchandising and furnishing. Staff uniforms were redesigned.

Promotional media. All promotional media incorporates the new identity. At the time of writing, the copy still retains the slogan "you bring out the best in us". Whether this changes or not is an advertising, rather than corporate identity, decision.

The cost of these changes is in the region of £1 million sterling. Such an investment requires sound management. To this end, the impact of the new identity is being researched — with two key groups, staff and customers. AIB Group managed to arouse much publicity for the new corporate identity. This was not all favourable. Irish newspapers published numerous letters from readers angry that a non-Irish design company was employed. AIB Group's response was that it is no longer a purely Irish company. This illustrates a difference in perception, ironically one which the new identity seeks to overcome.

AIB Group continues to monitor the impact of the new identity. The new image to which it aspires will take time to develop in the minds of the various publics. The company also perceives the new identity to be an integral part of something larger. Advertising copy reflects this: "At AIB, we've been changing. We've changed the way we look. The way we think. How we react. How we respond."

SUMMARY AND CONCLUSIONS

Corporate identity is of strategic marketing importance. It is one of the key dimensions used to construct image in people's minds. Image, in turn, may contribute to decisions about whether or not to do business with a company. Corporate identity must reflect organisational reality. If it does not, a negative image results. In services marketing, identity takes on increased importance because the evaluation process cannot rely on tangible qualities. When one considers the list of factors occasioning a need for identity change (Anspach. 1983), it is apparent that many of these pertain to the financial services industry. These changes, and those on a macro-environment level, have, and continue to have, an impact on a company-specific, and an industry-wide, basis. Strategic management thinking argues that companies must adapt if they are to be opportunely placed in such circumstances. There is evidence that this is what financial service businesses are attempting to do. By implication, the more "traditional" identities, based on the more "traditional" circumstances and values of industry, are out of date. Financial services companies therefore have a choice. They may treat corporate identity as inconsequential in the great scheme of things. Alternatively, they can treat corporate identity as a strategic marketing issue. This paper has shown why the latter choice is the only appropriate response. The adoption of the marketing concept must bring banks to the realisation that their "institutional" image must be disaffirmed and that corporate identity — what they project — can facilitate this objective.

The AIB Group case example illustrates how one company in the financial services industry treated corporate identity. Some unique circumstances, derived from the company's history, had combined with changes in the environment of all financial services companies. Allied Irish Banks plc was a substantially different organisation from that suggested by its name and origins. Following an extensive review, the company formally established a new mission and strategy. When corporate identity was examined, many of the signals that suggest the need for an identity change were found to pertain. In January 1990 the company unveiled its new identity, one which is a more accurate reflection of the new corporate reality.

This case demonstrates that a company's identity can facilitate positioning. The move, from being an Irish bank to an international financial services organisation, is one which needs to be communicated to many audiences, especially employees, customers and the financial community.

Corporate identity development is not mere "cosmetic tinkering". It is one vehicle, made up of many parts, whereby a company can articulate its mission and values to many publics. Given the growth in corporate identity development projects, it is disappointing that the mainstream marketing texts devote little attention to it.

REFERENCES

Abratt, R. (1989): "A New Approach to the Corporate Image Management Process", *Journal of Marketing Management,* 5(1): 63–76.

Allied Irish Banks plc literature (1990): "Banking in Ireland", "Ireland's International Banking Group", and "AIB Group News": Dublin: Allied Irish Banks.

Anspach, R.R. (1983): "Shaping Your Bank's Corporate Identity", *Bank Marketing,* October: 20–30.

Bateson, J.E.G. (1989): *Managing Services Marketing: Text and Readings,* Orlando, Florida: Dryden Press.

Berry, L.L. (1989): "The Employee as Customer", in *Managing Services Marketing: Text and Readings,* Orlando, Florida: Dryden Press.
Clarke, P.D., Gardener, E.P.M., Feeney, P. and Molyneux, P. (1988): "The Genesis of Strategic Marketing Control in British Retail Banking", *International Journal of Marketing,* 6(2): 5–19.
Clutterbuck, D., (1989): "Developing Customer Care Training Programmes", *Marketing Intelligence & Planning,* 7(1): 34–7.
Croft, M. (1990): "Design: After the Years of Plenty", *Marketing,* 9 February: 40–44.
Czepiel, J.A., Solomon, M.R., Suprenent, C.F and Gutman, E.G. (1985): "Service Encounters: An Overview", in J.A. Czepiel, M.R Solomon and E.G. Suprenent (eds), *The Service Encounter,* New York: D.C. Heath and Company.
Gray, E.R. and Smelzer, L.R. (1985): "Corporate Image: An Integral Part of Strategy", *Sloan Management Review,* 26(4): 73–8.
Gray, E.R. and Smelzer, L.R. (1987): "Planning a Corporate Facelift: Implementing a Corporate Image Programme", *Journal of Business Strategy,* 8(1): 4–10.
Hooley, G.J. and Mann, S.J. (1988): "The Adoption of Marketing by Financial Institutions in the UK", *Service Industries Journal,* 8(4), 488–500.
Howcroft, J.J. and Lavis, J. (1986): *Retail Banking: The New Revolution in Structure and Strategy,* Oxford: Basil Blackwell.
Kennedy, S.H. (1977): "Nurturing Corporate Images: Total Communications or Corporate Ego Trip?", *European Journal of Marketing,* 11(1): 120–64.
Kent, R.A. (1986): "Faith in the Four Ps: An Alternative", *Journal of Marketing Management,* 2(2): 145–54.
Kotler, P. (1988): *Marketing Management: Analysis, Planning, Implementation and Control,* sixth edition, Englewood Cliffs, N.J.: Prentice-Hall.
Levitt, T. (1960): "Marketing Myopia", *Harvard Business Review,* Vol. 38, July/August, pp. 24–7.
Levitt, T. (1981): "Marketing Intangible Products and Product Intangibles", *Harvard Business Review,* 59(3): 94–102.
Liswood, L.A. (1989): "A New System for Rating Service Quality", *Journal of Business Strategy,* 10(4): 42–5.
McIvor, C. and Naylor, G. (1980): *Marketing of Financial Services,* London: Institute of Bankers.
Morello, G. (1988): "The Image of Dutch Banks", *International Journal of Bank Marketing,* 6(2): 38–47.

Olins, W. (1989): *Corporate Identity,* London: Thames and Hudson.

Rathmell, J.M. (1974): *Marketing in the Service Sector,* Cambridge, MA: Winthorp, Cambridge.

Rushton, A.M. and Carson, D.J. (1985): "The Marketing of Services: Managing the Intangibles", *European Journal of Marketing,* 19(3): 19–42.

Sinkula, J.M. and Lawtor, L. (1987): "Positioning in the Financial Services Industry: A Look at the Decomposition of Image", *Proceedings, Development in Marketing Science Series,* Vol. X, US: Academy of Marketing Science.

Smith, D. and Harbisher, A. (1989): "Building Societies as Retail Banks: The Importance of Customer Service and Corporate Image", *International Journal of Bank Marketing,* 7(1): 22–7.

Southgate, P. (1990): "Researching Design", Market Research Society Conference Papers.

Sullivan, M.P. (1981): "Bank Services Promotion: Past, Present, Future", in J.H. Donnelly and W.R, George (eds), *Marketing of Services,* Proceedings Series, Chicago, Illinois: American Marketing Association.

Topalian, A. (1984): "Corporate Identity: Beyond the Visual Overstatements", *International Journal of Advertising,* 3(1): 55–62.

Watkins, T. and Wright, M. (1986): *Marketing Financial Services,* London: Butterworths.

Worcester, R.M. (1986): "Corporate Image Research", in R.M. Worcester and J. Downham (eds), *Consumer Market Research Handbook,* third edition, London: McGraw-Hill.

Zavoos, G. (1989): "EC Strategy for the Banking Sector: The Perspective of 1992", *European Affairs,* Spring: 100–108.

Zeithaml, V.A. (1981): "How Consumer Evaluation Processes Differ Between Goods and Services", in J.H. Donnelly and W.R. George (eds), *Marketing of Services,* Proceedings Series, Chicago, Illinois: American Marketing Association.

Zeithaml, V.A., Parasuraman, A. and Berry, L.L. (1989): "Problems and Strategies in Services Marketing", in J.E.G. Bateson (ed.), *Managing Services Marketing: Text and Readings,* Orlando, Florida: Dryden Press.

17

The Role of Sponsorship in the Marketing Communications Mix[*]

Tony Meenaghan

INTRODUCTION

The purpose of this paper is to examine the development of commercial sponsorship and its role in the marketing communications mix. It seeks to do so by focusing on two main areas.

The Development of Sponsorship

The following questions are examined:

(1) What is sponsorship?
(2) What factors are behind its past development?
(3) What is happening now in the sponsorship market?
(4) What developments are likely in the future?

Sponsorship in a Management Context

The following questions are examined:

(1) What is its role in marketing communications?
(2) Who are its audiences and what can sponsorship achieve with these audiences?
(3) How is the correct sponsorship programme selected?
(4) How must it be implemented and subsequently evaluated?

DEFINING COMMERCIAL SPONSORSHIP

Sponsorship is a relatively recent development and can truly be

---

[*]This paper originally appeared in *International Journal of Advertising*, Vol. 10, pp. 35–47.

described as an area of marketing in which basic principles are still being laid down. The following definition is appropriate at the present stage of sponsorship's development:

Commercial sponsorship is an investment, in cash or in kind, in an activity, in return for access to the exploitable commercial potential associated with that activity.

What this definition is saying is that from the sponsor's point of view the price paid is their investment in return for permission to exploit a particular activity. Essentially the sponsor is buying two things:

(1) The exposure potential which the activity has in terms of audience.
(2) The image associated with that activity in terms of how it is perceived.

It is important to regard sponsorship as similar to advertising, in that money is invested for commercial purposes. It must not be confused with other forms of corporate giving such as patronage or charity where the motives are altruistic, with the returns expected to be to society and not to the company itself.

THE SIZE OF THE SPONSORSHIP MARKET

Recent decades have seen the very rapid development of commercial sponsorship. An analysis of the UK sponsorship market provides a graphic illustration of this development with UK sponsorship expenditure showing a 10-fold increase between 1980 and 1991.

TABLE 17.1: UK EXPENDITURE ON SPONSORSHIP 1980–90 (£M)

Year	Total Expenditure
1980	35
1981	72
1982	105
1983	128
1984	145
1985	167
1986	191
1987	220
1988	250
1989	258
1990	287
1991	327

Source: Mintel 1991.

In 1974, expenditure on sponsorship in the UK was estimated at £18 million (Mintel 1980). In 1991 it was estimated that £327 million was spent on sponsorship in the UK (Mintel, 1991).

On a worldwide basis commercial sponsorship is increasingly recognised as a legitimate communications option for marketing management. In 1986 direct sponsorship expenditure worldwide was valued at $3.6 billion, a figure which represented between 2.5 per cent and 3.5 per cent of all advertising expenditure worldwide. In 1992, worldwide expenditure was estimated at $9.4 billion (Sponsorship Research International, 1993). Table 17.2 indicates the relative importance of the various world markets.

TABLE 17.2: WORLDWIDE SPONSORSHIP EXPENDITURE IN 1992

	Expenditure (Millions of US dollars)	Percentage of Work Expenditure
USA	3,550	37.8
Western Europe	3,520	37.4
Japan	1,550	16.5
Africa	50	0.5
Americas (excl. USA)	350	3.8
Asia (excl. Japan)	510	5.4
Australasia	150	1.6
Middle East	60	0.7
Worldwide total	9,400	100.0

Source: Sponsorship Research International Ltd. Annual Estimates of Sponsorship Markets, 1993.

The development of sponsorship however, is not equally distributed across all markets. In 1984 comparative figures for sponsorship as a percentage of total advertising spend showed considerable variation even among the more developed economies. As can be seen from Table 17.3, sponsorship in Italy was estimated at 9 per cent of total advertising expenditure compared with only 1.4 per cent in the US market (AGB, 1986). These estimates of sponsorship spending do not include the expenditure which is necessary to ensure the proper exploitation of the chosen sponsorship. The acknowledged industry norm is that expenditure at least equal to the direct sponsorship costs is necessary for adequate exploitation.

TABLE 17.3: SPONSORSHIP EXPENDITURE AS A PERCENTAGE OF ADVERTISING EXPENDITURE IN 1984 ($M)

Country	Advertising Expenditure	Sponsorship Expenditure	%
Italy	2,580	226	8.8
USA	73,380	1,000	1.4
UK	5,670	157	2.8
W. Germany	5,192	98	1.9
Netherlands	2,003	55	2.8

Source: Advertising Associations, AGB Intomart, 1986.

Driving Forces Behind Sponsorship's Development

The dramatic growth of commercial sponsorship as a marketing activity is probably due to the following:

(1) **Government policies on tobacco and alcohol.** Changing government policies on advertising for alcohol and cigarettes caused manufacturers of such products to seek alternative promotion media.

(2) **Escalating cost of advertising media.** Part of the attraction of commercial sponsorship is the belief that it provides a highly cost-effective marketing communications tool compared with traditional advertising.

(3) **The proven ability of sponsorship.** The proven ability of commercial sponsorship to achieve marketing objectives has been responsible for its increased usage.

(4) **New opportunities due to increased leisure activity.** Increasingly our leisure conscious society provides opportunities for sponsorship involvement. This is clear from the wide range of activities currently being pursued in both sports and arts compared with earlier decades.

(5) **Greater media coverage of sponsored events.** Increasingly, media coverage, particularly on television, is being directed towards sports and cultural activities, thereby creating opportunities for broadcast sponsorship.

(6) **Inefficiencies in traditional media.** A large part of the attraction of sponsorship for sponsors has been its potential as a way to overcome the inefficiencies of traditional advertising media. One such inefficiency is zapping, which decreases the actual audience for television advertising. A further attraction of sponsorship has been the opportunity to escape from the "clutter" associated with traditional media (although it must now be admitted that certain sports activities are themselves becoming increasingly cluttered).

CURRENT DEVELOPMENTS IN SPONSORSHIP

As a relatively youthful and dynamic industry, commercial sponsorship is undergoing several fundamental changes.

Patterns of Expenditure

There is evidence of a trend towards sponsorships which are more diverse than the traditional areas of arts and sport, as can be seen from Table 17.4. While sport remains the largest sector for sponsorship expenditures, new opportunities are opening up in emerging areas such as popular music, broadcast sponsorship and cause-related marketing activities.

TABLE 17.4: UK EXPENDITURE ON SPONSORSHIP 1980–91 (£M)

Year	Sports	Arts	Other	Total
1980	30	3	2	35
1981	60	7	5	72
1982	85	11	9	105
1983	100	15	13	128
1984	110	19	26	145
1985	125	22	20	167
1986	140	26	25	191
1987	160	28	32	220
1988	180	30	40	230
1989	210	33	15	258
1990	230	35	23	287
1991	250	45	32	327

Source: Mintel, 1991.

New Breed of Sponsor

While tobacco and alcohol companies may initially have been drawn to sponsorship for the reasons outlined above, the very success of their involvements has encouraged other entrants. Initially, commercial banking institutions entered the sponsorship fray. They were subsequently followed by other financial institutions such as merchant banks and building societies. More recently, sponsorship has been taken up by high-tech companies such as computer firms and Japanese electronic firms. Coincident with these changes has been a greater level of sophistication and commercial-mindedness in the choice of sponsorship programme.

Increasingly Sophisticated Support Services

A further development has been the improvement in support services available to the sponsor. Sponsorship consultants have increasingly become more specialised and professional, while advertising agencies which were initially sceptical have become more involved on behalf of clients. Research agencies have begun to respond to the needs of sponsors for information; several of them now provide profiles of audiences, images of sports and arts activities as well as various methods of measurement.

Future Prospects for Sponsorship

A continuation of the trends indicated earlier, coupled with the increased commercialisation of sports and the arts, the growth of new media, such as cable and satellite television, and the increasing sophistication of corporate sponsors, will ensure the continued growth of commercial sponsorship.

COMMERCIAL SPONSORSHIP IN THE MARKETING COMMUNICATIONS CONTEXT

Given the functions which commercial sponsorship is called upon to perform, it is clear that sponsorship must be viewed as an element of marketing communications within the broader context of the marketing mix of product, price, distribution and marketing communications — the traditional "4Ps" framework. Commercial sponsorship fits quite naturally alongside advertising, public relations, personal selling and sales promotion in that its basic function lies in achieving marketing communications objectives.

Each method of marketing communication assists in achieving

the overall marketing communications objective on behalf of the organisation. The task facing management is to evaluate the strengths and weaknesses of each method and to determine the ability of each method to assist in the achievement of objectives. The various methods of communication must then be combined to complement one another in the most cost-effective manner. The situation is analogous to the different sections of an orchestra being integrated to ensure the best possible overall performance.

SPONSORSHIP OBJECTIVES AND TARGET AUDIENCES

Businesses have a wide variety of audiences with whom they wish to communicate. These are indicated in Figure 17.1.

FIGURE 17.1: CORPORATE PUBLICS

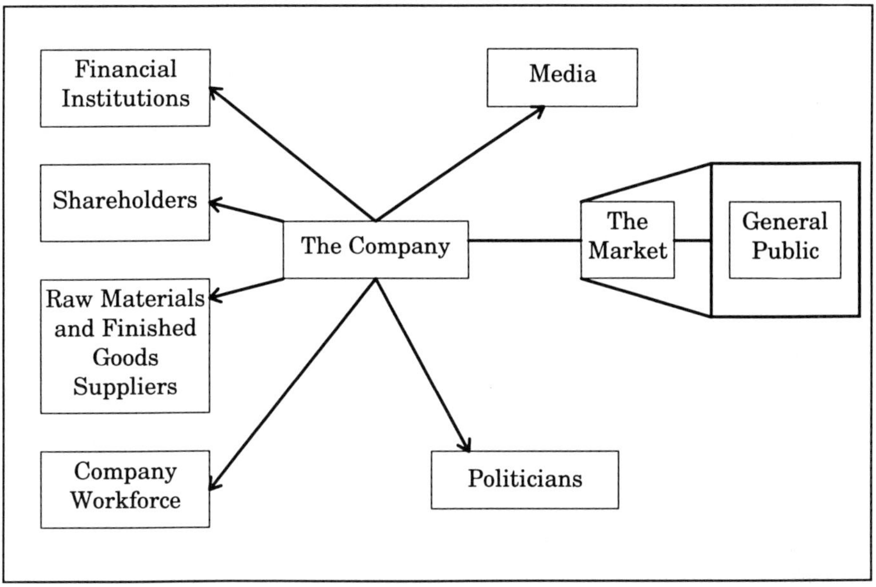

The Internal Public

Increasingly, organisations are recognising the importance of the internal staff public and the necessity to synchronise both the external strategy and the internal back-up systems and staff. With this in mind model organisations such as IBM, Digital, Marks & Spencer are developing "corporate culture" programmes. Within these programmes sponsorship has a major role to play in fostering staff pride, rewarding effort and in articulating the values of the organisation to its staff. The results in terms of staff morale and improved industrial relations are the major benefits of such programmes.

Key Decision-makers

Sponsorship allows us to build goodwill among opinion-formers and decision-makers. These can be business associates, government and trade union officials as well as opinion-formers in the media. Furthermore, as sponsorship is normally built around a particular event, it allows us to offer corporate hospitality to these key decision-makers as our guests. In this way, sponsorship is more subtle in its effects than other methods of marketing communication.

The Company's Target Markets

For the purposes of simplicity, objectives in relation to target markets can be subdivided into (1) corporate objectives and (2) brand objectives.

(2) **Corporate objectives.** Sponsorship is highly regarded for its ability to achieve certain objectives on behalf of a company. It can:
   (a) Increase public awareness of the company.
       There are numerous examples of companies achieving awareness objectives via the medium of sponsorship. Cornhill Insurance via its cricket sponsorship increased awareness in the UK market from 2 per cent to 16 per cent (Dinmore, 1980). Similarly, Canon increased its awareness level from 18.5 per cent to 79 per cent over the three-year period of its sponsorship of the English Football League. This result was achieved with considerable support expenditure in other media (Barrie, 1990).
   (b) Change the Corporate Image. Changing the corporate image is often a key objective for sponsorship involvement. By its association with Formula One Motor Racing, Yardley managed to dilute the feminine connotations of its name, enabling the introduction of male cosmetics as a result of this newer more macho image. Other corporate image objectives may require sponsorship to act as a medium of community involvement or to counter adverse publicity.

(3) **Brand objectives.** Sponsorship is highly regarded for its ability to achieve both brand awareness and brand image objectives. Recently Budweiser and Foster's have used sponsorship as a key element in gaining awareness for their products in European markets. Similarly, it can be used to position a brand on the market or to alter its image within that market. In the Irish market 7-Up have used an innovative popular music sponsorship programme to support nationwide tours by up-and-coming Irish rock bands who later featured in a series of television programmes entitled "7 Bands on the Up". This sponsorship had the effect of providing access to and repositioning the brand with the youth market (Byrne, 1990).

Within the marketing communications mix, commercial sponsorship can be regarded as a highly cost-effective medium to achieve awareness and image-related objectives at both the corporate and brand level.

SELECTING THE CORRECT SPONSORSHIP

Having identified the role sponsorship is expected to play, the next logical aspect of sponsorship management is the selection process. Potential sponsoring companies are inundated with requests for sponsorship funding. In 1984, Philips reported that they had received 10,000 such requests (Kohl and Otker, 1985). The existence of an agreed sponsorship policy provides an effective method of weeding out inappropriate proposals.

A sponsorship policy must of its nature be company-specific and reflect that company's vision of itself and its products. Generally, a sponsorship policy will clearly identify both acceptable and unacceptable areas of activity. For example, a company may decide not to sponsor individuals, blood sports, or a politically sensitive activity. Similarly, a policy may indicate acceptable areas of opportunity — the Arts, for example — at the upper, rather than the mass level. All potential sponsorships which have successfully passed the policy-screening stage must then be evaluated against selection criteria which have been determined in advance.

A Classification of Sponsorship Criteria

While individual companies must specify the selection criteria which they deem appropriate for their company overall or for particular audiences, the following criteria will generally be part of the selection decision.

The ability to fulfil objectives. A key criterion in the evaluation of any sponsorship proposal is its ability to fulfil stated objectives. These objectives, as indicated earlier, can be stated in both awareness and image terms at both the corporate and brand level. In the case of awareness objectives, success stories can be found at the corporate level (e.g., Cornhill and Canon) and at the brand level (e.g., Fosters and Budweiser).

A second major objective for sponsorship involvement lies in the area of image development. The very fact that a particular sponsorship has its own personality and perception in the public mind is a key criterion in sponsorship choice. This "image by association" effect is well established in marketing as different magazines display qualities of prestige, mood creation, credibility, authority and other characteristics, similarly there is obviously a "rub-off" or "halo-effect" from associating with a particular sponsorship. This image through association or "rub-off" effect is a central criterion in sponsorship selection.

At the corporate level, Gillette, a very American company, through its involvement with cricket, a traditionally British sport, effectively erased its American image. Similarly, at the brand level, Pepsi have sponsored concert tours by both Michael Jackson and Tina Turner, to suggest a more youthful image.

Coverage of the defined target audience. As stated, businesses can have a variety of audiences for their sponsorship activity and the ability of a sponsorship programme to match the defined target audience is a critical factor in selecting the particular sponsorship.

This matching process can take place at a number of levels.

(1) *Demographic.* To gain coverage of their particular markets Rolex sponsors polo while Lee Cooper sponsors rock music. In the past sponsorship selection has been bedevilled by poor profiling of audiences for sports, arts and other activities. However, the efforts of enlightened sports and arts bodies and certain research companies have considerably improved the quality of information, and sponsors are now able to evaluate potential sponsorships against their ability to reach their defined target audiences. One such research company, RSL Ltd., publishes a leisure monitor which indicates the profile of

audiences for major sports and arts activities in the UK (RSL, 1990).

(2) *Geographic.* The ability of the proposed sponsorship to cover the geographically defined market is also critical in selection. For a multinational company, the ability of the sponsorship to cover its various markets is important. For this reason Coca-Cola sponsors the Olympic Games while a domestically focused company such as Barclay's Bank sponsored the football league in the UK.

(3) *Life-style.* The ability of the sponsorship to reflect the life-style of the target audience is another important selection criterion. For this reason, Volvo selects both tennis and golf, while brewing and cigarette companies were more likely to sponsor soccer and snooker.

The level of coverage of the target audience. The amount of likely exposure and the audience size likely to be exposed to the company's message is an important selection determinant. Depending on the activity being proposed, the potentially exposed audience can be measured in terms of:

(1) Participants e.g., New York Marathon.
(2) On-site fans.
(3) Media coverage — e.g., the 1986 World Cup was seen in 166 different countries with a gross cumulative audience of 13,506,689,000 viewers (ISL Marketing, 1988).

Potential media coverage is often a key determinant in the selection process. For companies seeking corporate hospitality media coverage may represent a useful bonus; for major branded goods companies it may be the basis of their involvement.

The costs associated with the sponsorship programme. Affordability may be a key criterion. In costing any sponsorship the cost of "leveraging" the programme with support activity must be included. (Leveraging refers to the additional effort, largely promotional, which must be invested by the sponsor in order to exploit properly the opportunity provided as a result of securing particular sponsorship rights.)

Depending on the sponsor's rationale for involvement, various other criteria such as the opportunities for guest hospitality, staff knowledge of the proposed sponsorship, the organisation of the sponsored activity and the distraction factor involved may be employed to evaluate the various opportunities available.

The process of sponsorship selection can be rendered more systematic if the following approach is used. Each proposal, once short-listed following satisfaction of policy guidelines, is evaluated against the criteria deemed appropriate for the particular programme. To do this, each selection criterion should be ranked in terms of priority of preferred attainment and each proposal scored in terms of its ability to fulfil the stated criteria. A total score can thus be computed for each sponsorship proposal, enabling a more objective evaluation.

Implementing the Sponsorship Programme

The success of the sponsorship programme will be dependent to a large extent on how it is implemented. A critical factor is that the sponsorship be implemented as part of a marketing campaign and thus integrated with other elements of marketing communications. The sponsor must also support the sponsorship by additional advertising and promotions. It is commonly agreed that a figure of at least equal value to the direct fee payment must be used in leveraging the original sponsorship investment.

MEASURING SPONSORSHIP RESULTS

Having chosen the most appropriate sponsorship and ensured its proper implementation, it is then necessary to evaluate the sponsorship programme against the objectives stated at the outset. As is the case with all forms of marketing communication whether it is advertising or commercial sponsorship, the evaluation process is greatly facilitated if measurement is undertaken at several key stages.

(1) At the outset, measurement is required to determine the company's present position in terms of awareness and image with the target audience.
(2) Interim Tracking may be necessary if the sponsorship is longer term in order to detect movement on the chosen dimensions of awareness, image and market attitude.
(3) Final evaluation must take place when the sponsorship is completed, to determine performance levels against the stated objectives.

Bases for Measuring Sponsorship Effectiveness

There are five main methods of measuring sponsorship effectiveness.

(1) Measuring the level of media coverage/exposure gained.

The level of media coverage gained as a result of sponsorship involvement is frequently used by sponsors as an indicator of performance. Such evaluation constitutes measuring:

(a) The duration of television coverage
(b) Monitored radio coverage
(c) The extent of press coverage in terms of single column inches.

The monitoring of media coverage as a proxy measure of sponsorship effectiveness is widely used, essentially because it is practicable. However, it is important to recognise that the level of media coverage merely indicates the extent of the publicity resulting from the sponsorship and, as such, is basically similar to indicating the level of advertising time or space bought. As such, this measure on its own does not evaluate the effectiveness of the exposure gained.

(2) Measuring the communications effectiveness of sponsorship involvement.

As sponsorship is used to achieve basic communication objectives such as awareness and image, there is a tendency to evaluate sponsorship results in communications rather than sales terms. Levels of awareness achieved, attitudes created, perceptions changed or associations suggested are measured against stated objectives. One such example is provided by Cornhill Insurance in the UK, which decided to measure the effectiveness of its sponsorship using a research study every six months to establish the following:

(a) Unprompted name awareness
(b) Prompted name awareness
(c) Unprompted awareness of Cornhill as a sports sponsor
(d) Prompted awareness of Cornhill as a sports sponsor
(e) Attitudes towards sponsorship.

The results of four six-monthly research studies indicated that unprompted awareness increased from 2 per cent to 8 per cent to 13 per cent to 16 per cent with evidence of a fall-off in cricket's off-season. Its investment of £2 million returned an estimated £15–20 million worth of new business over a short period (Dinmore, 1980).

Sponsoring companies also attempt to evaluate sponsorship results by focusing on the degree to which respondents associate the company or the product with the sponsored activity. An example of this type of research in terms of levels of awareness and degree of association is provided in Table 17.5 (Mintel, 1980,1986,1988,1990).

TABLE 17.5: MOTOR RACING SPONSORSHIP AWARENESS

	Percentage of Respondents Mentioning Each Sponsor			
	1974	1977	1980	1988
Texaco	18	45	47	60
John Player	22	43	44	66
Marlboro	6	25	42	55
Rothmans	11	13	13	50
None/Don't Know	35	20	19	n/a

Source: Mintel.

It is particularly notable from Table 17.5 that there was a dramatic increase in the awareness level for Marlboro as a motor racing sponsor from 6 per cent to 55 per cent over a six-year period from 1974 to 1988.

The degree to which a sponsoring company is associated with a particular sponsorship activity can be correlated with classification variables such as sex, age and social class, thereby enabling sponsors to determine the level of awareness they have achieved with their identified target market.

Similar types of studies of corporate involvement in art sponsorship generally show low awareness and association levels. However, it must be recognised that arts sponsorship tends to offer high awareness levels within select minority populations, and thus the results of any awareness/association studies must be seen in this light.

As well as creating corporate or brand awareness, one of the particular capabilities of commercial sponsorship is in altering corporate or brand image. One such example is the case of IVECO trucks in the US market. IVECO established through research that the reason their trucks were not selling particularly well on the US market was because they were perceived as weak European vehicles compared with their more macho American competitors. The sponsorship of heavyweight boxing enabled IVECO to associate with a macho activity and reach key decision-makers. Subsequent research showed that this particular campaign was highly successful.

(3) Measuring the sales effectiveness of sponsorship. In commercial sponsorship, as is the case with advertising and marketing communications generally, the matter of keying sales results to given expenditures is highly problematic for a variety of reasons.

- (a) The simultaneous usage of other marketing inputs.
- (b) The carry-over effect of previous marketing communications effort.
- (c) Uncontrollable variables in the business environment such as competitor activity or changing economic conditions.

While these factors make the keying of sales results to sponsorship investment somewhat more difficult, many sponsors point to sales results as evidence of sponsorship effects, even if providing conclusive proof of this effect is difficult. American Express found that card usage rose by nearly 30 per cent during the period when it ran the Statue of Liberty campaign in the USA (Gottlier, 1986).

(4) Monitoring guest feedback. Where the objective of sponsorship involvement is the provision of guest hospitality, the monitoring of guest opinions can provide a measure of sponsorship impact. Similarly, where company staff or the local community are being targeted, the monitoring of feedback can also provide a useful measure of effectiveness. Other sources of feedback can be the participants, spectators and activity organisers, as well as the company's own sales force.

(5) Cost-benefit analysis. Where the motivation for sponsorship involvement is more philanthropic than commercially rational, it is necessary to go beyond conventional marketing measures to evaluate the effects achieved. In such instances, it may be necessary to utilise the collective opinion of senior management as the basis for evaluation.

CONCLUSION

Commercial sponsorship, while initially used in a rather cavalier manner by many sponsoring companies is today regarded as a highly cost-effective method of marketing communication. The increased sophistication of present day sponsors, the increasing range and standard of support services and the substitution by sponsorship recipients of a hard-nosed commercialisation for a previously held commercial naïveté have all ensured much more sophistication in terms of sponsorship usage. Such changes allied to accumulated learning experience have led to the current recognition of commercial sponsorship as a legitimate option within the marketing communications mix.

REFERENCES

AGB Intomart (1986): *Sport on Television and Sports Sponsorship,* Amsterdam: New Media Department.

Byrne, M. (1990): "The Public Relations and Marketing Opportunities of Music Sponsorship, Case Study: Seven-Up" Arts Council Seminar, Sponsorship and the Irish Music Industry, National Concert Hall, Dublin: 22 May.

Dinmore, F. (1980): "Cricket Sponsorship", *The Business Graduate (UK),* Autumn: 68–72.

Gill, B. CSS International Holdings Ltd. (1990): Personal Interview, London.

Gottlier, M. (1986): "Cashing In on a Higher Cause", *The New York Times,* 6 July.

ISL Marketing Ltd. (1988): *Sponsorship: Has the New Medium Come of Age?* Lucerne: lSL.

Kohl, F. & Otker, T. (1985): "Sponsorship — Some Practical Experiences in Philips Consumer Electronics", ESOMAR seminar. Address at Below-the-line and Sponsoring Seminar, Milan: Esomar.

Mintel (1980): *Sponsorship,* London: Mintel Publications.

Mintel (1986): *Sponsorship,* London: Mintel Publications.

Mintel (1988): *Sponsorship,* London: Mintel Publications.

Mintel (1990): *Sponsorship,* London: Mintel Publications.

Mintel (1991): *Sponsorship,* London: Mintel Publications.

RSL Leisure Monitor (1990): Harrow, Middlesex UK: Research Services Ltd.

Sponsorship Research International Ltd. (SRI) (1993): *Annual Estimates of Sponsorship Markets,* London: SRI.

PART VII

Pricing and Selling

18

Pricing Practices in Irish Companies[*]

Donal Keating

INTRODUCTION AND OBJECTIVES OF THE STUDY

It is a commonly held view that the setting of selling prices and output levels is an important decision which has implications for the allocation of resources at the level of both the firm and the economy (Scapens, Gameil and Cooper, 1983: p. 283). In the light of the foregoing, this study seeks to establish the pricing practices of the top 200 Irish companies. The specific objectives of the study are:

(1) To establish what methods firms use to communicate their prices to potential customers.
(2) To ascertain the precise basis on which the firms in the study group determine their prices.
(3) To establish the methods of calculating costs which firms use in their normal pricing decisions and to contrast this with the methods used for pricing special orders.
(4) To consider whether firms investigate the possible effect of potential prices on sales volume before setting their selling prices.
(5) To investigate the extent of the use of computers by firms in setting prices.
(6) To ascertain the non-cost factors which may be taken into consideration by firms in setting prices.
(7) To assess the impact of company size on pricing practices employed.

---

[*] This paper was first presented at the Irish Accounting Association Conference, Dublin, 1992.

(8) To present a comparative analysis of the pricing practices in Irish and UK companies.

Establishing why firms adopt specific pricing policies is not a primary objective of the study although, in the course of the discussion, certain suggestions will be advanced. The study is primarily concerned with establishing the nature of existing pricing practices in Irish companies, rather than providing explanations for such practices.

The paper is structured as follows. Initially, an overview of the literature on pricing policy will be presented. This will be followed by a discussion of the data collection process. The results of the study will then be discussed. Finally, some recommendations for further research will be suggested.

OVERVIEW OF THE LITERATURE ON PRICING POLICY

Among the factors which a firm should consider when setting its pricing policy are overall company goals, costs, consumer demand, competition and social responsibility (Brenner, 1971).

Dean (1951: p. 399) stated that "since pricing is not an end in itself, but a means to an end, an explicit formulation of the company's pricing objective is essential. The fundamental guides to pricing are the company's overall goals". Pricing decisions are normally short-run in nature, therefore the relationship between pricing decisions and long-run objectives must always be considered. For example, a firm with a long-run target rate of return objective may find that in the short run it has to price below the target rate to retain its market share (Brenner, 1971).

"The basic use of costs in pricing is ... to forecast the profit consequences of various alternative prices" (Dean, 1951: p. 454). Once a price has been set, costs establish whether the price–volume combination will give sufficient profits in the light of the firm's objectives. In many firms, the starting point in price setting is a formal consideration of costs.

> Two economic principles state this relationship (between price and consumer behaviour) in a manner helpful to marketing executives. The first is the law of demand, which states that more units will be purchased at low prices than at high prices. The second is known as price elasticity of demand. P.E.D. describes in a precise, quantitative manner the sensitivity of buyers to changes in price. (Oxenfeldt, 1961: p. 26)

Demand must always be considered regardless of what the firm's pricing objectives may be.

"Competition by its very nature tends to set an upper limit on pricing. Whenever a company desires to make any price move, it must anticipate the actions of its competitors" (Zober, 1964: p.. 76). This is true except in a perfectly competitive environment where the firm tends to be a price taker.

Social responsibility tends to be important when the firm sells large quantities of a product nationally (Brenner, 1971).

ROLE OF COST INFORMATION IN PRICING DECISIONS

Kaplan and Atkinson (1989: p 178) suggest that product cost information will have an important impact on the pricing decision where firms have flexibility in the prices they charge for their products; for example, when products are unique to individual customers. However, they also state that even when the firm is a price taker it needs to ascertain its scale of operation, production technology and method of marketing. These decisions will be influenced by product costs and by estimated profitability from product sales.

THE ECONOMIST'S PRICING MODEL

The economist suggests that the optimal price–output combination for a product is where its marginal cost equals its marginal revenue. This basic principle applies to all market structures (Drury, 1988: p. 296). A basic problem with the economist's model is that the economist is concerned with observing equilibrium behaviour in markets rather than observing firm behaviour. Therefore, economists tend to ignore the fact that individual firms do not equate marginal revenue with marginal cost in formulating optimal price output combinations (Kaplan and Atkinson, 1989: p. 179).

The economist's model tends not to be used by individual firms because, firstly, demand curves for a firm's products can be difficult to ascertain. Some firms have many products with complex inter-relationships, the estimation of demand curves in such instances is virtually impossible. Secondly, estimation of long-run marginal product costs is very difficult because in the long run if a product is to be profitable its marginal cost must cover, in addition to short-run variable costs, the costs of capacity resources required for the product, the indirect costs needed to support the product and the cost of fixed and working capital allocated to the product (Kaplan and Atkinson, 1989: p. 180). Thirdly, recent studies have shown that the single product model assumed in the economist's analysis is not representative of the economics of multi-product firms (Cooper and Kaplan, 1987). Companies with a diverse product line have higher costs, for the same output level, than single-product companies because of the increased indirect expenses needed to support the complexity of the firm's product line.

COST-BASED PRICING STRATEGIES

Among the most commonly used cost-based approaches to pricing are: cost-plus pricing, incremental pricing and return on investment pricing.

Cost-plus pricing involves adding a percentage mark-up over the absorption cost of the product in arriving at the selling price. Empirical studies have shown that cost-plus pricing is widely used (Skinner, 1970; Hague, 1971; Andrews and Brenner, 1975; Gabor, 1977; Lere 1980; Scapens, Gameil and Cooper, 1983; Hankinson, 1985; Mills and Sweeting, 1988).

Its main advantage is that when used in conjunction with standard costing systems it simplifies the pricing decision considerably. Moreover, the percentage mark-up can be varied by product or product line. In a study of pricing practices in small firms, Haynes (1964) found that constant percentage mark-ups were the exception rather than the rule. He suggests that full costs represent a starting point in setting a selling price. Once cost-plus prices are obtained they can be adjusted to reflect conditions in the marketplace.

However, cost-plus pricing has a number of drawbacks. Firstly, it ignores demand. Baxter and Oxenfeldt (1961) state: "Inability to estimate demand accurately scarcely excuses the substitution of cost information for demand information. Crude estimates of demand may serve instead of careful estimates of demand but cost gives remarkably little insight into demand". Secondly, it involves circular reasoning, in that activity levels are used to determine absorption costs which in turn determine selling prices which determine demand levels. Thirdly, if there is excess capacity in an industry, a firm using cost-plus pricing will be vulnerable to competition from competitors who are pricing on a contribution basis. This could result in a situation where a firm earns a profit on each product it sells but an overall loss arises because it fails to operate at budgeted activity levels. Fourthly, cost-plus pricing does not take into account the fact that different products make different demands on the capital resources of the firm. Cost-plus tends to coincide with return on investment pricing only where there is a high correlation between assets employed and costs incurred (Kaplan and Atkinson, 1989: p. 187).

Despite the foregoing weaknesses, cost-plus pricing is widely used in practice, Baxter and Oxenfeldt (1961) offer the following explanation:

> [T]hey offer a means by which plausible prices can be found with ease of speed, no matter how many products the firm handles. Moreover, its imposing computations look factual and precise, and its prices may well seem more defensible on moral grounds than prices established by other means. Thus, a monopolist threatened by a public inquiry might reasonably feel that he is safeguarding his case by using cost-plus pricing.

Incremental pricing is used to set a price floor for a product and is useful in special order pricing. If a firm had idle capacity, then any price above incremental cost will provide a positive contribution towards fixed cost recovery. Of course, in the long run a firm must recover all of its costs and earn a competitive return on its invested capital for it to remain viable. Therefore, incremental cost information enables a more flexible approach to pricing to be adopted by indicating the cost below which the price must not fall if the company wants to avoid decisions which will result in short-run losses.

Return on investment pricing has the advantage that the percentage mark-up over cost is directly related to the investment in the product line. The use of this cost-based method may increase in the future with the increasing use of new manufacturing technology in the production process (for example, automated or computer-assisted production lines). This approach can provide useful guidance to an industry price leader in that it provides a defensible price allowing the company to cover its costs and earn a competitive return on its invested capital.

Kaplan and Atkinson (1989: p. 190) suggest that this approach has a number of drawbacks. Firstly, it is noted that in firms using this approach management may not pay sufficient attention to potential competition. If a price is based on an optimistic return on investment, this may encourage competitors to expand their capacity, such increased capacity may put pressure on profit margins in the industry. Secondly, a variable target-return pricing strategy is rarely used in practice. This involves the use of a pricing strategy that yields a higher mark-up for those products making heavy use of the firm's scarce resources. Thirdly, the approach encourages an internal rather than an external orientation, in that little regard may be given as to whether target volumes can be achieved using the computed price. In this regard, the Japanese practice of target costing is noteworthy (Hiromoto, 1988). Japanese companies work backwards from a competitive market price to determine the target cost for the product. This approach may provide a greater incentive for cost reduction activities than the traditional cost-based pricing strategies.

ROLE OF ACTIVITY-BASED COSTING

Cooper and Kaplan (1987) contend that ideally all organisational costs (for example, costs of establishing distribution channels, costs of making sales, costs of servicing products for customers), not just factory costs, should be traced directly to products. They suggest that applying these costs to products using average mark-up percentages can create distortions and cross-subsidies between products. Costs arising from the introduction of new, low-volume products are shifted to high-volume products which may not use support department services extensively.

THE DATA COLLECTION PROCESS

A questionnaire was dispatched to the top 200 Irish companies on 26 September 1990. The companies were chosen based on the *Business and Finance* 1990 listing of the top 800 Irish companies (*Business and Finance*, January 1990). The questionnaire was addressed to the marketing director in each company. The deadline for the receipt of completed questionnaires was 26 October 1990. By the deadline, 112 completed questionnaires had been received, five additional replies were received subsequently.

Table 18.1 sets out an analysis of replies received. The valid replies percentage (50.5 per cent) compares favourably with similar studies carried out in the United Kingdom (22 per cent in the Atkin and Skinner study (1975) and 47 per cent in the Mills and Sweeting study (1988)).

Although the questionnaires were sent to marketing directors, over 40 per cent of them were completed by non-marketing specialists (see Table 18.2). Replies headed "marketing" arose from questionnaires completed by marketing managers (26 replies) and marketing directors (24 replies).

TABLE 18.1: ANALYSIS OF REPLIES

	Number	Percentage (%)
Total Questionnaires Posted	200	100
Total Questionnaires Returned	117	58.5
Valid Replies	101	50.5
Other Replies*	15	7.5
Post Office Return†	1	0.5

*   The other replies consist of firms who are engaged solely in manufacturing or where company policy does not allow them to participate in the study.
†   The post office return arose when the post office returned the questionnaire because the company to whom it was addressed was not known at that address.

Replies under accounting and finance resulted from questionnaires completed by financial controllers (10 replies) and finance directors (5 replies) while general management replies arose from questionnaires completed by managing directors (11 replies). Other replies consisted, in the main, of questionnaires completed in the planning department (7 replies).

In general, the questionnaires appear to have been completed by relatively senior management and, therefore, one can be reasonably confident that the information provided is accurate and authoritative.

TABLE 18.2: FUNCTIONAL SPECIALISM OF RESPONDENTS

	Number	Percentage (%)
Accounting and Finance	16	17
General Management	13	14
Marketing	53	58
Other	_12_	_11_
	94	100

Table 18.3 shows that 85 per cent of the respondents employ more than 100 people while some 17 per cent employ over 1,000.

TABLE 18.3: NUMBER OF EMPLOYEES IN RESPONDENT COMPANIES

	Number	Percentage (%)
Under 100	14	15
100–500	47	49
501–1,000	18	19
1,001–5,000	11	11
Over 5,000	6	6

Table 18.4 categorises the respondents by industry type. About 65 per cent of the respondents are involved in manufacturing, with the balance being service companies. Some 32 per cent of respondents are in the food, drink and tobacco sector.

TABLE 18.4: ANALYSIS OF RESPONDENTS BY INDUSTRY TYPE

	Number	Percentage (%)
Industrial and Manufacturing	16	16
Mining and Quarrying	1	1
Food, Drink and Tobacco	32	32
Chemical and Allied Industries	10	10
Metal Manufacturing	1	1
Engineering	4	4
Textiles, Leather and Fur	1	1
Construction	8	8
Paper, Printing and Publishing	4	4
Other Manufacturing	2	2
Service Industry	25	25
Retailing	10	10
Some Other	2	2

The results were analysed using the statistical package, MINITAB. Initially, empirical evidence regarding the pricing practices in Irish companies will be presented and then a comparative analysis of the pricing practices in Irish and UK

EMPIRICAL EVIDENCE REGARDING PRICING PRACTICES IN IRISH COMPANIES

Communication of Selling Prices to Customers

Table 18.5 shows the methods used by respondents to communicate their prices to customers.

TABLE 18.5: COMMUNICATION OF SELLING PRICES TO CUSTOMERS

	Number	Percentage (%)
Published (Customer) Price List	76	75
Internal Price List (used for quotation but not published to the customer)	37	37
Formal Tender	40	40
Some Other Method	20	20

The percentage column exceeds 100 because some companies use more than one method to communicate selling prices to customers. The published price list is by far the most popular method for communicating prices to customers. In general, fixed prices (112 per cent) are used more frequently than flexible prices (40 per cent).

Some of the answers received under the "some other method" category are:

- "Major section of our business is subject to government price control" (5 Companies).
- "Negotiation with customer" (3 Companies).
- "Prices are assessed on the basis of an opinion as to what the market can bear" (2 Companies).

Basis of Price Determination. Table 18.6 shows the basis on which the study companies determine their prices.

Among the replies under "some other method" were:

- "Government control and/or surveillance" (3 Replies).
- "Cost recovery only".
- "Maximum prices are governed by the current agreement between the Industry Federation and the Department of Health".

TABLE 18.6: BASIS OF PRICE DETERMINATION

	Number	Percentage (%)
Add a Percentage to Costs	34	34
Fix a Required Gross Profit Margin on Selling Prices	44	44
Market Forces	83	82
Some Other Method	8	8

Method of Calculating Costs Used for Normal Pricing Decisions

The study companies were asked to indicate what method of calculating costs they normally use in pricing considerations. Table 18.7 indicates the results.

TABLE 18.7: COSTS USED FOR NORMAL PRICING DECISIONS

	Number	Percentage (%)
Direct or Contribution Costing	42	43
Absorption of Full Costing	45	46
Return on Investment Pricing	14	14
Some Other Method	4	4

Some 60 per cent of respondents use either absorption costing or return on investment pricing for normal pricing decisions. This probably arises because in the long run the firm's selling price must recover all costs and earn a reasonable return on invested capital. For normal pricing decisions, 43 per cent of the study companies use contribution costing. This approach is useful where there is idle capacity in an industry and the firm wants to maximise its utilisation of capacity to maximise contribution. However, in the long run if a company uses contribution costing for pricing purposes the mark-up over cost would have to be considerably greater than if absorption costing were used. A positive feature related to the use of contribution costing is that under this approach the firm's cost behaviour patterns have to be carefully analysed.

Method of Calculating Costs Used for Special Order Pricing

Respondents were asked to indicate what method of calculating costs they would use if they received a special order which they could meet out of present capacity. Table 18.8 presents the results.

TABLE 18.8: COSTS USED FOR SPECIAL ORDER PRICING

	Number	Percentage (%)
Direct or Contribution Costing	59	66
Absorption or Full Costing	26	29
Return on Investment Pricing	10	11
Some Other Method	2	2

Contribution costing is ideally suited to a situation where a firm has idle capacity and where it receives a special order which will help it utilise some of its spare capacity. In this situation any selling price in excess of the firm's marginal cost will generate a contribution to the recovery of fixed costs and should be accepted. Therefore, it is not surprising to note that some 66 per cent of respondents use contribution costing when faced with special order pricing.

Absorption or return on investment costing is used in the special order situation by 40 per cent of firms. The danger with these approaches is that they can make the firm vulnerable to competition from competitors who are quoting prices on a contribution basis. The result may be that firms with idle capacity may lose special order business that could generate valuable contribution towards the recovery of fixed costs.

Non-cost Related Methods for Setting Selling Prices

Respondents were asked to indicate by which method prices are mainly fixed if they are not determined by costs. Seventy-five per cent of respondents use non-cost methods in arriving at selling prices. This reflects the importance which respondents attach to competitors' pricing practices and the investigation of possible customer reaction to a particular selling price.

TABLE 18.9: NON-COST METHODS OF PRICE SETTING

	Number	Percentage (%)
Follow the Market Leader	11	15
Reference to the General Level of Competitive Prices	52	69
Prior Investigation of Customer Reaction	19	25
Trial and Error	1	1
Consult the Sales Force	8	11
Some Other Method	3	4

Investigation of Effect of Proposed Prices on Sales Volumes

Respondents were asked to indicate whether their companies investigated the effect of proposed prices on sales volumes before setting their prices and, if so, by whom the investigation was carried out.

TABLE 18.10: INVESTIGATION OF EFFECT OF PROPOSED PRICES ON SALES VOLUMES

Does your company investigate the effects of potential prices on sales volumes before setting prices?

	Number	Percentage (%)
Yes	88	87
No	13	13

If yes, by whom is the investigation normally carried out?

	Number	Percentage (%)
Company Staff	85	97
Outside Organisation	3	3

Table 18.10 indicates that the vast majority of companies investigate the potential impact of sales prices on sales volumes and in virtually all of the companies in the study the investigation is

carried out by internal company staff rather than by an outside organisation.

Among the reasons given by those companies which did not investigate the potential effect of selling prices on sales volumes are:

- "Fixed prices are negotiated after tenders are submitted".
- "Rely on past trends of sales volumes and competitor prices".
- "Government control".
- "In many cases volume of sales is fixed or determined beforehand or tender is on a once-off basis".
- "Too wide a range of products to be able to assess".
- "Volume demand is not significantly influenced by price".

Use of Computers in Pricing

Table 18.11 sets out the extent to which computers are used in pricing in the study companies.

TABLE 18.11: USE OF COMPUTERS IN PRICING

Does your company use computers in any way when making price decisions?

		Number	Percentage (%)
List Prices:	Yes	73	78
	No	20	22
Tender Prices:	Yes	45	68
	No	21	32

The substantial minority of companies not using computers in pricing is surprising in view of the mechanical nature of many of the calculations involved.

IMPACT OF COMPANY SIZE ON PRICING PRACTICES EMPLOYED

The chi-square test was used to assess the impact of company size on pricing practices employed. The results are set out in Table 18.12.

From Table 18.12 we can conclude that there is no significant difference between the size of the respondent companies (measured in terms of numbers employed) and:

(a) The method used to communicate selling prices to customers.
(b) The basis for price determination.
(c) The method of calculating costs used for normal pricing decisions.
(d) The method of calculating costs used for special order pricing.
(e) The extent of the investigation of the effect of proposed selling prices on sales volumes.
(f) The extent of the use of computers in pricing decisions.

TABLE 18.12: IMPACT OF COMPANY SIZE ON PRICING PRACTICES EMPLOYED

	Computed X^2 Value	Critical X^2 Value at: 5% Level of Significance	1% Level of Significance
Communication of Selling Prices to Customers	8.47	12.59	16.81
Basis for Price Determination	7.99	12.59	16.81
Costs Used for Normal Pricing Decisions	1.01	5.99	9.21
Costs Used for Special Pricing Decisions	0.13	9.49	13.28
Non-cost Related Methods for Setting Selling Prices	21.39	9.49	13.28
Investigation of Effect of Proposed Prices on Sales Volumes	0.35	7.81	11.34
Use of Computers in Pricing: List Prices	2.49	7.81	11.34
Use of Computers in Pricing: Tender Prices	3.11	7.81	11.34

However, there is a significant relationship between the size of the respondent companies and the use of non-cost related methods for setting selling prices. It appears that smaller companies tend to follow the market leader in price setting while larger companies are more concerned with the general level of competitors' prices and, to a lesser extent, customer reaction to proposed prices.

The evidence also suggests that large companies tend to investigate the effect of proposed prices on sales volumes before fixing selling prices more frequently than do small companies; and that very large companies (over 5,000 employees) invariably use computers in the pricing decision irrespective of whether they use list or tender prices.

COMPARATIVE ANALYSIS OF PRICING PRACTICES IN IRISH AND UNITED KINGDOM COMPANIES

A similar study to the present one was carried out in 1986 in the United Kingdom by Mills and Sweeting (1988). Mills and Sweeting obtained their list of companies from the "UK's 7,500 Largest Companies 1986". From this list, they selected 100 manufacturing and 100 service companies at random. To assess whether significant differences in pricing practices exist between the two study groups of companies the statistical test for the difference between two proportions using the normal approximation was used and the results are as follows:

TABLE 18.13: BASIS OF PRICE DETERMINATION

	Irish Proportion	UK Proportion	Computed Z Value
Adding a Percentage to Costs	0.34	0.48	-1.99
Fixing a Required Gross Profit Margin on Selling Price	0.44	0.51	-0.98
Market Forces	0.82	0.27	7.71
Some Other Method	0.08	0.11	-0.73

Note: The critical value of Z at the 5% level of significance is +1.96 and at the 1% level +2.58.

A significantly greater proportion of the UK study companies add a percentage to costs in arriving at a selling price compared with the Irish study group.

The proportion of Irish study companies using market forces in price determination is significantly greater than the proportion of UK study companies. In this regard, it is important to note that the option "market forces" was not offered as a specific reply in the UK questionnaire. However, it was shown separately in the analysis of the UK results given that it was such a popular response. It may be that had "market forces" been offered as a response in the UK questionnaire, the proportion choosing it would have been considerably higher.

The proportion of UK study companies using cost-base methods in setting selling prices (99 per cent) is higher than the corresponding proportion of the Irish study group (78 per cent).

TABLE 18.14: METHOD OF CALCULATING COSTS USED FOR NORMAL PRICING DECISIONS

	Irish Proportion	UK Proportion	Computed Z Value
Direct or Contribution Costing	0.43	0.31	1.74
Absorption or Full Costing	0.46	0.58	-1.68
Return on Investment	0.14	0.18	-0.76
Other Method	0.04	0.03	0.36

Absorption costing is the most popular method of calculating costs for normal pricing decisions in both the Irish and the UK study companies. Return on investment pricing is more popular among the UK companies — this may reflect a greater investment in capital-intensive technology among the UK study companies.

TABLE 18.15: NON-COST RELATED METHODS FOR SETTING SELLING PRICES

	Irish Proportion	UK Proportion	Computed Z Value
Follow the Market Leader	0.15	0.16	-0.17
General Level of Competitors' Prices	0.69	0.82	-1.81
Investigation of Customer Reaction	0.25	0.39	-1.81
Trial and Error	0.01	0.10	-2.49
Consulting the Sales Force	0.11	0.27	-2.51
Other Method	0.03	0.07	-1.02

By far the most popular method used in both the Irish and UK study companies is reference to the general level of competitors' prices. The UK proportion is higher than the Irish proportion in all categories indicating a more extensive use of non-cost related methods in the UK as opposed to Irish companies.

These results coincide with the results of a study on pricing carried out in the UK in 1974 by Atkin and Skinner (1975). They concluded:

> Where prices were not determined by cost the most usual method seemed to be to refer to the general level of competitive prices. (Atkin and Skinner, 1975: p. 5)

TABLE 18.16: INVESTIGATION OF EFFECT OF PROPOSED PRICES ON SALES VOLUMES

	Irish Proportion	UK Proportion	Computed Z Value
Does your company investigate the effect of proposed prices on sales volumes before fixing sales prices?	0.88	0.65	3.76
Proportion of companies using an outside organisation to carry out the investigation	0.03	0.125	-2.07

The foregoing results show that a significantly higher proportion of the Irish study companies investigate the effect of proposed prices on sales volumes than the UK sample companies. The UK companies tend to use outside organisations to carry out this investigation to a significantly greater extent than the Irish study companies. In this regard it is interesting to note that in the Atkin and Skinner (1975) study in the UK, it was found that not a single company used an outside agency for formal price investigations.

The results confirm that companies in both countries view price as an important consideration in marketing their products indicating that demand must be relatively elastic for the majority of the products sold by the study companies.

SUMMARY AND CONCLUSIONS

This paper examined the pricing practices of the top 200 Irish companies as set out in the January 1990 edition of the *Business and Finance* magazine. A short questionnaire was sent to the marketing directors of the study companies and a response rate of over 50 per cent was achieved.

A number of conclusions can be drawn from the study:

(1) In communicating selling prices to customers the study

companies tend to use fixed (112 per cent) rather than flexible (40 per cent) prices.
(2) A broadly similar number of companies use cost-based methods (78 per cent) and market forces (82 per cent) as the basis of price determination.
(3) In normal pricing decisions more companies use absorption costing-based techniques (60 per cent) than contribution methods (43 per cent).
(4) Two-thirds of the study companies use contribution methods for pricing special orders in the presence of idle capacity. Some 40 per cent of companies use absorption-based techniques.
(5) The most commonly used non-cost methods for settling selling prices are reference to the level of competitors' prices and prior investigation of customer reaction to the proposed selling price.
(6) The majority of the study companies investigate the effects of proposed selling prices on sales volumes and use computers in pricing.
(7) In general, there is no significant difference between the size of the respondent companies (in terms of numbers employed) and the pricing practices employed by those companies. The only exception to this is in the use of non-cost related methods for setting selling prices.
(8) The pricing practices of Irish and UK companies were compared and significant differences were isolated and discussed.

The present study is very much exploratory in nature. Much additional work remains to be carried to establish further the pricing practices of Irish companies and the reasons why companies adopt specific pricing policies.

REFERENCES

Andrews, P.W.D., and Bruner, E. (1975): *Studies in Pricing*, London: Macmillan.

Atkin, B. and Skinner, R. (1975): *How British Industry Prices*, London: Industrial Market Research Limited.

Baumol, W.J. and Quandt, R.E. (1964): "Rules of Thumb and Optimally Imperfect Decisions", *American Economic Review*, 54(2): 23–46.

Baxter, W.T. and Oxenfeldt, A.R. (1961): "Costing and Pricing: The Cost Accountant versus the Economist", *Business Horizons*, Winter: 77–90.

Brenner, V.C. (1971): "An Evaluation of Product Pricing Models", *Managerial Planning*, July–August.

Cooper, R. and Kaplan, R.S. (1987): "How Cost Accounting Systematically Distorts Product Costs", in *Accounting and Management: Field Study Perspectives*, Boston: Harvard Business School Press.

Cooper, R. and Kaplan, R.S. (1988): "Measure Costs Right: Make the Right Decisions", *Harvard Business Review*, 66(5): 96–103.

Dean, J. (1951): *Managerial Economics*, Englewood Cliffs, N.J.: Prentice-Hall.

Drury, C. (1988): *Management and Cost Accounting*, London: Van Nostrand Reinhold.

Gabor, A. (1977): *Pricing: Principles and Practices*, London: Heinemann.

Gordon, L.A., Cooper, R., Falk, H. and Miller, D. (1981): *The Pricing Decision*, New York: The National Association of Accountants.

Hague, D.C. (1971): *Pricing in Business*, London: Allen and Unwin.

Hankinson, A. (1985): "Pricing Decisions in Small Engineering Firms — Some Interim Results", *Management Accounting*, June: 36–7.

Haynes, W.W. (1964): "Pricing Practices in Small Firms", *Southern Economic Journal*, April: 315–24.

Hiromoto, T. (1988): "Another Hidden Edge: Japanese Management Accounting", *Harvard Business Review*, 66(4): 22–6.

Kaplan, R.S. and Atkinson, A.A. (1989): *Advanced Management Accounting*, Englewood Cliffs, N.J.: Prentice–Hall.

Lere, J.C. (1980): "Observable Differences Among Prime, Variable and Absorption Costing Firms, *Journal of Business Research*, 10(3): 371–87.

Mills, R.W. and Sweeting, C. (1988): *Pricing Decisions in Practice: How are they Made in UK Manufacturing and Services Companies?*, London: The Chartered Institute of Management Accountants.

Oxenfeldt, A.R. (1961): *Pricing for Marketing Executives*, San Francisco: Wadsworth Publishing Company.

Scapens, R.W., Gameil, M.Y. and Cooper, D.J. (1983): "Accounting Information for Pricing Decisions", in *Management Accounting*

Research and Practice, I.C.M.A. Occasional Papers Series, London: I.C.M.A.

Skinner, R.C. (1970): "The Determination of Selling Prices", *Journal of Industrial Economics*, July 18(3): 201–17.

Zober, M. (1964): *Marketing Management,* New York: John Wiley.

19

Sales Force Management in Ireland*

Seán de Burca and Mary Lambkin

> For the first 70 years of this century the practice of sales management resembled the practice of medicine by tribal witch doctors. Sales managers had to rely on large doses of folklore, tradition, intuition and personal experience in deciding how to motivate and direct the performance of their sales forces. (Churchill, Ford and Walker, 1990: p. iii)

The quotation above, from the foremost academics in the field of sales management, seems to describe the past situation in Ireland and other European countries just as well as North America. Fortunately, things have improved considerably in the 20 years since, with an increasing volume of research evidence contributing insights into the factors which affect sales performance. It stands to reason that sales managers who try to exploit this knowledge base in carrying out their work are likely to be more effective than those who continue to rely merely on intuition. This paper sets out to review the theory and research evidence which have become accepted internationally as useful guidelines for various aspects of sales force management. Two recent surveys carried out in this country are particularly relevant for Irish sales managers and these are reviewed in depth.

The first section of the paper presents a general model of the job of sales force management which identifies the main tasks involved and the critical factors for success. The second section describes the two Irish surveys and outlines the research methodology employed. Subsequent sections summarise the

---

* © *Irish Marketing Review,* volume 6, 1993. This article is reproduced with kind permission from Mercury Publications Ltd.

results pertaining to each of the main dimensions of sales force management under the headings: sales force size and organisation, selection and training, motivation and performance, remuneration, evaluation. The final section offers some conclusions and guidelines for best practice by Irish sales managers.

SALES MANAGEMENT: A FRAMEWORK FOR ANALYSIS

The most general and most widely accepted framework for analysing the field of sales management is that of Churchill, Ford and Walker (1990) which is shown in Figure 19.1. This model divides the job of sales management into three broad categories of activities: strategy formulation, implementation and evaluation.

Formulating Sales Strategy

Personal selling is only one promotional tool, and promotion is only one element of marketing strategy. The sales function must be carefully integrated with the rest of the firm's marketing strategy if it is to be effective. This requires that the sales function be managed with clearly articulated objectives based on in-depth analysis of the firm's internal and external environment and of the needs of its products and markets. Churchill, Ford and Walker (1990) suggest that a sales strategy requires answers to five major sets of questions, as follows:

Market targeting. What customers should the firm target and what long-term objectives should be set for each of the major categories? What should be the firm's personal selling strategy?

Account management policies. How can various types of potential customers best be approached, persuaded or serviced? In other words, what account management policies should be adopted?

Sales force organisation. How should the sales force be organised to call on and manage various types of customers as efficiently and effectively as possible?

Sales planning. What level of performance can each member of the sales force be expected to attain during the next planning period? This involves forecasting demand and setting quotas and budgets.

Sales Force Management in Ireland

FIGURE 19.1: AN OVERVIEW OF SALES MANAGEMENT

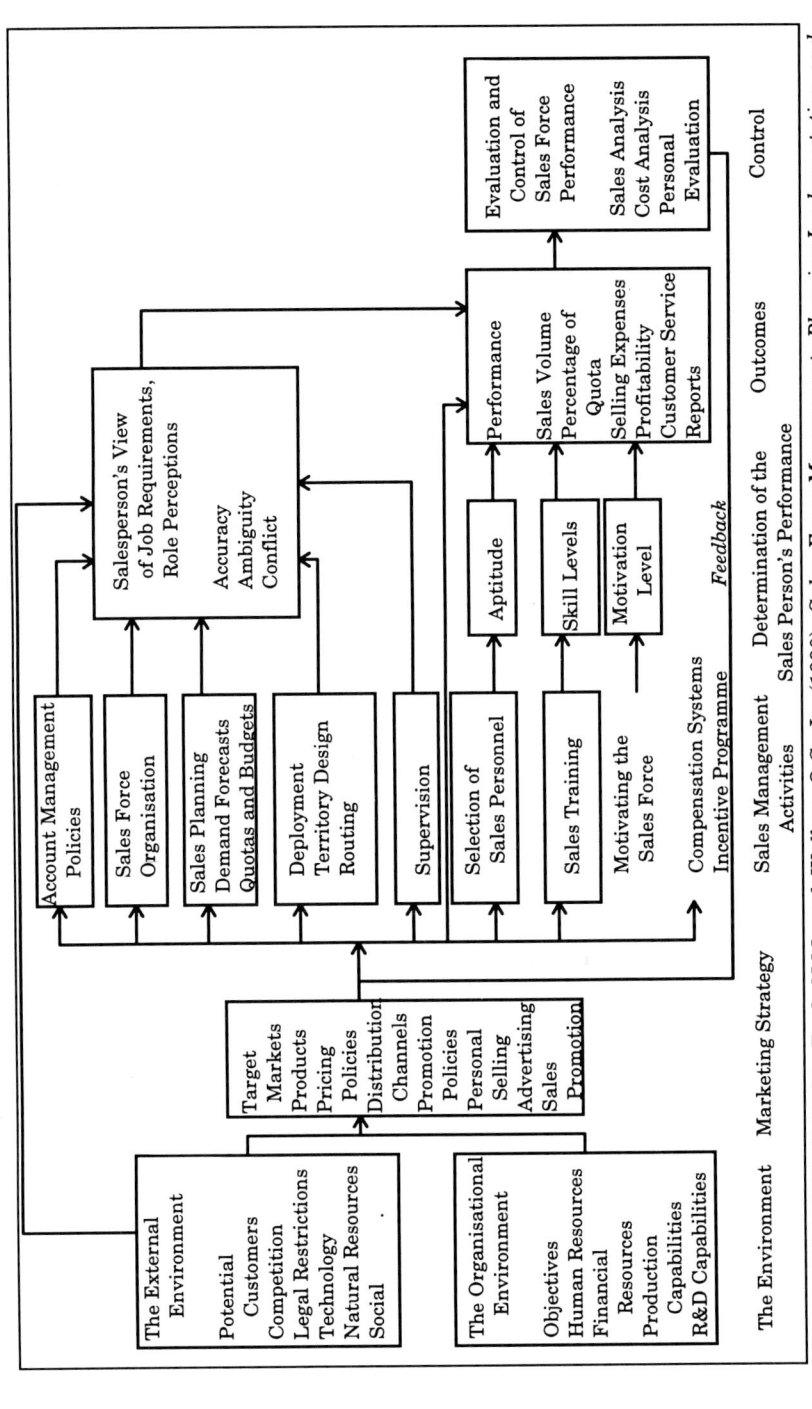

Source: Churchill, G.A. Jr, Ford, N.M. and Walker, O.C. Jr. (1990), *Sales Force Management: Planning, Implementation and Control*, third edition, Irwin, Homewood, Il.

Territory design and routing. In view of the firm's account management policies and demand forecasts, how should the sales force be deployed? How should sales territories be defined? What is the best way for each sales person's time to be allocated within their territory?

Implementing Sales Strategy

Implementing a sales strategy involves motivating and directing the behaviour of the sales force, which requires an understanding of how people think and why they behave as they do. The sales management model shown in Figure 19.1 suggests that four factors influence a sales person's job behaviour and performance:

Selection. The sales manager must decide what kinds of aptitude are necessary for the firm's salespeople to do the type of selling required to meet the sales objectives. Recruiting techniques and selection criteria can then be developed to ensure that salespeople with the required abilities are hired.

Sales training. Selling skills improve with practice and experience but, in most cases, it is not sufficient to let the salesperson gain the necessary skills simply through on-the-job experience. A preferable approach is for the sales manager to decide precisely what selling skills are needed to service the firm's customers and to find appropriate courses on which to send sales personnel.

Supervision. The salesperson's ability to perform is partly determined by their perceptions of the job that is required and of how to resolve conflicting demands between management and customers. A very important role of the sales manager is to define clearly what is required of the salesperson and to provide clear, unambiguous guidelines as to the appropriate trade-offs to make in conflict situations.

Motivation and compensation. A sales person cannot achieve a high level of job performance without being motivated to expend the necessary amount of effort. Motivation, in turn, is influenced by the types of rewards expected for a given level of performance — such as payment or promotion — and by the perceived attractions of those anticipated rewards.

Evaluation and Control of Sales

Setting objectives and planning strategy is a futile exercise unless managers follow through with a regular evaluation of actual performance compared to targets. This evaluation phase provides vital feedback to enable future strategies to be more finely tuned to market needs, and for the purposes of motivating and controlling the sales force.

Performance in this context has several elements, each of which is important. Firstly, one can distinguish between the *aggregate* performance of the sales force in achieving the firm's sales targets, and the performance of *individual* sales personnel in their respective territories. Secondly, one can distinguish between *objective* (output) and *subjective* (input) measures of performance. Objective measures include such obviously important variables as sales volume and profitability, while subjective measures refer to less obvious but no less important variables such as the level of customer service provided or the number of new accounts secured.

RESEARCH ON SELLING AND SALES MANAGEMENT

The discussion so far had identified the main tasks required of sales managers for the management of their sales forces, but it does not offer many insights into best practice in any of these tasks. This is the area in which research can be of help, to identify how firms typically handle the various sales management tasks and to indicate what has been found to work best in particular situations. Much of the research on these topics has been carried out in the US, which is a quite different market from the UK and the Republic of Ireland, not least because of the size disparity. Nonetheless, American studies have identified many variables affecting sales performance which have universal significance, because they refer to fundamental aspects of human behaviour, which we would ignore at our peril.

It is also useful, of course, to have local data reflecting the particular conditions in which a firm operates, and two recent studies carried out in the Republic of Ireland help to meet this need. The first of these is entitled *Profile of a Sales Force*, carried out by the authors of this article in 1991 under sponsorship from Sales Placement Ltd. The second is entitled *Buyer Perceptions of Irish and Overseas Sales People*, which was carried out by the Market Research Bureau of Ireland Ltd. (MRBI) on behalf of Creative Management Ltd., and was also published in 1991.

These studies take different but complementary perspectives

and, together, they provide a comprehensive body of knowledge about selling and sales management in Ireland. The remainder of this paper sets out to review the combined contributions of these studies and to validate their findings by reference to the evidence from studies carried out in other countries. Prior to discussing research results, however, it is necessary to review the research methodology used in the two Irish studies, and the corresponding biases and limitations.

Profile of a Sales Force

This study was based on a postal survey of sales/marketing managers. A self-completion questionnaire was sent to the Top 1,000 Irish firms listed by *Business and Finance* on 14 June 1991. The questionnaire was 15 pages long and contained 47 questions divided into 4 sections covering company profile, organisation for selling, recruitment, training and remuneration, and sales management.

A total of 321 companies returned their questionnaires, which represents an acceptable response rate (32 per cent of the population). Of these, 86 companies did not have a sales force of their own, and completed only the first section of the questionnaire. The survey analysis was restricted, therefore, to the 235 companies which have a sales force and completed the full questionnaire. Descriptive statistics on the analysis sample indicated that it was biased towards relatively large (74 per cent had more than 50 employees), long-established companies, operating mainly in the domestic market (63 per cent of turnover on average). The results are likely to be more applicable to similar companies, and are less likely to be typical of very small or new businesses or of those operating mainly in export markets.

Buyer Perceptions of Irish and Overseas Salespeople

The objective of this study was to determine what buyers think of salespeople in the Republic of Ireland. This was achieved by means of a telephone survey of 300 purchasing managers/officers, from a random sample of companies drawn from the top 1,000 companies listed by Dun & Bradstreet and *Aspect* magazine. A total of 208 interviews was completed from the initial sample and these were carried out by MRBI Ltd. between 18 November and 21 December 1991.

The sample populations for both surveys were the same therefore, and the analysis samples that emerged were also very close both in size and composition, as can be seen from Table 19.1. The size classification schemes differed slightly between the surveys but both were broadly similar. MRBI used a weighting scheme in their analysis to increase the representation of the smaller companies (weighting factor 1.45) and to reduce the impact of the very large companies (weighting factor 0.45), but this serves to bring their sample closer to the UCD one rather than farther apart. In sum, one could argue that these surveys represent the view points of two different constituencies from a similar sample of companies, one representing the sellers and the other representing the buyers. The similarity of the basic sample of companies is convenient because it should allow comparisons to be drawn between the two groups, and for generalisations to be made within a similar range.

TABLE 19.1: SIZE DISTRIBUTION OF THE COMPANIES IN THE TWO IRISH SURVEYS

Number of Employees	Profile of a Sales Force n = 235	Buyer Perceptions of Sales People n = 208
1<99	49%	42%
100–199*	26%	21%
200+†	25%	37%
TOTAL	100%	100%

* The MRBI study excluded companies with fewer than 35 employees.
† The UCD study classified this group as 101–250.

The discussion of research results below is presented under headings similar to those suggested by the Churchill, Ford and Walker (1990) framework discussed earlier.

RESEARCH FINDINGS ON SELLING AND SALES MANAGEMENT
Sales Force Size and Organisation

The strategic decision concerning how much emphasis to give personal selling relative to other elements of the promotional mix depends on the communication tasks which must be accomplished.

Among the important characteristics to consider are: the size and nature of the target market, the complexity and service requirements of the product, and other elements of the marketing mix for that product. The impact of these factors on the relative importance of personal selling is summarised in Figure 19.2.

FIGURE 19.2: IMPORTANCE OF PERSONAL SELLING AS A PROMOTIONAL TOOL

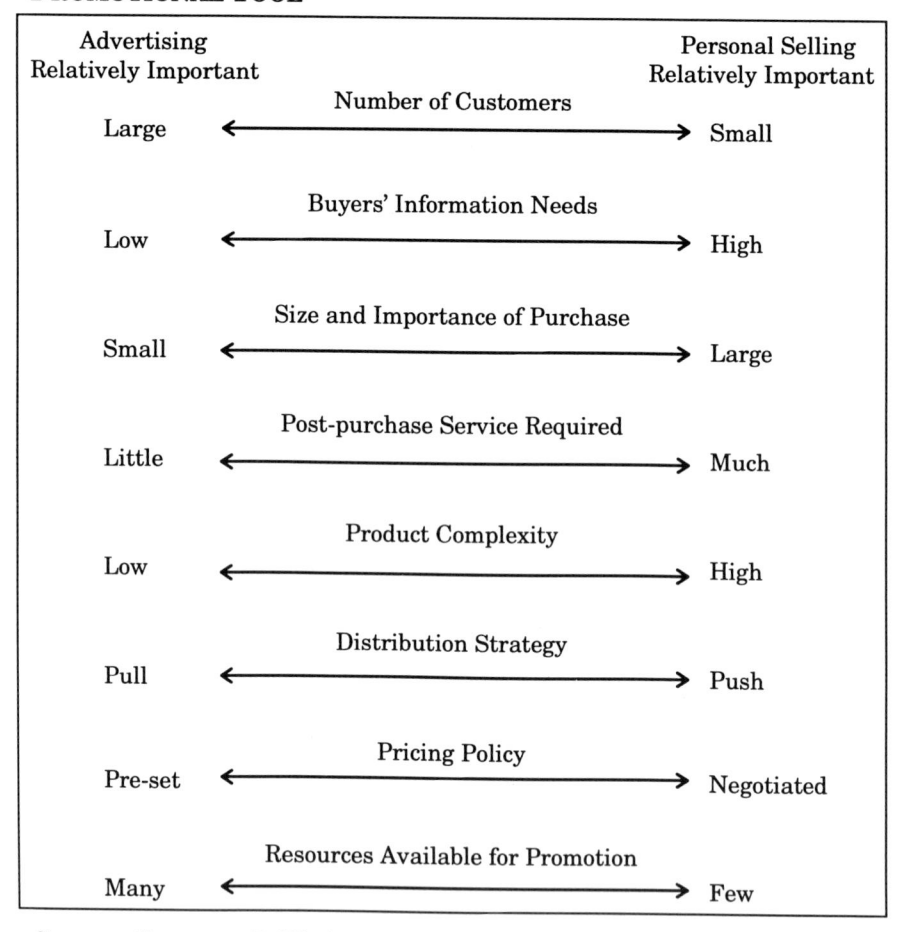

Advertising Relatively Important		Personal Selling Relatively Important
	Number of Customers	
Large	←——————→	Small
	Buyers' Information Needs	
Low	←——————→	High
	Size and Importance of Purchase	
Small	←——————→	Large
	Post-purchase Service Required	
Little	←——————→	Much
	Product Complexity	
Low	←——————→	High
	Distribution Strategy	
Pull	←——————→	Push
	Pricing Policy	
Pre-set	←——————→	Negotiated
	Resources Available for Promotion	
Many	←——————→	Few

Source: Cravens, D.W. (1987), *Strategic Marketing*, Homewood, IL: Irwin, p. 508.

In general, research evidence indicates that personal selling is more important and media advertising less important in industrial than in consumer goods companies (Udell, 1972; Harris et al., 1978). However, the same surveys emphasise that personal selling is considered the single most important promotional tool in both kinds of firms.

The size of sales forces operated by Irish companies is shown in Figure 19.3 (from *Profile of a Sales Force*). This shows that the most common size is between 5 and 10 (cited by 27 per cent of respondents), with significant proportions in the 1–5 and 10–15 categories. An analysis by industry sector did not produce any clear distinctions between consumer, industrial and service firms.

The ratio of sales managers to sales representatives for this sample averaged 1 : 4, so, for a sales force of 10 representatives, it would be typical to have three sales managers, perhaps one general sales manager and two regional or national account managers. The average age of sales representatives in this sample was 35 and the average length of service was 10 years. This suggests a relatively low level of employee turnover, which was found to be the case (68 per cent of respondents had a rate of turnover of less than 5 per cent, 87 per cent had less than 10 per cent).

FIGURE 19.3: SIZE OF SALES FORCES IN IRELAND

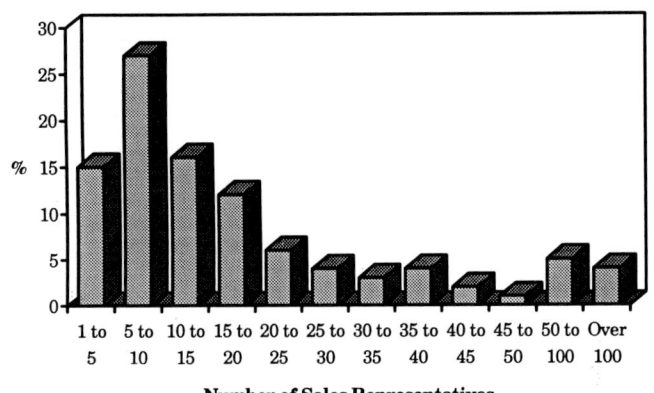

Source: Profile of a Sales Force.

Sales representatives in the surveyed companies averaged 28 calls per week, with a range from 19 to 40. This varied significantly by industry sector, however, with the agriculture and food/beverages/tobacco sectors having the largest number of calls (averages of 56 and 48 per week) and computers/information technology the lowest (8 per week). The mean number of calls per customer for the whole sample was 25 per year which equates to a call frequency of once a fortnight. This varied significantly across industries however, with monthly calls being cited by the largest proportion of respondents (37 per cent).

The average order size for this sample was £15,000, but this average conceals a wide degree of variation across companies and industries. The most frequently cited category was £1,000–£5,000 (27 per cent) and, in fact, orders of less than £5,000 were usual for over half of the companies (57 per cent).

In summary, the results of this section support the idea of a trade-off between the number and frequency of calls and average order size. The consumer goods companies conformed to the model of large numbers of customers, a high call frequency and small order sizes, while the industrial businesses had the opposite characteristics. Table 19.2 summarises the views of Irish sales managers with regard to the factors influencing the size and organisation of their sales forces.

TABLE 19.2: FACTORS INFLUENCING SIZE AND ORGANISATION OF THE SALES FORCE

	Mean Score
Sales Objective/Potential	4.3
Geographic Coverage	4.2
Number of Accounts	4.1
Frequency of Calls	4.0
Cost/Profit of a Salesperson	4.0
Type of Accounts	3.7
Competitor Activities	3.7
Level of Remuneration	3.3
Turnover of Personnel	2.8

Source: *Profile of a Sales Force.*

Selection and Training

Are good sales people born or are they made? This is a crucial question, which does not have a clear-cut answer. A survey of 2,000 American sales managers produced ambivalent responses on this issue (Bragg, 1988). While most of those surveyed believed that the things a company does to train its salespeople are the most critical determinant of future success, many also believed that that certain basic personal traits are necessary requirements. In sum, it seems that both aptitude and training are important for good performance, which suggests that careful selection and suitable training are equally important variables.

Selection. Aptitude and personal characteristics are generally thought to place an upper limit on an individual's ability to perform a given sales job (Churchill, Ford and Walker, 1990: p. 385). The task facing companies recruiting new sales personnel is to decide which personal characteristics to look for, and how to assess aptitude. A widely accepted principle for many years was that salespeople tend to be most successful when they are similar to their customers in as many dimensions as possible, such as age, sex, social status, educational attainment, etc. (Churchill, Ford and Walker, 1990). Recent research has cast some doubt on this relationship, but a review of American studies on this topic supports the general point that personal characteristics such as family background and marital status are the most important indicators of likely sales success (Ford et al., 1988). A major conclusion from this review is that evidence of initiative, responsibility and stability in a person's past and current life are key factors in assessing emotional maturity and motivation which, in turn, are important predictors of sales performance.

TABLE 19.3 SELECTION CRITERIA

	Mean Score
Personal Characteristics	4.6
Ambition/Potential	4.5
Sales Experience	3.9
Knowledge/Experience	3.8
Education Level	3.7
Personal Mobility	3.8
Age	3.4

Source: Profile of a Sales Force.

With regard to aptitude, a survey of top sales executives in 44 major American manufacturing firms ranked enthusiasm as the most important characteristic to look for in new recruits, followed by *organisation, ambition, persuasiveness, general sales experience*, and *verbal skill* (Moss, 1978). Interestingly, *recommendations* from previous employers or teachers were not seen as very important (ranked 8 out of 10), and *sociability* reflecting the "hail-fellow-well-met" type of personality — was ranked last on the list.

The *Profile of a Sales Force* survey shows that Irish sales managers have quite similar views to their American counterparts on this point, as shown in Table 19.3. *Personal characteristics* are ranked top of the list of selection criteria, followed by *ambition/potential* and *sales experience*.

Training. Training for sales people has two main dimensions: *product/market knowledge* and *selling skills*. The first of these dimensions is most appropriately provided through on-the-job training, because the requisite knowledge and information resides within the company. The second dimension may be more suited to external training, however, because professional selling can be enhanced by the application of sales techniques which may not be consciously known or practised in individual companies.

Research from several sources shows, however, that on-the-job training remains the main, and often the only, training that sales people receive. For example, a survey of 1,300 American and Canadian industrial firms, showed that 43 per cent provided no training for their sales forces, 34 per cent relied on internally developed programmes, and only 23 per cent used professional sales training services (*Marketing News*, 1989). The Irish evidence is very similar (*Profile of a Sales Force*, 1991). 91 per cent of companies give on-the-job training to their sales forces while 72 per cent provide formal courses, but a majority of the formal courses (77 per cent) last for one week or less. It does seem, therefore, that there is scope for improvement in this area.

Motivation and Remuneration

A salesperson's motivation to expend effort is determined by three sets of perceptions (Churchill, Ford and Walker, 1990: pp. 495–6):

(1) *Expectations* — the perceived linkages between level of effort and performance.
(2) *Instrumentalities* — the perceived relationship between improved performance and the attainment of increased rewards.

(3) *Valence of rewards* — the perceived attractiveness of the various rewards available.

Historically, sales managers and writers on motivating sales people have focused mainly on the third of these points — the *valence of rewards*, and the general assumption has been that monetary rewards have the highest value for salespeople.

But, is this assumption correct, or is it over-simplistic?

Several recent studies of industrial salespeople support the conventional view, but demonstrate that it is by no means universal, and is contingent upon many individual and organisational factors (Ingram and Bellenger, 1983; Ford et al., 1985). In particular, the value placed upon additional pay depends on the current level received, and on such factors as whether people reached their quotas and qualified for bonuses in previous years. The conclusion appears to be that the motivational effect of extra pay diminishes as the overall level of pay increases, so that highly paid salespeople would be less motivated to seek extra pay than less well-paid salespeople. Similarly, regular achievement of quota causes this factor to be taken for granted and to become less of a motivator, unless the quota is regularly increased to create new challenge.

The Irish study showed *remuneration* ranked third as a factor motivating salespeople, after *acknowledgement of effort* and *achievement of sales targets* (see Table 19.4). Furthermore, factors such as satisfaction of customers and being part of a team ranked equally with remuneration.

TABLE 19.4: FACTORS MOTIVATING THE SALES FORCE

Factor	Rank Order	Mean Score
Acknowledgement of Effort	1	4.6
Achievement of Sales	2	4.4
Remuneration	3	4.3
Satisfaction of Customers	4	4.3
Being Part of a Team	5	4.1
Meeting Management Expectations	6	3.9
Improvement of Lifestyle	7	3.6
Status Symbols	8	3.3

Source: Profile of a Sales Force.

This rank order may be specific to the type of companies in this sample, however, which probably represent the top end of the remuneration scale and also provide a range of other benefits.

The mix of rewards provided for salespeople is also an important influence on motivation. This refers to the relative emphasis on salary versus incentive pay (commission and/or bonus). The combination offered will influence the salesperson's instrumentality estimates, and will help determine which work activities and types of performance will receive the greater effort from that salesperson (Churchill, Ford and Walker, 1990). The question from a manager's point of view is how to design a suitable compensation plan to direct the sales force's efforts towards those activities that are most important to the overall success of the company's sales strategy.

American research indicates that most companies in that country (83 per cent) provide combination plans including salary plus some element of incentive pay, in the form of commission (21 per cent) or bonus (50 per cent), or both (11 per cent) (Alexander Group, 1988). The evidence also suggests that the average level of incentive pay is 20–25 per cent of total pay (McAdams, 1987). This rate varies, however, depending on whether commission or bonus is the chosen form of incentive. Another survey found that compensation plans combining salary and bonus have an average of 11 per cent incentive-related pay, while salary plus commission plans average 33 per cent incentive pay (Peck, 1982).

Commenting on this evidence, Churchill, Ford and Walker (1990) advise that when a company's primary objectives are related to short-term sales, such as increasing sales volume, or winning new customers, a large incentive component should be offered. When long-term sales and relationship building are the key objectives, a higher salary and lower level of incentive pay tied to appropriate performance targets (bonus) would be more effective. The *Profile of a Sales Force* report showed that sales force compensation plans in Ireland are quite similar to their American equivalents. As illustrated in Figure 19.4, 79 per cent of companies pay salaries plus some type of incentive payment. Of these, 21 per cent pay commission only, 24 per cent pay a bonus only, while 34 per cent pay both. The average rate of commission paid is 26 per cent while bonuses average 12 per cent of total pay, but it should be noted that both of these figures vary widely across industries.

FIGURE 19.4: COMPOSITION OF SALES FORCE COMPENSATION PLANS

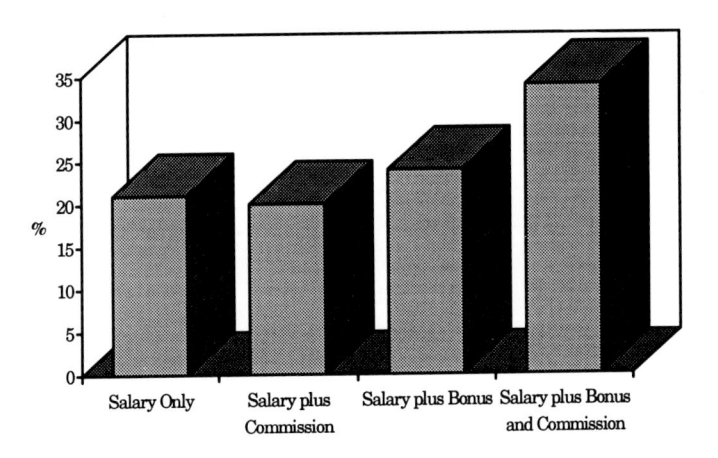

Source: Profile of a Sales Force.

Taking an average rate of incentive pay of 20 per cent together with an average salary for salespeople (£17,750) and estimates of other costs, the authors estimated that the total annual cost of a field sales representative currently in Ireland is approximately £43,500 (see Table 19.5). Extrapolating a bit further, it can be seen that the cost of an average-sized sales force of 10 representatives would be approximately £435,000 per year. Add to that the cost of sales management and sales administration at a ratio of, say, .5:1 and the total annual cost of selling would be £653,000. This would be a very significant level of overhead for many Irish companies and one whose productivity requires careful scrutiny.

Evaluation of Performance

Sales managers have many variables to choose from in judging the performance of their sales force, both objective and subjective, as shown in Table 19.6. In practice, however, most seem to opt for the simple, objective measures of output associated with sales volume and account profitability. One American study showed that 80 per cent of companies evaluate salespeople with respect to sales volume, and 75 per cent assess their performance relative to quota

(Jackson et al., 1982; 1983). Smaller proportions also focus on order and account data using some or all of the variables listed in Table 19.6.

TABLE 19.5: ESTIMATED AVERAGE COST OF A SALES REPRESENTATIVE

Basic Salary	£17,750
PRSI (12.2% of Salary)	2,355
Pension (10% of Salary)	1,780
Commission/Bonus (26% of gross earnings)	4,440
Travel Expenses	7,500
Car Purchase and Tax	6,000
Car Insurance	1,000
Service and Repairs	500
Postage & Telephone (£5 p/w; £75 p/m)	1,160
Training (1 x 1 week course)	500
Sundries (entertainment etc.)	500
TOTAL	£43,385

Source: Profile of a Sales Force.

Subjective measures of the quality of a salesperson's work are far more difficult, which probably explains why sales managers are reluctant to emphasise them in their formal evaluation procedures (Jackson et al., 1983). However, the relative emphasis on objective and subjective measures seems to depend on the purpose for which the evaluation is being used. A study by Patton and King (1985) suggests that objective sales performance measures are more important in termination and compensation decisions, whereas subjective assessments of product knowledge and customer relations are more important in transfer and promotion decisions.

The *Profile of a Sales Force* survey shows that Irish sales managers have a fairly similar view of the criteria that are important for evaluating sales performance.

TABLE 19.6: COMMON OUTPUT AND INPUT FACTORS USED BY SALES MANAGERS TO EVALUATE SALES PEOPLE

Output Factors	Input Factors
A. Sales	*A. Calls*
Total Sales Volume	Number of Calls to New Customers
Total Sales Value	Number of Planned/Unplanned Calls
Sales versus Target	Number of Calls
Sales by Product	
Sales by Customer	*Time Utilisation*
Sales by Region	Days Worked
	Calls per Day
B. Orders	Selling versus Non-selling Time
Number of Orders	
Average Size of Orders	*C. Non-selling Activities*
Number of Cancelled Orders	Job Knowledge
Number of Returned Orders	Management of Territory
	Administrative Efficiency
C. Accounts	Advertising Displays Set Up
Number of Active Accounts	Standing with Customers
Number of New Accounts	Number of Customer Complaints
Number of Lost Accounts	Number of Overdue Accounts Collected
Number of Overdue Accounts	
Number of Prospective Accounts	*D. Expenses*
Account Profitability	Total and Type
	As a Percentage of Sales
	As a Percentage of Quota

Source: Adapted from Churchill, G.A. Jr., Ford, N.M., and Walker, O.C. Jr. (1990), *Sales Force Management*, third ed., Irwin, Homewood, IL, pp. 731–40.

As can be seen from Table 19.7, *sales volume* ranks top of the list of performance measures, and *account profitability* is third. *Customer relations* comes second, however, and other subjective measures such as a *professional approach* and *product/technical knowledge* are also accorded a high priority. Interestingly, *new customers* are ranked 7 out of 9 which suggests that sales managers in the large mature type of businesses in this sample give a higher priority to the maintenance of existing business than to the generation of new business; this is consistent with their emphasis on good customer relations and account profitability. It is also consistent with the advice of Tom Peters who, in his book *Thriving on Chaos* (1988), cites research showing that it costs five times as much to win a new customer as to keep an existing one.

TABLE 19.7: EVALUATING SALES PERSONNEL

Factor	Rank Order	Mean Score*
Sales Volume	1	2.9
Customer Relations	2	3.5
Account Profitability	3	3.8
Professional Approach	4	3.9
Product/Technical Knowledge	5	5.3
Territory Management	6	5.6
New Customers	7	6.1
Number of Sales Calls	8	6.8
Order/Call Ratio	9	7.0

* Low mean scores indicate a high rank order and high scores mean the reverse.
Source: *Profile of a Sales Force*.

That same research study also produced interesting evidence on the behaviour of dissatisfied customers. In particular, it showed that 95 per cent of customers who have a bad experience with a supplier company do not complain or report it because they believe that it would not do any good. Furthermore, over 90 per cent of those who do complain do not repurchase the product about which they had reason to complain.

The lesson from this seems to be that companies cannot afford to take their customers for granted; otherwise the first evidence of a dissatisfied customer may be a lost account. Thus, another important dimension of performance evaluation rests with the views of the customers which may not necessarily match those of the sales managers. The second Irish survey *Buyer Perceptions of Irish and Overseas Salespeople* (1991) provides some useful insights on this topic. It specifically addressed the question of how purchasers evaluate salespeople and, particularly, how they rate the performance of Irish salespeople over those from abroad. The 208 purchasers interviewed see an average of 21 salespeople per month and four out of five of these are Irish.

The respondents were first asked to draw upon their own experience and name up to five qualities that they expect to find in a good salesperson. The combined responses to this question yielded a list of 17 qualities which are summarised in Table 19.8. From this it emerges that good *product knowledge* is the key quality expected of salespeople, particularly in manufacturing and processing industries. Other important factors are: *honesty, reliability, courtesy, professionalism, punctuality, communication skills and decisiveness.*

TABLE 19.8: EXPECTATIONS OF A GOOD SALESPERSON

Mentioned Spontaneously	%
Good Product Knowledge	65
Honesty/Integrity/Good Reputation	27
Reliable/Follows Up on What's Agreed	21
Not Pushy/Not a Pest	20
Good Manners/Polite/Courteous	18
Well Groomed/Neatness	17
Good Personality/Good Character	16
Knows Their Job/Business/Market	14
Punctuality/Time Keeping	14
Confident/Articulate/Can Communicate	12
Clear and Concise	10
Professional Approach	10
Directness/Decisiveness	9
Makes an Appointment	7
Comes Prepared	7
Good Quality Service/After-sales Service	7
Understands Customer Needs	7

Source: Buyer Perceptions of Irish and Overseas Salespeople.

On average, 50 per cent of Irish salespeople were said to have all or most of these qualities, but 75 per cent of overseas salespeople were said to possess them. Figure 19.5 provides a summary comparison of the ratings of Irish and overseas salespeople on six key qualities. Irish salespeople score less well on each of these variables but the widest margins are on product knowledge and general professionalism.

This comparison should be viewed with some caution because of the relatively limited experience of Irish purchasers in dealing with overseas salespeople (one out of five of the salespeople they see). However, a spontaneous listing of common failings of Irish salespeople identified similar points of weakness, such as lack of product knowledge (32 per cent of respondents), turning up without an appointment (25 per cent), lack of follow-up and back-up (16 per cent) and failure to deliver on time/unreliable (13 per cent).

It seems, therefore, that Irish sales managers and sales representatives would do well to question themselves on these important, although subjective points because, as we look to the future, it is obvious that Irish companies must be able to match international standards in their selling activities as well as in all other aspects of their operations.

CONCLUSIONS AND IMPLICATIONS

At the beginning of this paper it was pointed out that selling is only one element within the marketing mix — although a high cost element — and to manage it to best advantage, it must be subject to careful planning and strategic thinking. This requires a long-term focus and the specification of clear, measurable objectives which will provide clear guidance for all of the decisions made by sales managers and for specifying the tasks of the sales representatives. Without such clarity of purpose, it is easy to see how a sales force could become a costly overhead rather than a net contributor to the goals of the company.

The research reviewed in this paper yielded a number of insights which ought to be noted by companies which manage their own sales force. Firstly, in setting objectives for their sales personnel sales managers have to decide on the relative priority to be accorded to such variables as sales volume versus sales revenue, and maintaining existing business versus building new business. The results of this survey indicate that sales managers put primary emphasis on sales volume over account profitability and on existing business over new business.

FIGURE 19.5: SUMMARY COMPARISON OF IRISH AND OVERSEAS SALES REPRESENTATIVES: KEY SKILLS

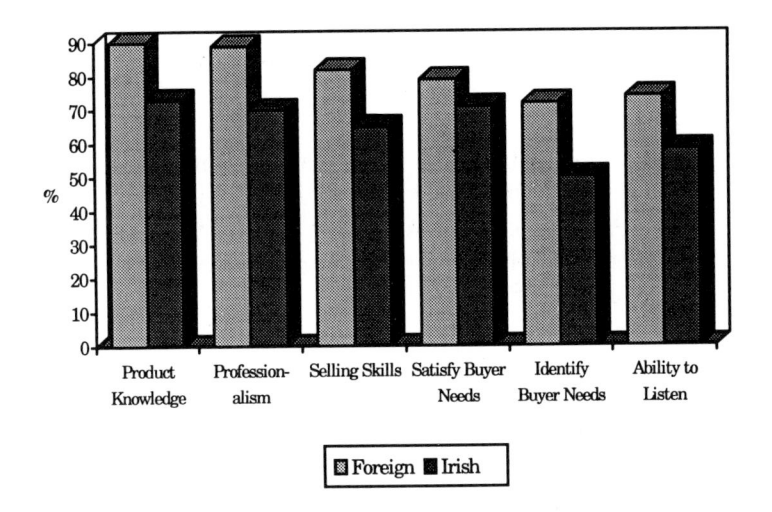

Source: Buyer Perceptions of Irish and Overseas Salespeople.

Secondly, objectives set by sales management should influence the nature and structure of the remuneration package given to sales personnel. If the emphasis is on maintenance of customer relations and sales volume, then a package based mainly on salary supplemented by a bonus tied to long-term performance targets would be optimal. On the contrary, if the objective is to build sales volume through new accounts, then a significant element of commission might be appropriate. Again, care must be taken to ensure that generous incentive payments are not being paid routinely without any demonstrable effect on sales.

Thirdly, for sales personnel to perform effectively requires not only that they be remunerated adequately, but also that they be equipped with skills and knowledge appropriate to their job. Research results seem to indicate that the level of formal training given to sales representatives is rather low, both in Ireland and internationally. It seems fair to argue that the increasingly professional nature of selling as a career would justify a more intensive training programme. Educators in sales and marketing and those involved in training and development would do well to recognise this need.

Finally, the necessity for further research on this important topic area needs to be highlighted. This study represents a starting point rather than a conclusive review, and it is hoped that other researchers and organisations may be interested in exploring in much greater detail various dimensions, touched upon here.

REFERENCES

Alexander Group (1988): *Sales Personnel Report, 1986/1987*, New York: Alexander Group.

Bragg, A. (1988): "Are Good Salespeople Born or Made?", *Sales and Marketing Management*, 140(12): 74–8.

Churchill, G.A. Jr. et al. (1985): "The Determinants of Sales Person's Performance: A Meta-analysis", *Journal of Marketing Research*, 22(2): 103–18.

Ford, N.M., Walker, O.C. Jr., and Churchill, G.A., Jr. (1985): "Differences in the Attractiveness of Alternative Rewards Among Industrial Sales People", *Journal of Business Research*, April 15(2): 123–38.

Ford. N.M., Walker, O.C. Jr., Churchill G.A. Jr., and Hartley S.W. (1988): "Selecting Successful Salespeople: A Meta-analysis of Biographical and Psychological Criteria", in M.J. Houston (ed.), *Review of Marketing*, Chicago, Illinois: American Marketing Association.

Harris, C.E. Jr., Still, R.R. and Crask, M.R. (1978): "Stability or Change in Marketing Methods", *Business Horizons*, 21, October: 35.

Ingram, T.N. and Bellenger, D.N. (1983): "Personal and Organisational Variables: Their Relative Effect on Reward Values of Industrial Sales People", *Journal of Marketing Research*, 20(2): 198–205.

Jackson. D.W., Keith, J.E. and Schlacter, J.L. (1983): "Evaluation of Selling Performance: A Study of Current Practices", *Journal of Personal Selling and Sales Management*, 3, November: 42–51.

Jackson, D.W. Jr., Ostrom L.L. and Evans K.R. (1982): "Measures Used to Evaluate Industrial Marketing Activities", *Industrial Marketing Management*, 11: 267–74.

Keenan, W. Jr. (1989): "The Nagging Problem of the Plateaud Salesperson", *Sales and Marketing Management*, 14(4): 36–41.

McAdams, J. (1987): "Rewarding Sales and Marketing Performance", *Management Review,* April: 33–8.

Marketing News (1989): "Study Reveals Sales Training Needs of Business Marketers", American Marketing Association, Chicago, 13 March: 6.

Moss, S. (1978): "What Sales Executives Look for in New Sales People", *Sales and Marketing Management*, March: 78.

Patton, W.E. III, and King R.H. (1985): "The Use of Human Judgement Models in Evaluating Sales Force Performance", *Journal of Personal Selling and Sales Management*, 5 May: 1–14.

Peck, C.A. (1982): *Compensating Field Sales Representatives*, New York: The Conference Board.

Peters T.J. (1988): *Thriving on Chaos: Handbook for a Management Revolution,* London: Macmillan.

Udell, J.G. (1972): *Successful Marketing Strategies in American Marketing,* Madison, WIS: Mimir Publishers.

PART VIII

Distribution Systems and Processes

20
Meeting Source Selection Criteria: Direct versus Distributor Channels*

David Shipley,
Colin Egan and
Scott Edgett

INTRODUCTION

Marketing performance is a function of marketing effectiveness (how well customer needs are satisfied) and marketing efficiency (at what cost) (Drucker, 1973; MacDonald, 1982). A key determinant of these factors is the choice of distribution channel. In broad and simple terms, producers can either perform the selling, service and physical distribution tasks themselves or recruit the specialist capabilities of intermediaries. Many factors influence which of these options is optimal for a particular producer. The prime considerations include market needs, size, and geographic dispersion; buy class; product complexity, bulk, and perishability; service needs; competitor channel designs; producers' channel competencies; and the availability and quality of intermediaries.

A prime purpose of using intermediaries is to generate efficiency through the exploitation of specialisation in sorting, assorting, storing, and transporting (Stern and El-Ansary, 1988; Walters and Bergiel, 1982). Efficiency is important because of its effect on costs, prices, and margins. However, overemphasis on distribution efficiency risks sacrificing effectiveness by trimming away the sources of customer satisfaction, which must be treated as the ultimate determinant of channel design and performance (Brown, 1987). Without effectiveness to win patronage there will be no sales to gain margins on, while price, a partial determinant of

---

* This paper was first published in *Industrial Marketing Management*, 1991, Vol. 20.

efficiency, is an important sourcing criterion, a wide range of other seller attributes are equally or collectively more important (Dempsey, 1978; Lehmann and O'Shaughnessy, 1974). Effectiveness, achieved through the provision of required product quality, delivery, information, service, choice, etc., must be appropriately prioritised, otherwise customers may source elsewhere. This is particularly likely where the prices of competing suppliers are closely matched, as in many industrial rebuy markets. Sacrificing too much channel effectiveness to gain channel efficiency will result in firms being, as Porter says, "stuck in the middle" with no competitive advantage (Porter, 1985).

Marketing principles hold that the selection and verification of channel design should be based on research to determine customer needs among other important factors. However, very few firms routinely perform customer satisfaction studies regarding specific vendor attributes (Churchill and Suprenant, 1982; Day and Wensley, 1988). Nevertheless, some general insights have been provided by supplier selection studies (Dempsey, 1978; Lehmann and O'Shaughnessy, 1974; Abratt, 1986; Banting, 1976; Brown and Purwar, 1980; Kassicieh and Roger, 1986; Kiser, Rao and Rao, 1975; McGoldrick and Douglas, 1983; Shipley and Prinja, 1988). These studies show that the identification of vendor selection criteria indicates requirements for effective marketing.

A key weakness of the source selection literature however, is that it has not addressed how well suppliers perform in providing attributes for customer satisfaction. In particular, it has not focused on the relative effectiveness of alternative channel designs. Accordingly, research is needed to determine the optimal designs for the achievement of competitive advantage through customer satisfaction. Findings would be of value to both educators and practitioners. Educators may develop more realistic and powerful theories and provide more appropriate training programmes, while practitioners may develop more effective channel designs and marketing strategies.

This study attempts to begin closing this empirical gap. The objective was to identify buyers' sourcing criteria and determine the absolute and relative performance in meeting them of industrial distributors and manufacturers serving customers direct. By studying rebuy buyers for British engineering companies, it addresses previously investigated and new potential sourcing criteria and investigates buyer perceptions of how well distributors and direct suppliers satisfy them.

METHODOLOGY AND SAMPLE

Data were gathered in a postal survey of senior buyers for companies chosen randomly from the *Directory of Engineering Companies, 1988*. A structured questionnaire was developed after a literature search and group discussions involving, respectively, seven and eight buyers for engineering companies. A pilot instrument was tested among ten additional buyers and subsequently amended to produce the final questionnaire. This contained 13 questions seeking 138 discrete pieces of data. The questions were easy to understand and sought multiple choice or scale evaluation answers. A range of response-building techniques was used. These included a clear statement of the research purpose, an offer to share findings, inclusion of a paid return envelope, a promise of confidentiality and opportunity for anonymity, a plea to altruism, and a second mailing of the questionnaire to non respondents.

Of 300 questionnaires, 28 were returned unopened, spoiled, or after the cut-off date. Usable responses numbered 112, providing a usable-response rate of 41.8 per cent. This compares well with the mean of 36.4 per cent for industrial mail survey response rates cited by Hart (1987). All of the responses were from engineering companies. Data concerning firm size showed that a large proportion of respondents were employed by small- to medium-sized firms. Of these, 80.4 per cent employ fewer than 200 people, while 70.6 per cent have annual revenues below £5 million.

Following Lehmann and O'Shaughnessy (1974), it recognised that industrial buying behaviour is strongly influenced by buyclass. To permit generalisable conclusions, therefore, respondents were asked to confine their responses to rebuy products only. The term "rebuy" was defined in the questionnaire and examples given of rebuy products included hand tools, fasteners, raw materials, lubricants, and simple office supplies.

Considerable support for the reliability of the findings obtains in the respondents' buying centre status and experience. Nearly 94 per cent of respondents had full authority for rebuy purchasing. 84.8 per cent were their firms' senior buyer, 84.1 per cent had more than 5 years' rebuy purchasing experience, and 61.8 per cent had more than 10 years' experience.

It was expected that buyers' perceptions of distributors and direct sellers would influence their purchasing decisions irrespective of where they were currently sourcing. However, given the comparative nature of the study, it was considered important to determine which sources are used for rebuys. Both of the sources under investigation are used extensively, with 93.8 per cent of respondents sourcing rebuys direct from producers and 97.3 per cent from distributors. It is not known what proportions of rebuy purchases are obtained from the two sources or what product differences exist, although it is reasonable to expect some variation. However, the prime purpose of this study was to determine the relative competitiveness of the two channel types in the supply of engineering rebuys generally. Statistical significance results shown in the following section were computed by x-square analysis.

RESULTS

Buyers' Source Selection Criteria

Respondents were asked to indicate on a 5-point scale the influence of each of 21 factors in their supplier selection decisions. Scale points ranged from 1 = no influence to 5 = very strong influence. The results show that all of the 21 variables are applied by much of the sample and most are influential in vendor selection. Fifteen factors were each cited by over 90 per cent of the sample, while the frequency for the least-cited criterion is 69 per cent.

Most of the analysis was conducted in terms of mean influence scores since these provide important insights. However, as Dempsey (1978) has warned, comparisons of sourcing criteria rankings should be treated with caution since there is a danger of forming misleading judgments from analyses of means which differ arithmetically, but not significantly. This is supported in the present findings. For example, Table 20.1 lists price competitiveness as the first-ranked criterion, but the mean influence of the tenth-ranked factor is only 9.8 per cent less than that of price. The other top 10 criteria are: keeps promises, helpful in emergencies, product quality, fair and trustworthy, previous performance, product availability, delivery service, technical know-how, and response to complaints. The narrow range of the mean influence of these variables strongly suggests that marketers should recognise their collective impact on supplier selection and strive to perform well on each variable, as well as to provide an attractive blend of all variables. This is reinforced by their high frequency values, which range only 3.5 per cent between 96.5 per cent and 100 per cent.

TABLE: 20.1 COMPARISON OF SOURCE SELECTION INFLUENCES AND BUYER PERCEPTIONS OF DISTRIBUTORS' AND DIRECT SELLERS' PERFORMANCE

\multicolumn{5}{c}{A. Buyers' Purchase Criteria}
Rank	Variables	Frequency %	Mean Influence	SD
1	Price Competitiveness	97.40	4.41	0.99
2	Keeps Promises	98.20	4.39	0.80
3	Helpful in Emergencies	98.20	4.36	0.80
4	Product Quality	96.60	4.34	0.99
5	Fair and Trustworthy	99.10	4.30	0.87
6	Previous Performance	98.30	4.23	0.93
7	Product Availability	97.40	4.21	0.97
8	Delivery Service	96.50	4.16	1.09
9	Technical Know-how	97.40	4.04	0.95
10	Response to Complaints	100.00	3.98	0.84
11	Capable and Helpful Sales Force	98.30	3.82	0.99
12	Reputation	94.90	3.68	1.11
13	After-sales Service	92.10	3.66	1.21
14	Adapt to Your Specification	89.30	3.55	1.36
15	Sales Quotation Service	89.30	3.55	1.29
16	Product Range	97.40	3.50	1.01
17	Personal Relationship with You	89.30	3.49	1.27
18	Credit Terms	85.20	3.27	1.36
19	Information Service	92.00	3.11	1.19
20	Informative Ads/Promotions	80.00	2.66	1.21
21	Product Demonstration	69.00	2.55	1.08

Rankings are by mean score. Frequency is the number of times a variable was rated higher than 1 (no influence) on 5-point scale.

B. Distributors' Performance			
Variables	**Mean Influence**	**SD**	**Rank**
Price Competitiveness	3.38	1.00	11*
Keeps Promises	3.39	0.87	10*
Helpful in Emergencies	3.59	0.80	4*
Product Quality	3.55	0.97	6*
Fair and Trustworthy	3.61	0.80	3*
Previous Performance	3.57	0.78	5*
Product Availability	3.79	0.85	2*
Delivery Service	3.96	0.83	1*
Technical Know-how	2.98	0.94	17*
Response to Complaints	3.27	0.86	15*
Capable and Helpful Sales Force	3.34	0.84	14*
Reputation	3.38	0.78	11
After-sales Service	3.16	0.91	16*
Adapt to Your Specification	2.57	1.16	21*
Sales Quotation Service	3.43	1.02	9
Product Range	3.50	0.85	7
Personal Relationship with You	3.49	0.93	8
Credit Terms	3.36	1.02	13
Information Service	2.95	0.94	18
Informative Ads/Promotions	2.89	0.95	19*
Product Demonstration	2.77	1.06	20*

Rankings are by mean score. Frequency is the number of times a variable was rated higher than 1 (no influence) on 5-point scale.

* Buyer mean influence significantly higher than perceived distributor performance at 95% level.

C. Direct Sellers' Performance

Variables	Mean Influence	SD	Rank
Price Competitiveness	3.71	0.93	3†‡
Keeps Promises	3.09	0.90	19†‡
Helpful in Emergencies	3.13	1.01	18†‡
Product Quality	3.82	0.88	2†‡
Fair and Trustworthy	3.59	0.78	5†
Previous Performance	3.45	0.78	7†
Product Availability	3.20	1.12	14†‡
Delivery Service	3.16	1.08	15†‡
Technical Know-how	4.00	0.83	1†
Response to Complaints	3.27	1.12	12†
Capable and Helpful Sales Force	3.39	0.68	8†
Reputation	3.46	0.87	6
After-sales Service	3.30	0.95	11†
Adapt to Your Specification	3.39	1.12	8†‡
Sales Quotation Service	3.66	0.86	4
Product Range	3.39	0.89	8
Personal Relationship with You	3.16	1.08	15‡
Credit Terms	3.16	0.93	15
Information Service	3.21	1.02	13
Informative Ads/Promotions	2.91	0.92	20†
Product Demonstration	2.88	1.11	21†

Rankings are by mean score. Frequency is the number of times a variable was rated higher than 1 (no influence) on 5-point scale.
† Buyer mean influence significantly higher than perceived direct supplier performance at 95% level.
‡ Significant difference between perceived performance of distributors and direct sellers at 95% level.

The results support earlier findings. For example, Lehmann and O'Shaughnessy (1974) reported reliability of supply and price as the most important criteria for sourcing routine-order products. Cameron and Shipley (1985) identified price, quality, and reliable delivery as the prime criteria for industrial raw materials rebuys, and Dempsey (1978) reported the primacy of the same three criteria. Dempsey (1978) concluded that industrial source selection decisions are substantially economic based and rational. However, he argued that other factors may be decisive when vendors' offerings are equal on explicitly economic criteria.

The present findings indicate that rebuy sourcing determinants are based on relationships as well as economics. The major role of economic criteria is clear. In addition to price, quality and delivery, high absolute means were recorded for the variables of product availability, technical know-how, after-sales service, adaptability to specifications, product range, quotation service, credit terms, and information service. The relatively low means attaching to informative ads/promotion and product demonstration probably reflect the low level of search usually associated with rebuy purchases.

However, high frequencies and means were also recorded for less directly economic criteria, supporting Dempsey's cautionary note. In particular, the variables keeps promises, helpful in emergencies, and fair and trustworthy attained means higher than those of all the economic criteria except price competitiveness. The eminence of these variables is consistent with studies of industrial marketing which advocate a strong need for sellers to establish effective relationships with buyers (Cameron and Shipley, 1985; Turnbull and Cunningham, 1981). Other relationships-based criteria given high means and frequencies by buyers are previous performance, response to complaints, capable and helpful sales force, reputation, and personal relationship with the buyer.

Absolute Performance of Channels

Buyers were asked to indicate how well distributors and direct sellers perform in meeting the 21 sourcing criteria using a 5-point scale (1 = performs badly; 5 = performs very well). The results displayed in Table 20.1 and illustrated in Figure 20.1 show clearly that both types of channels generally fail to match buyer needs for most of the criteria. Moreover, the failure gaps of both channel types widen as buyer requirements become more influential. Indeed, distributors underperform on 13 and direct sellers underperform on 12 of the 14 highest-ranking buyer influences. An inference is that buyers are obliged to satisfice to the extent of channel ineffectiveness. Both categories of suppliers need to improve effectiveness and there are clear opportunities for suppliers to improve their competitive positions.

Relative Performance of Channels

Table 20.1 and Figure 20.1 show the relative competitiveness of direct vis-à-vis distributor channels by comparing their absolute effectiveness as perceived by buyers. Although both channel types generally failed to meet buyer criteria in absolute terms, each type achieved advantage over the other on several of the top-ranking selection determinants. Distributors performed significantly better than direct sellers on keeps promises, helpful in emergencies, product availability, delivery service, and relationship with buyer variables. On the other hand, direct sellers significantly outperformed distributors on price competitiveness, product quality, technical know-how, and adapt to specifications variables. There were no significant differences in the remaining variables.

FIGURE 20.1: INFLUENCES OF PURCHASE CRITERIA AND PERFORMANCE OF DISTRIBUTORS AND DIRECT SELLERS IN MEETING THEM

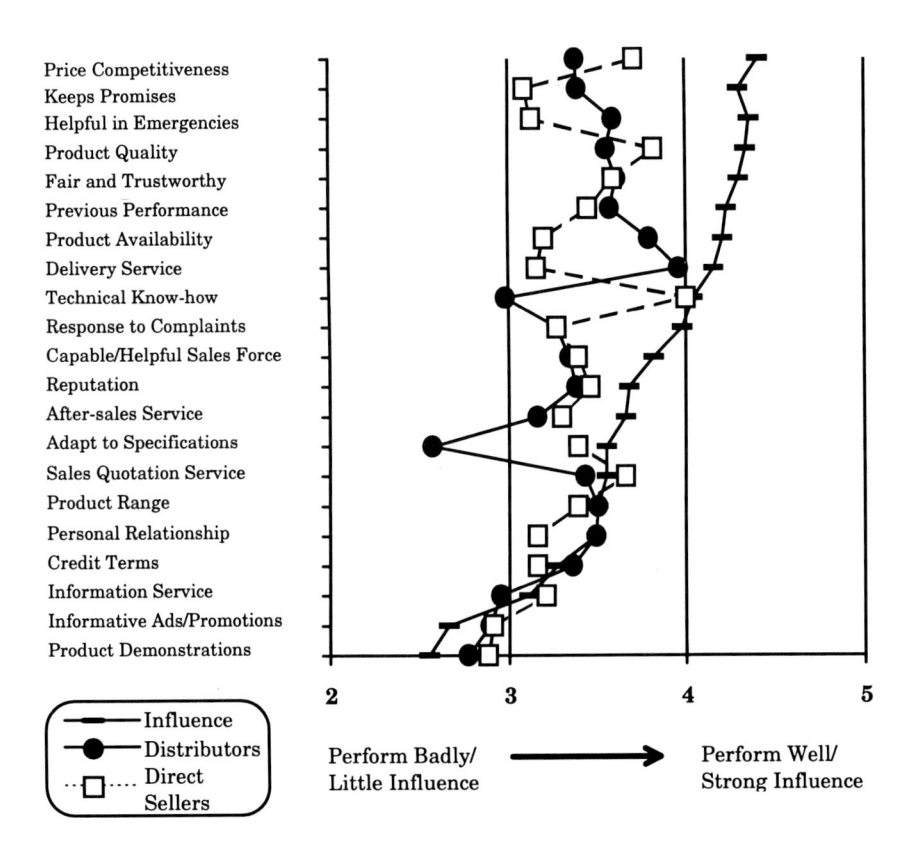

The significant differences are explained by the respective channel role specialisations of the two categories of suppliers. Distributors gain edge on variables associated with their prime distribution task of facilitating market coverage for the creation of customer relationships and the provision of products, services, and delivery (Shipley and Prinja, 1988). Specifically, four of the distributor advantages can be related to their typically narrow geographic market coverage and the consequent ability to build customer relations and react rapidly when required. Conversely, direct sellers perform significantly better than distributors on product-specific variables such as technical know-how, product customisation and quality, since these factors are within their primary domain of manufacturing. The price competitive advantage of direct sellers may be attributed to greater distribution efficiency, but this seems unlikely because of distributors' task specialisation. A more probable explanation is the lack of need for distributors' margins and less investment in building relationships.

As reported above, nearly all of the buyers purchase rebuys from both channel types. Respondents were asked to state whether they prefer to source rebuys from distributors or direct sellers or whether they have no preference. Nearly half (48.2 per cent) of respondents cited no preference. This may be because neither channel type meets buying criteria fully or because the competitive advantages of the two channels cancel out. However, 44.7 per cent of buyers cited a preference for purchasing from direct sellers, while only 7.2 per cent recorded a preference for distributors. Various explanations are possible. First, direct sellers may achieve an edge on influential sourcing determinants other than those researched in the study. Second, as manufacturers themselves, buyers may have inherent prejudices for trading with similarly configured suppliers, or against paying margins to intermediaries. Third, the magnitude of one or more of the competitive advantages recorded for direct sellers may be sufficient to give them overall advantage.

Extending this, the overall weight of economic criteria on which direct sellers generally perform better, although not reflected in buyers' mean scores, may exceed that of the relationships criteria on which distributors gain advantage. Finally, although buyers' needs are not fully met by either of the two channels, buyers may perceive better prospects than distributors for improvement among direct sellers. Irrespective of which of these or other explanations is correct, it is clear that distributors of engineering rebuys, and to a lesser extent direct suppliers, have in general failed to establish a decisive competitive position vis-à-vis the alternative channels.

DISCUSSION, CONCLUSIONS AND IMPLICATIONS

This study has emphasised the need to prioritise effectiveness in distribution channel design and performance. Its purpose was to compare the effectiveness of direct and distributor channels in industrial rebuy markets. Data presented address buyers' source selection criteria and buyer perceptions of distributors and direct sellers' effectiveness in meeting criteria. The results update the rebuy vendor selection literature and identify some previously neglected sourcing determinants.

Furthermore, the results corroborate the importance of economic criteria reported in earlier studies. However, the results also indicate that buyers are strongly influenced by factors associated with buyer–seller relationships. An important conclusion is that marketers should not focus on a few top-ranking sourcing criteria. Rather, sustainable competitive advantage accrues from the provision of each in a collectively important and extensive range of comparably influential economic and relationships attributes.

Both direct sellers and distributors achieve relative advantage on a small range of factors associated with their respective specialist functions in the supply chain. Direct sellers gain significant advantage on key economic criteria such as price, product, and technical attributes deriving from their prime role as manufacturers. Conversely, distributors gain a significant edge on delivery, availability, and relationships factors arising from their close geographic proximity to customers. However, nearly 50 per cent of buyers had no preference for either channel type. Fewer than 10 per cent of buyers favoured supply by distributors, whereas over 40 per cent preferred to trade with manufacturers directly. It is clear that neither channel type, particularly distributor channels, has established irresistible competitive position vis-à-vis the alternative.

A related issue, and the most important conclusion of the study, is that neither direct nor distributor channels adequately meet customer needs. Buyer perceptions are that both channel types significantly underperform on a wide range of important sourcing criteria. The reason for this is apparent. Buyers are strongly influenced by both economic and relationships criteria. Performance on the former is higher among direct sellers and on the latter among distributors. Having experienced supply from both channels, buyer perceptions have been shaped by what each is best at. Hence, as neither direct nor distributor channels perform better on both types of criteria, buyers perceive both channel types as suboptimal.

Both distributor and direct channels need to provide more customer satisfaction. However, operating as independent uncoordinated alternatives, both channels will encounter major barriers to improvement. Distributors' capability for offering more satisfaction, particularly on economic criteria, is likely to be constrained by their small size and resource base (Shipley and Prinja, 1988; Narus and Anderson, 1987). For example, building more technical competence and customisation will add to distributors' costs and, therefore, their relative price disadvantage. Equally, manufacturers' scope for creating and sustaining better direct customer relationships, delivery, and service is limited by their relative market remoteness.

A potentially more productive alternative to the independent operation of distributors and direct sellers is for them to cooperate with each other. This would enable them to enhance total customer satisfaction by exploiting their respective strengths and improving or nullifying their respective weaknesses. General consensus in the channels literature is that performance varies directly with channel co-operation (Dwyer, 1980; Hunt, Ray and Wood, 1985; Michie and Sibley, 1985). Recent literature has advocated an informal partnership approach for the achievement of effective co-operative channels (Narus and Anderson, 1986, 1987; Hlavacek and McQuiston, 1983; Rosson and Ford, 1982; Shipley, 1987). The philosophy of partnership is founded on mutual role recognition and co-operative role specialisation among producers and distributors, fairness, trust and respect, abundant communication and frequent personal interaction.

Partnership is recommended as the solution for the channel ineffectiveness identified in this study. Applying the partnership philosophy requires that all channel members recognise the channel as the unit of competition, not its constituent parts, and that customers are channel customers, not exclusive to either party. A key role for distributors in partnership is to identify and communicate precise buyer needs while the key role of manufacturers is to support distributors in satisfying them. Manufacturers should champion the co-ordinated attainment of high levels of effectiveness in the channels' provision of customer satisfaction on both economic and relationships criteria. Ensuring the latter should be largely the distributor's responsibility and manufacturers should take positive steps to reward and motivate distributors for high-level performance. Producers should also provide distributor training for meeting customers' economic criteria and offer technical help, sales force assistance, and other forms of support when required.

Finally, applying the partnership approach involves a less direct role in distribution for producers currently operating without intermediaries. Recommending partnership channels may, therefore, be considered strange given that a large minority of the buyers in this study prefer to source rebuys from direct sellers than from distributors. In cases where strong long-term customer alienation is likely to result from a switch to distributor channels, manufacturers are advised to continue with direct distribution and adopt a differentiated channels strategy so as to serve less-discerning customers with distributors. However, adverse customer reaction is expected to be small scale and short term. Customers ultimately buy satisfaction of needs, not supply channel designs. Their patronage can be expected to shift towards firms which implement the partnership approach in distribution and so offer improved effectiveness in delivering economic and relationships benefits.

REFERENCES

Abratt, R.L. (1986): "Industrial Buying in High-tech Markets", *Industrial Marketing Management*, 15(3): 293–8.

Banting, P.M. (1976): "Customer Service in Industrial Marketing: A Comparative Study", *European Journal of Marketing*, 10(3): 136–45.

Brown, J.R., and Purwar, P.C. (1980): "A Cross Channel Comparison of Retail Supplier Selection Factors", in *Marketing in the Eighties*, Chicago, Illinois: American Marketing Association.

Brown, R. (1987): "Marketing — A Function and a Philosophy", *Quarterly Review of Marketing*, 12(3/4): 25–30.

Cameron, S., and Shipley, D.A. (1985): "A Discretionary Model of Industrial Buying", *Managerial and Decision Economics*, 6: 102–111.

Churchill, G.A., and Suprenant, G. (1982): "An Investigation into the Determinants of Customer Satisfaction", in *Journal of Marketing Research*, 19: 491–504.

Day, G.S., and Wensley, R. (1988): "Assessing Advantage: A Framework for Diagnosing Competitive Superiority", in *Journal of Marketing*, 52(2): 1–20.

Dempsey, W.A. (1978): "Vendor Selection and the Buying Process", *Industrial Marketing Management*, 7(3): 256–67.

Drucker, P. (1973): *Management: Tasks, Responsibilities and Practices*, New York: Harper & Rowe.

Dwyer, R.F. (1980): "Channel Member Satisfaction: Laboratory Insights", in *Journal of Retailing*, 56(2): 45–65.

Hart, S. (1987): "The Use of the Survey in Industrial Marketing Research", *Journal of Marketing Management*, 3: 25–38.

Hlavacek, J.D., and McQuiston, T.J. (1983): "Industrial Distributors — When, Who and How", *Harvard Business Review*, 6(1): 96–101.

Hunt, S.D., Ray, N.M. and Wood, V.R. (1985): "Behavioural Dimensions of Distribution: Review and Synthesis", *Journal of the Academy of Marketing Science*, 13: 1–24.

Kassicieh, S.K. and Roger, R.D. (1986): "Microcomputer Purchase Criteria Across Industries", *Industrial Marketing Management*, 15: 139–146.

Kiser, G.E., Rao, C.P. and Rao, S.R.G. (1975): "Vendor Attribute Evaluations of Buying Centre Members Other than Purchasing Executives", *Industrial Marketing Management*, 4(1): 178–84.

Lehmann, D., and O'Shaughnessy, J. (1974): "Differences in Attitude Importance for Different Industrial Products", *Journal of Marketing*, 38(2): 36–42.

MacDonald, M. (1982): *Marketing Plans*, London: Heinemann.

McGoldrick, P.J. and Douglas, R.A. (1983): "Factors Influencing the Choice of a Supplier by Grocery Distributors", *European Journal of Marketing*, 17: 13–27.

Michie, D.A., and Sibley, S.D. (1985): "Channel Member Satisfaction: Controversy Resolved", *Journal of the Academy of Marketing Science*, 13: 188–205.

Narus, J.A. and Anderson, J.C. (1986): "Turn Your Distributors into Partners", *Harvard Business Review*, 64(2): 66–71.

Narus, J.A. and Anderson, J.C. (1987): *The Wholesale Distribution Channel: Building Successful Working Partnerships*, Washington D.C: Distribution Research and Education Foundation.

Porter, M.E. (1985): *Competitive Advantage: Creating and Sustaining Superior Performance*, New York: Free Press.

Rosson, P. and Ford, D.I. (1982): "Manufacturer–Overseas Distributor Relations and Export Performance", *Journal of International Business Studies*, 13(1): 57–72.

Shipley, D. (1987): "What British Distributors Dislike about Manufacturers", in *Industrial Marketing Management*, No. 16.

Shipley, D. and Prinja, S. (1988): "The Services and Supplier Choice Influences of Industrial Distributors", *The Service Industries Journal*, 8(2): 176–87.

Stern, L.W. and El-Ansary, A.I. (1988): *Marketing Channels*, Englewood Cliffs, N.J.: Prentice-Hall.

Turnbull, P. and Cunningham, M. (eds) (1981): *International Marketing and Purchasing: A Survey Among Marketing and Purchasing Executives in Five European Countries*, London: Macmillan.

Walters, C.G., and Bergiel, B.J. (1982): *Marketing Channels*, Glenview, Illinois: Scott, Foresman.

21
Value-adding Partnerships as Alternatives to Vertical Integration[*]

Emily Boyle

INTRODUCTION

Until recently, organisation theorists believed that organisational growth was natural (Robbins, 1987: p. 384). Various models of continuous growth and development were propounded (Greiner, 1972; Weinshall and Raveh, 1983). It was assumed that large businesses were superior to small ones, that the advantages of economies of scale and of the power and influence gained from size made large businesses not just desirable but inevitable (Galbraith, 1967; Peters, 1987). In the late 1960s Drucker asserted that "the large organisation is the environment of man in modern society", (1968: p. 173) and as late as 1980 Alfred Chandler and Herman Daems contended that the "large business firm and its managerial hierarchy are essential for organising modern industrial activity" (Chandler and Daems, 1980: p. 1). One way in which firms achieved their size was through the process of vertical integration.

However, by 1980 some theorists were also beginning to question these assumptions — to suggest that rather than experiencing infinite growth, organisations might have a "life cycle" and that they would at some stage inevitably go through a period of prolonged decline and shrinkage (Kimberly, Miles et al., 1980; Whetten, 1980).

The poor performance of many of the giant multinational corporations in recent years adds weight to this view. It also suggests that the advantages claimed for large organisations may

---

[*] This paper was first published in *IBAR*, 1993, Vol. 14, No. 2.

have been greatly overstated in the past and that small businesses have several significant advantages over large ones, particularly as far as flexibility and adaptation to a changing environment are concerned (Peters, 1987; Handy, 1989). Because of the problems which the giant corporations have recently encountered, many have turned to organisational restructuring, retrenching and down-sizing in an attempt to alleviate their position.

One way that this can be achieved is through what Peters refers to as "vertical deintegration" (1987: p. 8). However, downsizing and deintegrating can leave firms weak and vulnerable to takeovers. In order to prevent this from happening, some firms have begun to build up different types of inter-firm relationships, based on trust and co-operation rather than competition. Value Adding Partnerships (VAPs) are an example of this type of relationship. One way of creating a VAP is for a firm to lay off its full-time employees and contract out the work to them as self-employed business people.

This chapter provides an introductory discussion of this process. It examines the theory behind vertical integration and the reasons given as to why it is not an effective structure for businesses in the present economic conditions. The chapter goes on to consider the way in which some firms in Northern Ireland have used the process of deintegration to form VAPs with ex-employees. Other methods of forming VAPs, as well as factors which inhibit their creation, are also discussed. The evidence for the chapter has been derived entirely from newspapers and other secondary sources.

REASONS FOR VERTICAL INTEGRATION

The reasons suggested by academics for vertical integration being adopted are many and varied. Economists have concentrated on listing the specific factors that are likely to encourage firms to integrate vertically. For example, Alexis Jacquemin summarised the reasons for firms vertically integrating in the following way:

> Industries that are characterised by a close technological interdependence between successive stages of production and, moreover, that require a large volume of specific intermediate products or services are ... designated for operations of vertical integration. Because of the necessity for recurrent transactions with specialised suppliers (benefiting from accumulated experience), strict quality control, delivery according a precise frequency, and utilisation of complex information under uncertainty and more generally

because of close co-operation between users and suppliers, market mechanisms become rather inefficient (1987: p. 145).

In other words, where the conditions listed above exist, the administrative costs of having the various processes within the boundaries of the same firm are assumed to be less than the transaction costs involved if the processes are carried out by single sector firms, and the products bought and sold on the open market. Oliver Williamson (1975) has argued that the transaction costs are pushed up firstly by the bounded rationality of the firm's management, caused by uncertainty in the environment, and secondly by opportunism on the part of the firm's potential trading partners, when for some reason only a small number of possible trading partners exists. The existence of these two sets of characteristics will encourage "information impactedness" — that is, communication distortion — which will make the risks of relying on transactions in the market too costly and so lead to vertical integration as the alternative.

In contrast to the approach adopted by economists, organisation theorists have emphasised the control which vertical integration gives an organisation over its environment. For example, Khandwalla has argued that it is a means by which management "try to insulate the organisation from the external turbulence" of its environment (1977: p. 334), and Mintzberg has contended that it is used as a means for businesses:

> to bring some of the forces of supply and demand within their own planning processes and thereby regulate them ... thus the firm can extend its control into its environment, seeking to regulate whatever out there can disturb his routine operations (1979: p. 327).

REASONS FOR DEINTEGRATION

In the present economic circumstances, however, vertical integration can no longer act as a buffer against the vagaries of the environment. As Peters points out, as far as industry is concerned, "Nothing is predictable..... Predictability is a thing of the past" (1987: p. 9). Changing technologies, changing tastes especially for customised alternatives, and rapidly increasing competition all reduce the ability of vertically integrated firms to control their environments. Thus, the predominant advantage of vertical integration in the eyes of organisation theorists no longer exists.

In fact, Peters has argued that in the past the advantages of vertical integration have always been overstated and the disadvantages ignored (1987: pp. 16–17). One such disadvantage is the question of focus. As Johnston and Lawrence (1988) point out, most vertically integrated firms started out in one specific process — their area of "distinctive competences" (1988: p. 98). When the firm becomes integrated this can become a liability because "the strong culture that supports that focus makes it hard to perform tasks that require distinctly different orientations and values" (Johnston and Lawrence 1988: p. 99).

Another disadvantage of vertical integration is that the administrative costs rise steeply because of the increase in the size of the firm. As organisations grow larger, so the opportunities for problems of communication distortion and information impactedness to affect their performance adversely increase. In order to reduce the risk of this occurring and to ensure that the work of the firm gets done satisfactorily — "to ensure the machine like consistency that leads to efficient production", and "to ensure fairness to clients" (Mintzberg 1979: p. 83) without requiring constant communication between management and workers — various "coordinating mechanisms" are developed. These include such features as direct supervision, the standardisation of work process through the creation of formalised rules and procedures, and the standardisation of output, whereby the anticipated level of performance of each employee in terms of output, revenues, costs, material usage and so on is pre-ordained (Mintzberg, 1979). These co-ordinating mechanisms require the employment of a considerable number of supervisory and technical employees — work study people, training officers, cost and works accountants and so on — and their staffs (collectively termed the "technostructure" by Mintzberg) both to install and maintain. All of this pushes the firm's administrative costs upwards. Added to this are the costs of providing for the indirect services needed to maintain the goodwill of the workforce, usually in the form of a greatly expanded personnel function. There are also the costs of the dysfunctions caused by operating in this way, particularly as far as flexibility, motivation and employee–client relations are concerned. Finally, vertical integration does not provide any opportunities for synergy — in the way that horizontal diversification does — to compensate for the high administrative costs (Ansoff, 1965: p. 80 and Galbraith, 1988: p. 310).

Whilst the administrative costs of vertical integration have always been high, transaction costs between firms have recently been falling, thanks largely to the rapid diffusion and falling costs of information technology. This can increase the number of potential trading partners available to any firm by providing them with the expertise and knowledge to work closely with each other; it can ensure that rigorous standards of quality are adhered to; and it can enable firms to respond rapidly to each other when required. This technological development has spawned a considerable increase in the numbers of single sector companies, which in turn reduces the chances of any firm in the value-added chain — either supplier or user — behaving purely opportunistically towards any other firm.

Thus, in terms of the relative financial penalties incurred, the administrative costs of vertical integration have increased compared to the costs of operating through the marketplace. This seems to make deintegration increasingly attractive.

However, whilst the return to the traditional method of single sector firms operating through the market might seem logical, it also has its drawbacks. The traditional concept of competing in the market place for suppliers and customers breeds a selfishness in firms. Their main concern is that of maximising their own profits as far as possible. Therefore, instead of treating their trading partners as allies, they view them as rivals, and concentrate on trimming their own costs at the expense of their partners. As Johnston and Lawrence point out:

> If a company perceives a trading partner as an adversary, it may ship shoddy materials, squeeze margins, delay payments, pirate employees, steal ideas, start price wars, or corner a critical resource — all practices that reveal a lack of concern for the supplier's or customer's well-being (1988: p. 98).

These arguments imply that there are only two ways for firms to operate to ensure the fulfilment of the value-added chain: either through competing in the marketplace or through vertical integration. However, as Jacquemin points out, it is more realistic to consider these as the two extremes of a continuum in between which a variety of inter-firm and intra-firm structures exists. (1987: p. 147).

VALUE-ADDING PARTNERSHIPS

VAPs have been identified as one such inter-firm structure. According to Johnston and Lawrence, a VAP may be seen as:

> a set of independent companies that work closely together to manage the flow of goods and services along the entire value-added chain. It is an organisational form much like the putting-out

system of the early industrial revolution, whereby manufacturing was done in cottages and co-ordinated by a merchant-manufacturer who supplied the raw materials and sold the finished product (1988: p. 94).

In VAPs individual companies co-operate with each other: they appreciate that they have a stake in their partners' success, and that the financial soundness of their trading partners is of paramount importance to their own performance. They realise that they share common goals. They provide information for each other. They operate therefore through a system of close co-ordination for the benefit of all the members of the VAP. To a large extent, successful VAPs rely on "the attitudes and practices of the participating managers", who appreciate the importance of "the relationships along the entire value-added chain and the need for each link in the chain to be as strong as possible" (Johnston and Lawrence, 1988: pp. 94, 96). Furthermore, since VAP members are usually single sector firms, they can bring their own distinctive competences and focus — so often lost in vertically integrated concerns — to bear in their operations. Overall it can be argued that VAPs combine many of the advantages of vertical integration — for example, facilitating a certain degree of planning, research and development, sharing information, and economies of scale — with those of smallness, including fewer administrative costs, greater flexibility and adaptability, closer personal relations, less problems of motivation, easier control and improved focus.

The concept of VAPs (if not the name) is by no means new. Writing in 1967 J.K. Galbraith commented on the mutual advantages for firms of establishing long-term contracts with each other (Galbraith, 1967: p. 40) A year later, Drucker noted:

> Increasingly major organisations farm out to each other the very performance of their own functions. Increasingly each organisation is using the others as agents for the accomplishment of its own tasks (Drucker, 1968: p. 166).

In 1976 Herbst talked of organisational networks of which the basic characteristic is "the maintenance of long-term directive correlations, mutually facilitating the achievement of a jointly recognised aim" (1976: p. 33). More recently Morgan has identified an organisational structure called the "loosely coupled network", which:

> has a small core of staff who set a strategic direction and provide

the operational support to sustain the network, but it contracts other individuals and organisations to perform key operational activities (1989: p. 67).

Handy describes a similar organisation structure which he classifies as a "shamrock organisation" which consists of a small full-time organisational core, the contractual fringe and an abundance of part-time and temporary employees (1989: pp. 72–81). The core and the contractual fringe are in fact value-adding partners. The advantages cited for this system over the traditional organisation structure include the fact that the threat from a slump is dissipated by spreading the risk over several firms (what Handy (1989: p. 74) refers to as "exporting the uncertainty"), and that the core organisation only pays the contractual fringe "for results, not for time" (1989: p. 77).

EXAMPLES OF DEINTEGRATION AND THE FORMATION OF VAPS

Handy implies that the contractual fringe is often made up of ex-employees who have been laid off by the core organisation and then contracted by it to carry out work for it (1989: pp. 77–8). In Northern Ireland the dairy industry provides an example of this very process. Until recently the dairies bought their milk from farmers at prices set by the Milk Marketing Board. They then processed it mainly into liquid milk. For example, in 1964 Northern Dairies had nine plants, all producing liquid milk (*Business Telegraph*, 1991a). The milk was then delivered to the customer — usually the final consumer — at prices set by the Milk Marketing Board. In the days before mass refrigeration was common, the dairies employed full-time roundsmen to ensure rapid delivery of the milk to the consumers' doorstep. This method of operating remained the norm until 1984/5, despite considerable changes in the industry. Firstly, demand for liquid milk began to fall, largely as a result of an increase in demand for soft drinks. (Sales of milk have been declining for the last ten years, although in 1989 there was a slight rise on the previous year [*Business Telegraph*, 1991b].) The dairies therefore diversified into other products — yoghurt, cheese, butter, ice cream, lollies, pre-packed salads and now even *fromage frais* (*Business Telegraph*, 1991a; *Business Telegraph*, 1991c). Thus, in 1989 only 14 per cent of the milk bought by the dairies was used for liquid milk (*Belfast Telegraph*, 1989). A further change has been the rapid increase in refrigerated space in shops and supermarkets, facilitating the sale of milk through these outlets. Indeed, in 1989 a quarter of the province's liquid milk was sold through supermarkets (*Belfast Telegraph*, 1989). Finally, qualified drivers are no longer as scarce as they used to be. Thus the dairies are no longer constrained as they were in the past by the "smallness of numbers" of potential milkmen qualified to drive.

Under these circumstances in 1984/5 the dairies decided to lay off their roundsmen and enfranchise them as self-employed milkmen, thus in effect creating a number of VAPs. The VAPs consist of the farmers who provide the milk, the dairies who buy it and process it and sell it to the roundsmen, the Milk Marketing Board which still sets the price of unprocessed milk and now recommends the price to be charged to the final customer, and the Dairy Council for Northern Ireland which "represents the processors and producers of milk" and is responsible for its marketing (*Business Telegraph*, 1991b). This body has recently embarked on a major advertising campaign "supporting doorstep delivery of the pinta".

The creation of these VAPs has provided benefits for both the dairies and the milkmen. The dairies have benefited from reduced costs in several areas. With fewer employees there is less administration to be done, and less labour welfare costs to pay. Control of the milkmen is now through the price recommendatory mechanism rather than by supervision or by specifying the customers for each roundsperson. At the same time, demand for milk delivered to the door has in no way been diminished by the change. As for the milkmen, they have gained from greater freedom and flexibility as well as gaining financially. Such matters as when to deliver the milk and to collect the money and how many assistants to have are now their own personal decision. Yet they can still rely on the dairies to provide the milk, on the Milk Marketing Board to recommend prices, and on the Dairy Council to promote their product and their role.

Another very similar set of VAPs was created by Moy Park Ltd., one of the largest poultry producers in the United Kingdom, which sells processed poultry products to such supermarket chains as Tescos, Asda and Waitrose in Britain and to Stewarts in Northern Ireland. Its headquarters are situated in Craigavon; and it has two modern hatcheries in Northern Ireland and one in Yorkshire; two processing factories in Northern Ireland and one in Southport; a factory in France; and its sales and marketing "nerve centre" in Crewe. The number of people employed directly by the firm has risen from 1,500 in 1985 to 2,000 in 1990, 1,100 of whom are in

Northern Ireland (*Business Telegraph*, 1985a; *Business Telegraph*, 1990). It also provides work for 800 others indirectly (*Belfast Telegraph*, 1988). Its turnover has increased from £60 million in 1987 to £60 million in 1990 (*Belfast Telegraph*, 1988; *Business Telegraph*, 1990).

Until 1984 Moy Park had been part of the Courtaulds Group and was losing money heavily. In that year Courtaulds decided to divest and sold it to the then management team. A five-year plan of restructuring the organisation was then introduced. The firm claims to be an "integrated food production" concern "beginning with the elite breeding stock, which leads to parent stock, then to broiler chickens" (*Business Telegraph,* 1990). However, this is not completely accurate. One aspect of the restructuring was the laying off of the farmers who had previously been employed to tend the broilers. As Anne Ferguson points out:

> One quality that distinguishes Moy Park from its peers is that instead of owning broiler houses it contracts farmers within a twenty mile radius to grow for it (1988: 79).

The farmers are sold day-old chicks which have been specially bred to Moy Park's specifications — originating as hatching eggs from Ross breeders, which become the grandparents of the broilers that the farmers buy. These are very pure in strain, disease free, and with the large flat breast structure and white meat that consumers demand. Moy Park also provides the feed for the birds (Ferguson 1988: p. 79). According to the production director, Eric Reid the system works as follows:

> We pay a base Grade A price plus a bonus for good farming. They (the farmers) don't get anything for birds below that grade. This stops all the bad farming and monkeying about ... over my dead body would I go back to managed houses. This way there's no guaranteed wage of any description — they are totally self-motivated and have total ownership (cited in Ferguson 1988: p. 79).

Clearly, there are similarities between the milk roundsperson's and the broiler farmer's situations. Both have changed from being full-time employees to being self-employed small businesses, with a very close relationship with their former employers. Both know precisely what results are expected of them by their VAP partners. Both have been trained in the way to do the job during their years as employees of their respective companies. Neither has any worries about the quality of their inputs — this being guaranteed by their VAP partners. Finally, both have made available to them the means of providing themselves with the required capital to carry out their tasks satisfactorily. The milk roundspeople can either hire their lorries from the dairies or buy them outright; while Moy Park provides small grants and "puts in a good word for a grower with his bank" if that person needs money to maintain a broiler house or to build a new one (Ferguson, 1988: p. 79).

Where conditions such as these do not exist, however, the creation of VAPs is less probable. For example, television is an industry in which the core organisations have increasingly become single sector firms. Ten years ago the majority of programmes shown on British television were produced by the television companies themselves. Now, however, many of them are made by independent producers. At present, more than ten independent programme making concerns are operating in Northern Ireland. Some of these, like Brian Waddell Productions, have been formed by former employees of the local television companies, yet there has still been no discernible evidence of VAPs developing between them and the television companies. Indeed, the independent producers spend a great deal of time and energy trying to get partners, both to help pay for their proposed projects and to screen them (*Business Telegraph*, 1991d). Suggested reasons for the lack of development of VAPs in this area include the non-routine nature of the work of the producers, and the problems for the television companies of trying to ensure the quality of the inputs and of specifying the desired end results.

OTHER METHODS OF CREATING VAPS

The VAPs identified here have been created by vertically integrated firms laying off employees in one specific part of the process, and contracting them individually to do the work that they were previously employed to do. However, it is not equally possible for a firm to divest of a process as a unit and then to become a value-adding partner to that unit. Management buy-outs are one way of achieving this. This method of VAP creation is particularly useful when the capital requirements for doing the job are beyond the means of an individual. Indeed, VAPs need not be derived from vertically integrated firms at all. They can just as easily occur from the coming together of a number of single sector concerns who realise the benefits of operating in this way. For example, since the early 1950s Desmond's, the major Northern Ireland clothing manufacturer, has built up a very effective VAP with Marks and Spencer (*Business Telegraph*, 1985b). Similarly,

Henderson's, the grocery wholesaler, has recently become sole provider for all the Spar and VG stores in Northern Ireland. (*Belfast Telegraph*, 1991a). Again, Shorts, the plane maker which was sold in 1989 to Canadian multinational Bombardier, has established a very close relationship with Maydown Precision Engineering, investing £4.5 million in it in March 1991. Maydown provides "quality machined parts" for Shorts (*Belfast Telegraph*, 1991b).

As already noted, the use of VAPs in business is not new. Where vertical integration is illegal, then such an inter-firm relationship is commonplace. For example, in the property business prior to the passage of the Building Societies Act in 1987, most estate agencies were partners in a VAP with a building society or an insurance company. With the passage of the Act, restrictions on building societies and insurance companies owning estate agencies were lifted, and many estate agencies were swallowed up by their financial partners. In Northern Ireland the most successful example was the takeover of Brian Morton's by the Halifax Building Society. However, other takeovers were less successful. The buy-out of Ulster Property Sales by the Nationwide Anglia Building Society was the first to take place in Northern Ireland after the Act came into operation, but it was an unmitigated disaster for the building society; within two years the estate agency had been sold back to the management team (*Business Telegraph*, 26 February 1991). Moreover, the relationship which had existed between the companies prior to the takeover had been destroyed and could never be rebuilt. In 1991, therefore, Ulster Property Sales was appointed Northern Ireland representative for Hambro Guardian Assurance — thus creating the potential, however, for the creation of a new VAP.

CONCLUSION

The concept of VAPs — as an inter-firm relationship which combines many of the advantages of vertical integration with the benefits of small-firm size — might seem very appealing to managers struggling to cope with the problems facing large organisations today. However, both Johnston and Lawrence 1988: p. 100) and Handy (1989: p. 91) agree that this type of working relationship can be very difficult to maintain. If it is not handled satisfactorily, suggest Johnston and Lawrence (1988: p. 100), it can easily either degenerate into anarchy or revert to vertical integration. How this can be prevented bears examination in its own right.

REFERENCES

Ansoff, H.I. (1965): *Corporate Strategy*, London: McGraw-Hill.
Beresford, P. and Butler, D. (1991): "Behind the Irish Troubles", *Management Today*, March: 109–12.
Belfast Telegraph (1988): 19 April.
Belfast Telegraph (1989): 9 August.
Belfast Telegraph (1991a): 12 April.
Belfast Telegraph (1991b): 21 March.
Business Telegraph (1985a): 10 December.
Business Telegraph (1985b): 19 November.
Business Telegraph (1990): 4 December.
Business Telegraph (1991a): 16 April.
Business Telegraph (1991b): 5 March.
Business Telegraph (1991c): 26 March.
Business Telegraph (1991d): 7 April.
Business Telegraph (1991e): 26 February.
Chandler, A. and Daems H. (1980): *Managerial Hierarchies*, Harvard: Harvard University Press.
Drucker, P. (1968): *The Age of Discontinuity*, London: Heinemann.
Ferguson, A. (1988): "Pennies from Poultry", *Management Today*, December: 74–82.
Galbraith, J.K. (1967): *The New Industrial State*, London: Pelican Edition.
Galbraith, J.K. (1988): "Strategy and Organisation Planning", in J. Quinn, H. Mintzberg and R.H. James (eds), *The Strategy Process*, Englewood Cliffs, N.J.: Prentice-Hall.
Greiner, L. (1972): "Evolution and Revolution as Organisations Grow", *Harvard Business Review*, 50(4): 37–46.
Handy, C. (1989): *The Age of Unreason*, London: Business Books.
Herbst, P.G. (1976): *Alternatives to Hierarchies*, Leiden: Martinus Nijhoff.
Jacquemin, A. (1987): *The New Industrial Organisation*, translated by Fatemeh Mehta, Oxford: Clarendon Press.
Johnston, R. and Lawrence, P.R. (1988): "Beyond Vertical Integration — The Rise of the Value-Added Partnership", *Harvard Business Review*, 66(4): 94–101.
Khandwalla, P. (1977): *Design of Organisations*, Orlando, Florida: Harcourt, Brace, Jovanovitch.
Kimberly, J.R. and Miles, R.H. et al. (1980): *The Organisational Life Cycle*, London: Jossey Bass.
Mintzberg, H. (1979): *The Structuring of Organisations*, London: Prentice-Hall.

Morgan, G. (1989): *Creative Organisation Theory*, London: Sage Publications.

Peters, T. (1987): *Thriving on Chaos*, New York: Harper and Rowe.

Robbins, S. (1987): *Organisation Theory, Structure, Design and Applications*, Second Edition, London: Prentice-Hall.

Weinshall, T. and Raveh, Y. (1983), *Managing Growing Organisations*, Chichester, UK: John Wiley and Sons.

Whetten, D.A. (1980): "Sources, Responses and Effects of Organisational Decline", in Kimberly, Miles, et al., *The Organisational Life Cycle*, London: Jossey Bass.

Williamson, O. (1975): *Markets and Hierarchies*, New York: The Free Press.

22

Manufacturer–Middlemen Relationships: A Case of Balancing the See-saw?*

Sean Ennis

INTRODUCTION

The question of how a manufacturer should address the problem of achieving greater effectiveness in the management of its relationships with middlemen has begun to receive greater attention from researchers in recent years. (Gassenheimer et al., 1989). This is a welcome situation given the paucity of studies in this area as noted by Gattorna (1978).

This paper examines alternative approaches to the management of such relationships. Specifically, it reports on a study carried out in 1990 on manufacturer–dealer interfaces in the office-equipment industry in the United Kingdom. As a result of this study a number of recommendations are made as to how a manufacturer can develop a successful channel strategy based on the notion that middlemen need to be positioned according to their individual requirements and on the level of support activities necessary from the perspective of the manufacturer.

The study highlights the often neglected fact that manufacturers still retain a belief that:

(a) There is little need to research the disparate requirements of middlemen.
(b) Differing strategies are required as a consequence.
(c) A reluctance to grasp the reality that in the future,

---

* This paper was first published in *Proceedings of the 1991 Annual MEG Conference*, Vol. 1.

successful management of channel relationships will place a greater emphasis on the establishment of partnerships with selected middlemen.

CHANNEL-MEMBER RELATIONSHIPS

Narus and Anderson (1986 and 1987) note that as distributors move to a more professional management style, their role in working relationships with manufacturers must become more proactive as opposed to reactive. This perception raises a number of dilemmas which face the typical manufacturer in its dealings with middlemen. The most basic of these dilemmas must be: "What functions do I expect my intermediaries to perform?" In turn, this poses the strategic issue of how dependent a manufacturer should be in such relationships with middlemen. In this regard, Reddy and Marvin (1986) consider that accelerating direct sales costs, prohibitive inventory carrying costs, intensifying domestic and foreign competition and higher levels of service demanded by customers ensure a growing reliance by manufacturers on middlemen. Magrath and Hardy (1987) also cite the shortening of product life cycles and the consequent fact that channels need to expose the products to their widest possible customer base before their benefits become outdated, as another compelling reason for recognising a heightened role for middlemen.

In essence, it is no longer logical to accept that the push and effort must come solely from the manufacturer in an attempt to develop a market — with the middleman playing a passive, docile role. This does not imply that it is sufficient to ply the middleman with a series of basic elements of support, such as brochures, co-operative advertising, training seminars and price discounts. Many companies mistakenly assume that such support activities will be adequate to ensure that distributors and dealers will be motivated to such an extent that they will "push" their product at the expense of the competition. In a more recent article Magrath and Hardy (1989) reflect that such support services as those highlighted above are almost without exception provided anyway by the competition. At the very least, it ensures that a manufacturer is on a par in such areas with its main competitors. However, it is unlikely that a competitive advantage can be attained. Extensive research with the distributor/dealer base is necessary to pinpoint areas where improvements in support are required and can consequently be delivered by the manufacturer.

THE SEE-SAW ANALOGY

In many ways the simple see-saw which can be seen in a children's playground acts as a useful analogy to describe the relationship between the manufacturer and the dealer/distributor base. The situation where the middleman plays a passive role, with only the minimum level of support activities and, more importantly, individual attention from the manufacturer is represented in Figure 22.1.

FIGURE 22.1: LEVEL OF SUPPORT PROVIDED (MINIMAL)

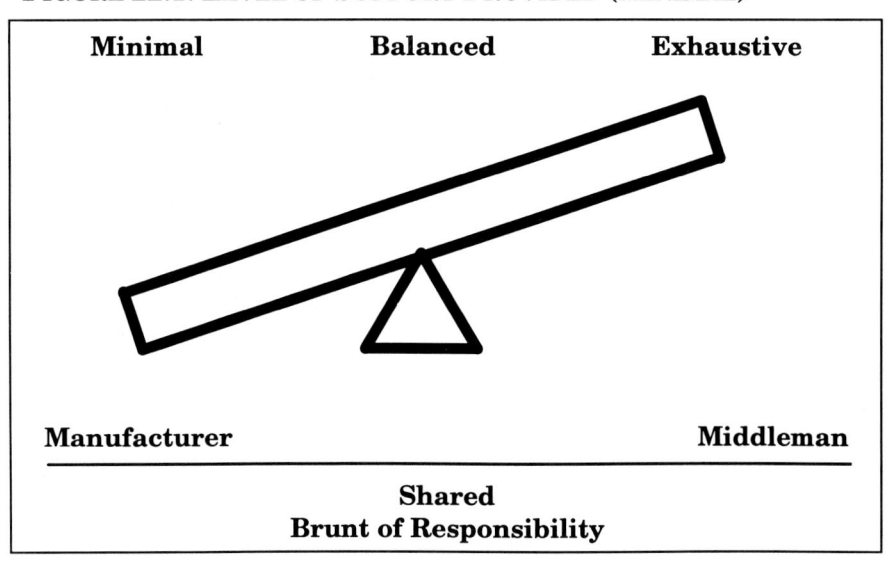

Minimal	Balanced	Exhaustive
Manufacturer		Middleman
	Shared Brunt of Responsibility	

In this case the manufacturer is the main driving force, with the middleman not putting much effort into the pre-sales, marketing and post-sales of the manufacturers' brand. This situation may occur for a number of reasons. It may be because the manufacturer feels that the minimum level of support provided is enough and has failed to realise the apathy that such an approach creates in the attitudes of the intermediaries. It could be as a result of the nature of the product. Typically for low-involvement products which are not technically complex and where the end user has a clear understanding of the prices and reputations of the respective brands on the market, the contribution required from the middleman may not be of a sophisticated or exacting nature. Clearly, the onus will be on the manufacturer to encourage end users to buy its brands in preference to the competition. Using the "see-saw" analogy, it might be acceptable for the manufacturer to take the main brunt of the support activities. In summary, Figure 22.1 represents situations where the manufacturer is the proactive, initiating influence on activities, with the middleman adopting a reactive, passive position.

However, for many products, where the end-user is reliant upon the middleman for advice, information and all-round guidance, such an unbalanced position will be detrimental from the point of view of the manufacturer. In the case of high involvement products of a technically complex nature, the middleman will be expected to become much more proactive in the relationship with the manufacturer. As a result, the latter party in the relationship will have to give much greater thought to precisely what improved levels of support need to be provided to the middleman in an attempt to achieve a "balanced position on the see-saw". This is represented in Figure 22.2.

FIGURE 22.2: LEVEL OF SUPPORT PROVIDED (BALANCED)

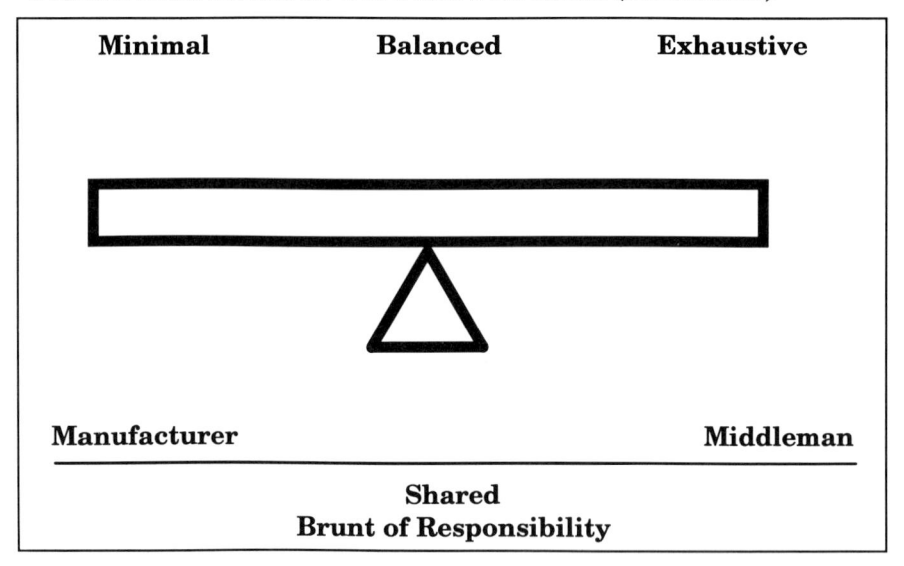

| Minimal | Balanced | Exhaustive |

| Manufacturer | | Middleman |

Shared Brunt of Responsibility

Here the relationship is based on the assumption that only a balanced, shared allocation of tasks and responsibilities is necessary for successful representation to the end-user base. Who then is responsible for creating the imbalance in Figure 22.1? Also who should be proactive in redressing the balance? It is too simplistic to suggest that the fault lies with the middleman for not actively seeking a more proactive role in the equation. In order for the middleman to do so it will be necessary for the manufacturer to assess the specific support activities required to motivate the middleman and ultimately achieve a greater sales penetration in the marketplace. This is especially the case where the middleman does not have (or want) exclusive representation for a particular manufacturer's product range.

It is equally difficult to apportion blame to the manufacturer. The answer is not one which advocates that the middleman should be provided with an exhaustive, all-encompassing range of support activities. This leads to the unbalanced situation depicted in Figure 22.3.

In this case the manufacturer is tempted to "shower" the middleman with a wide range of supports — many of which are not actively sought, and again with little attempt being made to research the specific requirements of the intermediary base. The net result can end up in an expensive, undifferentiated strategy for the manufacturer which fails to achieve a situation where the middleman performs effectively.

FIGURE 22.3: LEVEL OF SUPPORT PROVIDED (EXHAUSTIVE)

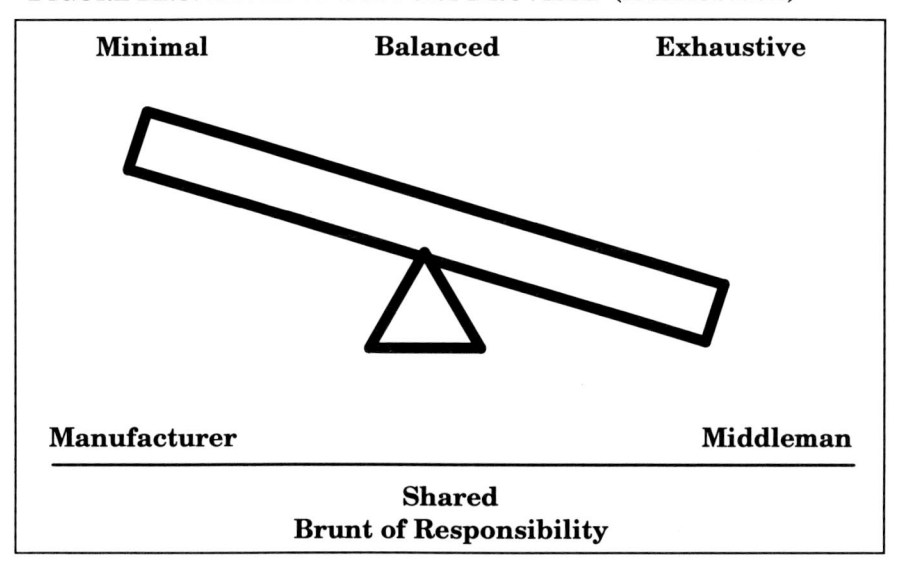

Minimal	Balanced	Exhaustive
Manufacturer		Middleman
	Shared Brunt of Responsibility	

ACHIEVING THE CORRECT BALANCE OF SUPPORT SERVICES TO MIDDLEMEN

Magrath and Hardy (1989) report on research carried out by a manufacturer who decided to examine the attitudes of his small, medium and large distributors to his standard support programme. Not surprisingly perhaps, he discovered variations in satisfaction levels between the categories of distributors. This was evidenced by the reaction of the small distributors who felt that the training, lead generation and incentive programmes would be more suitable for larger distributors with larger staffs, more professional management and better financing. Typically, small manufacturers were headed by individuals who of necessity had to take responsibility for a number of business functions and with little time to follow up sales leads or attend training programmes. In contrast, the larger distributors were more concerned with the development of just-in-time inventory systems and generally creating faster order response times. Because they had already developed their own sales force which necessitated the need for in-house training programmes, they were less concerned with these issues. The medium-sized distributors did, however, perceive a very real need for these support programmes.

The main lesson to be gleaned from this study was that by virtue of basic interviews with the distributor base, the manufacturer was able to uncover discrepancies in satisfaction levels with his support programme. The research also proved that the assumption made by many manufacturers that distributors would speak up and express their disquiet about those aspects of the support programme with which they were dissatisfied, is an erroneous one.

THE COMPOSITION OF SUPPORT SERVICES

Typically for technically complex products which require equal involvement from both manufacturers and middlemen, the range of support services which need to be supplied can be broken down into the following categories.

(1) Sales Training.
(2) Marketing Supports:
 (a) Brochures
 (b) Mail Shots
 (c) Exhibition Support
 (d) Advertising.
(3) Technical Training:
 (a) Seminars
 (b) Training Manuals
 (c) Refresher Courses.

(4) Installation Support:
  (a) Approved Installers
  (b) Monitoring Procedures
  (c) Standards.
(5) Maintenance Support:
  (a) Procedures
  (b) Warranties
  (c) Frequency
  (d) Quality of Repair and Maintenance.
(6) Customer Service:
  (a) Handling and Processing of Orders
  (b) Delivery
  (c) Response to Faulty Product
  (d) Sharing of Customer Information
  (e) Nature of Communication with Middlemen
  (f) Dealing with Emergency Orders.
(7) Pricing Support
  (a) Discount Policy
  (b) Level of Flexibility
  (c) Discount Competitiveness.

One of the strategic challenges facing manufacturers is the need to assess the distributor/dealer base to ascertain firstly, whether there are significant differences in the perceived level of importance of the various elements of support activities between the middlemen, and secondly, whether profiles can be developed of the distributor/dealer base, with a view to developing specific tailor-made strategies for each group as opposed to simply devising a generic strategy which would be applied in all cases.

BACKGROUND TO THE STUDY

In early 1990, a study was carried out on behalf of a large multinational company which operates in the British key-systems equipment industry. For the purposes of confidentiality it is not possible to identify either the company or the dealer base which was used in the survey. The company involved wished to carry out research with its dealer base with the objective of gaining a clearer understanding of the disparate needs and requirements. This information could then be used to revise their existing approach to the management of channel relationships. The particular sector of the key-systems industry under examination was that which addressed the telecommunications needs of small- to medium-sized businesses. Traditionally this was an industry which was controlled by British Telecom, until its privatisation in the early 1980s. Since then a number of large companies such as Panasonic, Philips, Ferranti, Toshiba, STC and GPT have entered the market with a comprehensive range of products.

The current position of the industry can best be described as *emergent*. It is still a "young" industry, but is beginning to mature in terms of the attitudes of the various players. What was once a commodity product dominated by one large company (British Telecom), has become a sophisticated product which has been prone to a bewildering number of "add-ons" and features enhancement over the past five years. This has led to a dramatic reduction in the life cycles of many of the products on the market. The telecommunications system is an essential element of any company's business operations. The technical complexity of the product is dependent upon the size of the business. As the company expands its operations, it is fair to say that the requirements inherent in this product will become more sophisticated. Likewise, the costs involved will increase in relation to the more exacting demands associated with a bigger operation — for example, as the company grows, there will be a greater demand for extra telephone lines. The company contemplating the purchase of such a product will tend to rely to a large extent on the expertise and product range recommended by the dealer. Developments such as the "least-cost routing system", digitalisation, and the movement towards technological convergence of voice and data communications ensure that this is the case. Because of the technical nature of the product, there are three elements relating to the buyer–seller interface: installation, maintenance and product upgrading (when appropriate).

THE DISTRIBUTION STRUCTURE IN THE UNITED KINGDOM

The way in which the product is sold to the end-user is depicted in Figure 22.4. The distributor base constitutes five large distributors who cover the UK. They deal with secondary dealers; that is, dealers who do not deal directly with the manufacturers but instead purchase their requirements from distributors. Those in the second category of dealers are referred to as direct dealers. As their title suggests, they deal on an individual basis with the manufacturers. This study is concerned with the dealer base.

FIGURE 22.4

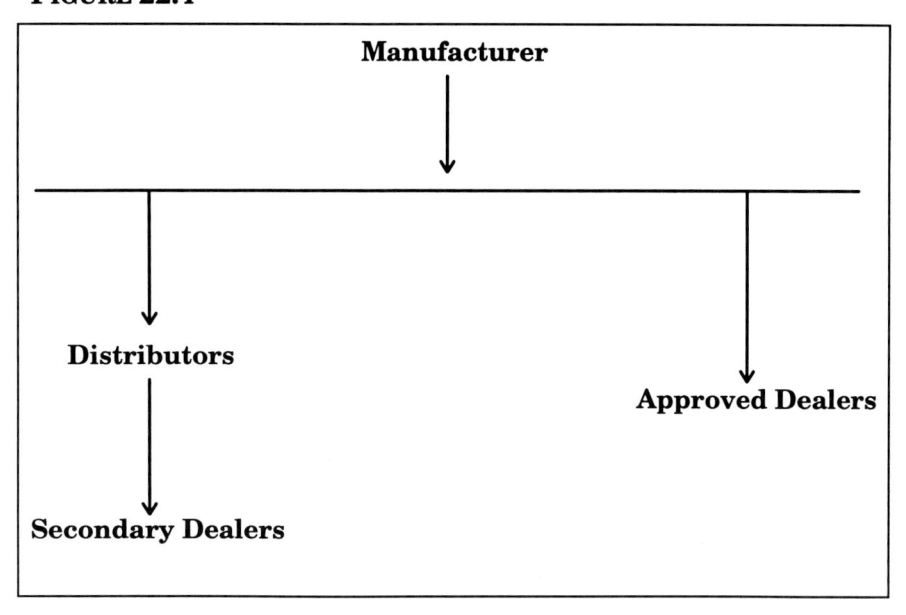

```
                    Manufacturer
                         |
                         ▼
    ┌────────────────────────────────────────┐
    │                                        │
    ▼                                        ▼
Distributors                         Approved Dealers
    │
    │
    ▼
Secondary Dealers
```

RESEARCH METHODOLOGY

The main task of this section of the research was to examine the structure of the dealer network which currently exists in the industry. Specifically, the following areas were examined:

(1) The dealers' perception of the role which manufacturers and dealers play in the industry.
(2) Areas of current dissatisfaction in the manufacturer–dealer interface.
(3) Criteria used by the dealers in the selection of manufacturers.
(4) Evaluation by the dealers of the current business strategies employed by manufacturers.
(5) Their long-term perspectives on future trends in the industry.

RESEARCH DESIGN

The depth interview was chosen as the most effective means of assessing and probing the opinions and attitudes of the respondents. This method enables the interviewer to be flexible in the approach to the interview and also to examine the extent and scale of the dealers' operations "on site".

Interviews were conducted with 16 dealers who stocked the manufacturers' product range. The dealer base for inclusion in the sample was determined after consultation with the manufacturer in question and after interviews with the five distributors and two other manufacturers who were deemed to be major players in the industry. The overall objective was to examine whether dealers could be categorised according to their specific requirements in the relationship with middlemen, and concurrently to evaluate whether the manufacturer could tailor specific strategies to particular groups of dealers as a result.

A feature of this sector of the office equipment industry is that no dealer seeks or is offered exclusive representation of any one manufacturer's product range. Rather, they prefer to carry a number of different manufacturers' brands, thereby ensuring that a level of choice can be offered to the end-users.

The dealers chosen for participation in the survey were representative of those operating in the industry. They were selected on the basis of:

(a) Size and extent of business operations
(b) Nature of their relationship with the client company (i.e., whether they were direct or secondary dealers)
(c) Non-client-company dealers (i.e., dealers who did not stock the client company's product range).

MAIN FINDINGS

Dealers' Perceptions of Manufacturers' Support Activities

The dealers were highly critical of the range of supports provided by the manufacturers. Many felt that the strategy employed by them could best be described as "minimal". This was reflected particularly in the areas of technical and sales training programmes. The more professional dealers tended to run their own in-house programmes. Another major criticism expressed was the lack of personal attention received from manufacturers. Only one manufacturer appeared to encourage the concept of joint sales calls on customers. The area of promotional support activities also did not escape criticism. The point was made that in this case support again was minimal — brochures were basic in terms of content; when dealers ran out of them, manufacturers were slow to provide new supplies; while support was provided for co-operative advertising, it was minimal and no help was provided in terms of identifying suitable media for targeting potential customers.

These issues raise an interesting dilemma for manufacturers. It is clearly not feasible from a financial point of view to provide equal support to each dealer on a generic basis. Not every dealer warrants or indeed deserves such a high level of treatment. There is consequently a need to evaluate the contributions (both existing and potentially) of each dealer in the network.

This will allow the manufacturer to assess the degree of support which would be appropriate in each case. Figure 22.5 represents a continuum on which the manufacturer can place dealers according to the level of support to be provided.

FIGURE 22.5: DEALER SUPPORT CONTINUUM

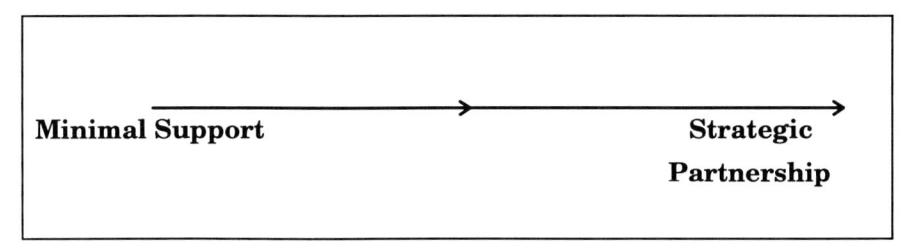

Minimal Support ⟶ Strategic Partnership

This continuum highlights the need for different strategies to be employed according to the relative importance given to individual dealers. Thus, dealers on the right hand side would typically be dealers who meet the following requirements:

- High sales levels of the client manufacturer's product
- Dedicated sales team
- Full support provided in terms of installation and maintenance
- Willingness to develop technical and training programmes in tandem with the efforts of the manufacturer
- Existence of (or willingness to invest in) a professional Management Information System.

This differentiation of dealers will indicate to the manufacturer those likely to be worthy of greater investment in support activities which ultimately might even lead to the situation where a strategic partnership could exist. This section of the research clearly indicated that dealers tend to have no allegiance to any one manufacturer. Thus, a situation can arise where a particular brand of product may be "pushed" by a dealer simply because it is "fashionable" at that particular point in time. As soon as an "upgraded" brand of product appears on the market, then it in turn becomes the "flavour of the month". One dealer referred to this phenomenon as the "Hotbox Theory". It indicates the potentially damaging situation which manufacturers face in this industry. Because of the perceived minimal approach to support activities, it is clear that dealers have great difficulty in expressing any loyalty to an individual manufacturer's product range. Even when they do, they will be quick to switch support to a more fashionable brand. This area of the research emphasised the need for manufacturers to "profile" and position dealers to help them develop a more differentiated, focused channel strategy.

The Dealers' Perceptions of End-users

(1) There was a general agreement that the end-user is still relatively unsophisticated in terms of product knowledge and awareness of which products are available and which manufacturers supply them.
(2) This can be explained largely because of the nature of the industry. Prior to deregulation in 1984, British Telecom sold the product on a commodity basis. The customer had no choice, and what choice there was, was limited by the bland approach to marketing adopted by BT.
(3) There is also the problem that while the telephone system which a company uses is critical to the basic way in which it operates, it is still last on the list of priorities when a company is purchasing office equipment.
(4) The small- to medium-sized company relies almost exclusively on the dealer for guidance.
(5) The design and aesthetic features relating to key-systems are becoming more important to end-users. Aspects such as weight, colour and size are taken into account.

These points serve to highlight the critical role which the dealers play in the channel system.

POSITIONING THE DEALER BASE

The interviews revealed a number of significant differences between the dealers. It was possible as a result to develop specific profiles of dealers which could, if used properly by manufacturers, be appropriate for improving the level of support required. The following profiles were developed.

Category 1: The "Box Shifters"

This category of dealer best describes the company which is

typically small in terms of size — often being a "one-man-band" operation. They can be classified as "dabblers" in so far as they engage in other business activities in addition to this sector of the office equipment industry. They engage in little formal marketing and selling effort, apart from a standard advertisement in the *Yellow Pages*. They buy from distributors and have little formal or informal contact with the respective manufacturers. Some — not all — attend training courses organised by manufacturers. This category can be further subdivided into those who are genuine operators who have the necessary skills in the area of installation, and those who are of dubious quality, where end-users can have problems with the product when installed.

Category 2: "Middle-of-the-Road Merchants"
Dealers in this category tend to be larger companies who, in many cases, deal directly with a number of the manufacturers. Their essential approach to selling key-systems is, however, basic, to say the least. In most cases, they are companies which have specialised in selling photocopiers and fax machines and have acquired the key-systems product as part of a general expansion of their office equipment portfolio. In many cases they do not have a dedicated sales team. As a consequence, they have a young, inexperienced sales staff and/or they use the same selling techniques to sell key-systems as they would when selling photocopiers.

Category 3: "The Business Communications Consultants"
Dealers in this category view themselves as the "sophisticates" of the key-systems industry. In many cases they have received industry approval (BSI approved), and provide a complete service to the end user of the product, installation and maintenance. Many of these dealers were started by former British Telecom personnel who spotted the opportunity in the early days of deregulation and have developed their business in line with industry changes. They are highly funded companies (in contrast to categories 1 and 2). This is an essential prerequisite because they have to carry high levels of stock to enable them to gain BSI approval.

There are variations within this overall category. Those in the first sub-category see the need to carry a range of product which will allow them to tailor-design a specific product for an individual end-user. They tend to deal with a maximum of up to five separate manufacturers. This allows them to cover the spectrum in terms of price competitiveness, state of the art technology and the variety of applications. As a result, a comprehensive choice is presented to the end-user, they see their role as one of "selling solutions to problems". If the manufacturer base with which they deal cannot come up with a solution, then this category of dealer will deal with the distributor in an attempt to satisfy the customer. Those in the second sub-category have similar attitudes, except that they prefer to deal with a very small number of manufacturers — usually a maximum of two. Here, great emphasis is placed on building up a very strong working relationship with a particular manufacturer. The underlying philosophy is that this type of dealer can never hope to be "an expert in every make of key-system on the market", and furthermore the dealer sees no need to be in this situation.

IMPLICATIONS FOR THE MANUFACTURER?

The most salient issue to emerge from the exploratory discussion above, is the need to recognise the fact that each category of dealer *requires a different approach in the area of relationship management.*

Category 1: "The Box-Shifters"

The small dealer falling into this category is best served by the *distributor*. It is too expensive and time-consuming to warrant personal attention from the manufacturer in the form of direct visits on a frequent basis. However, there is scope to improve the level of support to this category of dealer by focusing in particular on seeking improvements in the following areas:

- Quality of training manuals.
- Back-up support — e.g., audio visual cassettes.
- Periodic sales seminars.
- Regular news bulletins/information packages on new product developments/product upgrades.

The main criticism expressed by dealers in this category was that they felt that they were receiving only the most minimal of attention from individual manufacturers. Thus, slight upgrades in the above four areas would have the effect of creating a more positive response from such dealers. The overall thrust of the business strategy here should be one of working closely with the distributor. After all the distributor is the direct link with these dealers.

Category 2: "The Middle-of-the-Road Merchants"

The key areas of weakness with this category of dealer lie in the level of technical and sales support provided by manufacturers. The level of product knowledge as to what is available on the market is not high among these dealers. Manufacturers need to be seen to be supportive in a *visible* manner. More frequent visits need to be made to such dealers by both technical and sales personnel. Manufacturers must also be seen to be quick in terms of responding to problems encountered by dealers, particularly in the areas of faulty product and difficulties encountered in installation. Also, the idea of the manufacturer's salespeople making joint calls with the dealer's representatives should be explored more fully. This again stresses the "visibility and credibility" aspect of relationship between the manufacturer and dealer. A strategy which is based on providing the minimal level of support necessary is one which is guaranteed to irritate the dealer and ensure poor representation.

Category 3: "The Business Communication Consultants"

This third segment represents the most difficult and challenging area for manufacturers. Dealers in this category have developed a detailed knowledge of the existing product ranges and innovations which are currently on the market. They also tend to be proactive in terms of developing their own "in-house" technical and sales training programmes. Likewise, they place great emphasis on establishing dedicated salespeople within their field of activity. The dealers interviewed in this survey who fall into this category were highly critical of the standard of training provided by manufacturers, this being the main reason for them developing their own induction programmes. If a particular manufacturer's key-system fails to measure up in terms of features/attributes, then it will not be considered by this dealer. Thus, there is an even greater need to form much closer working relationships.

THE NEED FOR LONG-TERM CHANGES IN CHANNEL MANAGEMENT

The research conducted with the dealer base suggests very strongly that the manufacturer in this case should look very closely at how to manage relationships. In particular, it reinforces the belief expressed earlier that it is no longer appropriate to consider adopting a single, generic strategy for the entire dealer base. The profiling of the dealer base into three distinct subgroups or segments clearly indicates the need for selective strategies for each category.

Given the increasing sophistication of key-system products on the market and the resulting demands on the part of dealers in terms of selling such products, a more systematic channel management approach is required on the part of manufacturers.

The industry itself is changing. The major manufacturers have concentrated on product design and development at the expense of general marketing issues. The structure of the dealer base is also beginning to mature. The more far-sighted dealers (Category 3) have recognised this trend and have become more professional in their approach to selling key-systems As standards begin to be implemented, the more spurious operators in the field find themselves under pressure to compete. The manufacturer in turn needs to be more selective in dealings with the dealer base. On the basis of this research it is recommended that dealers should be selected on the basis of:

- The range of overall services which they provide to the end-user.
- The level of experience and commitment of their sales team.
- The degree of financial backing/funding available.
- The current range of key-systems which they stock.

The level of support provided is dependent upon which category the particular dealer is included in. Thus, for the "Box-Shifters", greater use is made of the distributor base, with basic support being provided by the manufacturer. The concept of a "strategic partnership" should be explored in the case of the "Business Communications Consultants". Because of their greater sophistication, expertise and knowledge, a far closer working relationship is needed. The alternative strategies are depicted in Figure 22.6.

SUMMARY AND CONCLUSIONS

This paper has addressed the question of how a manufacturer should most effectively manage relationships with its distributor/dealer base. It stresses the need for a balanced approach in the area of support services which it needs to provide. The analogy of the "see-saw" is used to demonstrate what can happen when such a balanced approach is not achieved.

FIGURE 22.6: ALTERNATIVE STRATEGIES

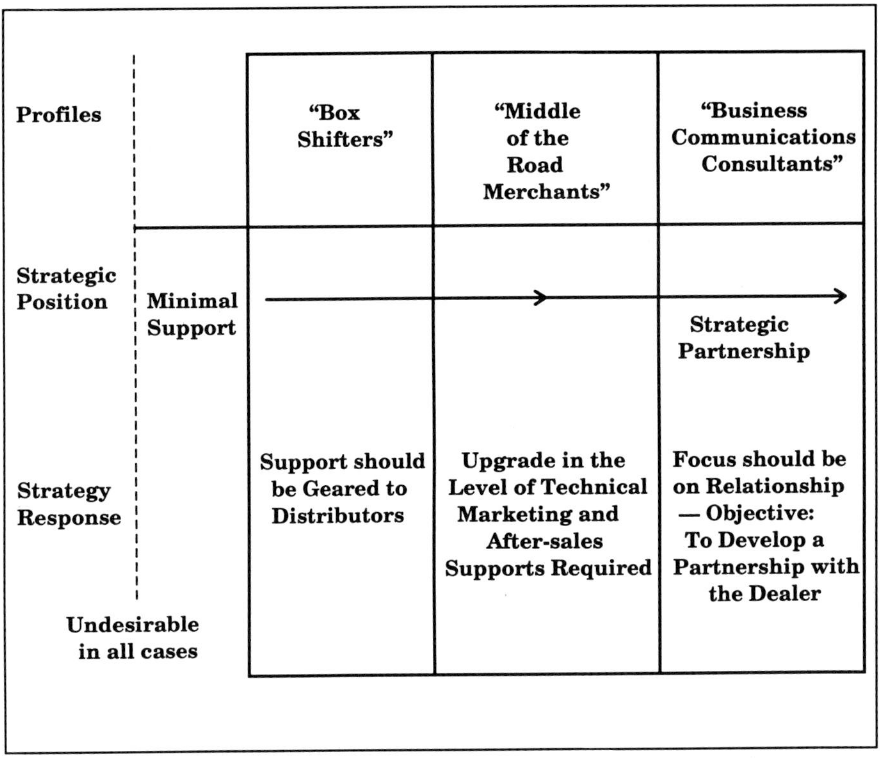

Profiles		"Box Shifters"	"Middle of the Road Merchants"	"Business Communications Consultants"
Strategic Position	Minimal Support	──────────────⟶ ──────────────⟶		Strategic Partnership
Strategy Response		Support should be Geared to Distributors	Upgrade in the Level of Technical Marketing and After-sales Supports Required	Focus should be on Relationship — Objective: To Develop a Partnership with the Dealer
	Undesirable in all cases			

The need to research the middleman is also emphasised, focusing on the notion that middlemen can be profiled or segmented on the basis that they have different needs and requirements. As a result this paper identifies the danger of applying a generic channel management strategy.

Empirical research is presented based on interviews undertaken with dealers in the key-systems industry in the UK. The findings support the contention that manufacturers can achieve a more positive response from middlemen if a focused differentiated channel strategy is pursued.

REFERENCES

Gassenheimer, J.B., Stirling, J.U., and Robicheaux, R.A. (1989): "Long-term Channel Member Relationships", *International Journal of Physical Distribution and Materials Management*, 19(12): 15–28.

Gattorna, J. (1978): "Channels of Distribution Conceptualisations : A State-of-the-Art Review", *European Journal of Marketing*, 12(7): 471–512.

Magrath, A.J. and Hardy, K.G. (1987): "Avoiding the Pitfalls in Managing Distribution Channels", *Business Horizons*, 30(5): 29–33.

Magrath, A.J. and Hardy, K.G. (1989): "Gearing Manufacturer Support Programmes to Distributors", *Industrial Marketing Management*, 18: 239–44.

Narus, J.A. and Anderson, J.C. (1986): "Industrial Distributor Selling: The Roles of Outside and Inside Sales", *Industrial Marketing Management*, 15: 55–62.

Narus, J.A. and Anderson, J.C. (1987): "Distributor Contributions to Partnerships with Manufacturers", *Business Horizons*, 30(5): 34–42.

Reddy, N.M. and Marvin, M.P. (1986): "Developing a Manufacturer–Distributor Information Partnership", *Industrial Marketing Management*, 15(2): 157–63.

Part IX

Marketing Research

23

Quantitative Research

Tom Harper

INTRODUCTION

There are abundant textbooks on marketing research but most of them are theoretical in focus and are written from a British or American perspective. The objective of this paper is to present a brief practical introduction to marketing research in Ireland today. The paper should be read as a supplement to textbook material on the theory and methods of marketing research. It will not review qualitative research (groups and in-depth interviews) nor will it cover areas related to social and cultural research — for example, opinion poll research.

THE MARKETING RESEARCH INDUSTRY

The marketing research business in Ireland is relatively small with an estimated annual turnover of £13 million (1994). The Marketing Society of Ireland publishes a register of research companies every two years listing about 25 different companies. The top five companies in Ireland, however, account for about 90 per cent of the total turnover and are listed in Table 23.1. Aside from Nielsen, which is an American multinational, the companies are mostly Irish owned. Many have some affiliation with UK- or European-based companies.

All of the companies in Table 23.1 belong to the Organisation of Irish Market Research Companies (AIMRO). This body meets about six times a year to discuss issues related to the Irish market research industry. Membership of AIMRO is restricted to suppliers of research with a certain level of turnover. Other organisations which have marketing research concerns in Ireland include the Marketing Society and the Marketing Institute. Many executives in the research business have membership with the UK Marketing Research Society or the European Society for Opinion and Marketing Research (ESOMAR), which has just under 3,000 individual members and acts to promote the development and use of marketing research across Europe.

TABLE 23.1: TOP IRISH RESEARCH FIRMS

Company	Number of Employees
IMS	25
Lansdowne	26
Nielsen	38
AGB	45
MRBI	17
B&A	16
Wilton	7

Source: The Marketing Society.

Each year the research subcommittee of the Marketing Society provides information on the Irish research market to ESOMAR, which then compiles a report on the size and nature of marketing research in each European country (see Table 23.2).

TABLE 23.2: RESEARCH METHODS

Method		% of Business
Ad Hoc Studies		43
	Quantitative	28
	Qualitative	15
Continuous Research		57
	Omnibus	9
	Panel	41
	Other	7

Source: ESOMAR/Marketing Society.

The broadest classification of marketing research distinguishes between ad hoc studies and continuous research. Ad hoc research can be divided into quantitative research — mostly face to face interviews at home or in the street — and qualitative research —

groups and in-depth interviews. Continuous research can be broken down into omnibus, panel and other long-term surveys.

CONTINUOUS RESEARCH

Continuous research can be defined as measurement on an ongoing basis with no defined "end" to the process and is not geared to any specific client company. It is designed to monitor changes that are occurring in the market. Most manufacturing and service companies who subscribe to continuous research would be primarily interested in trends and share movements over time.

Two kinds of continuous or syndicated methods can be used:

(a) Regular interval surveys (Omnibus and Market tracking)
(b) Panels (households and retail outlets).

Regular Interval Surveys (Omnibus)

Omnibuses are surveys run by the research companies. Clients buy space in the questionnaire by adding questions to meet their requirements. Field work can be organised on a weekly, biweekly or monthly basis. The sample can be accumulated over time to produce quite a large sample base. Clients have the option of flexible periods or rolling survey periods together. Target audiences can be anything from housewives to young adults. Types of information gathered in this way may include types of brands consumers purchase and the reason why (price, quality, etc.), or how often they travel abroad.

Aside from regular Omnibus surveys, some Irish research companies run continuous surveys dedicated to one client's needs or in one particular area — for example, MRBI run a Business Financial Services Monitor.

Tracking surveys are a series of interviews which are determined by the research agencies and sold to as many clients as possible. For example, some advertising tracking is conducted in Ireland by Millward Brown (a UK-based research company), to measure awareness of brands which may or may not be advertising on TV, radio or some other medium.

PANELS

In terms of market measurement, there are two major types of panel techniques in Ireland: the AGB Attwood household panel and the Nielsen retail panel. A third major panel research contract is the TAM panel which is discussed below. Panels consist of homes or shops which have been statistically selected in order to be representative of the population as a whole. The owners of the homes or shops approached agree to participate in the survey on an ongoing monthly or bimonthly basis. The panels are representative of the total population and the data collected is used for estimates of the market as a whole.

Nielsen operates a retail audit service. It monitors the performance of Fast Moving Consumer Goods (FMCGs) by collecting data in a sample of retail outlets spread throughout the country. The sample outlet data is grossed up to the total number of outlets in the country to give estimates on volume of sales, market share, average retail selling price, distribution and out of stocks. A number of different services, or Indexes, is provided. For example, Food, On-licence, Chemists and Confectionery are all separate services. Nielsen is the larger of the two market measurement panels and an example of some of its output is shown in Table 23.3.

Attwood sends diaries to a continuous sample of housekeepers who provide information based on their household purchases. The consumer records type, size, price and place of purchase for each item printed in the diary. The data is used to estimate total market size and share. Attwood, however, is able to say what type of consumer is buying the product where Nielsen shows information relating to performance in the shop. Other analyses can also be run on Attwood data such as brand switching, repeat buying and consumer loyalty.

NON-CONTINUOUS RESEARCH

Non-continuous, or ad hoc, research is "once-off" research commissioned to help solve specific problems of companies. It is usually customised to meet the needs of the client. The leaders in this field in Ireland are IMS, Lansdowne, B&A and MRBI.

These types of studies are normally conducted by asking a large sample of respondents a few questions in a short time period. Formal and structured processes are employed. These include problem definition, method selection, questionnaire design, sampling, data entry, data processing and analysis and reporting, as shown in Table 23.4. The theory underlining the method of these surveys is well documented and the reader is referred to any of the standard marketing research texts (see references). For the purpose of this paper, we will touch on areas which extend the theory into the practical world of Ireland.

Quantitative Research

TABLE 23.3

MARKET SHARES

R.O.I. FOOD

466   5-51 M8CB-00015 BABY RUSKS

R.O.I

KILOGRAMMES IN ACTUALS

Sales Y% CH	-11	13	*	*	-3	-3	-6	-10	-24	-17	-22	-19	-10	-17
	71191	74930	76758	69388	74147	71718	66590	67735	58606	57771	58161	58241	60253	360767
F.ORG 150 GM	8.5	8.8	10.2	9.6	8.7	9.3	9.5	9.1	10.5	10.4	9.9	10.7	8.6	9.8
F.ORG 300 GM	19.1	20.2	16.7	18.6	20.6	19.5	18.8	18.7	22.6	21.4	22.2	20.5	19.1	20.7
F.L.S. 150 GM	1.9	2.5	2.9	2.8	2.8	2.8	3.0	3.3	3.8	3.7	4.1	3.7	3.4	3.6
F.L.S. 300 GM	4.1	3.9	3.1	4.8	2.8	4.2	4.0	4.9	5.7	3.9	3.4	4.0	3.9	4.3
F.BAN/FT RK	.3	.3	.3	.3	.3	.4	.4	.4	.4	.3	.3	.3	.3	.3
LIGA	65.0	62.9	66.1	63.2	63.7	63.2	63.6	62.9	56.4	59.5	59.0	59.6	64.0	60.3
ALL OTHER	1.1	1.4	.7	.7	1.1	.6	.7	.7	.6	.8	1.1	1.2	.7	.8
F.ORG CONS	27.8	29.2	27.0	28.2	29.4	28.8	28.4	27.9	33.1	31.8	32.1	31.2	27.7	30.5
ALL OTHER	1.1	1.4	.7	.7	1.1	.6	.7	.7	.6	.8	1.1	1.2	.7	8.0
FARLEYS TOT	34.0	35.9	33.3	36.2	35.3	36.1	35.8	36.5	43.0	39.7	39.9	39.2	35.2	38.8
Latest 12 Mths	FM	AM	JJ	AS	ON	DJ	FM	AM	JJ	AS	ON	DJ	FM	FM
	1992												1994	1994

FM
1993

Source: A.C. Nielsen Company.

TABLE 23.4: SURVEY PROCESS

> ⇒ **Questionnaire Design**
> ⇒ **Data Collection**
> ⇒ **Key-punch**
> ⇒ **Validation**
> ⇒ **Weighting**
> ⇒ **Calculation**

Survey Method

The Questionnaire design or interviews can be classified as follows:

- Face to Face
  — fully-structured
  — open-ended
  — fixed-choice
  — pre-coded or scaled
  — semi-structured
  — unstructured
- Telephone (CATI)
- Self-completion
  — mailed
  — personally-placed
  — machine-input

In Ireland most of the data collection is through face to face interviews. Ireland lags behind most other European countries in telephone interviewing because of the low rate of telephone penetration — currently about 75 per cent of private homes in Ireland have a phone.

CATI stands for Computer Assisted Telephone Interviewing and there are many powerful PC computer packages available which make this data collection method very cost effective. This research area will certainly grow along with telephone penetration growth. Self-completion questionnaires are also popular because of the low cost, but non-response bias can make the results misleading. Self-completion techniques tend to be used more by companies gathering information on their own consumers or subscribers. Telecom Éireann, for example, carries out postal surveys on its customers.

Most surveys use quota control sampling as opposed to probability sampling. Quota samples are chosen to match the structure of the population on one or more predetermined criteria. Each interviewer is given quota controls for their assigned area, as shown in Table 23.5. The quota variables are usually obtained from the CSOs Census which has the required data at a very detailed level, that is, for each District Electoral Division (DED). The advantages of quota sampling are cost, speed, and ease of use. The disadvantages are that they have a larger sampling error than probability-based methods and they could also suffer from bias as the final selection of interviewees lies with the interviewers. It will also give a sample of people who are more available for interview.

TABLE 23.5: QUOTA SAMPLE WITHIN DED

40 Interviews Required

Age	Male	Female	TOTAL
Under 35	11	9	20
35 (+)	8	12	20
TOTAL	19	21	40

Some larger Irish surveys use probability methods for sample selection. For example, the readership survey (called the JNRR — see below) and the annual TAM Establishment Survey are designed by multistage probability methods. These surveys use Probability Proportional to Size (PPS) methods to select areas or DEDs (stage 1), and then use Systematic Random Sampling to select names from the electoral register (stage 2). Nielsen and Attwood also use probability methods in the sample design of their panels.

In terms of data entry, processing and reporting, the methods used by Irish marketing research companies vary. As most surveys can be easily processed on PCs with any number of packages, some firms do all the work in-house. Others choose to send the data to a bureau for data entry and processing. Some of these processing bureaux are in the UK, but recently, Irish-based bureaux have been doing very well here; for example, Infocorp Ltd. based in Dún Laoghaire. Research results can either be printed to hard copy (paper) or copied to disk so that clients can easily transfer the data to their own PC package for reporting or analysis.

So far we have concentrated on the non-media side of marketing research; in many ways media research can be quite technical and as a result it is treated separately.

MEDIA RESEARCH

Marketing research which measures market shares involves the collection of data on what is purchased. Media research, on the other hand, is a method to measure or quantify what is watched on TV, what is read by the public, what posters are seen on the street and what is listened to on the radio. Hence, along with the usual research problems of sampling error, bias, and accurate data collection, media research data collection is often reliant on the memory of the interviewee.

Media research contracts usually "go out to tender" and are for durations of three or more years. At time of publication (1994), the media research market breaks down as follows:

TV

Television measurement in Ireland is done through a continuous panel of homes with one or more televisions (currently about 96 per cent of private homes have a television). The contract to measure the television-viewing audience is currently held by AGB TAM. This is by far the most sophisticated marketing research measurement technique used in Ireland. Special "peoplemeters" are installed in a sample of homes throughout the country. Each night a computer dials all sample homes and collects the TV viewing data from the previous days viewing for all people who live in the home. As a result, ratings are available on-line the next day. (A rating is an estimated percentage of all people within the target audience who viewed a specific programme or commercial). Because of the level of detail and frequency of data collection, the usage and analysis of the results has evolved into a very complex science, as illustrated by some of the terms and concepts defined in Table 23.6.

TABLE 23.6: TV MEDIA TERMINOLOGY

⇒ **Rating (TVR) = No. Of Viewers/Universe Total**
⇒ **GRP (Gross Rating Point = AVE. TVR x No. of Spots**
⇒ **Gross Impressions = GRP x Universe**
⇒ **Cost per Thousand = Cost of Schedule/Gross Impressions**
⇒ **Station Average Price = Revenue/Gross Impressions**
⇒ **Frequency = GRP/Reach**

Source: Media Audits.

Radio

A number of organisations in the radio industry who were interested in the Irish radio audience came together to form the Joint National Listenership Research (JNLR) Committee and employed a research company to provide estimates of national and local radio audiences. The current contract is with MRBI and they have had the contract since 1989. They use a method called "24-hour aided recall". Sample respondents are taken through the activities of the previous day to determine when and what stations they listened to on a quarter-hour basis. Programme prompts are used to "aid" interviewees. Separate surveys are conducted for weekdays and weekends.

READERSHIP

The Joint National Readership Research (JNRR) Committee controls the readership contract which now resides with Lansdowne Market Research. Each person chosen for interview is asked to go through a booklet of "mastheads" or titles of a large number of publications. For each title, respondents are asked to say how often they read or looked at it recently. In this way the JNRR strives to measure any exposure to the press medium. The aim of the survey is to measure the "average issue readership", for both Irish newspapers and magazines. Non-Irish publications are not measured.

OUTDOOR

Outdoor media includes the 6,000 poster panels, roadside sites or bus shelters spread throughout Ireland. As with other media, the research is commissioned by a committee, in this case it is called the ORAC Committee. First, sites are classified by town size, road type and visibility. Then data are collected on travel patterns of the adult population and tied back to the panel sites. This is quite a difficult research contract and it is currently held by IMS.

OTHER MEDIA

Various methods are used to measure other media. For example, cinema is measured both on the JNRR and through a specially commissioned tracking survey. Most recently, an Irish Target Group Index (TGI) was started by London-based agency BMRB in association with IMS. The TGI measures market size, shares, brand loyalties, buyer demographics and media selection of the adult population. It is a very big survey (large sample and 70 plus pages of questionnaire) which will provide a link between media exposure and product purchase. Hence, manufacturers will know not only who consumes their products but what they read or what they watch on TV.

THE ROLE OF COMPUTERS

The growth of the powerful PC over the last ten years has had a significant effect on the Irish research market. Because Irish data bases are small in comparison with the UK or the USA, key-punching, processing and reporting can all be quickly accomplished on personal computers. Packages exist which specialise in questionnaire validation and processing; for example, SPSS, Quantum, Foxpro and SAS. Some companies even have their own packages to help users analyse marketing research data. Nielsen have a package called "The Nielsen Workstation", and television ratings and radio research can all be accessed through a number of packages which allow the user to manipulate the database to suit their needs. Computers will certainly continue to play a role in the future of the Irish research market.

FUTURE TRENDS

Although trying to predict the future is always risky, one area of clear futuristic change is in data collection. Most of the major supermarket chains, have point of purchase bar code scanning checkouts. About 40 per cent of FMCG business goes through scanners and about 85 per cent of goods have a bar code issued by the ANAI (Article Numbering Association of Ireland). Using this data has the advantage of being very clean (but not error free!) and quickly gathered. This would allow for quick reporting and allows for sophisticated data modelling. With the movement to scanning, the door will be open for what is known as "single source" databases. That is, media selection and product purchase measured electronically through the same sample.

In addition to technology playing a role in the future, Irish marketing research companies will continue to become more service-oriented. Benefits can be achieved by moving from being gatherers and reporters of data to becoming analysers who can help clients solve their marketing problems. To do this they will not only have to understand the data they are supplying but also the nature of the business of their clients.

REFERENCES

Crimp, M. (1985): *The Marketing Research Process,* Englewood Cliffs, N.J.: Prentice-Hall.

Emory, C.W. and Cooper, D.R. (1991): *Business Research Methods,* Boston: Richard D. Irwin.

ESOMAR (1994): *ESOMAR Annual Market Study 1993,* August, Amsterdam: ESOMAR.

Hoinville, G. and Jowell, R. (1985): *Survey Research Practice,* Hants, UK: Gower Publishing.

Kent, R.A. (1991): *Continuous Consumer Market Measurement,* London: Edward Arnold.

Kinnear, T.C. and Taylor, J.R. (1987): *Marketing Research — An Applied Approach,* London: McGraw-Hill.

Marketing Society (1993): *Marketing Society Register of Marketing Research Organisations,* Dublin: Marketing Society.

Mercer, A. (1991): *Implementable Marketing Research,* London: Prentice-Hall.

Rossi, P.H., Wright, J.D. and Anderson, A B. (1983): *Handbook of Survey Research,* San Diego: Academic Press.

Worcester, R. and Downham, J. (1986): *Consumer Market Research Handbook,* London: McGraw-Hill (ESOMAR).

24

Qualitative Research: Where it's At, Where it's Going*

Phelim O'Leary

Throughout the past decade there has been consistent growth in the volume of qualitative market research conducted in Europe. At home this has been driven by Irish companies which have a consumer marketing focus, and more recently it has been added to by a widening range of organisations and institutions somewhat outside the classical marketing field; this would include government agencies, voluntary charitable groups, schools, political parties and the churches. In itself this latter development is a reflection of the integration of marketing thinking into the mainstream social organisation of Irish life but, from the perspective of this writer, it is the fact that qualitative research should have been chosen as a useful tool by so many disparate sources that is of primary interest. It seems an appropriate point at which to reflect on where qualitative research stands at present, and to offer some thoughts on its future.

Some history would help to set a context, but even the history of qualitative research emerges as a qualitative analysis. There is not an ordered sequence of events leading to its current position, rather an array of factors of influence which have combined to fuel the practice. Rena Bartos, in an address to the Advertising Research Foundation's Qualitative Workshop in 1985, pointed out that qualitative research grew out of several streams of theory and practice in the social sciences, but also that political theory has been essentially qualitative in its evaluation of political systems since the time of Aristotle. The assumption that qualitative research is newfangled is belied by the existence of such papers as

---

* © *Irish Marketing Review,* volume 6, 1993. This article is reproduced with kind permission from Mercury Publications Ltd.

"The Art of Asking Why", originally published by Paul F. Lazarsfeld in 1934.

This author's own experience as a practitioner, and observations drawn from conversations with clients and research colleagues, suggest that qualitative research in Ireland has moved through three broad periods.

EARLY PHASE

In the 1960s, marketing had little structure in this country. I stand open to question, but remember it being said that there were but 14 marketing management positions existing in 1963. With this background, it is hardly surprising that qualitative research had little presence.

It was classified under the intimidating title of "Motivation Research" and only existed at the outer fringes of formal market research. Because its techniques were known to be drawn from psychoanalysis, it had an esoteric and unknown quality; an image, it should be said which did not aid its incorporation into the mainstream of commercial activity, and which provided a residue of inhibition that continues to this day.

MID-PERIOD

During the 1970s market research as a discipline was up and running, served by a cluster of highly professional Irish companies which are still to the fore. The emphasis was on the collection of fairly basic marketing data, most often through quantitative survey techniques. However, the term "Motivation Research" had now been replaced by "Qualitative Research", an important shift in semantic terms. It was frequently used as a forerunner to sample surveys, mapping out salient areas of interest and refining questionnaire design. Moreover, it began to be employed as a discrete and self-contained function, and this was largely connected to the realisation that it was necessary to understand consumers at an emotional level, and that this understanding, once achieved, could actually affect marketing action and pay commercial results. Once this realisation had been reached, there was consistent and rapid growth in qualitative research, and an unfortunate (and essentially meaningless) side effect in a minor war breaking out between proponents of qualitative and quantitative methods.

This period was also marked by two important features. Qualitative research became more accessible to management in general, and presentations of qualitative findings were made to boards of companies, not just the immediate marketing team. Secondly, qualitative research formally entered the world of advertising. Advertising agencies found that, rather than being an irritant and a hindrance, qualitative research and, particularly, insightful qualitative analysis, could actually further the goal of producing great advertising, and give creative personnel new avenues for development. (This is not axiomatic; the potential for qualitative research to contribute positively to creative advertising continues to be a point of debate, and is queried by not a few advertising people.)

CURRENT PHASE

Superficially the third period may not appear markedly different from the growth phase described above. Yet, under scrutiny, there have been important movements. Most important is the incorporation of qualitative research into the mainstream not alone of market research as a discipline, but into marketing management and education. It has become an accepted and familiar tool of management, as likely to be considered by a chief executive of a large Irish company as by the planning director of an advertising agency. In this context, it has also become fully international. Witness this researcher involved in a joint multicultural analysis of washing motivations with nine other qualitative researchers from different countries, ranging from Austria to Turkey, with each having conducted a similar study in the home territory. The goal? A pan-national marketing strategy (if valid and if possible) with proper allowances for individual country status.

This integration of qualitative research into the structural mainstream of management has had two significant effects. Firstly, it has generated sophistication amongst buyers and users of qualitative research; in the experience of our company, Irish marketing management is at least as sophisticated in its demands of qualitative research as its international counterparts.

Secondly, this has resulted in an increased rigour applied to the various stages of any qualitative research project, from the recruitment of respondents (who may, for instance, be recruited for interview on psychographic criteria), to techniques of interviewing and moderation in discussion groups, and perhaps most significantly, to the analysis of qualitative data. Analysis has become truly multidisciplinary, and not only involves established psychological and sociological constructs as frames of reference, but draws on such areas as linguistics and anthropology. But these, of course, are only tools themselves; the requirement of contemporary buyers of qualitative research is, above all, an analysis which details the implications for marketing action (or indeed, inaction).

Thus, it seems that the current phase of qualitative research is characterised by consolidation of developments remarked in earlier periods. There is not a great deal of fundamental change, but, rather, shifts in emphasis. A renewed, and welcome, emphasis is the more frequent collaboration of qualitative research with quantitative methods, in the pursuit of solutions and valuable market intelligence. The philosophy of the company in which this author works, for example, is centred on problem solving; it really is immaterial (within limits) which disciplines are applied to resolve the objective. The other emphasis which is noteworthy is that of qualitative research being required to contribute to strategy and planning; major Irish companies and institutions may use qualitative research as part of a future strategic design at the corporate level; a brand strategy for, say, a five-year period may be developed with the help of qualitative research.

NEW TECHNIQUES

By and large, qualitative research continues to have basic functions similar to those it has always had. These are, firstly, exploring the emotional nature of attitudes, motivations and decision-making, and secondly, an emphasis on answering the question "why?" There are two current projects which may be used to illustrate the fundamental orientation.

(1) A major Irish company observed that it was held in great respect, but that underneath this respect lay a syndrome of complex negative emotions directed at the company. There was a marked difference between "public" and "private" attitudes to the company. The long-term strategic problem was the possibility of ever-declining corporate status, and the operational difficulties which could ensue. The immediate problem was the potential for "secret" negative attitudes to the company, hindering the development of the company's products. Here, research facilitated the development of strategic plans at both corporate and product levels and, as importantly, guided the implementation of these plans.

(2) A food brand continued to lose share to a competitor, although the elements of its total marketing mix (product, packaging, price, advertising, etc.) were deemed and found to be in good

health. Answering the question "why?" became critical in the knowledge that refining elements of the mix would be unlikely to change the situation. (The most plausible answer, and most actionable insight, was found in the evidence that consumers had come to conceptualise the brand as being in a different product sector than that in which it was assumed to be, leading to a fundamental rethink about the brand, and how it should behave and speak).

To achieve its function, qualitative research deals directly with people, often at an individual level, or in pairs and small groups. The management of these interactions is obviously crucial, as they provide the raw material for analysis. Within the dialogues which form the fieldwork for qualitative market research projects, there are layers of accessibility to attitudes and motivations. Figure 24.1 is used to illustrate this layering of accessibility.

FIGURE 24.1: LAYERS OF ACCESSIBILITY

	Self	
Others	Known Public	Private
	Unknown Public	Subconscious

- There is the known and overt public self which is shared with others. (Top LHQ)
- There is a private self, not shared or presented to others. (Top RHQ)
- There is a public self, accessible to others, of which the individual is unaware at a conscious level. (Bottom LHQ)
- There is a subconscious self, unavailable to the individual and not presented to others. (Bottom RHQ)

In an ideal world, qualitative research would have total access to each of the quadrants illustrated. In reality, this is impossible. However, much may still be achieved. The known public self will be expressed, and a skilled qualitative researcher will access through observation, including body language, the public self unknown to the individual. This leaves two areas: the private self and the subconscious. Surprisingly, it is consistently found that much of the private self is shared, especially in the relatively intimate and confidential surround of qualitative interviews and discussions.

Still, there are no "tricks" which can be performed here to pry into the private world, and it is an absolute condition that respect for the individual is maintained; consumers in qualitative research are not laboratory animals, and an approach which treats them as such is in itself a mark of shoddy and faulty practice.

As ever, entry into the subconscious self will create both methodological and philosophical debate. The essential point is that, in this author's experience, it is possible, and it can provide meaningful and actionable findings. That being said, caution must be exercised in analysis and extrapolation, and the limitations of such excursions must be recognised.

This latter area has led to much contemporary interest in what are known as "new techniques" in qualitative research, which are variously described as projective techniques, non-verbal techniques and creative techniques. In truth, these are not new at all, but have, as it were, been re-invented to meet demands of the current marketplace for deeper insight. A warning note should be sounded in this context. It is obvious that use of these techniques can represent the sexy end of qualitative research, but their use is meaningless unless they further the objectives of the study. In unskilled hands, they are dangerous, insofar as that analysis of findings becomes cock-eyed. There is also the considerable danger of an emphasis on techniques getting in the way of high quality qualitative research; a moderator who arrives in a focus group with a bag of verbal and non-verbal tricks can become more involved with the tricks than with what is occurring in the group. If the techniques appear to be "techniques" to respondents, an unwanted and distracting dynamic will be introduced.

With these caveats, projective techniques can facilitate examination of subconscious attitudes and emotions, and in the circumstance where either high or low verbal articulation skills among respondents form barriers to exploration (for instance, highly articulate respondents can unwittingly employ their ability to intellectualise as a screen to truer and more fundamental emotions and feelings). Projective techniques are particularly useful in developing creative and innovative avenues for a brand, product or service; they can provide guidance on the symbolic nature of the subject; for example, where certain colours, shapes and visual codes are key elements of a brand's make-up.

There is now a great range of creative techniques which may be drawn upon. A more recent development has been the tailoring of specific techniques to illuminate very particular areas of interest. A description of some of the more commonly used gives a flavour of their usefulness.

PSYCHODRAWING

Respondents produce abstract paintings of their feeling about the subject — for example, a brand, a company, a service. The painting is titled and personally signed. An art gallery is constructed, with each "artist" explaining the emotions and meanings of their painting for the others in a small group.

It is very instructive to observe how the paintings are constructed during the exercise. How slow or fast are the movements? Is the painting painstaking or produced with spontaneous verve? How precise are the drawing activities? In a recent such exercise, for example, we found competitive brands to be drawn one with clinical precision, the other with passion and emotive intensity.

TIME TRAVEL

We enter an imaginary time capsule, and can move back or forward in time, to defined years — for example, "It is 1937, we are in the bathroom of a suburban house in Dublin ... picture this in detail" (verbal and visual exercise).

This is useful for establishing historical contexts, life cycles and future projections Time boundaries are also limitless, and we have found that "going back" thousands of years has provided insights into the current status of a brand. A more recent example indicated how a brand held more attraction in its current mature adulthood; the "infancy" was subsequently explored and led to relaunch of key appeals without drawing on stereotypical nostalgia.

ROLE PLAYING

This involves the "acting out" of brands, stereotypes, fantasies, and so on, and it may be an individual or group activity. Recently, we had a group act as the board of directors of a company discussing the future of one of its key brands. Each member had been assigned a distinct role, such as, finance director, marketing director, production director, and so on. The resulting highly charged three-hour debate illustrated how consumers understood and perceived the brand being pulled and tugged in conflicting directions (it has now been made far more coherent).

Role-playing can be especially useful in exploring issues of gender. For instance, gender reversal can be employed to examine brands which are dominantly male or female in an innovative way. (We have had a group of men "become" women buying bath oil. A group of women "became" man in a trendy pub chatting up women with fascinating aspects of alcohol brands becoming apparent).

THE MUSEUM

The key subject of interest must become the centrepiece of a museum, designed, outfitted and furnished with artefacts by respondents. This can be a visual exercise, and allows detailed verbal descriptions. The museum must have potential meaning to the people who visit it in the future, who would come away with a deep understanding of the product, brand, institution, service, etc., under examination. Although this exercise can produce a simplistic picture at the beginning, with skill it can produce an illuminating view of the reference field in which the subject lives. We have used this technique successfully as a starting point to brainstorming about brands, especially to gain insight into the wider culture of a brand's existence.

WHERE IT'S GOING

At the end of the day, techniques are just that — techniques. They constitute nothing novel in the field of qualitative research, but their contemporary integration and judicious use indicates perhaps what is the most significant trend in the field for the future. This is the simple objective of higher quality, especially in the richer analysis which is itself geared towards action on the part of the research buyer. This orientation to higher quality, which this author believes is already in train, will also be likely to encompass the following:

A Necessity to Achieve a More Holistic Picture

Even the most straightforward qualitative research study on a brand will indicate that it exists in a wider world than, for instance, immediate competitive brands, its consumers and non-consumers, and its advertising. More attention will be paid to this wider world.

Multidisciplinary Analysis
To achieve a more complete picture in itself will require more wide-ranging analytical tools. Psychological and sociological concepts will continue to be primary disciplines, but constructs drawn from social anthropology, semiotics and linguistics will, this author suggests, be more frequently employed.

A Greater Focus on Culture
This is very much connected with the two preceding points, but is deserving of a mention on its own. High quality qualitative research will be sensitive to cultural mechanisms in our reference system. Our own culture in Ireland, it may be contended, is becoming increasingly complex, and more difficult to decode. Products, services, brands, advertising campaigns, companies, government departments will all exist within this culture, and be influenced by it, underlining the requirement for qualitative research to take account of it. This orientation will also probably be spurred by events such as the Single Market, and continuance of pan-European and even world brand strategies. Multicultural studies may also become more common, and these can now readily be directed from an Irish base. In turn, this will contribute to knowledge of Irish culture, as understanding one's own country often comes from discovering that reality is constructed in a wholly different way by one's neighbour.

More Attention to Brand–Consumer Dialogue
Qualitative research has become very adept at providing an understanding of brands, and many studies are conducted to explore and detail the personalities and images of brands. Similarly, research has become highly skilled in documenting consumers, and providing psychographic and lifestyle analyses. Customer segmentation is an area in which much work has been progressing. To some extent, a focus on both the brand and the consumer can inhibit examining what goes on between them. Qualitative researchers such as Judie Lannon have been to the fore in emphasising attention on the "dialogue" between brand and consumer. She has, for example, with great insight explained how advertising is part of this dialogue, and can be evaluated as

such; to borrow her words: "it is not so much what advertising does to people, as what people do with advertising".

In this author's own recent experience, there has been increasing emphasis on understanding the brand–consumer dialogue, and it is to be expected that this trend in qualitative research will increase.

A Deeper Involvement with Change and Innovation

Historically, qualitative research has been used as a tool in the assessment of change; for example, a "new" product or advertising campaign is developed to a workable ideas stage and is evaluated within focus groups. But this type of approach can have its defects. First, it brings in research only at certain points in a continuum of development, and, second, research in this context tends to be used as a filter; filters can unwittingly hinder true innovation.

A more profitable and progressive approach is the integration of the research function into the broad continuum of innovation itself wherein it can collaborate and harmonise with other disciplines such as product research and development, financial systems, marketing and advertising. On a number of projects, this type of team approach to change and innovation has already been active, with beneficial results. This general orientation will also be likely to force a greater examination of what innovation really is, and the kinds of implications this has for design of research projects and their implementation.

Many so-called innovations are only modifications which fit easily into the established order of perception. They are reckoned to be "new" because they have meaning within an existing reference frame. While this kind of change is often a key to survival of a product or brand, it does not encompass real innovation and novelty; something which could not have been imagined beforehand. Qualitative research is beginning, at last, to deal with the latter area and the issues it raises. (One, for instance, is the likelihood of immediate rejection of innovation by consumers because it is not decodable in terms of existing structures; this requires other ways of examining observed knee-jerk rejection in qualitative research).

Consideration is being given to the meaning of innovation, and the cycle of innovation. The idea, for example, that innovation brings disorder (one of the reasons it is resisted) is an interesting one; it also suggests that research should focus on the disorder rather than the existing order challenged by the innovation. In a similar vein, it can be observed that innovation is more likely at the beginning to attract a "neophile" élite while the mass market has a neophobic bent. The innovation only stands a chance of being adopted if the larger market is permeable to the values of the neophile segment. These considerations can significantly influence the design of qualitative research projects dealing with change and innovation in, for instance, leading with a study of neophile attitudes and values, and evaluating the potential for permeability of these to the mass market.

As always, the non-existent future stands right by us.

REFERENCES

Bartos, R. (1985): "What it Is and Where it Came From", *Address at the Advertising Research Foundation,* November, US: Advertising Research Foundation.

Byrne, D. (1991): "Changing Attitudes in Ireland 1991", IAPI, Dublin: Behaviour and Attitudes.

Durgee, J.F. (1986): "Richer Findings from Qualitative Research", *Journal of Advertising Research,* 26(4): 36–44.

Fleury, Pascal (1992), "Quoi de neuf?", *Trilogy,* Paris.

Lannon, J. (1992): "Asking the Right Questions", *Admap,* 327(3): 11–16.

Lazarsfeld, P.F. (1934), "The Art of Asking Why?", *National Marketing Review.*

O'Leary, P. (1991): "Verbal and Non-verbal Techniques in Group Discussions", *Address at the Marketing Society of Ireland Seminar,* November, Dublin: Marketing Society of Ireland.

Part X

International Marketing

25
An Analysis of Competition in the New Europe[*]

John Fahy

The much-hyped 1992 turned out to be a turbulent year for the European Community but not for the reasons that were originally envisaged. The momentum towards completion of the Single Market bringing with it fears of a "Fortress Europe" was replaced by some confusion and uncertainty. The year saw the rejection by Denmark of the Maastricht Treaty on greater integration, its narrow passage in France, uncertainty in Britain and all of this against a background of the demise of the ERM and the instability during and after the GATT talks. However, as we enter a new era in Europe's history firms, both inside and outside the EU, are facing a radically changing business environment. Commentators from a number of fields, including management (Higgins and Santalainen, 1989; Mitchell, 1989; Weihrich, 1990), economics (Bennett and Hakkio, 1989; Calingaert, 1989; Krugman and Verbeke, 1990), finance (Hexter, 1989; Haufbauer, 1990; Simpson and Korbel, 1990) and marketing (Bertrand, 1989; Quelch, Buzzell and Salama, 1990) have all alluded to the notion that the new Europe will be significantly more competitive. However, this contention has not been subjected to any theoretical rigour. Though it might be argued that such a theoretical base has not been established, a solid body of thought on competitive analysis is emerging in the management and strategy literature, which in turn draws from the fields of organisation theory, industrial organisation economics, marketing, finance and others. The key contribution, to date, has been the work of Porter (1980), who provided a conceptual model of the forces driving competition. It is proposed

---

[*] This paper first appeared in *European Journal of Marketing*, Vol. 27, No. 5, pp. 4–53.

to use this model to analyse the new competitive situation emerging in the EU and to assess the consequent impact on the strategies of incumbents and potential entrants.

This analysis will incorporate a number of stages. First, to provide a backdrop to the discussion, it will be necessary to assess the progress being made towards the attainment of the ambitious targets set out with the passing of the Single European Act in 1986. Changes are taking place almost every day as directives are passed, obstacles are encountered and unforeseen events begin to make an impact. Thus, an assessment of progress, problems and opportunities in the EU is provided. Second, though the outcome of many of the Commission's initiatives is subject to speculation, an analysis of the initial response of companies provides valuable clues to likely changes in the competitive environment. Finally, the strategic implications of these environmental changes are outlined.

THE SINGLE MARKET: AN ASSESSMENT OF PROGRESS

There has been a great deal of misconception about the changes taking place in Europe. Now that it has come and gone, it is clear that 1992 was not a magic year. It was merely a continuance of the progress which can be traced back to 1961 when the Treaty of Paris created the European Coal and Steel Community (ECSC), a supranational body overseeing the two industries and comprising Belgium, France, Italy, Luxembourg, The Netherlands and West Germany (Lynn, 1992). The landmark Treaty of Rome in 1967 consolidated the process of integration with the formation of the European Economic Community. But progress was slow until a radical new step was taken towards integration of the then 12 member states with the passing of the Single European Act in 1986. Other dates may become equally noteworthy in the future. The second stage of European Monetary Union begins in 1994 with the establishment of a European Monetary Institute as a forerunner to an EC central bank, to be followed by a fixing of the ECU in relation to other currencies (*Irish Times*, 11 December 1991). A single currency for Europe is due for introduction on 1 January 1999.

In addition, several other developments have added to the air of uncertainty about the Union's future. Four EFTA (European Free Trade Association) countries — Austria, Finland, Sweden and Norway are in the process of joining. Along with the 12 members of the EU they formed the European Economic Association (EEA) in 1993. Thus, the Union will effectively have another four new members by 1996. The prospects of further integration with Eastern European countries, like Poland, Bulgaria and Hungary, look slimmer in the short term as these economies would be scant net recipients of both structural funds and funds from CAP (Common Agricultural Policy) (*Wall Street Journal*, 22 September 1989). However, the break-up of Eastern Europe will continue to make an impact on developments in the Union. The collapse of the Berlin Wall and the resulting cost of German unification is viewed in many circles as having given rise to the current turmoil in the currency markets. Prospective entrants like Finland have seen their export earnings drastically reduced by the break-up of the Soviet Union. Movements of labour into the EU from the East continues to cause controversy as unemployment in the EU pushes towards 10 per cent. These economic and political changes will be paralleled by changes in industry structures which will redefine the bases for competition.

Despite the difficulties encountered in the ratification of the Maastricht Treaty and the break-up of the ERM because of speculation in member currencies, the progress towards completion of the Single Market remained steadily on course. The momentum gained by attempts to meet the 1992 target date has been significant in radically accelerating the pace of change in the EU. A distant memory, it seems, are the days when it took 14 years of negotiations to agree a jam standard (*Wall Street Journal*, 22 September 1989). The output of European standardisation bodies has risen spectacularly over the last few years. Decisions have already been taken by the Council of Ministers on 95 per cent of the 282 proposals in the Commission's initial White Paper and 85 per cent have been adopted in national legislation.

But despite this progress the Single Market was not completed on schedule by 31 December 1992. Not all proposals were put into force, with some countries dragging their heels in implementing proposals adopted by Council. Worst offenders to date include Italy, Ireland, Luxembourg, Belgium and Spain (Lynn, 1992). Ironically, the two countries leading the implementation table are Denmark and France (who have ratified approximately 150 proposals), despite their difficulties with the Maastricht Treaty. In addition, though standards may have been put into force and implemented by governments, the scope for cheating is great and the power to enforce is weak (*The Economist*, 26 September 1992). Governments which violate Single Market rules can be taken to the European Court. Some countries, most notably Italy, but also

France, Germany and Belgium, have had a number of court rulings against them. Several of the most contentious issues have been left until last and agreement cannot be expected for a number of years. Foremost among these are trademark/patents, international mergers, social policy and the harmonisation of VAT rates.

Thus, the process of change will be equally problematic in future years as will the industry environments in which companies operate.

FORCES DRIVING COMPETITION

Industries display varying degrees of competitiveness. Some, like financial services, air travel and retailing seem to be particularly competitive and advantages tend to be short-lived (Bhide, 1986). Others, particularly those showing rapid growth, such as health foods and mineral water, seem to sustain a larger number of profitable players.

A number of parameters have been used to measure the degree of competitiveness in an industry: for example, the four-firm concentration ratio (which measures the combined market share of the top four companies). But it was not until a seminal piece by Porter (1980) that a comprehensive explanation of why some industries are more competitive than others was provided. Porter contended that some industries were inherently competitive, depending on their structural make-up. This framework and subsequent supporting literature (Wright, 1986; Miller, 1988), while not representing a theoretical base, has stood the test of time and a great deal of scrutiny very well. It remains the best accepted framework for diagnosing competition.

Porter identified five key groups of forces which drive competition, namely rivalry among existing competitors, the existence of barriers to entry, the threat of substitutes, the bargaining power of buyers and the bargaining power of suppliers. Various key elements underlie each of these dimensions and are summarised in Table 25.1.

The economic and regulatory changes in the EU are likely to affect the forces driving competition in every industry. Some industries, such as duty-free shops at airports, will disappear. Others are likely to be radically altered. The following section assesses the changes taking place in each of the forces driving competition in the new Europe.

TABLE 25.1: THE FORCES DRIVING COMPETITION

Rivalry Among Existing Competitors Determined by:	Threat of New Entrants Determined by:	Threat of Substitutes Determined by:	Bargaining Power of Buyers Determined by:	Bargaining Power of Suppliers Determined by:
Number and Size of Competitors	Cost Advantages of Incumbents	Relative Price Performance of Substitutes	Buyer Concentration	Supplier Concentration
Fixed or Storage Cost Levels	Product Differentiation by Incumbents	Switching Costs	Buyer Volume	Importance of Volume to Supplier
Intermittent Overcapacity	Capital Requirements	Buyer Propensity to Substitute	Buyer Margins	Input Differences
Product Differences	Switching Costs		Product Differences	Buyer Switching Costs
Brand Identity	Access to Distribution Channels		Brand Identity	Number of Substitute Inputs
Switching Costs	Government Policy		Buyer Switching Costs	Threat of Forward Integration
Industry Growth Rate			Availability of Substitutes	
Exit Barriers			Level of Pull Through	
			Ability of Buyers to Backward Integrate	
			Buyer Information	

Source: Adapted from Porter, M. (1980): *Competitive Strategy,* New York: The Free Press.

COMPETITIVE CHANGES IN THE EU

The process of harmonisation currently taking place in the EU and the resulting impact on companies operating there has a range of implications for the forces driving competition. A likely growth in the level of competition in the EU's major industries has been the focus of much attention since this process began. Van der Hoop (1988) notes that a vocal minority of business and political leaders are claiming that the Single Market will cause predatory competition, widespread business failure and catastrophic unemployment. Insights from the structural forces driving competition suggest a more balanced perspective, as shown in Table 25.2 below, and discussed in the following paragraphs.

Rivalry among existing firms. Rivalry among firms in an industry occurs at both the strategic and operational level. Operational level rivalry is very familiar, for example, advertising battles, price competition, etc. At a strategic level, firms jockey for positions of competitive advantage by manipulating a variety of drivers (Porter, 1985). A number of structural forces helps to accentuate this rivalry.

In particular, intermittent overcapacity, switching costs and exit barriers are likely to increase competitive rivalry within Europe's industries. Many industries, such as steel, detergents, pharmaceuticals and banking are already characterised by significant overcapacity (Friberg, 1989). Indeed, preparations for the Single Market have served to heighten overcapacity as acquisitions and significant capital investment, in industries such as paper and chemicals in 1989 and 1990, met with the downturn in the world economy in the past two years (Mason, 1992). This problem is likely to be accentuated by fluctuations in exchange rates, particularly for companies also operating outside the EU. Exit barriers are also significant in many European industries. For example, the Single Market is unlikely to be able to support 12 national airlines.

But government shareholdings in these companies, and nationalistic tendencies, will ensure that they continue to operate, in some cases as a cross-border alliance such as that proposed between British Airways and KLM (Netherlands). Finally, the opening of borders and particularly the harmonisation of technical standards are likely to reduce switching costs, thereby intensifying competition.

On the positive side, the intensity of competition is likely to be reduced as fixed/storage costs are lowered. Companies operating within the EU are rationalising their operations in preparation for more open markets.

An Analysis of Competition in the New Europe 399

TABLE 25.2: COMPETITIVE CHANGES IN THE EU

Direction of Change	Rivalry Among Competitors	Threat of New Entrants	Threat of Substitutes	Bargaining Power of Buyers	Bargaining Power of Suppliers
Increase	Intermittent Overcapacity	Government Policy	Relative Price Performance of Substitutes	Buyer Concentration	Supplier Concentration
	Switching Costs			Buyer Margins	Input Difference
	Exit Barriers			Availability of Substitutes	
Decrease	Fixed or Storage Costs	Cost Advantages of Incumbents	Switching Costs	Buyer Volume	Threat of Forward Integration
		Capital Requirements		Buyer Switching Costs	Supplier Switching Costs
		Switching Costs			
		Access to Distribution Channels			
Neutral	Number and Size of Competitors	Product Differentiation by Incumbents		Threat of Forward Integration	Substitute Inputs
	Industry Growth Rates				
No General Changes	Product Differences		Buyer Propensity to Substitute	Product Differences	Importance of Volume to Supplier
	Brand Identity			Brand Identity	
				Level of Pull Through	
				Buyer Information	

For example, Jacobs Suchard, the Swiss packaged-goods manufacturer, has recently consolidated production of individual brands at specific factories to achieve scale benefits, closed facilities in Stuttgart and Paris and equipped remaining plants with state-of-the-art automation and flexible manufacturing systems. The harmonised market will allow greater economies in production and distribution, thus reducing fixed and storage costs (Berger, 1989).

A number of authors have alluded to the notion that competition will intensify as a result of an increased number of rivals in the marketplace (Bertrand, 1989; Van der Hoop, 1988). However, conflicting forces serve to neutralise this variable. On the one hand, there is the suggestion that new competitors will be arriving from the US and the Pacific Rim as well as from within Europe. Particularly noteworthy is the threat from Japan. By the end of 1988 there were 392 Japanese manufacturing plants in operation in Europe, an increase of 116 on 1987 (Berger, 1989). On the other hand, as integration with EFTA countries increases, there is a threat of greater competition from several significant players, like Nestlé, BBC Brown Boveri and CIBA-Geigy, in Switzerland, and Volvo, Electrolux and Stora in Sweden. However, this trend will be counterbalanced by the increasing consolidation occurring within European industry. A wave of mergers and strategic alliances continues to sweep Europe. In the first nine months of 1990 alone, some 1,190 European concerns changed owners, for a total value of $32.7 million (Berney, 1990). Similarly, the industry growth rate variable is somewhat neutral. The Cecchini report forecast a 4.5 per cent annual growth rate in Gross National Product (GNP) in the Community, though the recession experienced during 1992 saw growth rates of 2 per cent or less being more prevalent in the Community. However, it is difficult to project the likely effect of any level of growth on specific industries, though one outcome could be an increased number of growth industries with a consequent reduction in the intensity of competition.

Overall, a number of conflicting forces are at work. One very probable outcome is a significant shake-out of marginal competitors in many industries (Mitchell, 1989; Bennett and Hakkio, 1989). Many European industries are characterised by a large number of small competitors; for example, the German timber industry has 3,000 firms, though it is expected that by the mid-1990s no more than 800 will remain (Samiee, 1990).

The threat of new entrants. High barriers to entry lessen the intensity of competition and can result in the achievement of high economic rents by some firms (Rumelt, 1987). As many as 19 different market entry barriers have been identified in the literature (Karakaya and Stahl, 1989). Porter (1980) proposed six major sources of barriers to entry: namely, cost advantages of incumbents; product differentiation by incumbents; capital requirements; switching costs; access to distribution channels; and government policy.

Removal of entry barriers is the main target of the harmonisation process. However, the extent of their reduction is contingent on the successful implementation of all the proposed directives. Each broad set of proposals will serve to reduce entry barriers significantly (Fahy, 1990).

Cost advantages of incumbents are likely to be reduced through the removal of border posts and the harmonisation of technical standards. The successful removal of technical barriers will also reduce customer switching costs, increasing access to distribution channels particularly in the industrial goods sector. All facets of the harmonisation process will serve to reduce the capital requirements necessary for entry into new markets.

However, these changes will be diluted if many of the current problems facing the EU's legislators are not resolved. The reciprocity clause in many EU directives, irrespective of whether it seeks national or "mirror image" treatment, will continue to remain a barrier to entry. Lack of mutual recognition, in both product standards and testing and certification procedures, will create a barrier to entry for non-EU firms (Mosbacher, 1990). Barriers will also be created because of a lack of agreement on local content and country of origin rules (Farren, 1990) and on patenting laws (Linville, 1990). The *à la carte* approach of domestic governments to EU legislation will serve to exacerbate market barriers. For example, France has been embroiled in an argument with the Commission over industrial subsidies, while many firms feel that they are being denied a fair chance to win government business in other countries, in line with proposed changes in public procurement practices (*The Economist*, 26 September 1989). Selective adoption extends to different industries, further complicating analysis. For example, Greece, Italy and Luxembourg are hindering EU-wide application of over half the directives adopted in the banking industry, while member states have adopted over 80 per cent of directives relating to insurance.

Finally, counterbalancing forces are at work in the area of product differentiation of incumbents. Technical harmonisation should serve to reduce differentiation barriers which provided incumbents with artificial advantages over new entrants. But many cultural and language barriers will persist long after the harmonisation process is complete, thus counteracting these changes.

The threat of substitutes. Despite the attention given to market share, few companies do a good job of defining their market boundaries (Abell, 1980). Narrow market definition may result in potential substitutes being overlooked. Though the issue of substitutes is usually industry-specific some broad insights can be gained. As noted earlier, the harmonisation process is likely to have a significant impact on consumer switching costs, particularly in the industrial goods sector. Union-wide technical standards will make switching between suppliers easier for companies, thus increasing product substitutability. The relative price performance of substitutes could be a very significant factor during the early stages of the development of the internal market. This is because of variation resulting from the harmonisation of fiscal barriers. For example, excise rate harmonisation would dramatically reduce liquor prices in Ireland, Denmark and the UK, while vastly increasing them in Italy. In the UK the price decrease in wine would be greater than that for beer which would be likely to give rise to substitution (Quelch, Buzzell and Salama, 1990). In addition, the present exchange rate instability within the Union would give rise to significant price performance differences, unless currencies are realigned before borders become fully open.

The bargaining power of buyers. The ability of large powerful firms to extract concessions from suppliers has the effect of reducing industry profitability. As outlined in Table 25.1 a wide variety of factors have an impact on the bargaining power of buyers in any given industry. The changes taking place in the EU will affect the buyer bargaining power in different industries in different ways. However, a number of general predictions can be made. Overall buyer bargaining power is likely to increase mainly because of increased buyer consolidation, reduced buyer volume, increased efficiency and the availability of substitutes.

Mergers and alliances are also increasing significantly in the retailing and wholesale sectors. A number of EU-wide co-operative buying groups have been formed, for example, the alliance between the Argyll Group (UK), the Ahold Group (Holland) and Casio of France. Furthermore, the Ahold Group has expanded into Portugal by acquiring a 49 per cent stake in the Pingo Doce supermarket chain (*International Management*, 1992). The importance of particular suppliers to any one buyer is likely to decrease for two reasons. Differential pricing may no longer be possible as importers and buyers look to import from the cheapest source, increasing the potential sources of supply and available substitutes (Mitchell, 1989). Furthermore, exclusive trade agreements are likely to come under increased antitrust scrutiny (Linville, 1990). Finally, reduction in transportation and distribution costs is likely to create opportunities for increased buyer efficiencies and profit margins.

At this stage, there appear to be very few forces having a negative effect on buyer bargaining power. The increased size of companies will create a very viable threat of forward integration. In fact, some companies are already bypassing distributors and taking advantage of direct distribution opportunities (Van der Hoop, 1988). However, attempts to forward-integrate may meet with some regulatory resistance; for example, the recent changes in the UK brewing industry have sought to reduce the role of "tied houses" in the distribution of beer.

Bargaining power of suppliers. A similar pattern of effects is likely to take place on the supply side of industries. Increasing consolidation will strengthen supplier bargaining power. Furthermore, a number of factors is likely to increase the importance of European suppliers. Many US and Japanese companies are aware of the importance of developing local linkages within EU member countries. Thus many companies are seeking to localise design, R&D and production in the EU (Berger, 1989). The desire to be a "good citizen" (Bertrand, 1989) will strengthen domestic supplier bargaining power. However, unlike the situation with buyers, several strong forces are likely to reduce supplier bargaining power. As technical standards are harmonised, buyer switching costs are reduced. Increased consolidation and rationalisation will reduce the threat of forward integration by suppliers. In fact, much of the rationalisation process includes the sources of supply; for example, Philips Inc. has dropped 10,000 suppliers in the past few years. Such activities by major companies will have the effect of reducing supplier bargaining power.

Finally, the issue of substitute inputs is somewhat neutral. As noted in the case of buyers, reduction in the opportunities for differential pricing will increase the availability of substitute inputs, thus decreasing supplier bargaining power. However in certain sectors, particularly the supply of labour, bargaining power will be significant. Adoption of the Social Charter and the possibility of a German model of worker participation will have a significant impact on human resource deployment.

DISCUSSION

There has been a great deal of general comment on the possible impact changes in the EU will have on the activities of companies both inside and outside the Union.

TABLE 25.3: A FRAMEWORK FOR DIAGNOSING CHANGES IN INDUSTRY COMPETITIVENESS

Factors	Relative Weighting	Factor Change	Weighted Change
Rivalry Among Competitors Number and size of Competitors Level of Fixed Costs Intermittent Overcapacity, etc.			
Threat of New Entrants Cost Advantages of Incumbents Capital Requirements Switching Costs, etc.			
Threat of Substitutes Relative Price Performance of Substitutes Switching Costs, etc.			
Bargaining Power of Buyers Buyer Concentration Level of Pull Through, etc.			
Bargaining Power of Suppliers Supplier Concentration Threat of Forward Integration, etc.			Total Change

For example, significant levels of deregulation in the aviation industry are likely to increase the intensity of competition in this sector, while, for the foreseeable future, quotas restricting the number of Japanese cars coming into the Union look likely to remain in place. But the foregoing has shown that a good understanding of the nature and extent of competition in particular industries requires a rigorous analysis of a wide variety of elements. The process of integration is likely to effect all of the players in the industry chain. The Porter model is a suitable basis for analysing these changes. An illustration of how the model might be applied in any given industrial situation is provided in Table 25.3 above. The scope of such an analysis may be very wide ranging, including an analysis of related industries or dimensions of the industry in different parts of the EU.

The value of this framework is that it allows planners to quantify the extent of change in an industry and more importantly to identify clearly where the locus of change will be.

CONCLUSIONS AND IMPLICATIONS

This paper provides a more rigorous analysis of the competitive changes taking place in the EU than has been available to date. It has shown that suggestions of more aggressive competitor activity are only the tip of the iceberg; significant changes are affecting all the structural forces driving competition in different ways. Corporate planners and managers need to analyse all elements of competitive activity to get a clearer view of the challenges that lie ahead. The framework provided here is an essential blueprint for such an analysis.

On a general level we can conclude that the drive towards harmonisation will serve to increase the intensity of competition in the EU. This will be as a result of increased rivalry among competitors and particularly because of the increased bargaining power of buyers. Conflicting arguments exist as to whether European or US firms — with the latter's economic strength derived from a large home-market base, and the notion that they are better organised to operate in a large transcontinental market — will be more successful (Farren, 1990). Some authors note that many European firms are cash-rich, quite the opposite of their highly leveraged US counterparts, and that the extensive rationalisation being undertaken will make them more competitive (Higgins and Santalainen, 1989). The next few years should provide some answers to this debate.

In conclusion, several strategic implications emerge from this discussion. Firstly, access to good information will be paramount in the new Europe. The rapidly changing business environment will require very close monitoring and particular attention needs to be paid to progress on directives impacting a firm's particular industry. Furthermore, access to the legislative process through the lobbying platforms will also be essential (Hunter, 1989). Second, the importance of strategic positioning has been recognised (Mitchell, 1989). Companies need to know where they stand in the market, have a clear vision of where they want to be and know how to get there. However, flexibility will also be critical as changes in the regulatory environment mandate new strategies (Delachaux, 1990). Finally, strategic alliances may play an important role in managing the competitive environment. The implications from this analysis are that alliances which alter competitive rivalry or the bargaining power of buyers should be considered.

The new Europe will be a challenging one for incumbents and new entrants alike. However significant rewards exist for companies aggressive enough to meet the challenge.

REFERENCES

Abell, D.F. (1980): *Defining the Business: The Starting Point of Strategic Planning*, Englewood Cliffs, N.J.: Prentice-Hall.

Aron, D. (1990): "Where Are the Americans?", *Industry Week*, 239(4): 67–9.

Bennett, T. and Hakkio, C.S. (1989): "Europe 1992: Implications for US Firms", *Economic Review*, 74(4): 3–17.

Berger, M. (1989): "The Paranoia Gripping Japanese Business", *International Management*, 44(4): 24–8.

Berney, K. (1990): "Europe's Merger Mania", *International Management*, 45(1): 4–5.

Bertrand, K. (1989): "Scrambling for 1992", *Business Marketing*, 74(2): 49–59.

Bhide, A. (1986): "Hustle as Strategy", *Harvard Business Review*, 64(5): 59–65.

Calingaert, M. (1989): "What Europe 1992 Means for US Business", *Business Economics*, 24(4): 30–36.

Delachaux, F.B. (1990): "The Effects of 1992 on European Business", *Business Horizons*, 33(1): 33–6.

Economist, The (1992): "After 1992", 324(7778): 71–2.

Economist, The (1992): "Will More be Merrier", 325(7781): 73.

Economist, The (1992): "After 1992", 324(7778): 71–2.

Fahy, J. (1990): "Market Entry Strategy in the New Europe", in L.M. Capella, H.W. Nash, J.M. Starling and R.D. Taylor (eds), *Progress in Marketing Thought*, Mississippi State, MS: Southern Marketing Association.

Farren, J.M. (1990): "US–EC 1992 Trade Issues", *Business America*, 111(1): 4–5.

Friberg, E.G. (1989): "1992: Moves Europeans are Making", *Harvard Business Review*, 67(3): 85–9.

Haufbauer, G.C. (1990): "Europe 1992: Opportunities and Challenges", *Brookings Review*, 8, Summer 13–22.

Hexter D.R. (1989): "Europe 1992: How Will it Affect International Competition?", *Financial Executive*, 5(5): 20–24.

Higgins, J.M. and Santalainen, T. (1989): "Strategies for Europe 1992", *Business Horizons*, 32(4): 54–8.

Hunter M. (1989): "Bold Strategies in a Brave New Market", *Business Month*, No. 134, August: 42–4.

International Management (1992): "Ahold Follows in Le Lion's Footsteps", 47(9): 26.

Irish Times, The (1991): "Single Currency Road Clearly Mapped Out", 11 December: 7.

Karakaya, F. and Stahl, M.J. (1989): "Barriers to Entry and Market Entry Decisions in Consumer and Industrial Goods Markets", *Journal of Marketing*, 53(2): 80–91.

Krugman, A.M. and Verbeke, A. (1990): "Corporate Strategy After the Free Trade Agreement and Europe 1992", in *Regional Integration in the World Economy: Europe and North America*, Kiel: Joint Canada-Germany Symposium.

Linville, D. (1990): "Marketing in Europe in 1992", *Business America*, 111(1): 14–6.

Lynn, M. (1992): "Countdown to Completion", *International Management*, 47(1): 10–15.

Mason, J. (1992): "The Storm Breaks Over Europe", *International Management*, 47(4): 34–7.

Miller D. (1988): "Relating Porter's Business Strategies to Environment and Structure: Analysis and Performance Implications", Academy of Management Journal, 31(2): 280–308.

Mitchell, D. (1989): "1992: Implications for Management", *Long Range Planning*, 22(2): 32–40.

Mosbacher, R.A. (1990): "US–EC Co-Operation Increases as the Single Market Takes Shape", *Business America*, 111(1): 2–3.

Porter, M. (1980): *Competitive Strategy*, New York: The Free Press.

Porter M. (1985): *Competitive Advantage*, New York: The Free Press.

Quelch, J.A., Buzzell, R.D. and Salama, E.R. (1990): *The Marketing Challenge of 1992*, Reading, MA: Addison-Wesley.

Rumelt, R.P. (1987): "Theory, Strategy and Entrepreneurship", in *The Competitive Challenge: Strategies for Industrial Innovation and Renewal*, Cambridge, MA: Ballinger.

Samiee, S. (1990): "Strategic Considerations of the 1992 Plan for Small Exporters", *Business Horizons*, 33(2): 48–52.

Simpson, C.D. and Korbel, J.J. (1990): "Getting US Companies Ready for 1992", *Journal of Accountancy*, 169(May): 60–76.

Thomson, I. (1990): "Internal Market Developments September–November 1990", *European Access*, 6 December: 15–17.

Van der Hoop, H. (1988): "Europhobias or Europhoria?", *Distribution*, 87(10): 38–46.

Weihrich, H. (1990): "Europe 1992: What the Future May Hold", *Academy of Management Executive*, 4(2): 7–18.

Wright, P. (1986): "The Strategic Options of Least-Cost, Differentiation and Niche", *Business Horizons*, 29(2): 21–6.

26

Successful SME Strategies for International Markets[*]

*Frank Bradley and
Seán Ó Réagáin*

INTRODUCTION

How successful exporting companies allocate resources to international product-markets and critical cost areas of the business system with a view to developing competitive advantage in international markets is the subject of this paper. From a management perspective, internationalisation is often synonymous with achieving rapid company growth. In their study of fast-growth businesses in the UK, Storey et al. (1989) found that one of the main characteristics which distinguished growth companies was the importance of exports in their sales. The need to internationalise in order to grow is all the more acute in the case of a small open economy like that of Ireland, because of the small size of the domestic market (O'Grady, 1987). Despite the obvious need for Irish companies to go international, only a small number of indigenous companies have succeeded in establishing a significant presence in export markets. The research on which this paper is based is described in greater detail in Ó Réagáin (1991).

THEORETICAL BACKGROUND FOR THE RESEARCH

There is an extensive literature on the barriers to internationalisation faced by the SME, and the propensity of such firms to internationalise. Less attention has been given to ways in which successful international marketing companies initially establish

---

[*] This paper first appeared in *EMAC*, Barcelona, 1992.

themselves in international markets to achieve the crucial mass required for export growth.

The central argument of this paper is that concentration on strong products and markets, and on critical cost areas of the business system, is the route to international market success for SMEs in small open economies. Concentration on strong products and markets is concerned with the company's marketing strategy while concentrating on the critical cost areas of the business deals with the importance of the business system for competitive advantage in international markets.

Regarding product-market resource allocation, the choice is between diversification and concentration (Ayal and Zif, 1979). The first implies fast penetration of a large number of product-markets and diffusion of effort among them. The second is based on concentration of resources in a few product-markets and general expansion into new areas. Product-market concentration appears to be a rewarding route to success in international markets for the SME because it allows attractive markets to be targeted and resources to be focused on these markets only. Using a market concentration strategy, the first international market then acts as a bridgehead both for diversification into other international markets and for launching other products internationally.

Underlying its second contention is the assumption that the key success factor is to find a source of competitive advantage through a reorganisation of the business system. The objective of this reorganisation is to achieve a superior cost-quality combination in a way that makes it difficult for a larger competitor to emulate. The argument to be tested is that the key to competitive advantage is to avail of the flexibility which a small firm enjoys to unbundle the business system so as to focus on those elements of the chain which yield the greatest return in value-added terms, while rearranging the provision of the other elements of the chain as cost-effectively as possible.

BARRIERS TO INTERNATIONALISATION AMONG SMEs

For an SME, internationalisation involves a gradual progression over a relatively long period, rather than a rapid increase in activities through spectacular investment (Bradley, 1983; Cavusgil, 1980). The international progression of a typical SME takes place in clearly identifiable incremental steps (Johanson and Wiedersheim-Paul, 1975; Johanson and Vahlne, 1977; Bilkey and Tesar, 1977; Cavusgil, 1980).

Critical to the growth of the SME is its ability to surmount the barriers to internationalisation at each stage. These barriers may be classified as external or internal (Cavusgil and Nevin, 1981). External barriers can be considerable. Most international market environments are highly dynamic because of changing foreign government policies, unpredictable shifts in the economy and exchange rates and unexpected changes in customer demands and competitor positions (Bradley, 1985). Internal barriers are also important. Inadequate access to information (Douglas, et al., 1982), apprehension about export marketing (Cavusgil, 1980), management and organisational weaknesses, exacerbated by the absence of marketing assets (Bradley, 1983), and lack of top management determination to export (Cavusgil and Nevin, 1981) are among the internal impediments identified.

In addition to these obstacles to internationalisation, SMEs in Ireland face a number of additional constraints (Buckley, 1988) arising from the country's peripheral island location, the small scale and openness of the domestic market (Consultative Committee on Marketing, 1984), late industrialisation (National Economic and Social Council, 1982), and the lack of tradition in exporting (Department of Industry and Commerce, 1987).

Market and Organisational Barriers Identified

Working with growth companies in its Company Development Programme, the Industrial Development Authority (IDA) (now Forbairt) in Ireland has highlighted a number of market related difficulties faced by small- and medium-sized Irish firms in taking the initial export marketing step. The market-related issues identified were:

- Opportunistic sales-driven approach
- No clear pricing policy
- Lack of knowledge of real selling costs
- Lack of influence over agents and distributors due to a lack of clear objectives.

Broader organisational-related difficulties encountered by these companies when trying to establish an international market position were:

- Inadequate spread of management capabilities across functions
- Insufficient attention to financial controls

- Absence of a product development strategy
- Inadequate planning of working capital and cash-flow requirements
- "Management stretch" on operational issues with insufficient attention to strategic issues.

RESOURCE ALLOCATION IN INTERNATIONAL MARKETS

Once the decision to grow through internationalisation has been made, it is necessary to determine the international marketing resource allocation to be adopted to achieve the required critical mass. The elements of this decision represent the "basic strategies in international marketing" (Segler, 1987). The resource allocation decision determines the distribution of the company's resources among specific countries and products. Determination of the international marketing resource allocation begins by establishing the number of markets in which to operate and the desired characteristics of these markets. Once the international market portfolio of the firm has been determined, individual geographic markets may be chosen which are consistent with it. In deciding the scope of its desired export market coverage, two generic strategies are available to an SME: product-market concentration and product-market diversification (Ayal and Zif, 1979).

Product-Market Concentration

Market concentration initially involves the purposeful selection of a small number of the most promising markets for more intensive development (Hirsch and Lev, 1983; Ayal and Zif, 1979; Piercy, 1982). It has been argued that for a small firm serving up to six export markets is considered a concentration strategy, while for larger established exporters, concentration suggests a maximum of ten markets (Piercy, 1982). For an SME going international for the first time out of a small home market such as Ireland, two or three markets would appear to constitute a reasonable span for a concentration strategy.

A concentration strategy may be particularly attractive for the SME as it requires a relatively low initial investment in marketing facilities, avoids the cost of dealing with small orders to little-known markets, limits the span of managerial control and enables more visits to be made to each market. It also keeps the costs of international market research within the limits of the company's resources (Ryans, 1988). Market concentration may also provide a springboard for subsequent diversification and consequent stabilisation of the firm's exports (Hirsch and Lev, 1973). The issues regarding product concentration may be developed in an analogous way.

Product-Market Diversification

Market diversification involves the simultaneous entry into as many markets as possible (Hirsch and Lev, 1973). A market diversification strategy normally implies more than twelve country markets and marketing resources divided equally among all markets (Piercy, 1982).

The objective of a market diversification strategy is to obtain a high rate of return through market development rather than market penetration, while maintaining a low level of resource commitment by selecting more accessible target markets (Bradley, 1991). A market diversification strategy involves a greater risk for the exporter since it requires a larger initial investment in markets. Greater risk attaches to market spreading, but where it is successful it has been shown to be more profitable (Hirsch and Lev, 1973). In the longer term, a market spreading strategy is usually followed by a period of market consolidation in which the number of markets is reduced as less profitable ones are abandoned (Ayal and Zif, 1979).

In practice, a firm is unlikely to select a position at either extremity of the spreading–concentration spectrum, but more probably will pursue a mixed strategy, selling to a relatively large number of markets while concentrating resources on a selection of these (Bradley, 1991). The advantage of such a mixed strategy is that it allows a firm to focus its strategy on the most promising markets, while leaving sufficient flexibility to accept opportunistic business in other markets (Piercy, 1982). The issues regarding product diversification may be developed in a similar manner.

Feasible Product-Market Resource Allocation Strategies

Investment in product-markets usually occurs between the extremes of complete concentration and complete diversification. Product-market allocation strategies are closely interlinked; market allocations impose constraints on the range of feasible product allocation strategies if the firm is to sustain its competitive position in international markets.

If an SME combines market and product diversification

strategies, it is unlikely to have sufficient resources to make the required marketing effort for all markets and products. This is the risk of under-investing in markets, a problem which arises in rapid growth markets especially (Figure 26.1).

FIGURE 26.1: CONSTRAINTS ON COMBINING MARKET AND PRODUCT ALLOCATIONS

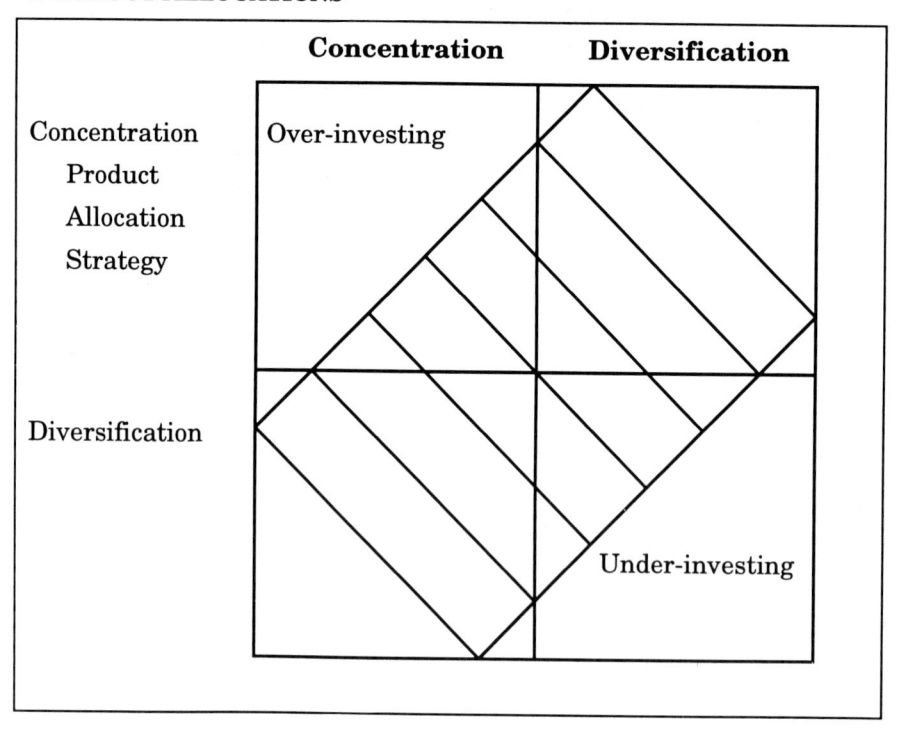

	Concentration	Diversification
Concentration Product Allocation Strategy	Over-investing	
Diversification		Under-investing

The risk of over-investing arises if the company serves only a few markets with a small range of products which may leave some important markets open to competitors. This difficulty is most likely to occur in companies with new innovative products for which it is important to be the first mover in international markets. To avoid the risk of under- or over-investing it may be necessary to balance product and market allocation strategies, represented by the shaded area above (Figure 26.1).

International Marketing Strategies for SMEs

International expansion strategies similar to those used in the domestic market are known to be successful (Bradley, 1991). The smaller the firm and the more limited its export experience, the greater are the benefits from using a strategy based on existing products in the domestic market (Doyle and Gidengil, 1977). In many instances SMEs depend on price-based competition in one or two markets only and neglect other elements of the marketing mix (Bradley, 1983). As a result, they fail to establish critical mass in international markets. Indeed, some firms follow an extreme form of concentration strategy by serving one market only. Other firms, spreading themselves too thinly across many markets, fail to achieve the minimum level of market penetration required to cross the critical mass threshold.

The appropriate route to international markets for SMEs hypothesised here is in the pre-export stage, the successful company exploits domestic market opportunities to build up company resources, focusing particularly on developing a high-capability, broadly-based management team and an efficient integration of the business system for a small number of products, say three: A Product, B Product and C Product in which the company has particular strengths (Figure 26.2).

FIGURE 26.2: APPROPRIATE INTERNATIONAL MARKETING STRATEGIES FOR SMEs

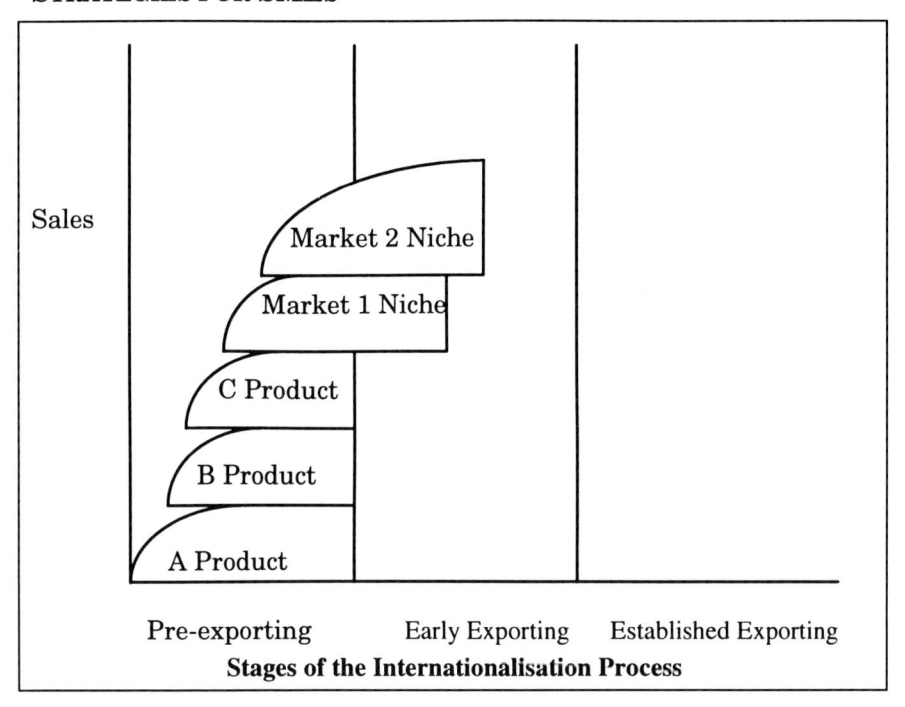

Company strategy for internationalisation would be concentrated on the product-market segment where the core competences of the company give it a competitive advantage.

The approach should be to open up each market based on the market or product niche in which the company has unique strengths. The process might evolve step by step, taking one market at a time, Market 1, Niche 1, learning from it and then using it as a bridgehead to transfer that learning to the same niche in the next market (Market 2, Niche 1). Consolidation and profitability should be achieved in each market before developing new ones. The company may develop its international operations by continuing to develop new markets in a step by step manner, ensuring consolidation before moving on. The extent to which this model fits with the approach taken by successful exporting SMEs is the subject of this research. These value chain relationships, based on market and marketing investments, allow firms to establish and change positions in business networks (Mattsson, 1985) to produce competitive advantage.

PROCESS POSITIONING IN THE BUSINESS SYSTEM

Process positioning concerns ways of sourcing manufactured components and launching products included in the firm's portfolio. The core of the process positioning concept is that the firm should be viewed as competing within a business system, not an industry (Gilbert and Strebel, 1988). A productive activity is viewed as a chain of many parts, ranging from design to use by the final consumer. The various parts of this chain can be ordered in terms of stages of perceived value-added.

The objective of a firm's process positioning is to organise the business system to achieve an increase in the level of perceived value-added or a reduction in the price charged so that the total perceived value to the customer exceeds the collective cost to the firm of performing the value activities embodied in the final product. Process positioning for competitive advantage is based on the company's ability to organise the business system to provide the final customer with the desired perceived value at the lowest delivered cost which requires superior performance in at least one of the business system activities.

High perceived value strategies are more appropriate in the emerging stages of the product life cycle when the manufacturing process is not a significant competitive factor. Technology is still evolving, the business system has not stabilised and competition tends to be confined to product innovation and development at this stage. High perceived value strategies tend to favour product-markets with short life cycles. Low delivered cost strategies, however, are more appropriate at the standardisation phase of the product life cycle which is characterised by rapid market development. Attention is focused on the production process and resources are directed to the entire business system with process technology, market positioning and distribution efficiency becoming critical.

By following a planned sequence of moves emphasising high perceived value now and low delivered cost at a later stage, where one set of circumstances creates the conditions for implementation of the other, the firm successfully develops a proactive outpacing strategy which identifies elements of perceived value which are not worth the delivered cost. These can then be unbundled and produced outside the firm at a lower cost. Additional elements of perceived value desired by the served segment can be included in the competitive formula at acceptable cost (Gilbert and Strebel, 1988).

RESEARCH METHODS

Research Objectives and Hypotheses

The two specific objectives of the research were to identify and describe:

- The scope, type and mix of markets and products developed in the early stages of internationalisation by successful SMEs.
- The strategy for achieving competitive advantage in chosen international markets.

From the literature reviewed, a number of hypotheses were developed. In regard to the first objective, four hypotheses were formed. International marketing success is likely to depend on:

(1) Market concentration rather than diversification.
(2) Narrow market segment focus and non-price competition.
(3) Development of markets similar to the home market.
(4) Small number of markets and products initially.

Concentration is defined as devoting effort and resources in at most three markets. Implied in the fourth hypothesis is the need to achieve critical mass in international markets. In regard to the second objective, two hypotheses were formed. Successful exporters are more likely to:

(5) Pursue strategies aimed at high perceived value for market segments selected ("proactive outpacing strategies").
(6) Contract out parts of the value chain in seeking competitive advantage.

Data Collection

The research involved the collection of data on the internationalisation strategies of SMEs in Ireland. Some of the data was available in records maintained by the Industrial Development Authority (IDA). Additional data were collected directly from the companies themselves using a questionnaire. A two stage approach to data collection involving a combination of mail, telephone and personal interviewing was used. Project Officers in the IDA supplied much of the detailed background data from records. In this way part of the questionnaire was completed. The remainder of the questionnaire, referring mainly to strategic planning issues, was completed in direct interviews. To minimise the likelihood that companies might convey to IDA executives an overly optimistic view of their activities, all information relating to company performance was based on externally audited data drawn from IDA records. Questioning of company management was confined to the development of marketing strategies. Unstructured personal interviews were also held with known authorities in international marketing to gain a better understanding of the situation facing successful exporting SMEs.

Survey Firms

The sample universe consisted of wholly Irish-owned manufacturing firms with up to 500 employees who had received grants from the IDA, and which had passed the stage of initial exporting. It is believed that this experimental stage refers to the first two years of exporting (Wiedersheim-Paul, Olsen and Wesch, 1978). The definition of an SME is that accepted by the Commission of the EU: all companies employing 500 people or less. The sample frame was confined to successful companies, where success was defined as having at least one third of total company sales in each of the two previous years derived from export markets. The firms in the sample may, therefore, be regarded as committed exporters.

A non-probabilistic sampling method was used. Sample selection was based on the shares of different sectors in the total exports of Irish-owned manufacturing industry. It was decided to use data from the IDA's Irish Economy Expenditures Survey (IEES) as a proxy for exports of Irish-owned companies by sector. This survey has the advantage that it discriminates between exports of indigenous and multinational companies and allows a breakdown at sectoral level, thus overcoming limitations of data on exports available from other sources.

Data on sales, components of sales and the destination of sales of manufacturing companies in Ireland and available in the IEES were used in the study. Use of these data has a number of limitations: it is a survey rather than a census, which has implications for the representativeness of the data, particularly at NACE-sector level. Only companies employing 30 or more people are included in IEES. The IEES is, however, the best available source of data on exports of Irish-owned companies.

Given the concern about representativeness, it was decided to sample three sectors: the modern sector; the traditional sector and the natural resource-based sector taking account of the share of each in the total exports of Irish-owned companies. A sample size of 100 was selected. Details of the 82 completed questionnaires returned are shown below according to their NACE sector (Table 26.1).

TABLE 26.1: DETAILS OF SAMPLING AND RESPONSES

NACE Sector	Companies Sampled	Companies Responding		Response Rate %	
	No.	No.	No.	No.	No.
Modern	28	26		32	
Chemicals			3		4
Engineering			23		28
Traditional	16	17		20	
Non-metallic minerals			3		4
Textiles			2		2
Clothing, Footwear and Leather			6		7
Paper and Printing			2		2
Miscellaneous			4		5
Natural Resources	56	39		48	
Food			30		37
Drink and Tobacco			3		4
Timber and Furniture			6		7
TOTAL	100	82		100	

The natural resource-based sectors are slightly under-represented given their share of exports and the modern and traditional sectors are over represented. Since natural resource based companies still constitute almost half of the sample responses, this imbalance is not regarded as serious.

There were three principal reasons for the 18 non-responses:

(1) The project officer was not sufficiently familiar with the company to complete the questionnaire having only recently assumed responsibility for the company.
(2) Though agreeing in principle to participate, the project officer became too busy with other matters to complete the questionnaire.
(3) The company refused to participate for undisclosed reasons. In each case no further attempts were made to collect information on the companies involved.

Given that 89 per cent of indigenous manufacturing companies in Ireland employ fewer than 50 people and 97 per cent employ less than 200, the sample may appear over-representative of larger SMEs. In the absence of an accurate breakdown of indigenous exporting companies by size, it could be expected that successful exporting companies would tend to fall into the larger employment size. Accordingly, the sample is taken to be broadly representative.

Almost three quarters of companies in the sample started up within the last 20 years, reflecting the radical restructuring which the Irish industrial base went through following EEC entry in 1973, leading to the closure of many older, uncompetitive indigenous companies. Almost all companies in the sample have less than 20 years exporting experience, reflecting the relative youthfulness of the indigenous industrial base referred to above, coupled with the protected nature of the Irish market prior to EEC entry in 1973. More than half the companies in the sample had sales of £1 million or less. Exports accounted for between one and two thirds of total sales for most firms in the sample.

RESEARCH RESULTS AND DISCUSSION

The research findings in relation to the resource allocation of successful exporting companies and the way they use the business system to achieve competitive advantage in international markets are discussed in this section.

The research findings on international marketing allocation are discussed under the following headings:

- Strategic Spread of Markets and Products
- Market, Segment and Competitive Positioning Strategy
- Types of Market and Products
- Approaches to Internationalisation.

The research findings on developing an international competitive advantage among SME exporters relate to the way elements of the business system are organised within a Gilbert and Strebel (1988) low delivered cost – high perceived value framework. The research also considers the extent to which unbundling the business system by subcontracting elements is used as a competitive weapon to achieve a superior cost-quality advantage over larger international competitors.

Strategic Spread of Markets and Products

Two generic strategies are open to a firm seeking to internationalise: concentration and spreading (Hirsch and Lev, 1973; Ayal and Zif, 1979; Piercy, 1982). According to these researchers, firms allocate resources and effort close to one or other end of the continuum represented by these extremes. Given the barriers to internationalisation faced by all SMEs and particularly the obstacles faced by those in Ireland, as described, it was hypothesised that market concentration, involving a focus on at most three international markets and products, was more likely to be associated with success in the early stages of exporting than was diversification. The research findings suggest strong support for this hypothesis. In relation to markets, on each of the three variables used to measure concentration or spreading, the majority of responses were consistent with a concentration approach (Table 26.2).

TABLE 26.2: MARKET SERVED AT INITIAL PRODUCT LAUNCH

Market No.	Responses (N=81)
	%
One Market Only	70
Few Selected Markets	17
Any Attractive Market	4
All Markets where Firm has a Presence	9
Total	100

The vast majority of respondents were found to focus on a few markets only: 70 per cent of respondents initially launch a product internationally in one market only; 87 per cent concentrate their market investment in one or a few markets only. These findings are similar to those of Irvine (1988). In a survey of 72 firms, in which concentration was defined as selling into at most six geographical markets, he found that 54 per cent of firms indicated that they were pursuing a concentration strategy.

In order to identify the product-market combinations selected, the market and product concentration and diversification variables were combined. Almost two-thirds (65 per cent) of companies combined product and market concentration while 22 per cent combine market concentration with product diversification (Table 26.3).

TABLE 26.3: PRODUCT MARKET CONCENTRATION AND DIVERSIFICATION (N=81)

Range of Products	One Market Only %	Few Selected Markets %	Any Attractive Market %	All Markets with a Presence %	Total %
Significant Variation (Diversification)	16	6	0	1	23
No Significant Variation (Concentration)	54	11	4	8	77
Total	70	17	4	9	100

The risk of over-investing arising from a strategy of product-market concentration was discussed above. To test for evidence of this, the performance of companies pursuing various strategy combinations in relation to their export market penetration targets was examined (Table 26.4). No significant difference in achievement of export market objectives was found in the proportion of companies pursuing each of the strategy combinations which achieved their export market penetration objectives. For all combinations significantly over half of the firms were on target.

TABLE 26.4: PRODUCT-MARKET DIVERSIFICATION AND EXPORT MARKET PENETRATION OBJECTIVES (N=81)

Export Market Penetration Objectives	Product-Market Concentration (N=53)	Product Diversification Market Concentration (N=18)	Product Concentration Market Diversification (N=9)	Product-Market Diversification (N=1)
On Target	72%	83%	67%	1%
Off Target	28%	17%	33%	0%

The association of concentration with export success found in this research bears out findings in other countries (Cunningham and Spiegel, 1971; Piercy, 1981a). Moreover, it is consistent with the Doyle and Gidengil (1977) view that exporters are unlikely to be successful unless they have a market concentration strategy, since resources are dissipated over a range of marginal markets.

This research shows that most respondents combine a market concentration strategy with a product concentration strategy. According to Segler (1987), such a strategy combination leads to the risk of being caught in the "overspending" trap by leaving some important markets open to competitors. Examining product-market positioning combinations and company performance against export market objectives, however, provides no significant evidence of an "over-spending" problem in the case of those combining product and market concentration.

Three possible reasons may be advanced as to why no substantial basis for sustaining the "over-investing" hypothesis was found. First, consumer products companies in the sample appear to combine a highly concentrated market strategy with a somewhat broader spread of products, while industrial products companies appear to adopt a strategy of high product concentration across a somewhat larger spread of markets. The degree of flexibility within these overall concentration strategies appears to be sufficient to avoid the "overspending" trap.

A second possible reason for the absence of an overspending problem among "concentrators" is that the problem is most likely to occur in the case where a company is a first mover in international markets. Many Irish SMEs do not fit this profile, being followers into established markets. The third possible explanation is that, being successful, these exporters may have protected themselves against the dangers of over-concentration in other elements of their strategies; for example, by selecting segments of greatest potential for them.

Market, Segment and Competitive Positioning

The findings on market and competitive positioning concur more with Piercy's (1982) view that price and non-price competition can be combined with concentration or with spreading, rather than with Ayal and Zif's (1979) view that concentration is associated with penetration pricing and spreading with price skimming. Most respondents seem to combine non-price strategies with market concentration strategy (Table 26.5). The explanation behind this may lie in the large proportion of respondents pursuing a niche or differentiation strategy to target particular segments within their narrow geographic market range.

TABLE 26.5: MARKET SEGMENT AND COMPETITIVE POSITIONING

Competitive Strategy	Narrow Market Concentration	Segment Focus Market Diversification	Broad Market Concentration	Segment Focus Market Diversification	Total
	(N=67)	(N=2)	(N=11)	(N=2)	(N=82)
	%	%	%	%	%
Niche Strategy	36	0	5	0	41
Differentiation	24	1	2	0	27
Price Competition	14	1	3	1	19
New Product-Market	1	0	1	1	3
Other	8	0	2	0	10
Total	83	2	13	2	100

Almost three quarters of firms which pursue niche or differentiation strategies serve a narrow range of customer groups. Moreover, for most of the firms the segment focus was not found to vary across geographic markets, reinforcing a preference for a narrow segment focus approach.

In this regard, Ayal and Zif's (1979) model of generic strategies relating geographic market scope and segmentation to competitive position appears to be borne out by the research. Most of the firms pursuing a narrow segment market concentration combination indicated that they were competing on non-price factors (Table 26.5). This research supports the hypothesis that export success is more likely to be associated with a narrow segment focus and with non-price-based competitive strategies.

Types of Markets and Products Selected

Most firms sampled focus their export strategies on markets which are similar to existing markets, thus supporting the hypothesis (Table 26.6). This is also consistent with the findings regarding markets chosen by successful SME exporters in the early stages of internationalisation (Madsen, 1988).

TABLE 26.6: NATURE OF EXPORT MARKET

Similarity of Export Market	Product Group		Total
	Consumer Products	Industrial Products	
	(N=45)	(N=37)	(N=82)
	%	%	%
Very Similar	12	6	18
Similar	34	26	60
Not Relevant	6	9	15
Different	2	5	7
Total	54	46	100

There is some evidence, however, that a higher proportion of industrial products companies sell into diverse markets than consumer products companies, perhaps because, for specialist industrial products companies, similarity of customer needs rather than similarity of geographic market is the key criterion determining type of market chosen.

Based on evidence in the literature, it was hypothesised that export success was more likely to be associated with a conservative market and product development strategy than with a strategy which combined entry into diverse markets with significant new product development. The research evidence indicates that while this hypothesis can be supported, the majority of firms follow some degree of product-market development.

Two major factors dominated the international market selection decision: geographic proximity and stage of development of the market. A third factor, size relative to the domestic market, was also important (Table 26.7). It would seem that successful exporters, by emphasising proximity, similarity and size, choose international markets with the implied intention of enlarging the domestic market incrementally. In addition, this approach also economises on the use of scarce resources. The market selection strategy of successful exporting firms seems to fit the concentric circles mould described by Segler (1987).

TABLE 26.7: MOST IMPORTANT FACTOR INFLUENCING MARKET CHOICE

Factor Influencing Choice	First (N=82) %	Second (N=67) %	Third (N=63) %	Top 3 (N=212) %
Geographic Proximity	34	31	21	29
Stage of Development	33	36	14	28
Size Relative to Domestic Market	12	15	21	16
Location of Customers	9	3	21	10
Market Similarity	5	12	21	12
Other	7	3	2	5
Total	100	100	100	100

Approaches to Internationalisation for the SME

It was hypothesised that the appropriate way of establishing a foothold in international markets for the SME is to focus initially on a small number of markets and products to achieve subsequent international market penetration objectives in a planned, sequential manner, using existing markets and products as "bridgeheads". A large majority of respondents indicated that their initial move into export markets involved a highly concentrated market and product strategy combination, thereby supporting the hypothesis (Table 26.8). This supports the findings in other studies regarding the initial internationalisation step, most notably, that of Madsen (1988) for Denmark, a country similar to Ireland where SMEs are "forced" to export at an early stage of their development.

TABLE 26.8: INITIAL MARKET CONCENTRATION (N=82)

Products	Markets 1 %	2–3 %	>3 %	Total %
1	50	6	4	60
2–3	22	4	1	27
>3	6	2	5	13
Total	78	12	10	100

International Competitive Arena for SME Exporters

In terms of Gilbert and Strebel's (1978) framework, the companies in the sample would be expected to follow proactive outpacing strategies aimed at delivering higher perceived value to satisfy the particular expectations of selected market segments, rather than aiming at a mass market with a pre-emptive low delivered cost strategy, as a large industry leader might be expected to do. An analysis of the competitive positioning strategies suggests that most companies pursue a proactive strategy: for the large majority of respondents, strategy is built on non-price factors rather than direct price competition.

There is evidence that successful SME exporters pursue proactive outpacing strategies. Product quality, a critical element in any high perceived value strategy, was cited most often by respondents as one of the three most important elements in their strategies (Table 26.9). Moreover, of the other five elements commonly cited, three — on-time delivery, customer relations and product design and features — are all elements which contribute to high perceived value. While price, which may be taken as an indicator of a low delivered cost strategy, was identified by the majority of respondents as a significant element, it was the most important element for only 28 per cent of respondents and in no case was strategy based only on price. This suggests that the basis of the competitive advantage lies in the achievement of a superior perceived value position, often in combination with low delivered cost, rather than through the pursuit of low delivered cost only.

The predominance of perceived value-related factors over delivered cost-related factors is a consistent finding in other research into sources of international competitive advantage for SMEs (Dobrydnio, 1988; Keng and Jiuan, 1989; Madsen, 1988; Piercy, 1981a; Christensen, de Rocha and Gertner, 1987).

TABLE 26.9: KEY ELEMENTS OF COMPETITIVE ADVANTAGE

Competitive Factors	First (N=82) %	Second (N=81) %	Third (N=78) %	Top 3 (N=241) %
Quality	29	40	19	29
Price	28	17	17	21
On-Time Delivery	16	18	22	19
Product Design & Features	12	4	0	5
Customer Relations	8	10	28	15
Distribution Network	1	6	12	6
After Sales Service	1	1	2	3
Other	5	4	0	3
Total	100	100	100	100

Significance of the Business System for International Competitive Advantage

Most of the firms surveyed acknowledge the importance of superior performance of critical functions in the business system in achieving a competitive advantage over larger international competitors. The four elements of the business system identified most frequently as directly relevant to the attainment of a superior perceived value position were: research and development, production, marketing and purchasing (Table 26.10).

The lower priority attached by respondents to the quality control function is interesting: it was the activity cited most often as being important, but, in most cases, it was the second or third most important element of the business system. This suggests that it is perceived as a necessary but not sufficient condition for a strategy based on high perceived quality to be effective. The quality control function in effect acts as a check that other important activities of the business system have been performed to the required standard. In a number of other studies, the quality control and design functions have also been identified by SME exporters as the most significant factors in the achievement of international competitive advantage (Piercy, 1981a; Joynt, 1982; Dobrydnio, 1988).

TABLE 26.10: KEY ELEMENTS OF VALUE CHAIN

Elements of Value Chain	First (N=75) %	Second (N=72) %	Third (N=74) %	Total (N=221) %
Research	32	11	3	15
Development	23	10	20	18
Production	16	19	11	15
Marketing	16	8	14	13
Purchasing	8	33	28	24
Quality Control	4	3	5	4
Sales	1	3	0	1
Transportation	0	13	19	10
Distribution	=	=	=	=
Total	100	100	100	100

Contracting Out in International Competitive Advantage

The key to achieving international competitive advantage through pursuit of a proactive outpacing strategy is to isolate and unbundle those elements of the business system for which the perceived value is not worth the delivered cost. The research findings support the hypothesis that such contracting out of elements of the value chain can play a significant role in efforts to achieve international competitive advantage. A significant proportion of respondents acknowledged the role of contracting out in their strategies. Cost is the principal reason given for contracting out (56 per cent of respondents). Quality was cited by 4 per cent of companies while cost and quality together was cited by 30 per cent of companies.

Of the elements of the business system most frequently outsourced by respondents, four are functions which specialist subcontractors could be expected to provide more cost effectively than the firm itself: sub-assembly, distribution, processing and installation (Table 26.11).

TABLE 26.11: ELEMENTS IN VALUE CHAIN CONTRACTED OUT

Elements in Value Chain	Respondents (N=50)* No.
Sub-assembly	18
Distribution	14
Production	10
Processing	7
Design	2
Installation	2
Sourcing of Raw Materials	1
Transport	1
Testing	1
Marketing	1
After-sales Service	1

* Responses sum to more than 50 because some companies contracted out more than one element of the value chain.

The other two functions which some respondents indicated they contracted out are production and design. Production was also identified by respondents as a critical element in a high perceived value strategy and so might be expected to be carried out in-house. It may be, however, that having a subcontract capability allows the firm flexibility in managing fluctuations in market demand, thus facilitating achievement of international competitive advantage through the attainment of a unique perceived value and delivered cost combination.

Only a small proportion of firms subcontract the design function. These cases would appear to depart from the hypothesised strategy framework in that a function associated with achievement of high perceived value is being outsourced.

The positive response of the majority of respondents indicates that subcontracting plays an important part in strategies to facilitate the achievement of a high perceived value strategy more cost effectively.

CONCLUSIONS

This paper has sought to contribute to an understanding of the process of successful internationalisation by SMEs. Based on the analysis, a number of conclusions may be drawn:

- The internationalisation step is more likely to be successful if a highly concentrated approach is taken, focusing on a few markets and products.

- In seeking to achieve competitive advantage over larger, and often more centrally located competitors, strategy should reflect quality rather than price-related factors and should target a narrow range of customer groups. This was the strategy pursued by 68 per cent of established successful firms surveyed.

- Effective organisation of the key activities of the business system can contribute an important competitive edge in the pursuit of quality-based strategies.

- Contracting out of business system activities not critical to the quality of the final product, can facilitate international competitive advantage by allowing SME exporters flexibility to deliver a superior quality product more cost effectively.

These conclusions have a number of implications for the management of SMEs seeking to develop export markets for the first time and for those already in the early stages of internationalisation.

In the initial export market step, the SME should concentrate its resources and effort on a small number of familiar markets and on products matching customer requirements in the selected market, which may be different from the home market. With increasing export experience, the focus may then be widened gradually to encompass more demanding markets and products.

Within the selected export markets, the focus should be on selected market segments with which the firm can achieve a strong competitive position based on non-price factors.

In seeking to achieve international competitive advantage, management should try to identify those parts of the production process which contribute most to final product value for their selected customer segment, and concentrate efforts on these.

At the same time, they should explore the potential for providing more cheaply those elements of the product which cost the firm more to produce than their value to the customer. The potential for contracting out these activities to specialist subsuppliers should be investigated.

REFERENCES

Ayal, I. and Zif, J. (1979): "Market Expansion Strategies in Multinational Markets", *Journal of Marketing*, 43(2): 84–94.

Bilkey, W.J. and Tesar, G. (1977): "The Export Behaviour of Smaller-Sized Wisconsin Manufacturing Firms", *Journal of International Business Studies*, 8(1): 93–8.

Bradley, M.F. (1983): "A Public Policy for International Marketing", *Journal of Irish Business and Administrative Research*, 5(2): 57–75.

Bradley, F. (1985): "Key Issues in International Competitiveness", *Journal of Irish Business and Administrative Research*, 7(2): 3–14.

Bradley, M.F. (1991): *International Marketing Strategy*, London: Prentice-Hall International.

Buckley, A.P. (1988): *International Market Entry and Development: The Role and Impact of the State Support System*, (unpublished) MBS dissertation, Department of Marketing, University College Dublin.

Cavusgil, T. (1980): "On the Internationalisation Process of Firms", *European Research*, 6: 273–80.

Cavusgil, S.T. and Nevin, J.R. (1981): "Internal Determinants of Export Marketing Behaviour: An Empirical Investigation", *Journal of Marketing Research*, 18(1): 114–19.

Christensen, C.H., de Rocha, A. and Gertner, R.K. (1987): "An Empirical Investigation of the Factors Influencing Exporting Success of Bean Firms", *Journal of International Business Studies*, 18(3): 61–77.

Consultative Committee on Marketing (1984): *Ireland and Marketing, Report to the Sectoral Development Committee*, Dublin: Stationery Office.

Cunningham, M.T. and Spiegel, R.I. (1971): "A Study of Successful Exporting", *British Journal of Marketing*, 5(1): 1–12.

Department of Industry and Commerce (1987): *Review of Industrial Performance 1986*, Dublin: Government Publications.

Dobrydnio, R. (1988): "Marketing Strategies and Export Performance of Small Peruvian Manufacturing Firms", *Journal of International Business Studies,* 19(2): 315.

Douglas, S.P., Samuel, C.C. and Keegan, W.J. (1982): "Approaches to Assessing International Marketing Opportunities for Small and Medium-Sized Companies", *Columbia Journal of World Business,* 17(3): 26–32.

Doyle, P. and Gidengil, Z.B. (1977): "A Strategic Approach to International Market Selection", *AMA Proceedings,* Chicago, Illnois: American Marketing Association.

Gilbert, X. and Strebel, P. (1988): "Developing Competitive Advantage", in B.J. Quinn, H. Mintzberg, and R.M. James (eds), *The Strategy Process,* Englewood Cliffs, N.J.: Prentice-Hall.

Hirsch, S. and Lev B. (1973): "Foreign Marketing Strategies — A Note", *Management International Review,* 13(6): 81–8.

Irvine, D. (1988): Competitive Strategies in International Marketing, (unpublished) MBS dissertation, Department of Marketing, University College Dublin.

Johanson, J. and Wiedersheim-Paul, F. (1975): "The Internationalisation of the Firm, Four Swedish Case Studies", *Journal of Management Studies,* 12(3): 305–22.

Johanson, J. and Jan, E.V. (1977): "The Internationalisation Process of the Firm — A Model of Knowledge Development and Increasing Foreign Market Commitments", *Journal of International Business Studies,* 8(1): 23–32.

Keng, K.A. and Jiuan, T.S. (1989): "Differences Between Small and Medium Sized Exporting and Non-Exporting Firms: Nature or Nurture", *International Marketing Review,* 6(4): 27–40.

Madsen, T.K. (1989): "Successful Export Marketing Management: Some Empirical Evidence", *International Marketing Review,* 6(4): 41–55.

National Economic and Social Council (NESC) (1986): *A Review of Industrial Policy,* Dublin: NESC.

O'Grady, N. (1987): *Open-Minded Management and Exporting Activity in Small Manufacturing Firms,* (unpublished) MBS dissertation, Department of Marketing, University College Dublin.

Ó Réagáin, S. (1991): *Towards an Understanding of Successful Internationalisation by Small and Medium Sized Enterprises in Ireland,* (unpublished) M.B.A. dissertation, University College Dublin.

Piercy, N. (1980): "Export Marketing Management in Medium-Sized British Firms", *European Journal of Marketing,* 17(1): 48–67.

Piercy, N. (1981a): "Company Internationalisation: Active and Reactive Exporting", *European Journal of Marketing,* 15(3): 26–40.

Piercy, N. (1982): *Export Strategy, Markets and Competition,* London: George Allen and Unwin.

Ryans, A.B. (1988): "Strategic Market Entry Factors and Market Share Achievement in Japan", *Journal of International Business Studies,* 19(3): 389–409.

Segler, K.G. (1987): "The Challenge of Basic Strategies", *European Journal of Marketing,* 21(5): 76–89.

Storey, D., Keasy, K., Watson, R. and Wynarczyk, P. (1987): *The Performance of Small Firms,* London: Croom Helm.

Wiedersheim-Paul, F., Olsen, S.C. and Wesch, L.S. (1987): "Pre-Export Activity — The First Step in Internationalisation", *Journal of International Business Studies,* 9(1): 47–58.

27

The Exporting Activities of Small Firms in Northern Ireland[*]

William Clarke

INTRODUCTION

For many years, the main thrust of industrial development policy in Northern Ireland has been aimed at attracting inward investment, but substantial difficulties have been encountered with this approach. These difficulties stem primarily from the poor image of the region as a result of the continuing civil unrest which has persisted since 1968, and partly from the severe competition for increasingly scarce large-scale mobile investment projects emanating from many other economically deprived regions offering broadly similar inducements. In consequence, considerable attention has been given in recent years to the stimulation of indigenous enterprise, both through the development of existing companies and the creation of new ones.

Primary responsibility for the design and implementation of measures aimed specifically at small firms (arbitrarily defined as those having less than 50 employees) rests with the Department of Economic Development and with the Local Enterprise Development Unit, normally referred to as the DED and LEDU respectively. The realisation that growth opportunities are severely limited within the context of a small and peripheral regional economy led to a greater interest in the possibilities of export-led growth. A wide divergence of views is apparent within the local community on whether or not it would be worthwhile to allocate scarce resources to promote export development within the small business sector. At one extreme, it is suggested that very few small firms export, that few of them are capable of doing so even

---

[*] This paper first appeared in *IBAR*, Vol. 12, pp. 88–103.

with substantial assistance, and that the net contribution in terms of additional income and employment generated is likely to be minimal. A rather different view is that, given the limited size of the domestic market, there really is no viable alternative growth path available. Public debate and policy formulation were inhibited by a lack of up-to-date information on a number of key issues. For that reason, LEDU commissioned a major study of the current exporting activities of small firms, the fieldwork for which was completed during the period April–September 1988.

This paper reports and analyses the main findings of that enquiry, discusses their implications for future policy, and seeks to place them within the context of other recent research into the problems encountered by small firms attempting to export.

Definition of Exporting

For the purposes of this paper, "exporting" is defined as selling goods or services to customers located outside Northern Ireland. Exporting is normally defined as selling goods or services to customers located outside the country of origin. However, in the case of Northern Ireland, this definition is in some respects too simplistic. In some cases, a sale to a customer a few miles down the road is, technically and legally, true exporting. Selling to customers located in the Republic of Ireland is for many firms relatively straightforward, and represents a fairly easy process of expansion within their natural geographic expansion area. In contrast, selling to customers situated in other parts of the United Kingdom presents many of the problems associated with exporting, although technically and legally these sales should not truly be regarded as exports. It is acknowledged that including sales to mainland Britain as "exports" is strictly-speaking inaccurate, but it is suggested that this approach is more meaningful in terms of offering a better insight into the actual problems encountered by small firms located in Northern Ireland when they seek to expand the scope of their activities beyond the limited regional home market.

Scope and Methodology of the Enquiry

The population studied was defined as all companies currently in receipt of LEDU assistance (i.e., "LEDU clients") excluding those being assisted under the Enterprise Grants Scheme. In effect, this definition includes the great majority of small firms engaged in manufacturing and employing between 5 and 50 people. According

to lists supplied by LEDU, this comprised a total of 1,638 firms.
The research was conducted in two stages as follows :

Stage 1. All 1,638 firms were included in the LEDU mailing list and were contacted by letter and invited to indicate whether or not over the preceding 12 months they had sold any of their output to customers located outside Northern Ireland. A total of 1,091 valid (i.e., usable) responses were received, representing a response rate of 66.7 per cent.

Stage 2. Those companies which replied indicating that they had exported some proportion of their output were contacted again and invited to supply additional information concerning their exporting activities. A total of 247 valid responses to this initial postal enquiry were received. Subsequently an additional 100 companies were contacted by telephone. In addition, more detailed personal interviews were conducted with the managing director (or another senior manager) of 50 companies identified by LEDU as major exporters. This procedure yielded a total sample of 397 LEDU exporters — that is, approximately 25 per cent of all LEDU client companies, and more than 50 per cent of the LEDU client companies identified as exporters during Stage I.

The procedure set out above was designed to gather data on the basis of as comprehensive a coverage of LEDU's current client base as possible. As with all enquiries of this kind, the basic difficulty arising is the extent to which the responses actually received are truly representative of the population as a whole. The key issue is to what extent the information given and the views expressed by those companies which responded to the enquiry is also typical of those companies which did not respond. Subsequent comparison revealed a very close symmetry between the sample and the population as a whole in terms of industrial sector and geographical location, which tends to suggest that a representative sample was in fact obtained, and that results based on the sample may be applied with confidence to the total population.

PROFILE OF LEDU EXPORTERS

Incidence of Exporting

On the basis of the information obtained in the survey it may be concluded that at least 42 per cent of LEDU clients are exporters;

in other words, during the previous 12 months they had sold at least some proportion of their output to customers located outside the province.

This estimate is based on the results of Stage 1. Valid (i.e., usable) replies were received from 1,091 firms out of a total of 1,638 contacted, representing a response rate of 66.7 per cent. A total of 687 of the firms responding indicated that they had exported some of their output in the preceding 12 months. The most pessimistic assumption possible is that none of the non-respondents are currently exporting; on that basis, Stage 1 established that 687 firms out of the 1,638 initially contacted (i.e., 41.9 per cent) are currently exporting.

Value of Exports

The best estimate that can be made from the data collected during the course of the enquiry is that during the financial year 1987/88 LEDU-assisted firms sold approximately £150 million of goods and services to customers located outside Northern Ireland.

Given that 70 per cent of respondents recorded export sales of less than £250,000, it is felt that the "best estimate" that can be provided is to assume that the average exports of non-respondents is equivalent to the average of responding companies with annual export sales of less than £250,000. This approach implies annual average exports for non-respondents of approximately £85,000 per company, yielding a total estimate of approximately £50 million, as follows:

Value of exports reported by respondents	£122,992,500
Estimated value of exports by non-respondents	£ 26,435,000
TOTAL	£149,427,500

The spread of export sales by value as reported by respondents is summarised in Table 27.1. It is clear that a substantial proportion of small exporters are operating at a very low level. Roughly a quarter of those firms which provided information reported annual exports of less than £20,000; just over half of them exported less than £100,000. At the other end of the spectrum, a total of 21 firms reported export sales in excess of £1 million.

TABLE 27.1: VALUE OF EXPORTS

Export Sales (£000)	% of Firms (N=376)
Less than £20,000	25.7
21–50	12.2
51–100	13.7
101–250	19.8
251–500	16.2
501–£1m	6.9
More than £1 million	5.5
Total	100.0

Exports and Employment

It is clear that the exporting activities of small firms make a significant contribution to maintaining employment in Northern Ireland. The best estimate that can be provided from the information available is that approximately 2,100 jobs in LEDU-assisted companies are directly attributable to exports.

TABLE 27.2: NUMBER OF EMPLOYEES LAID OFF IF EXPORT ORDERS WERE UNOBTAINABLE

No. of Employees	% of Firms
None	37.7
1	8.4
2	11.3
3	9.0
4	5.4
5	4.6
6–10	15.8
More than 10	7.8
TOTAL	100.0

A total of 321 companies provided information in response to the question: "How many of your current employees would you have to lay off if for some reason you were unable to obtain any more orders from outside Northern Ireland?" In line with other findings which indicate that a substantial proportion of LEDU companies are exporting on a very limited scale, more than a third (38 per cent) of respondents indicated that they would not have to lay off any of their staff if export orders were not forthcoming. At the other end of the spectrum, a total of 26 companies of varying sizes stated that they would have to close down altogether in that situation). An average of 3.68 jobs per company are attributable to exports (Table 27.2 above).

The estimate is based on the assumption that the non-respondents tended to be those companies which are less involved in exporting, and is derived by excluding only those respondents indicating job losses in excess of 10 in calculating an average figure for job losses per company in non-exporting companies, as follows:

No. of jobs attributable to exporting in companies
    providing information   1,182
Estimated no. of jobs attributable to exporting in
    companies which did not provide information   366
Companies x 2.49 jobs per company   911
                                   TOTAL   2,495

Importance of Exports

The importance of exporting was assessed by inviting respondents to indicate what percentage of their total sales is accounted for by exports (Table 27.3).

TABLE 27.3: EXPORTS AS A % OF TOTAL SALES

Per Cent of Total Sales	% of Firms (N=382)
Less than 10	32.9
11–25	16.7
26–50	20.1
51–80	19.6
81–100	10.7
TOTAL	100.0

Here again the information reported is consistent with other findings which suggest that a substantial proportion of LEDU-assisted companies are not deeply involved in exporting. For roughly a third (32.9 per cent) of those exporters providing information in this point, exports account for less than 10 per cent of their total sales. Exports comprise less than 25 per cent of turnover for roughly half (49.6 per cent) of the firms contacted; exports represent less than 50 per cent of total sales for just under 70 per cent of small exporters. A total of 8 companies reported that 100 per cent of their sales are exported.

Attitudes to Exporting

A more subjective indication of the importance of exporting was obtained by asking respondents to indicate how important they regarded export business for the future prosperity of their company (Table 27.4). Just under 60 per cent of respondents stated that they believed exporting to be very important in these terms; a further 30 per cent regarded exporting as quite important.

TABLE 27.4: IMPORTANCE OF EXPORTS FOR THE FUTURE PROSPERITY OF THE COMPANY

	% of Firms (N=392)
Very Important	59.7
Quite Important	30.4
Not Very Important	7.7
Not At All Important	2.2
Total	100.0

These findings are slightly at odds with the more objective measures of the importance of exporting (Table 27.3), which would tend to suggest that for many small firms exporting is not in fact of such major importance. The key to this apparent contradiction may well lie in the inclusion of the phrase relating exporting to the future prosperity of the company. It seems reasonable to conclude that the great majority of small exporters hold a generally positive attitude to the idea of developing their exports in the future, even though they may only be exporting to a very limited extent at present. The importance of this conclusion, if indeed it is valid, should not be overlooked. Virtually all the research undertaken in other areas concerning export development suggests that a key success requirement is the pre-existence of a positive attitude at the level of the individual manager. (Miesenbock, 1988; Kaynak et al., 1987; Verhoeven, 1988.) It is suggested that this evidence that many small firms are favourably disposed to export development represents a major advantage in terms of LEDU's future activities in this field.

Respondents in general display a very positive attitude to exporting; with a substantial majority (75 per cent) agreeing that exporting is essential to the long-term survival of any small firm located in Northern Ireland. More than 80 per cent hold the very sensible view that the export market is very competitive, but less than 20 per cent were prepared to agree that there are so many problems associated with marketing that it is simply not worth the effort. However, a much less positive view is taken when government agencies are referred to in the context of exporting, with only a third of respondents (36 per cent) agreeing that, if you want to get into exporting, there is plenty of support available from government agencies.

TABLE 27.5: ATTITUDES TO EXPORTING

	Strongly Agree	Agree	Don't Know	Disagree	Strongly Disagree
	% of Firms (N = 391)				
Exporting is essential to the long-term survival of any small firm located in Northern Ireland.	39.4	36.2	5.5	18.1	0.8
The export market is very competitive.	37.5	46.9	10.2	5.4	
There are so many problems with exporting that it is simply not worth the effort.	8.6	9.4	14.8	40.6	26.6
If you want to get into exporting there is plenty of support available from government agencies.	0.8	35.2	30.5	27.3	6.2

Destination of Exports

The notion that for most small firms exporting means selling to Great Britain is not supported by the evidence received from respondents concerning the destination of their export orders. Just over 10 per cent of the companies contacted export only to customers located in Great Britain. The converse of this finding is of course that 90 per cent of them are engaged in "true" exporting (i.e., to customers located outside the United Kingdom).

Roughly a quarter export only to the Republic of Ireland, and a further quarter restrict their exporting activities to the British Isles. On the information available it would appear that about a third of LEDU exporters are selling to EU member states other than the UK and/or the Irish Republic, and about 10 per cent currently sell at least some proportion of their output to customers located elsewhere in the world.

TABLE 27.6: DESTINATION OF EXPORTS BY BROAD GEOGRAPHICAL AREA

	No. of Firms	% of Firms
Great Britain Only	44	11.2
Republic of Ireland Only	95	24.2
Great Britain and Republic of Ireland	88	22.5
EU*	125	31.9
Other Areas†	40	10.2
TOTAL	392	100.0

* Defined as Britain and/or Ireland plus at least one other member state.
† Defined as Britain and/or Ireland plus at least one other market outside the EU.

A more detailed analysis of the export markets serviced reveals some interesting indicators of broad trends. Sales to the EU appear to be concentrated in the nearer and more prosperous markets — West Germany, the Netherlands, France and Belgium. Exports further afield display a similar pattern of concentration on the nearer and more prosperous markets of North America and Scandinavia.

A number of studies (Cannon and Willis, 1983; Piercy, 1984) suggest that success in exporting is more likely if a company's efforts are concentrated on a limited number of markets, as opposed to being dissipated ineffectively over a large number of widely different markets. It would appear that the great majority of small exporters are applying this strategy, in that roughly 85 per cent of them have limited their activities to date in only one or two export markets. It is of course a matter for debate whether or not this has be largely fortuitous and dictated by limited resources, or is the result of a deliberate policy decision. The 31 companies which reported sales to a large number of export markets (6 or more) are all larger and more experienced companies with a substantial track-record in exporting.

TABLE 27.7: NUMBER OF EXPORT MARKETS SERVICED

No. of Markets	% of Firms (N = 367)
1	45.1
2	31.7
3	5.4
4	5.1
5	4.3
6 or more	8.4
TOTAL	100.0

Difficulties Encountered

The exporting companies identified in the survey were invited to state what are the main difficulties they have encountered in developing and maintaining export business.

Factors which may be classified as major problems for small exporters are:

- The high cost of maintaining regular contact with customers
- Exchange rate fluctuations
- Difficulties in obtaining payment
- Identifying suitable agents/distributors
- High transport costs and the perceived unreliability of transport services
- Customs clearance difficulties
- Cash-flow problems
- Lack of management time to devote to export development
- The perceived remoteness of Northern Ireland and associated communications problems
- Lack of financial resources required.

The most frequently mentioned difficulty encountered is the substantial costs involved in maintaining regular contact with existing and potential; customers, which most respondents regard (correctly) as being of vital importance. Most respondents expressed the problem simply in terms of travel and subsistence costs, but a few also included the costs of maintaining a sales office and/or distribution facilities elsewhere. It is noticeable that this problem was highlighted by a substantially higher number of "large" as opposed to "small" exporters. Problems caused by fluctuations in the exchange rate were also more common amongst larger exporters. The great majority (over 95 per cent) of problems associated with customs clearance were encountered in exporting to the Republic of Ireland; it would appear that the hoped-for improvement in this area resulting from the introduction of SAD has not yet occurred at ground level.

Cash-flow problems were caused both by the long lead time between dispatch of an order and the eventual receipt of payment for it, and by the costs associated with increasing output to cater for exports (including equipment costs, higher stock levels of raw materials and finished goods, and initial marketing expenditures). It is perhaps significant that these problems were noted only by large exporters; the most obvious explanation is that the smaller exporters are operating on such a limited scale that these problems have not yet arisen.

In contrast, a relatively higher proportion of small exporters cited the sheer lack of senior management time as a major difficulty, and a lack of the financial resources required for export development was noted only by smaller companies.

Less serious problems noted by substantial numbers of LEDU exporters include:

- Limited production capacity
- Lack of knowledge about marketing and exporting
- Identifying potential customers
- Price competition from overseas suppliers
- Obtaining information about export markets
- Technical or legislative barriers to trade.

LEDU Assistance

Respondents were also invited to suggest specific ways in which LEDU could help them to develop their export business further. It was anticipated that a high proportion of respondents would request additional financial assistance, and this indeed was the case. By far the most important single area where firms feel that additional financial help is needed is in reducing the costs of maintaining adequate representation in export markets, either through frequent visits, or by opening a permanent sales office. Most other finance-related suggestions were aimed at simply increasing the amount of grant that can be obtained in connection with various schemes which already exist. The only "new" areas of possible grant aid identified were:

- Assistance in respect of direct advertising costs
- Insurance cover — i.e., LEDU-backed indemnity against default.

In terms of non-financial help, most companies would like LEDU to supply them with information on possible export opportunities. A significant number of the larger companies expressed a need for some kind of exporting unit within LEDU which could advise on a wide range of export-related matters.

In general, the larger exporters offered more suggestions than the smaller companies, and identified several specific areas where more assistance is, in their view, needed:

- A translation/language training service
- A credit-rating checking service
- A documentation advice service.

The Mechanics of Exporting

In order to probe more deeply into the detail of exporting activity at the level of the individual firm, personal interviews were conducted with 50 companies identified by LEDU as major exporters. The main findings of this element of the research are summarised below:

(1) The notion that it takes a very long time to become an established exporter is not supported by the experience of the 50 companies interviewed. Roughly half of them obtained their first export order within the last five years, and only six companies had more than ten years' experience of exporting.

(2) All but one of the companies interviewed stated that their exporting activities were the result of a deliberate policy decision, rather than something which happened more or less by chance. The factors which led companies to take this decision include:

- Limited size of NI market
- Too much competition in NI market
- NI market in decline
- Company became aware that opportunities existed, and followed them up
- Company was approached by a potential customer from outside NI.

(3) Most companies reported that they obtain their export orders by a combination of their own direct sales efforts and through agents or distributors; two-thirds of them operate in association with an agent or distributor.

(4) Only 6 of the 50 companies contacted have a separate export sales executive/department; for the great majority of them, primary responsibility for obtaining export business rests with the managing director.

(5) Roughly half of those contacted believe that exporting is more profitable than sales in the home market. A further third rated the profitability of export sales as about the same as sales in the domestic market. Most of the companies stated that although in general they can obtain higher prices for their exports, the extra revenue is offset by higher transport, packaging and administrative costs.

(6) In spite of the fact that they believe the export market is very competitive, 90 per cent of respondents insist that they do not compete primarily on price; the quality of the product and the service they offer are just as important. Most respondents expressed the view that top quality in both the product and its associated pre- and after-sales service is essential for success in exporting. These attributes are of paramount importance in obtaining export orders in the first place, and subsequently in developing a strong relationship with customers overseas. Higher prices are necessary to cover the additional cost involved, but the constant pressure of competition in terms of price cannot be ignored.

(7) Over 80 per cent of companies interviewed draw up their quotations for export orders in pounds sterling and roughly 10 per cent normally quote in US dollars; only 10 per cent of them as a matter of course do so in the currency specified by the customer.

Only about a third of the companies interviewed require payment by means of irrevocable letter of credit; 40 per cent ask for a bank draft and 25 per cent are paid by means of an open cheque. This has not created any major problems for most of them, although isolated cases of default were recorded. Slow payment, especially by customers located in France and the Republic of Ireland, is a much greater problem than non-payment. To try and counteract this, some companies require customers to pay 30 per cent of their invoice before goods are dispatched.

Half the firms interviewed prepare quotations on a CIF basis, 30 per cent quote their prices ex-works, and the remainder quote FOB. Most respondents emphasised that they make substantial efforts to ensure that the transport arrangements they make are reliable, and best suited to the customer's needs. In general the transport system itself is not a problem, but the possibility of strike action severing links is an ever-present worry.

(8) Roughly half of the companies contacted process their export documentation in-house. A third have it done for them by a transport company, and the rest use a freight-forwarder. None of the respondents reported any major problems in respect of documentation, although several pointed out that occasional minor difficulties arise as a result of simple clerical errors. Most of them, however, pointed out that in the initial stages of their export development, documentation was a major headache, and complained that at that stage there was no help whatever available to them, whether from government agencies, the banks, or any other source they could discover. In effect, they learned from their own mistakes. It was felt that this was bound to be a continuing problem for new exporters, which may require attention.

(9) It is perhaps surprising to note that 27 of the 50 companies interviewed (i.e., 54 per cent) claim that they do not normally obtain insurance cover against the risk of non-payment on export orders. Those companies which obtain credit insurance do so primarily via the ECGD or a commercial insurance company, rather than through the banks. The companies not covered by credit insurance have by and large experienced no major problems as a result. They do not feel they are at risk primarily because:

- Their customers are well known to them.
- They carry out informal checks on the current credit-rating of customers ("through the grapevine").

- The costs of insurance are felt to be too high.

However, many of them acknowledged a growing need for credit insurance as their business expands and they find themselves dealing more and more with customers unknown to them.

(10) Just over half the companies contacted reported that they had to undertake some modification to their product to make it acceptable in the export market. The nature of the modifications required range from a complete redesign to fairly marginal alterations in specifications, labelling and packaging. Product adaptation was usually described as "quite expensive", but it was pointed out that this is both necessary and unavoidable and frequently results in a final price much higher than could otherwise be obtained.

(11) Nearly all the companies contacted had been assisted by a government agency (the IDB) in respect of their exporting activities; the five companies which had not done so to date are currently in negotiation. All but two of the recipients of assistance classified it as "very valuable" to them; only one company felt it was "not at all valuable". The most common types of assistance received was in respect of attendance at a trade fair or exhibition and to conduct market research.

CONCLUSIONS

It is clear that a substantial proportion of LEDU-assisted companies are already engaged in exporting, and that their exporting activities make a useful contribution to the overall level of economic activity in Northern Ireland, particularly in terms of the creation and maintenance of employment. It is also clear that there is considerable potential for further export-led employment generation. Given the broad parameters of the relationship between exporting and employment in the small firms sector identified in this study, it is by no means unrealistic to think in terms of setting a short-term target of creating an additional 1,000 full-time jobs in LEDU-assisted firms over a three-year period, by means of an increased level of exporting activity. Specifically, it has been established that, in broad terms £150 million of exports supports approximately 2,000 jobs; in other words £75,000 worth of export sales generates one job. On that basis, the creation of an additional 1,000 jobs would require an additional £75 million of exports, which represents an increase of 40–50 per cent over present estimated levels.

On the basis of the various enquiries completed during the research project as a whole it may be suggested that LEDU's existing client base could be subdivided into five broad categories in terms of their exporting activities, as follows:

(1) **Non-exporters** — companies which are not currently exporting and have no intention or desire to do so. Many of these firms are in the service sector.

(2) **Potential exporters** — companies which are not currently exporting but have expressed interest in doing so.

(3) **Small-scale exporters** — companies which are currently exporting, but only to a limited extent (defined as less than £50,000 a year and/or less than 15 per cent turnover).

(4) **Established exporters** — companies which, are currently exporting in excess of £50,000 a year and/or more than 15 per cent of turnover.

(5) **Large-scale exporters** — companies currently exporting more than £1 million a year, of which there are at least 20.

It is suggested that three broad strategic options are available to LEDU in respect of developing the exports of its clients:

(1) Attempt to provide all existing and potential exporters with whatever assistance may be required to help them develop their exports. This option would present LEDU with an enormous and complex task even if substantial additional resources were made available. The likely outcome is that effort and resources would be spread too thinly, and would therefore be ineffective.

(2) Concentrate effort and resources on developing potential and small-scale exporters, on the grounds that established and large-scale exporters no longer require assistance. This option also runs the risk of spreading resources too thinly, and of producing results which are rather disappointing in terms of the level of effort required.

(3) Concentrate effort and resources on further developing established and large-scale exporters. This option is likely to be far and away the most cost-effective strategy to generate a significant increase in export related employment in a relatively short period of time. It is acknowledged that options (2) and

(3) imply introducing an element of selectivity into the export assistance provided by LEDU. This is felt to be necessary, and justifiable in terms of the general principle of parity of opportunity for access to LEDU assistance. It is not suggested that LEDU should cease to make available as widely as possible its general package of assistance measures, but rather that additional higher levels of assistance should be more closely targeted on those firms which are most likely to maximise the yield on the assistance provided, in terms of additional jobs created. Again, it is acknowledged that some existing measures do in fact include provision for selective assistance to "high-fliers" along the lines suggested. The point is rather that, as things stand at present, it would appear that the possibilities for providing additional assistance on a selective basis are not being utilised to maximum effect in terms of export development. Whichever strategic option is finally chosen, there will still remain a number of problems and obstacles to be overcome. In the case of potential and small exporters, the major problems identified are associated with the acquisition of knowledge and the availability of advice about marketing and exporting, rather than the provision of increased or additional types of financial assistance. In the case of established and large exporters, the major problems are partly financial (the higher costs of maintaining a presence in export markets) and partly the need for access to more sophisticated levels of advice (for example, checks on the credit-rating of potential customers).

It is often suggested (Fell, 1986) that Northern Ireland companies as a whole are too grant-oriented in their thinking. That assertion is not entirely supported by the findings of this research project. Provided it is acknowledged that any business manager anywhere in the world would, as a matter of principle, prefer to receive more rather than less financial assistance from government agencies, it is remarkable that the major thrust of the views expressed by so many of the LEDU clients contacted is their pressing need for more non-financial assistance.

It is beyond the scope of this paper to provide a detailed review of the very wide range of assistance measures available to small exporters in Northern Ireland. However, an objective overview suggests that they are, taken together, more than adequate to meet the likely needs of even the most active small exporter. The difficulties they encounter would appear to be associated more with: a certain confusion and lack of knowledge of precisely what is available; a lack of expertise in preparing requests for assistance in accordance with the regulations approved for each specific scheme; and an impatience with the perceived bureaucracy and delay associated with actually obtaining assistance.

The soft option would be to conclude that the procedures and regulations should be greatly simplified, but this neglects two key points. Firstly, many of the various schemes have been designed in a way which is designed to force small firms to operate within a coherent long-term plan; that approach has much to commend it. Secondly, there will always be a need to ensure that scarce resources are used for the purposes intended; there is always the possibility of fraud. A more balanced conclusion therefore is that there is a pressing need to facilitate maximum effective use of existing schemes, rather than to oversimplify them, or devise new ones.

REFERENCES

Cannon, T. and Willis, M. (1983): "The Smaller Firms in Overseas Trade", *European Small Business Journal,* 1(3).

Cheong, W.K. and Cheong, K.W. (1988): "Export Behaviour of Small Firms in Singapore", *International Small Business Journal,* 6(2).

Fell, D. (1986): "Northern Ireland: Building a Stronger Economy", *Business Outlook and Economic Review,* 1(3).

Kaynak, E., Ghausi, P.W. and Olopson-Bredenlow, T. (1987): "Export Behaviour of Small Swedish Firms", *Journal of Small Business Management,* 25(2): 26–32.

Kaynak, E. and Kothani, V. (1984): "Export Behaviour of Small and Medium-Sized Manufacturers: Some Policy Guidelines for International Marketers", *Management International Review,* 24(2): 61–70.

Miesenbock, K.J. (1988): "Small Businesses and Exporting: A Literature Review", *International Small Business Journal,* 6(2): 42–61.

Piercy, N. (1984): "Export Marketing Management in Medium-Sized British Firms", *European Journal of Marketing,* 18(1).

Seringhaus, R. (1986): "The Role of Information Assistance in Small Firms Export Involvement", *International Small Business Journal,* 5(2).

Verhoeven, W. (1988): "The Export Performance of Small and Medium-Sized Enterprises in the Netherlands", *International Small Business Journal*, 6(2).

Verhoeven, W. (1988): "The Export Performance of Small and Medium-Sized Enterprises in the Netherlands", *International Small Business Journal*, 6, 2.

Index

**Tables shown as (T0.0);
Figures as (F0.0)**

Aaker, D.A., 101, 205
Abannat, R.F., 135
Abell, D.F., 402
Abernathy, W.J., 189
Abratt, R., 242, 244, 246, 247, 322
action learning
   implementing, 94–6
advantage
   competitive, 123–33
   layers of, (F9.10)
advertising
   Advertising Association of Ireland, 224, 231
   agency, the traditional, 233
   costs in UK, (F15.1)
   element of marketing communications, 221–38
   production costs, 234
   Research Foundation, 380
   television, 179–81, (T12.3)
AGB Attwood, 371, 375
   Intomart, 259
   TAM, 376
age distribution
   Ireland, 37, (T3.4)
   Europe, 37, (T3.4)
   projected trends, 43
age structure, 37–9
ageing trends, 39
agricultural revolution, 100
agriculture, Irish
   economic dependence on, 3
   employment, 3, (T1.1)
   percentage of merchandise exports, 3, (T1.2)
   exports, 24
agri-food sector, Irish
   indigenous firms, 21, 24
   EC market penetration, 24
   impact on balance of payments, 24
   low import propensity, 24
AIB
   Bank, 252
   Group, 252, 253, 254
   Group Treasury, 252
   Investment Managers, 252
AIMRO, 369
Alexander Group, 308
Allied Irish Banks plc, 249–54
Anderson, C.R., 135, 136
Anderson, J.C, 332, 350
Andrews, K.R., 135
Andrews, P.W.D., 278
Ansoff, H.I., 135, 339
Anspach, R.R., 243, 246, 247, 253
Antenna Report on Broadcasting, 227
anti-trust legislation, 72
Armstrong, S., 236
Arnold, D., 174
Article Numbering Association of Ireland (ANAI), 379
Asia
   branding for, 175
   Southeast, 9
Aspect, 300
Assael, H., 150
Atkin, B., 280, 291
Atkinson, A.A., 277, 278, 279
Atkinson, P.E., 186
attitude orientation, cycles in, 73–6, (F6.1/2)
attitudes to customers, 73–6, (F6.1/2)
audience
   control of media, 235, 236
   fragmentation, 237

(audience *continued*)
  sophistication, 236
  target, 266-7
Audit Bureau of Circulation, 226
automobile industry, 189
Avonmore, 111-14, 170, 171,
  (F12.1), 182
Ayal, I., 410, 412, 413, 421, 424

baby products
  decline in future Irish demand
    for, 44
Bailey's Irish Cream, 70, 178, 183,
  216
Bain, J.S., 203
balance of payments, Irish, (T2.1)
  causes of improvement in, 16,
    17
  deficit in , 14
  growth of industrial exports
    effect on, 26
  impact of agri-food exports on,
    24
  importance of overseas firms
    in, 26
  importance of competitiveness
    in, 26
  factors involved in, 26, 27
  surplus in, 28
balance of trade, Irish, 24
Ballygowan Spring Water, 178,
  179, 182, 183
B & A, 372
Bank of Ireland, 244
banking (see also financial
  services), 105
banks
  Irish retail, 179
Banting, P.M., 322
bar codes, 379
Barclays Bank, 267
bargaining
  power, 176
Barnes, J.G., 78
barriers to entry and mobility, 203
Bartos, R., 380
Barwise, P., 176
Bateson, J.E.G., 247
Bauer, R.A., 236

Baxter, W.T., 278, 279
BBDO, 232
Belfast 12, 67, 154, 159
  /Dublin economic corridor, 12
Belfast Telegraph, 342, 343, 344,
  346
Belgium
  price rises, 23
Bell Laboratories, 188
Bennett, T., 393, 400
Benson, R., 236
Berger, M. , 400, 403
Bergiel, B.J., 321
Berney, K., 400
Berry, L.L., 247
Bertrand, K., 393, 400, 403
Bhide, A., 396
Biggadike, E.R., 204, 212
Bilkey, W.J., 410
birth rate, Irish
  decline since 1980, 8, 34
  highest in Europe, 34
  influence of Catholic Church
    on, 35
  influence on household size, 41
  influences on, 35
  Northern Ireland, 35
birth rate, European, 37
Blackmon, K.L., 193
Bodinson, G.W., 193
Boggis, F., 76, 82
Bond, R.S., 203
Bonoma, T., 62
Bord na Móna, 182
Boston Consulting Group, 203
Bower, J.L., 135
Bradley, F., 410, 413, 414, 415
Bradley, J., 28
Bradley, M.F., 411, 413
Bragg, A., 304
brand
  building, international, 174-8
  concept, 169-71
  corporate benefits of, 171-4
  development in Ireland
    impediments to, 178-81
  equity, 171
  extensions, 173
  functionality, 169

Index 457

(brand *continued*)
  knowledge, 171, 172 (F12.2)
  names, 167–84
  personality, 169
  representationality, 169
  strategy, 167–84
branding
  in the Irish market, 177–81
brands
  Irish, options for developing
    internationally, 181–3
  world, (T12.1), 167–9
Brenner, V.C., 276, 277, 278
Briggs, M., 233
British Airways, 132, 398
British Rate and Data (BRAD), 226
British Telecom, 356, 360, 361
Broadcasting Act 1990, 230
Broom, H.N., 147, 148
Brown, J.R., 322
Brown, W.R., 321
BS 5750 Quality System Standard, 191
BSI, 361
Buck, S., 237
Buckley, A.P., 411
Buckley, D., 228
budget deficit, Irish, 27
Building Societies Act, 346
business objectives
  and Information Technology
    and customer service, 108, 109, (T8.3)
  in small enterprises, 147
business plans
  and information technology
    and customer service, 106–7, (T8.2)
Business and Finance, 280, 291, 300
Business Telegraph, 342, 343, 344, 345, 346
businesses
  high growth small, 134–43
  small, 146–61, 435–52
  small- to medium-sized (SMEs), 103–9, 409–32
Butler Cox, 101

Buyer Perceptions of Irish and Overseas Sales People, 312
buyers
  purchase criteria of, (T20.1), (F20.1)
Buzzell, R.D., 135, 136, 190, 209, 393, 402
Byles, D., 234
Byrne, M., 265

cable broadcasting, 228
Calingaert, M., 393
Campbell, M., 179
Cameron, S., 327, 328
Cannon T., 443
Canon, 216, 266
Cantillon, S., 57
Cantrell & Cochrane's, 182
Carat International, 232
car sales, new,
  Ireland, 48, 50, (T4.4)
  Europe, 50
Carson, D., 87, 148, 247
Cashback, 68
Catholic Church
  influence on Irish birth rate, 35
Cavanagh, R.E., 135
Cavusgil, T., 410, 411
Cawley Nea Ltd., 234
Cement Roadstone Holdings (CRH), 65
Census
  of Industrial Production, Irish, 22
  of Population, Irish, 43
  Reports, Irish, 43
Central Bank of Ireland, 14, 47, 48
  Annual Report, 14
Central Statistics Office (CSO), Irish, 20, 21, 43, 142, 375
Challenge (of Customer Focus), the, 79
channel management, 349–63
Chandler, A.D., 135, 336
Chanelle Veterinary, 66, 69
Channon, D., 136
Checkout magazine, 26

chemicals
  Irish exports of, 21
chemical industry, Irish
  organic, 27
  other, 27
Child, J., 135
children's products
  decline in future demand for, 44
Christensen, C., 135, 423
Christopher, M., 102
Churchill, G.A., Jr., 295, 296, 301, 305, 306, 308, 322
Clarkin, E., 170
Clifford, D.K., 135
clothing
  Irish exports, 22, 27
  Irish imports, 26
  industry, use of information technology, 105
Clutterbuck, D., 247
CocaCola, 20, 177, 215, 267
Cohn, T., 136, 148
College of Marketing and Design, 62
Combs, L.J., 87
Committee for Economic Development, 146
Common Agricultural Policy (CAP), 28, 395
communications services sector, Irish
  need to expand, 28
competition
  absence of, 72
  analysis of in the new Europe, 393–406
  a barrier, 118
  forces driving, 396, 397, (T25.1)
  in the European Union, 397
  pricing and, 277
  speed as a factor in, 125
competitive
  advantage, 123–33, 174
  devices, 136
  game plays, 124–33, (F9.4)
  supremacy, 127
competitiveness
  diagnosis of changes in, 404, (T25.3)
  Irish
    and import propensity, 25
    as a factor in balance of payments, 26
    effect on balance of payments, 17
    enterprise as a response, 7
    efficiency on supply side as a response, 7
    improvement in, 27
    loss of, 23
    need to maintain, 28
    price comparisons, 23
competitor
  strengths and weaknesses, 128
computer-assisted television interviewing (CATI), 374
computer firms, 262
computer software
  Irish exports, 20
consumer
  confidence, 47
  decision-making, 171
  durables
    increase in demand, 44
  expectations
    Ireland/Europe, 47, (T4.2)
  global, 235
  goods, light, 22
  optimism, 48
  perceptions, 171
  price index, 53, (T4.3)
  reactions to pricing, 53–6
  saving and credit
    trends, Irish, 47–50, (T4.3)
    future trends and expectations, 56–7
  spending
    composition of, Ireland/EU 51–3, (T4.5)
    trends, Irish, 47–50 , (T4.3)
    future trends and expectations, 56–7
consumption, Irish
  import share, 25, (T2.7)
consultancy services, Irish
  need to expand, 28

Consultative Committee on
  Marketing, 411
Cooper, D.J., 275, 278
Cooper. P., 236
Cooper, R., 278, 280
Co-operation North, 62
Córas Tráchtála Teoranta (CTT),
  24
Cornhill Insurance, 266, 269
corporate
  core values, 77
  culture, 71
  flexibility, 136, 137
  goodwill, 167
  image
    management process, 242–4,
      (F16.1)
    identity, 241–54
      rationale, 244–6
      development process, 246–7
      in financial services sector,
        247–53
  mission statements, 77, 102
  philosophy, 91, 102
  relatedness, 136, 137
  vision, lack of, 118
corporate-environment
  relationship, external, 71
cost
  control, 23, 24
  lower delivered, 125
  production, 125
costing. see pricing
Coughlan, C., 69
Courtaulds Group, 344
cream liqueur
  Irish exports, 20
Creative Management Ltd., 299
credit advances, personal, 48,
  (T4.3)
Croft, M., 241
Crosby, P., 87, 189
Culliton Report, 6, 11, 12
culture, corporate, 71
Cudennec-Poon, C., 102
Cunningham, M., 328, 423
currency, hard, policy, 7
current account, Irish, 14
Curtis, J., 57

customer
  attitudes to, 73–9, (F6.1/2)
  base, protecting the, 102
  care groups and panels, 76
  expectations, 87
  focus, 73, 77–9
  information system (CIS),
    111–18
  integrating all company
    activities around, 67
  labelling the, 76, 77, (F6.3)
  loyalty, 172
  orientation, 72–9
  perceived value, 124–33
  perceptions, analysing, 91
  programmes, 76
  relations and quality, 85–87,
    (F7.2)
  resistance, 118
  responses to, selected, (F6.2)
  satisfaction, 77, 102
customer needs
  in competitive advantage, 128
  understanding, 64
customer service, 65, 101, 105–18,
  355
  and Information Technology,
    105–18, (T8.1/2)
  plans, 106–7, (T8.2)
  relative importance of
    activities, 65
Czepiel, J.A., 247

Daems, H., 336
Dairy Council for Northern
  Ireland, 343
Dale, B.G., 193
Daly, M.E., 6, 12
data processing equipment
  expected growth in demand, 28
  Irish exports, 20
  industry in Ireland, 27
  sector prices, 28
Day, G.S., 101, 135, 136, 138, 203,
  205, 322
DDB, 232
dealer base, 360–62
dealers. see distributors
Dean, J., 276

debt, Irish national, 6
de Chernatony, L., 169, 176
Deere, John, 216
deficiencies, facing, 68
Delachaux, F.B., 406
Delivery, Innovative, System, the, 133
demand
   private and public sector, 16
   aggregate vis-à-vis budget deficit, 16
   Irish domestic, 16, 27
   foreign, 17
demographic trends and expectations, future, 43
Dempsey, W.A., 322, 324, 327, 328
Department of Economic Development (N.I.), 435
Department of Industry and Commerce, 411
dependency levels
   Ireland, 5
   Denmark, 5
deregulation, 72, 73
de Rocha, A., 428
Dervis, K., 9
design industry, 241
Desmond's, 345
detergent market, 175
Development Committee, Sectoral, the, 28
differentiated strategies, 135–8
Dinmore, F., 264, 269
direct selling
   v. using distributors, 321–33
Directory of Engineering Companies, 323
distribution
   channels, 321–33
   system, 102
   structure in the United Kingdom, 356
distributor
   –manufacturer relationship, 349–65
   level of support needed by, 351–62
   support services for the, 354
dividends, 16

divorce, 40
DKM Ltd., 231
Dobrydnio, R., 428, 429
Dodge, H.F., 188
Doherty-Wilson, L., 235
domestic appliances, ownership of, (T4.6)
Donaldson, B., 65, 102
Douglas, R.A., 322
Douglas, S.P., 411
Doyle, P., 63, 173, 415, 423
Drucker, P., 321, 336, 341
Drury, C., 277
Dublin
   /Belfast economic corridor, 12
   population trends, 39
   Area Rapid Transit System (DART), 25
Dun & Bradstreet, 300
Dwyer, R.F., 332

Earl, M.J., 100
economic corridor, Dublin/Belfast, 12
economies
   of scale, 173, 176
   of scope, 176
Economic and Social Research Institute, 12, 57
economies of Ireland, the two, 12
Economist, The, 177, 395, 401
economy, Irish
   development of, meagre record, 4
   future trends and expectations, 56–7
   long-term achievements, 3
   need to regenerate, 7
economy, world 9
education, Irish
   improvement since 1920s, 3
   reduction in future demand for, 44
efficiency on supply side
   response to competitive pressure, 7
El-Ansary, A.I., 321
elderly people
   factor in household size, 41

(elderly people *continued*)
    increase in market needs, 44
elasticity
    income, 53
    in ten product groups, 56, (T4.8)
Electronic Data Interchange (EDI), 109–13
electronic sector
    expected growth in demand, 28
    prices, 28
Electronics, Consumer, Ownership of, (T4.7)
emigration, Irish
    absorbing surplus labour, 4
    acceptance of and consequences, 7
    cause of population decline, 33
    curtailment of opportunities for, 4
    effect of unemployment on, 35
    N.E.S.C. Report on, 8
    Northern Ireland, from, 36
    patterns of, 34, (T3.1)
    projected trends, 43
    safety valve, 10
employment levels
    by sector, 3, (T1.1)
    less than in 1920s, 4
    lowest in Europe, 5
energy
    consumption as factor in balance of payments, 27
    shift in sources, 24
engineering
    electrical, growth in demand, 28
    exports from Ireland, 21
    industry, 27
entrepreneurs
    Irish supply of, 7
enterprise
    Irish level of, 10
    need for, 11
    response to competitive pressure, 7
enterprises. *see* businesses

Era of Deregulation, the, 72, 73
Eurobrands, 175, 176
Euromarket, 175
Euromonitor, 50, 176
Europe
    birth rate in, 35
Europe, Eastern, 10, 72, 395
European Economic Community (EEC), 420
Europe, Western
    employment, 50
    media buying, 232
    new car sales, 50
Europe, Western Continental
    income per capita, 4
    living standards, 4
    Irish merchandise exports to, (T1.2)
    difficult market to penetrate, 23
European Community (EC)
    age distribution, 37, (T3.4)
    average spending per capita (PPS), 45, 46, (T4.1)
    export performance, 18
    income per capita, (T1.3)
    life expectancy, 38, (T3.5)
    ownership of domestic appliances, 53, (T4.6)
    ownership of consumer electronics, 53, (T4.7)
    productivity, 5, (T1.3)
European
    Coal and Steel Community, 394
    Currency Unit (ECU), 394
    Directory of Consumer Brands, 176
    Economic Association (EEA), 394
    Free Trade Association (EFTA), 394
    Market, Single, 175, 193, 393, 394
    Monetary System (EMS), 23, 25, 27
    Monetary Union, 394
    Social Charter, 403

(European *continued*)
    Society for Opinion & Market Research (ESOMAR), 369, 370
European Union (EU)
    ageing trends, 39, 43, (T3.4)
    and quality standards, 193
    buyer bargaining power in, 402
    changing business environment, 393
    competition in, 393–406
    competitive changes in, 397
    consumer expectations 47, (T4.2)
    consumer expenditure, 51–3, (T4.5/6/7)
    dismantling trade barriers, 175
    geographic distribution of population, 39
    home ownership, 53
    household size, 41, (T3.8)
    income per capita, 10
    intervention system, 61
    life expectancy, 39, (T3.5)
    living standards, 57
    population, 36, 43, (T3.3)
    unemployment, 5
    youth population, 38, 39
excellence in marketing, 62
exchange rate, 7, 23
Exchange Rate Mechanism (ERM), 8, 23
expenditure
    consumer, Ireland/EU, 51–3, (T4.5)
expenditure survey, IDA's, 21
expenses, future-orientated, 136, 137
experience curve, 203
export markets, Irish
    dependence on United Kingdom, 22
    diversification, 23
    expansion of, 17
    failure to retain of United Kingdom, 23
    Irish share of United Kingdom, 22, (T2.6)

exports, Irish
    buoyancy of, 23
    cost competitiveness of, 23
    expansion, 27
    geographical pattern of, 19
    growth of, 17, 21
    growth and overseas firms, 17–21
    high-tech products, 19, (T2.3)
    increase in, since 1950s, 3
    indigenous firms, by, 21, (T1.5)
    industrial, 26
    manufacturing, 3, 19, 22, 23
    performance, 18
    prices, index of, 28
    ratios, indigenous and overseas firms, 27, (T2.5)
    types of firm, 19, 20
exports, merchandise, Irish
    agricultural percentage of, 3, (T1.2)
    commodity composition of, 19
    commodity/destination statistics, 3, (T1.2)
    fall in value of, 28

Fahy, J., 401
family size, 35. *see also* household size
Famine, the Great Irish, 33
farm size, 43
farmers, 43
Farren, J.M., 401, 405
Fast-moving Consumer Goods (FMCG), 372, 378
feedback, 76
Feigenbaum, A.V., 186
Fenwick, P., 234
Ferguson, A., 344, 345
Ferrell, O.C., 152
fertility rates. *see* birth rates
film and video industry, Irish
    need to expand, 28
financial services sector
    corporate identity in, 247–54
    need to expand, 28
    special characteristics, 248
    use of information technology, 105

First Maryland Bankcorp, 252
fiscal
  expansion, 6
  policy, 27
firms. *see* businesses
firms, Irish
  computer, 262
  foreign-owned, export sales, 17, (T2.4&5)
  high-tech, 262
  indigenous, export sales, 17, (T2.4&5)
  Japanese electronic, 262
Fitzgerald, J., 25, 28, 57
flexibility, corporate, 136
Fletcher, K., 101
focus strategy, 137–41
food
  expenditure, 51, 52
  processing industry, 27
  product, 61
food and drink industries, 3, 26,105
  imports, 26
  percentage of manufacturing labour force, 3
food sector prices, 28
footwear and travel goods industries, 27, 68
Forbairt, 411
Ford, D.I., 332
Ford, N.M., 295, 296, 301, 305, 306, 308
foreign exchange earnings, 21
foreign investment, 5, 61
foreign takeovers, 21
Fornell, C., 203
Foxpro, 378
Freeling, A., 174
French market, 68
freight services, trade in, 15
Friberg, E.G., 378
Friesen, P.H., 143
fully extended product and quality, 88–94, (F7.1)
furniture industry, 27, 105
future trends and expectations
  demographic, 43
  consumer spending, savings and credit, 56–7
  future-orientated expenses, 136–7

Gabor, A., 278
Gaedeke, R.H., 148
Galbraith, J.K., 336, 339, 341
Gale, B.T., 135, 136, 190
Gameil, M.Y., 275, 278
Garvin, D.A., 187, 190
Gassenheimer, J.B., 349
GATT, 393
Gattona, J., 349
General Electric, 216
geographical distribution of population, 39–40, (T3.6)
George, F.H., 83
Gertner, R.K., 428
Gidengil, Z.B., 415, 423
Gilbert, X., 416, 417, 421, 427
Gilmore, A., 87
Global consumer, 235
Gottlier, M., 271
Government. *see also* policy
  borrowing policy, 5, 27
  budget deficit, 16
  limits of power, 7
  policy on international trade, 16
  rôle vis-à-vis economic enterprise, 11
  spending, 11
GPT, 356
Gray, E.R., 243, 244, 245, 250, 252
Greenley, G.E., 151
Greiner, L., 336
Gronroos, C., 71, 85, 86, 87
Gross Domestic Product (GDP)
  European Community, 5, (T1.3)
  Ireland, 5,(T1.3)
Gross National Product (GNP)
  current account surplus related to, 28
  growth in Europe, 9
  growth rate needed, 9
  growth to mid-1990s, 9
  per worker, Ireland and EC, 6, (T1.3)

(Gross National Product (GNP) *continued*)
  and balance of payments, 14, (T2.1)
  and public sector borrowing requirement, 27
growth
  matrix, 135
growth rates
  comparative, 9
  needed, 10
Guiltinan, J.P., 150

Hagan, J.T., 189
Hague, D.C., 278
Hakkio, C.S., 393, 400
Hambrick, D.C., 135, 136, 138
Handy, C., 337, 342, 346
Hankinson, A., 278
Harbisher, A., 244, 248
Hardy, K.G., 350, 353
Harper, T., 235
Harris, C.E., Jr, 302
Harris, J.E., 135
Hart, S., 323
Haufbauer, G.C., 393
Hawthorne (Western Electric), 188
Hayden, F., 223
Haynes, W.W., 278
health
  improvement since 1920s, 3
  expenditure, 51, 52
Henderson's, 346
Henley Research Centre, 57, 236
Henry, H., 234
Herbst, P.G., 341
Hexter, D.R., 393
Higgins, J.M., 393, 405
Higher in Perceived Value (HPV), 125–33
high-tech exports, Irish, 19
high-tech firms, 262
Hiromoto, T., 280
Hirsch, S., 412, 413, 421
Hlavacek, J.D., 332
home ownership, 52, 53
homogenisation of wants, 174

Hooley, G.J., 248
Horner, C., 101
Horovitz, J., 102
Hounshell, D.A., 188
households, Irish
  future increase in formation of, 44
  numbers of, 40, (T3.7)
  single person, 42
  size and composition, 40–42, (T3.7)
housing in Ireland
  improvement in since 1920s, 3
housing mortgages, 48
Howcroft, J.J., 243, 245, 248
human resource, investing in the, 69
human resources in Ireland
  need to upgrade quality of, 11
Humble, J., 102
Hunt, S.D., 32
Hunter, M., 405

identity. *see* corporate identity
image. *see* corporate image
immigration to Ireland, 34
imports, Irish
  compared with exports, 24
  competing with domestic suppliers, 25, 26
  growth, 16, 24
  growth and the trade balance, 24–6
  penetration, 25, 26, (T2.7)
  share of domestic consumption, 26, (T2.7)
income
  effect on family size, 35
  effect on marriage rate, 34
  per capita, Ireland and EC, 4, 5, (T1.3)
  restraint, 15
  trade-off against jobs, 8, 11
independent television
  programme makers, 345
Independent Radio and Television Commission (IRTC), 223, 227
Index Optical Company, 115–7

Index

indigenous firms
   in Ireland and France, use of information technology, 105
   Irish, 6, 20, 21, (T2.4)
indigenous sector and competitiveness, 21–4
Industrial Development Authority (IDA), 21, 26, 411, 418, 419
   Irish Economy Expenditure Surveys, 21, 419
Industrial Development Board (N.I.) (IDB), 449
industrial development policy (N.I.), 435
industry, Irish
   composition of new firms, 28
   lack of development, 6
information revolution, 100
information technologies
   top three, 109–10, (T8.4)
   planned, 111, (T8.5)
Information Technology (IT)
   and business plans, 106–7
   and customer service, 100–118
   and marketing, 101, 105–6, (T8.1)
   and sales, (T8.1)
   managers' perceptions, 100
   plans, 106–7, (T8.2.)
initiative, 232
innovation
   as a strategy, 135
innovative delivery system, 133
Institute of Advertising Practitioners in Ireland (IAPI), 233, 235
intervention system, 61
International Fund for Ireland, 12
International Management, 402
intra-industry trade ratios, 27
inflation, 7
infrastructure, physical, Irish
   need to upgrade quality of, 11
insurance industry, 105
Institute of Practitioners in Advertising (UK), 43
integrating all company activities around the customer, 67
interest rates, 7

International Organisation for Standardisation (ISO), 191
international transfers, 16
investing in people, 69
investment
   income, 15
   inward foreign, 5, 61
Ireland
   age distribution of population, 37, (T3.4)
   ageing trend, 39
   alcohol expenditure, 51, 52
   average spending per capita (PPS), 45, 46, (T4.1)
   balance of payments, 14
   consumer expectations, 47, (T4.2)
   consumer expenditure, 45–57, (T4.5/6/7)
   current account, 14
   demographic statistics, 34, (T3.1)
   economic performance, 3–12
   employment, 3, (T1.1)
   exports, 15, 18, (T2.2)
   family size, 40, (T3.8)
   financial services consumer expenditure, 53
   food expenditure, 51, 52
   future effects on demand, 44
   future population trends, 43
   geographic distribution of population, 39, (T3.6)
   health expenditure, 51, 52
   home ownership, 53
   household size statistics, 38, 40, (T3.7)
   housing expenditure, 51, 52
   life expectancy, 38, (T3.5)
   liquor prices, 402
   market penetration, 53
   merchandise trade, 5, 14, 15, 16, (T1.2&2.1)
   motor industry, 50
   new car sales, 48, 50, (T4.4)
   population size, 33–7
   pricing practices in, 275–92
   productivity per capita, (T1.3)
   trade patterns, 19

(Ireland *continued*)
    vital population statistics, 36, (T3.3)
    social class categorisation, 43, (T3.9)
    use of information technology in customer service, 100, 18
    weakness of marketing in, 61
Irish
    Bankers' Federation, 12
    Dairy Board, 178, 182
    Distillers Group, 21, 182
    Economy Expenditure Surveys 21, 419
    International Advertising Agency, 170
    market
        branding in the, 177–8
        top brands, 183
    Independent, 226
    Marketing Journal, 177
    Marketing Review, 61
    Marketing Surveys (IMS), 372, 378
    Press, 226
    Target Group Index (TGI), 378
    Tam Establishment Surveys, 235
    Times, The, 226, 235
    Trade Board, 24
Irvine, D., 442
Ishikawa, K., 186, 190
ISL Marketing, 228, 267
ISO 9000
    and quality standards, 186–201
    benefits from implementation, 196, 197
    costs and savings associated with, 191–3
    financial model for cost savings, (T13.1)
    issues of motivation, 195, 196
    marketing considerations, 197, 198
    vendor relationships, 198, 199, 200

Jackson, D.W., 310

Jacquemin, A., 337, 340
Japan
    top brands in, 177
    Industrial Standards Mark (JIS), 190
    lean manufacturing in, 126
    Ministry of International Trade and Industry, 190
Japanese
    cars, EU quota on, 404
    companies, 68, 125
    cost advantage, 125
    target costing in pricing, 280
    electronic firms, 262
    reliability, 189
Jiuan, T.S., 428
jobs
    creation of, 4, 11
    scarcity of, 4
    trade off with income restraint, 8, 11
Johanson, J., 410
Johnston, R., 339, 340, 341, 346
Joint National Listenership Research (JNLR), 53, 377
Joint National Readership Research (JNRR), 53, 375, 377, 378
joint ventures, 130
Juran, J.M., 82, 87, 188, 190
Justis, R.T., 152

Kaizen, 190
Kanter, R., 72
Kaplan, R.S., 277, 278, 279, 280
Karakaya, F., 401
Kassicieh, S.K., 322
Katz, R.L., 136
Keen, P., 103
Keller, K.L., 171, 172
Kendrick, J.J., 193
Keng, K.A., 428
Kennedy, S.H., 242, 244, 245
Kerrygold, 178, 182, 183, 216
key-systems equipment industry, 355
Khandwalla, P., 338
Kieser, A., 135
Kimberly, J.R., 336

Index

King, R.H., 236, 310
Kinsale Head Gas Field, 24
Kiser, G.E., 322
knowledge
  of market, 128, (F9.7), 159
  of competition, 128, (F9.7)
  of the company, 128, (F9.7)
Kohl, F., 265
Kotler, P., 101, 150, 152, 169, 245
Korbel, J.J., 393
Krugman, A.M., 393
Kuhn, A.H., 83, 87, 135, 136
Kuriloff, A., 147, 148, 152
Kyj, M.J. and L.S., 102

labelling the customer, 76, 77, (F6.3)
labour force, Irish
  agricultural content, 3, (T1.1)
  increase in, 8
  surplus, 4, 10
language training services
  need to expand, 28
languages, foreign
  poor command of, 23
Lannon, J., 236
Lansdowne Market Research, 170, 372
Lawrence, P.R., 339, 340, 341, 346
Lavis, J., 243, 245, 248
Lawtor. L., 243
layers of accessibility, (F24.1)
Lazarsfeld P.F., 381
lean manufacturing, 126, 127
Lees, C., 228
Lehmann, D., 322, 323, 327
Leppard, J., 147, 153
Lere, J.C., 278
Lev, B., 412, 413, 421
Levitt, T., 174, 207, 246
Liebster, L., 101
life expectancy, 39
life cycle of a small firm, 152–4
Linane, C., 178, 179, 181
Lindberg, R., 136
Lintas, 232
Linville, D., 401, 403
Lismona Wear plc, 110–11
Liswood, L.A., 247

living standards, Irish, 3, 4, 8, 53
  compared with UK and Europe, 4
  need to raise, 8
  rise in since 1920s, 3
Local Area Networks (LAN), 109–10
Local Enterprise Development Units (N.I.) (LEDU), 435–52
logistics system, 102
long-term economic challenges 8–9
long-term economic record, 3–12
long-term view, taking the, 67, 68
Lynn, M., 394, 395

Maastrict Treaty, 393, 395
MacDonald, M., 321
MacMillan, I.C., 135, 136, 138
macroeconomic framework, need for a sound, 11
Madsen, T.K., 425, 427, 428
Magazine News, 226
Magaziner, I.C., 189
Magrath, A.J., 350, 353
Mallot, R.H., 189
management
  marketing, *passim*
  silo, 127
  style in small enterprises, 147–61
Mann, S.J., 248
manufacturer-middlemen
  relationships, 349–65
manufacturing
  lean, 126, 127
  world class, 127
manufacturing, Irish
  as percentage of labour force, 3, (T1.1)
  linkage with Northern Ireland, 12
  need to expand exports, 28
  sector in international trade, 17
  volume of output, 3
market
  attractiveness, 33
  composition, 33

(market *continued*)
  entry, 203–17
    and profitability, 206–17
    barriers to, 203
    early followers, 204, 212, 213
    later entrants, 204, 214, 215
    pioneers, 204, 211, 212
  segments, 138
  share, 142, 173, 205, 206, 276
  size, 33
  variables, 33
  Irish
    composition, 33
    size, 33
    potential, 46
market research, 43, 76, 369–90
  continuous, 371
  industry, the, 369, 370
  methods, 370
  non-continuous, 372
  panels, 371, 372
  social class groupings, 43
  Society (UK), 369
  Bureau of Ireland (MRBI), 299, 300, 301, 371, 372, 377
Market Research Europe, 53
Marketing, 234
marketing
  Action Programme (AIB Group), 250
  analysts, 33
  characteristics of small firms, 148–9
  communications, 221–38
    costs in UK, (F15.1)
  concept, 71, 85,102
  considerations re IS 9000, 197, 198
  Development Programme (MDP), 224, 226
  effectiveness, 62, 321
  efficiency, 62
  education, 71
  evolution of a small firm, 152–4
  excellence in, 62, 69, 70
  function, 61, 67
  fundamentals, ten, 63
  implicit, 156–60
  information systems (MIS), 69
  internal, 72, 78
  international, 409–34
  Irish, state of, 61, 62
  mix, the, 82, 83,102, 155, 262
  myopia, 71
  -oriented companies, 63
  orientation, 102
  planning, 107,(T8.2)
  planning for small firms, 146–61
  performance, 91, 321
  position, 135
  practice, quality, 62
  practice in small enterprises, 147–61
  principles, 322
  skills, 62, 179
  Society of Ireland, 229, 369, 370
  strategic, 67–8
  strategies for SMEs internationally, 409–34
  target, 66, 67
  total quality, 71
Marketing News, 306
Marketing Week, 236
markets
  barriers to internationalisation of, 411, 412
  target, 66, 67
marriage
  age as factor in population decline, 33
  rate decline, causes, 34
  rate as factor in population decline, 33
  legal separation, 40
Marvin, M.P., 350
Mason, J., 398
Maydown Precision Engineering, 346
McAdams, J., 308
McCarthy, A., 24
McCoy, D., 28
McGoldrick, P.J., 322
McIvor, C., 248

McKenna, R., 61, 67
McKinsey, 237
McNulty, P., 183
McQuiston, T.J., 332
meat products, 27
media
    buying, 231
    changes in the, 223–31
    costs, 230
    expenditure, 224–6
    expenditure in UK, (F15.1)
    fragmentation, 226, 227
    in Ireland, 223–31
    International, 233
    Partnership, 232
    penetration, 227, (T15.5)
    research, 376
    specialists, 231–3
    super-highway, 226
Medico-Social Research Board, 43
merchandise trade, Irish, 5, 14, 15, 16, 28
metals
    exports, 21
    industry, 27
Michie, P.A., 332
middlemen. *see* distributors
Miesenbock, K.J., 442
migration statistics, Irish, 34, (T3.1)
Miles, R.H., 336
Milk Marketing Board, 342, 343
milk products, 27
Miller, D., 143, 396
Mills, R.W., 278, 280, 283, 289
Millward Brown, 236, 371
MINITAB, 282
Mintel, 228
Mintzberg, H., 143, 338, 339
mission statements, corporate, 77
Mitchell, D., 393, 400, 403, 405
Mittal, B., 229
Mjoset, L., 7
Montgomery, D.G., 203
Moran, J., 179
Moranco Strategic Marketing, 179
Morello, G., 248
Morgan, G., 341

Morgan, N., 81, 82
mortgages, housing, 48
Morton's, Brian, 346
Mosbacher, R.A., 401
Moss, S., 326
motivation research, 381
Moy Park Ltd., 343, 344, 345
multinational investment in trade, 21
Munster and Leinster Bank, 249
museum, the, 387
music industry, Irish
    need to expand, 28

NACE sector, 419
Narus, J.A., 332, 350
narrowcasting, 237
National Economic and Social Council, 8, 13, 17, 27, 411
National Register of Certified Products and Companies, 193, 194
National Standards Authority of Ireland (NSAI), 191, 193, 194
Naylor, G., 248
needs, customer, 64, 87
    understanding, 64
network services
    need to expand, 28
Nevin, J.R., 411
new cars, sales of, 48, (T4.4)
new firms
    industrial composition, 28
New York Marathon, 267
Nielsen, A.C., 369, 371, 373, 375, 378
non-marketing, 156–60
Non-media Advertising (NMA) 224, 225, 226, 237
North America
    ageing trend, 39
    television viewing habits, 229
Northern Dairies, 342
Northern Foods, 182
Northern Ireland
    Dairy Council for, 343
    Department of Economic Development, 435

(Northern Ireland *continued*)
    deintegration in, 342–5
    export activities of small firms, 435–52
    Industrial Development Board, 449
    industrial development policy, 435
    Local Economic Development Units (LEDU), 435–52
    need for cross-border economic co-operation, 12
    population statistics, 35, (T3.2)
    prices, 26
    profile of small exporters, 437–49
    value-added partnerships in, 342–6
Northern Ireland Bankers' Association, 12
Northern Ireland Economic Research Centre, 12

Oakland, J.S., 186
occupations
    Irish census data, 43, (T3.9)
O'Donoghue, R., 182
office equipment industry, 27, 28
Ogilvy & Mather, 175, 232
O'Grady, N., 409
oil
    prices, 25, 27
    shift to coal from, 24
Olins W., 241, 243, 246, 249, 250
Olsen, S.C., 418
Olympic Games, 267
O'Malley, E., 23
options for economic progress, 9–10
ORAC Committee, 378
Ó Réagáin, S., 409
Organisation for Economic Co-operation and Development (OECD), 17
Organisation of Irish Market Research Companies, 369
Organisation and Systems Innovations Ltd. (OASIS), 101
O'Shaughnessy, J., 322, 323, 327

Otker, T., 265
O'Toole, G., 193
outdoor media, 377, 378
overseas companies in Ireland 17, 20, 22, 26 (T2.4/5)
Oxenfeldt, A.R., 276, 278, 279

Pacific Rim, 9
paper and printing
    Irish imports, 26
    industry, use of information technology, 105
parents, adults living with
    effect on household size, 41
Pareto Principle, 63
participation, 93
passive palsies, 236
Patton, W.E., III, 310
Paul, G.W., 150
Payne, A.F., 102
Peck, C.A., 308
people, investing in, 69
people management, 88
perceived value, 125–33
performance standards, 87
peripherality, 12
Pernod Ricard, 182
Perry, J., 227
personal savings ratio, 28
Perspectives, 229
Peters, T.J., 102, 312, 336, 337, 338
Petrie, P.A., 9
pharmaceutical industry, Irish, 27
Phillips, L.W., 82
Piercy, N., 81, 82, 413, 423, 424, 428, 429, 443
PIMS, 204, 206, 212
Plunkett, J.J., 193
Point of Sale (POS), 109–10
policy, Irish government
    borrowing, 5, 7, 27
    budget deficit, 16
    cost control, 23, 24
    devaluation, 16
    emigration, 7
    fiscal, 6, 27, 28
    hard currency, 7
    income restraint, 16

Index 471

(policy, Irish government
  continued)
  industrial, 6
  industrial enterprise, 11
  international trade, 16
  inward investment, 5
  principles, 10
  private *v.* public sector
    demand, 16
  productivity, 16
  protectionism, 6, 61
  unemployment, 11
policy principles, 10–11
Pollay, R.W., 229
population, European Community
  age distribution, 37, 38, (T3.4)
  ageing trend, 39
  life expectancy, 38, 39, (T3.5)
  median age, 39
  vital statistics, 34, (T3.1)
population, Irish
  age distribution, 37, 38, (T3.4)
  ageing trend, 39
  decline, 33
  factors, 33
  future trends, 43
  geographic distribution, 39,
    (T3.6)
  growth, 33
  household size, 41, (T3.8)
  life expectancy, 38, 39, (T3.5)
  median age, 39
  Northern Ireland, 35, (T3.2)
  natural increase, 34
  social categories, 43, (T3.9)
  vital statistics, 34, (T3.1)
population size, 33–7
Porter, M.E., 135, 189, 191,192,
  195, 203, 322, 393, 396, 398,
  401, 404
portfolio analysis, 203
Premier Periclase, 65
price
  determination, 283
  premium, 173
prices, Irish
  competitiveness, 23, 26
  export, index, 28
  sensitivity of, 27

pricing
  activity-based costing, 280
  cost based strategies, 278, 279
  cost-plus, 159, 278, 279
  decisions, 284–5
  economist's model, the, 277
  effect on sales volumes of, 286,
    291
  effect of company size on
    287, 288
  incremental, 279
  in Ireland compared with UK,
    289–91
  management team, 92
  non-cost related methods,
    285–6
  policy, 276, 277
  practices, 275–92
  return on investment, 279
  special order, 285
  target costing, 280
  use of computers in, 287
Prinja, S., 322, 330, 332
printing industry, 105
private sector demand, 16, 25
privatisation, 72
problems experienced with
  suppliers, 64–6
process positioning, 416, 417
product
  fully extended, and quality,
    the, 82–5, (F7.1)
  dimensions, 92
  life cycle, 135
  orientation, 136, 137, 16
  quality, improving, 82
  management, 88, 92, 95
    team, 95
  -market resource allocation,
    410
  -market, international
    marketing strategies, 414
  placement, 228
production
  orientation, 72
productivity, Ireland and EC, 5,
  (T1.3)
Profile of a Sales Force, 303, 306.
  308, 310

Profit Impact on Marketing
    Strategies (PIMS), 204, 206,
    212
profit performance, improving, 63
profits, 16, 28
property market, residential, 48
protectionism, Irish, 6, 61, 249
psychodrawing, 386
public sector borrowing
    requirement, 27
public relations
    an element of marketing
    communications, 221
publishing industry, 105
purchase stages, 83, 84, (F7.1)
Purchasing Power Standard
    (PPS), 45, 46, (T4.1)
Purgavie, B., 178
Purwar, P.C., 322

qualitative research, 380-90
    history, 381, 382
    new techniques, 383-6
        museum, the, 387
        psychodrawing, 386
        role playing, 386
    Time Travel, 386
quality
    as a management function, 187
    assurance, 188, 189
    assurance system, 193, 200
    construct, 87
    control, 188, 189
    cost of, 189
    definition of, 186
    eras, 187
    improvement, 81-98, (F7.3/4/5)
    improvement model, 88-98,
        (F7.3/4/5)
    improvement programmes,
        90-98
    improvement benefits, 97, 98
    inspection, 187
    Japanese manufacturers, of,
        189
    levels, acceptable (AQL), 190
    management, evolutionary
        process of, 187, (F13.1), 193

management, strategic, 189,
    190
Management, Total (TQM), 72,
    198
marketing practice, 62, 63
performance, 62
service, 71, 87-98
standards, 186-201
    and IS 9000, 186-201
    in Europe, 191
    System Standard BS 5750, 191
    value chain, 190
quantitative research, 369-79
Quantum, 378
Quelch, J.A, 393, 402
Quigley, W.G.H., 12
Quimby, C., 93

Radford, G.S., 188
Rao, S.R.G. and C.P., 322
Rathmell, J.M., 247
Raveh, Y., 336
Ray, N.M., 332
Raymont, T., 228
Rayner, P., 191, 192, 195
readership surveys, 377
reasons for economic
    improvement, 15
Read, G., 179
Reddy, N.M., 350
Reich, R.B., 189
Reichfield, F.F., 76
relatedness, corporate, 136, 137
reliability
    engineering, 189
    standards, 87
repatriation of profits, 28
Research and Development (R &
    D), 131, 136, 139, 140
resource allocation, product-
    market, 410
restrictive practices, 11
reliability
    of Japanese manufacturers,
        189
*Retail Banking: The New
    Revolution in Structure and
    Strategy*, 248

Index

Revans, R., 93, 94
Riesenbeck, H., 174
Riordan, E.B., 24
Risky Business, 228
Robbins, S., 336
Roberts, J., 175
Robertson, T., 176
Robinson, W.T., 203
Roger, R.D., 322
role playing, 386
Rosenberg, L.J., 150
Rosson, P., 332
royalties, 16
RSL Ltd., 266, 267
RTE, 230, 252
Rumelt, I.R., 135, 136
Rumelt, R.P., 400
Rushton, A.M., 247
Ryans, A.B., 413

Saatchi & Saatchi, 232
Salama, E.R., 393, 402
sales
  force
    management, 295–316
    motivation and
      remuneration of, 298, 306–9
    perceptions of, by buyers, 300, 301
    performance evaluation of, 299, 309–14
    profile of, 300
    selection and training of, 298, 304–6
    size of, 301, 303, 304
  incentive scheme, 113, 114
  information, 111
  management, 296–316, (F19.1)
  promotion, 221
  representatives, 113
    comparison of Irish and overseas, (F19.5)
    cost of, (T19.5)
    evaluating, (T19.7/8)
    use of information technology in, 106, (T8.1)
Samiee, S., 400
Santalainen, T., 393, 405

SAS, 378
Sasser, W.E., Jr, 76
satellite broadcasting, 228
savings, personal, ratio, 28
Scapens, R.W., 275, 278
Scherer, F.M., 135
Scheuring, E.E., 186
Schmalensee, D.H., 81
Scholhammer, H., 147, 148, 152
sectoral development committee, 28
Sedgwick, L., 179
Segler, K.G., 412, 423, 426
selecting focused target markets, 66
self-support teams, 93
selling
  an element of marketing communications, 221
  personal
    importance of, (F19.2)
semi-conductor market, 189
separation, legal, 40
service, customer
  relative importance of activities, 65, (T5.1)
  levels, 75
service quality, 72, 86, 87
  total, 86, 90
  characteristics and quality, 87–90
  dimensions of, 87–90
services
  employment in, (T1.1)
  for empty nesters, increasing demand, 44
  need to expand, 28
  trade in, 15, 28
"shamrock organisation", 342
Shaping the Future: Business Design through Information Technology, 103
shared resources, 130
Shergill, S., 224
Shewhart, W.A., 188
Shipley, D.A., 322, 327, 328, 330, 332
Short's, 346
Sibley, S.D., 322, 332

silo management, 127
Single European Market, 175, 193
single person households, 42
Sinkula, J.M., 243
Skinner, R.C., 278, 280, 291
small enterprises
   export activities (N.I.), 435–52
   high growth, 134–43
   marketing planning in, 146–61
small- and medium-sized
   enterprises (SMEs), 103–7,
     409–34
Smelzer, L.R., 243, 244, 245, 250, 252
Smith, D., 244, 248
Smith, R., 72
Smith, S., 87
social class statistics
   Ireland, 42–3, (T3.9)
   scales, 43
Society of the Irish Motor
   Industry, 50
socioeconomic groups. *see* social
   class
soft drink concentrates
   exports, 20
Southgate, P., 241
spending
   amount of, 45
   average per capita – European
     Union, 45, 46, (T4.1)
   pattern of, 45
   power, 45–6
Spiegel, R.I., 423
sponsorship
   costs, 267, 268
   implementing the programme 268
   in the marketing
     communications mix, 257–72
   measuring the results, 268–71
   objectives and target
     audiences, 263, 264, 265
   Research International (SRI), 228, 259
   selection, 265
   size of market, 258, 259

UK market, 228, (T17.1 & 5)
US expenditure, 259, (T17.2/3)
world expenditure, 259, (T17.2)
Sport on Television and Sports Sponsorship 259
SPSS, 378
staff management, 88
Stahl, M.J., 401
Star, The, 227
STC, 356
Steinberg, S., 228
Steinhoff, D., 147
Stena Line, 90–97
Stern, L.W., 321
Stewart's, 343
Storey, D., 409
strategic alliances, 130
strategic
   change, 143
   positioning, 134–43
strategy
   differentiated, 135–43
   focus, 135–43
   for high growth small firms 134–43
   international marketing, for
     SMEs, 409–34
Strebel, P., 416, 417, 421, 427
strengths, building on, 68
Structural Funds, 11
Sullivan, M.P., 249
Sunday Business Post, 69, 227
Sunday Tribune, 227
Sunday World, 227
suppliers, problems experienced
   with, 64–6
Suprenant, G., 322
surplus – will it last?, 28
Swan, G., 228
Swan, J.E., 87
Sweeting, C., 278, 280, 283, 289

Tailoring Products/Service
   Packages for Target Markets, 66, 67
TAM, 375
targeted population, (CPT), 230
Tate, C.E., 147

Index

taxation
    as an incentive, 11
    changes in law, 21
    corporate profits, 21
Taylor, F.W., 188
teamwork, 93
television
    advertising, 179–80, (T12.3)
    audience measurement
        375, 376
    market, colour, 189
    media terminology, (T23.6)
Telecom Éireann, 374
Tesar, G., 411
Textiles
    Irish imports, 26
Thomson, J. Walter (JWT), 232, 236
thoughtful butterfly, the, 236
Thriving on Chaos, 312
time travel, 386
Tootelian, D.H., 148
Top Gun, 228
Topalian, A., 246
Total quality management (TQM), 72, 82
total marketing effort, 81
total service quality, 86
tourism, 15, 28
Toyoda system, 127
Trade, Balance of, Irish
    deficit in, 27
    ratios, intra-industry, 27
    surplus, merchandise, 28
trade patterns, Irish, 19
trade unions
    and internal marketing, 78
trading income, 15
transfer pricing, 21
travel abroad
    Irish reluctance to, 23
travel goods industry, 27
travel services, 105
Treaty of Paris, 394
    of Rome, 394
Turnbull, P., 235, 328
Tyebsee, T.T., 152

Udell, J.G., 302

Ulster Property Sales, 346
understanding customer needs, 64
unemployed, long-term, 11
unemployment in Ireland
    effect on family size, 35
    effect on marriage rate, 34
    effects, 10, 34, 35
    highest in Europe, 8
    need to reduce, 8
    Northern Ireland, 12
    policy towards, 11
    related to emigration, 35
United Kingdom
    AIB Group in, 249
    competitiveness, 23, 26
    consumer spending, 51–3
    economic development, 3
    export performance, 3, 17
    food and beverage expenditure, 51, 52
    football league, 264
    health expenditure, 51, 52
    Irish exports to, 5, 24, (T1.2)
    key-systems equipment industry, 355
    liquor prices, 402
    manufactured goods market, Irish share, 22, (T2.6)
    market, Irish dependence on, 27
    marketing communications costs, (F15.1)
    pricing practices, 289–91
    sponsorship market, 228, 258, (T17.1 & 4)
    subsidiaries in Ireland, 20, 23
    use of information technology in customer service, 103–8
United States
    AIB Group in, 249
    companies, use of information technology, 105
    Irish merchandise exports to, (T1.2)
    Irish shops in, 159
    market buoyancy, 9
    sponsorship expenditure, 259
War Department, 188

value
  chain, 430
  perceived, 124–33
Value-Added Partnerships (VAP), 336–46
Vancil, R.F., 150
Van der Hoop, H., 398, 400, 403
Verbeke, A., 393
Verhoeven, W., 442
video and film industry, Irish
  need to expand, 28
vendor relationships and TQM, 198, 199, 200
  vertical integration, 337-8
Voss, C.A., 193

wage bargaining system, 7
Walker, O.C., Jr, 295, 296, 301, 305, 306, 308
Wall Street Journal, 395
Walters, C.G., 321
Ward, J., 61
Waterford Crystal, 70, 178, 182, 183, 216
Waterman, R.H., 102
Waters, J.A., 143
Watkins, T., 248
Weihrich, H., 393
Weinshall, T., 336
Wensley, R., 203, 322
Wesch, L.S., 418

Whetten, D.A., 336
Whitten, I.T., 203
Wiedersheim-Paul, F., 410, 418
Wiersema, F.D., 136
Williamson, O., 338
Willis, M., 443
Witcher, B.J., 81, 186
Wood, V.R., 332
Woodward, H., 136
Worcester, R.M., 246
World Bank, 9, 13
world class manufacturing, 127
World Cup, 267
world
  markets, buoyancy in, 23
  population, 36
    259, (T17.2)
Wright, J.D., 396
Wright, M., 248

Yip, G.S., 206
youth population, Ireland and Europe, 38

Zavoos, G., 248
Zeithmal, C.P., 135, 136
Zeithmal, V.A., 247
Zenith, 232
zero defects, 189
Zif, J., 410, 412, 413, 421, 424
Zober, M., 277